THE COMMON HOURS OF PRAYER OF THE ARMENIAN APOSTOLIC CHURCH ENGLISH TRANSLATION (THE SINGING OF THE HOURS)

DURING THE PATRIARCHY OF:

HIS HOLINESS KAREKIN II
CATHOLICOS OF ALL ARMENIANS
OF THE HOLY SEE OF ETCHMIADZIN

HIS HOLINESS
ARAM I CATHOLICOS
OF THE GREAT HOUSE OF CILICIA

HIS BEATITUDE ARCHBISHOP
NOURHAN MANOUGIAN
ARMENIAN PATRIARCH OF JERUSALEM

HIS BEATITUDE ARCHBISHOP
SAHAK II MASHALIAN
ARMENIAN PATRIARCH OF CONSTANTINOPLE

BY

DEACON GREGORY (KRIKOR) R. ERITZIAN
HOLY TRINITY ARMENIAN APOSTOLIC MOTHER CHURCH
FRESNO, CALIFORNIA
2023

All photos are new, remastered hand drawings, based on etchings from the Adeni Zhamakirk with Saghmosaran and Donatzooytz St. James' Press, Jerusalem, fourth edition 1915, drawn by my daughter Anastasia Ava Eritzian, Graduate of Terlemezian Art College in Yerevan, Armenia.

A great thanks to my lifelong friend and brother in Christ Rev. Dr. George A. Leylegian for all of his encouragement, prayers, advice, and for the proofreading of this text.

Publication made possible by
Holy Trinity Armenian Apostolic Church
Church Christian Education Committee
Fresno, California

Services provided by Antioch Media, Fresno, California.

Free PDF download available at
www.AntiochMedia.com/ArmenianPrayer.

©2023 Copyright by Gregory R. Eritzian.
All rights reserved. Protected under copyright laws of the United States of America and safeguarded by the Author, Fresno, California, 2023.

ISBN: 979-8-9900290-9-5
The Common Hours of Prayer of the Armenian Apostolic Church English Translation (The Singing of the Hours) by Gregory Richard

No part of **THE COMMON HOURS OF PRAYER OF THE ARMENIAN APOSTOLIC CHURCH ENGLISH TRANSLATION (THE SINGING OF THE HOURS)** may be reproduced, stored in a retrieval system, or transmitted in any form or by any means, electronic, mechanical, photocopying, recording or otherwise, except as may be expressly permitted by the applicable copyright statutes or in writing by the Author.

*This book is dedicated to all Armenians
throughout the millennia who have
been killed and massacred through
wars and genocides, committed by
enemies of the True and Living God
Jesus Christ,
because of their faith in Him and
in defense of their fatherland.
May He resurrect them in His glory
on the final day
in His glorious second coming.*

PEER REVIEW

"Deacon Gregory Eritzian has gifted the Armenian faithful in the English-speaking world his labor of love, a tangible version of Armenian spirituality expressed in The Common Hours of Prayer, this commendable translation that speaks to the laity and the clergy alike."

Abraham Terian
Emeritus Professor, St. Nersess Armenian Seminary

AUTHOR'S NOTE

This text was diligently prepared by Deacon Gregory (Krikor) Richard Eritzian Pharm D. of Holy Trinity Armenian Apostolic Church of Fresno Ca. whose life objective is to serve God, the Church, and the Armenian people faithfully by spreading the Good News of our Church's faith to the Armenian people both in the diaspora and the Fatherland; so they may, as lost sheep, rejoin the shepherd's flock, which is our Mother Church. Gregory (Krikor), the grandson of genocide survivors, was born in Fresno Ca. in 1966 and was raised in the Armenian Congregational Church although his family always had close ties with the Mother Church. He is a direct descendant of three Armenian priests who served in their local villages prior to the Armenian genocide. His great great grandfather Der Harootyoon was actually martyred in the genocide. He began serving the Mother Church at the age of 19 on a summer study program to the Armenian Patriarchate of Jerusalem. Upon his return to Fresno, he continued studying about the Armenian Apostolic Church, began taking Diaconate classes and began serving at Holy Trinity. After receiving his Bachelor of Arts Degree in Chemistry from California State University Fresno in 1988, he moved to San Francisco where he also served for four years at St. Gregory the Illuminator's while he was attending the University of California San Francisco School of Pharmacy. After obtaining his Doctorate of Pharmacy Degree in 1992, he moved back to Fresno and began practicing pharmacy. He was ordained a Stole-Bearer in 1994 by Archbishop Datev Sarkisian. He married Karolina Petrossian of Yerevan, Armenia in 1997 and has a daughter Anastasia and son Dikran. The family makes their second home in Yerevan where he serves at various churches in Armenia. He was ordained a Deacon at Holy Trinity in Fresno Ca. in December 2001 by Bishop Moushegh Mardirossian. In 2003 he took a sabbatical from work and studied the spring semester in Armenia as a student of the Diocese of Yerevan headquartered in the St. Sarkis Cathedral and the Yerevan State University's Theological Department under the auspices of Bishop Navasart Kojoyan.

As a part of his service to the Armenian Church he gives presentations on numerous church topics to adults as well as the youth for both Armenian Church audiences and non-Armenian ecumenical audiences including television broadcast commentaries of the Divine Liturgy, and has semi-regularly delivered the Sunday Sermons both in the Western Prelacy of the Armenian Apostolic Church of America and in the Republic of Armenia.

The Common Hours of Prayer is his specialized area of study because in his opinion it is the most spiritually inspiring and theologically rich aspect of the Armenian Apostolic Church. He fell in love with the Common Hours of Prayer while participating in them twice a day while in a summer study program at the Sts. James' Armenian Patriarchate of Jerusalem in 1986.

He has dedicated his life to the continuous study and service of the Armenian Apostolic Church.

PREFACE

This book "The Common Hours of Prayer of The Armenian Apostolic Church English Version (The Singing of the Hours) is actually the second related book in a series by the author.

The first book "Zhamakirk The Common Hours of Prayer of the Armenian Apostolic Church (Transliterated Version with Explanation of the Rubrics) was first published by Antioch Media, Fresno, Ca. 2006. The purpose of the first book was mainly as a study guide for all deacons and as practicum for non-Armenian reading acolytes and deacons. However, numerous laity also use the book either to follow along or as a private devotional. In both books, the transliteration and translation is from the text of the "Chancel Book of Hours" Adeni Zhamakirk, Armenian Patriarchate of Jerusalem Sts. James' Press 4th Edition 1915, but the page layout is meant to follow as closely as possible the St. Vartan Press 1986 edition which textually is the same version. The standard hand held books of the Common Hours of Prayer printed by both The Great House of Cilicia and the Armenian Patriarch of Jerusalem Sts. James' Press follow page for page the St. Vartan Press 1986 edition. The font of the St. Vartan Press 1986 and Jerusalem edition is slightly larger and easier to read. Being that these three Armenian font versions are the most commonly used editions in the United States and Canada, to be consistent and making it easier to follow along whether the participant be lay, acolyte, or deacon, with some minor exceptions the same text will appear on corresponding pages of both books as in the Armenian font editions.

The complete Translation of the Common Hours of Prayer of the Armenian Apostolic Church with biblical verse citations was a monumental task. (COVID delayed its publication by one and a half years.) The Common Hours of Prayer (Zhamakirk) being used as the original was the Chancel Book of Hours (Adeni Zhamakirk 4th Edition printed by Sts. James Press, Jerusalem 1915.) The Common Hours of Prayer contain nine Hours of Prayer (or ten depending how they are being counted) which are to be performed in their entirety 365 days a year. Its original content is as old as King David of the Old Testament who wrote the Psalms which are extensively used and form the base of the Common Hours of Prayer. The development of the prayers was then gradually expanded by: the Apostles and the Christians of the First Century A.D., the early Church Fathers of the Universal Church, the Hermitic Desert Fathers, St. Gregory the Illuminator, St. Sahag, St. Mesrob, Movses Khorenatzi, Kuid Arahezatzin, Hovhannes Mantaguni, Stepanos Suinetzin, Hovannes Sargavak, Tovma Medzopetzin, Krikor Datevatzi, and most notably by St. Gregory of Nareg and St. Nerses

PREFACE

the Graceful of the 11th and 12th century respectively. There are many other authors both known and forgotten. With few modifications, the Common Hours of Prayer is the same as the 12th century version.

The main purpose of the translation is for not only the Armenian Apostolic Church faithful but for the entire world to know what exactly the Armenian Apostolic Church confesses and believes in while using modern American English with an understandable vocabulary. This book was translated giving the utmost importance to correct word selection to convey the intended meaning in the Classical Armenian. It is the Classical Armenian that conveys the Armenian Apostolic Church's theology. It is the author's goal that the reader will feel as if they are reading the Classical Armenian while actually reading modern American English. Special consideration was given as to predict whether the English vocabulary chosen will still be in use and have the same meaning one hundred years from now because the last time serious original but only partial translations of the Common Hours of Prayer were made were in the beginning of the twentieth century.

All biblical passages were originally translated by the author. This includes Psalms, Epistles, and Gospels. It is a disservice to use another English biblical translation such as King James, Revised Standard Version, or even the Douay-Rheims. The Classical Armenian is unique and on occasion may be very close to the above translations but more times than not it is noticeably different especially with the Psalms. The reader will be reading a precise translation. There are instances where the reader may think that the author made grammatical mistakes such as using a singular subject with the verb in the plural or there not being a verb in the sentence; the author followed the Classical Armenian and purposely did not make adjustments for this. He remained adherent to the Classical Armenian but without compromising comprehension of the English.

This book was not written to eliminate the Classical Armenian from the Common Hours of Prayer. It was written to keep the Classical Armenian as the language of the Armenian Apostolic Church. The spirituality and beauty of the various liturgies of the Armenian Apostolic Church are in the Classical Armenian. These aspects are not conveyed fully in any other language whether it be English or even Modern Armenian. All of the Church's melodies, hymns, chants, and poetry are structured exclusively for Classical Armenian. This book is an excellent private devotional that Armenians and non-Armenians alike, of all denominations, may take spiritual inspiration or comfort in.

TABLE OF CONTENTS

When necessary, contents begin with the Armenian Titles because the English Translated Titles are unfamiliar to most clerics and laity alike.

X=Beginning Chancel	PAGE	SENIOR CHANCEL	STUDENT CHANCEL
Renunciation	5		
Profession of Orthodox Faith	5-7		
The Order of Confession and Acquittal	7-10		
Procedural Instructions	11-13		
NIGHT HOUR			
Lord's Prayer	15		
Der yete shrtoons im (Lord, if you open my lips)	16		
Der zi pazoom (Lord, for my oppressors are many)	16-24		X
Hishestzook (Let us remember)	24-27	X	
Zartootzyalks (The awakening of all)	28-31		X
Ashkhar Amenayn (All of the world)	31-35	X	
or Arravod Looso (Morning of Light)	35-38	X	
Prayer Uzken Kohanamk (From You we are satisfied)	38-40	X	
Ganonaklookh (Primary Canon Psalm)	41-64	X	
Hanksdyan Sharagan (Hymn of Rest)	65 or 86	X	
or Aysor Anjarr (Today the Inexpressible Dawn)	65	X	
Psalms before the Gospels	65-100	X	
Gospel of Crucifixion (found in the Chancel Gospel)	86	X	
or **Gospel of Rest** (Hanksdyan)	100-109	X	
or **Gospels of Holy Friday**	67-86	X	
(Good Friday: Psalms, Introits, Hymns, and Gospels are easily found in the Holy Week Book (Avak Shapat)			
Norokogh Diezeratz (Regenerator of the Universe)	81-86	X	
(Total of 4 Hymns by St. Nerses each followed by a connecting **Gospel** all read on Holy Friday morning)			
Hanksdyan Sharagan (Hymn of Rest)	86	X	
Asdvadz Anegh (God Uncreated)	109-126	X	
(and other hymns according to tone of the day by St. Nerses remembering those resting in Christ)			
Petition Hokvotzn Hankootzelotz	126		
(For the souls of those who are at rest)			
Proclamation Vasn Hankootzyal	126		X
(For the sake of the souls who are resting)			
Prayer Krisdos Vorti Asdoodzo (Christ Son of God)	126		X
Petition Krisdos Asdvadz mer (Christ our God)	127		
Orhnootyoon Sharagan (Blessing Hymn)	127		X
Petition according to type of and tone of the day	128-130		
Proclamation according to tone of the day	131-142		X
Prayer and Petition according to tone of the day	132-144	X	
Takavor Havidyan (Eternal King) by day and tone	145-167	X	
Alleluias according to type of and tone of the day	168-215	X	

TABLE OF CONTENTS

	PAGE	SENIOR CHANCEL	STUDENT CHANCEL
MORNING HOUR			
Lord's Prayer	217		
Ltzak (In the morning we were filled)	217		
Oorakh yeghak (We became glad)	217		X
Orhnyal yes (Blessing, Three Boys in the furnace)	218-224		X
Petition	224		
Hartz Sharagan (Hymn of the Fathers')	224-231		X
Proclamation Yegyalks (We all having come)	232		X
Petition	233-234		
Introit Medzatzoose (Song of Mary the God-Bearer)	235	X	
Orhnootyoon of Zechariah (Song of Zechariah)	236-237	X	
Prayer of the Elderly Simeon	237	X	
Medzatzoostze Sharagan (Hymn of Magnification)	238-241	X	
Proclamation Soorp Zasdvadzadzinun (Holy God-Bearer)	241	X	
Prayer Ungal Der zaghachans (Receive Lord)	242	X	
Proclamation Vasn soorp deghvooys (For the sake of this holy place)	243		X
Prayer Too yes Takavor (You are king)	243	X	
Yeghitzi anoon dyarrn (Song of Oil Bearing Women)	244	X	
continuation Ari Der oknya (Rise Lord help)	244		X
continuation Ari yev mi merzher (Rise and do not reject)	244	X	
continuation Takavorestze (Lord shall rule as king)	244		X
continuation Orhnya antzn im (My being, bless the Lord)	244	X	
Gospel of The Oil Bearing Women	245-256	X	
Hymn after the Gospel of The Oil Bearing Women	257-259		X
Proclamation Zvarjatzyalks (Having rejoiced)	260		X
Prayer Amenagetzooytz (True most life giving)	260	X	
Psalm 50 before Hymn of Mercy	261-263	X	
Voghormya Sharagan (Hymn of Mercy)	263-267	X	
Proclamation Yergrbakemk (We bow down)	267	X	
Petition	268-269		
Introit Psalm before Der Hergnitz Sharagan	269-272		X
Der Hergnitz Sharagan (Lord of the Heavens Hymn)	273-278		X
Parrk i partzoons (Glory to God in the Highest)	279-280		X
Yev hamenayn zham (At all hours)	280-281	X	
Petition	281		
Arravodoo yerk (Morning Song)	282-290	X	
Proclamations Asastzook (Let us all say in unison)	290-293		X
or Asdvadz medz (Great God)	294-296		X
or Arrachnortk yeghen (They became leaders)	296-297		X
or Uzjknootyoon (The resistance of the holy martyrs)	298-299		X
or Mayr soorp (Mother holy)	299-301		X
or Parravorestzook (Let us glorify)	302-303		X
Petition Parekhos oonimk (We have as advocates)	292		

TABLE OF CONTENTS

	PAGE	SENIOR CHANCEL	STUDENT CHANCEL
Prayer Kohanamk uzken (From You we are satisfied)	303-304	X	
Soorp Asdvadz (Thrice holy)	305-306	X	
Petition Prgel uzmez (To save us)	306		
Proclamation Vasn lseli (For the sake of the voice)	307	X	
Psalm 112 Yeghitzi anoon dyarrn (The Name of the Lord shall be blessed)	307-308	X	
Gospel of Healing *(For Feast days of the Lord, the Psalm, Prophetic, and Epistle readings are read by the Student Chancel. The special Gospel for the day is read from the Lectionary by the Senior Chancel.)*	308-313		X
Sunday Hymn of Creation Norasdeghdzyal (From the beginning the Word)	313-315	X	
Proclamation for Sundays Khntrestzook (Let us request)	315		X
Getzo Der (Give life Lord)	315	X	
Prayer Koom amenazor (Your most powerful)	316	X	
Antasdan (Blessing the four corners of the earth)	317-319		
Introit Psalm before the Mangoonk Sharagan	319-320	X	
Mangoonk Sharagan (Hymn of Children Serving the Lord)	321-324	X	
Proclamation Vasn Khaghaghootyan (For the sake of peace)	324	X	
Prayer Soorp yes Der (You are holy Lord)	325		X
Prayer of Manasseh (Lent)	334-337		X
Proclamation (Lent) Yegyalks i khosdovanootyoon (Having come in confession)	337-338		X
Prayer Der Asdvadz (Lord God)	338	X	
Recitation of Sargavak Vartabed (Saints) Hisha Der (Remember Lord Your ministers)	332		X
continuation to end Hisha Der yev voghormya (Remember Lord and have mercy)	332-333	X	
Psalm 114 (Saints days) Siretzi (I loved)	325-328	X	
or Psalm 5 (All Fasting) Panitz imotz (Give ear to my words)	339-344	X	
Hymns of Creation	344-357	X	
Petition Door mez Der (Grant us Lord)	329-330	X	
Proclamation Soorp Jknavorokn (Holy hermits)	330		X
Prayers Vor undretzer (You Who chose)	330-331	X	
or Bsagich srpotz (Crowner of saints)	331-332	X	
Recitation of Sargavak Vartabed (Fasting) Hisha Der. (Remember Lord Your ministers)	359		X
continuation to end Hisha Der yev voghormya (Remember Lord and have mercy)	359	X	

TABLE OF CONTENTS

	PAGE	SENIOR CHANCEL	STUDENT CHANCEL
SUNRISE HOUR			
Lord's Prayer	360		
Yeghitzi anoon Dyarrn (May the Name of the Lord)	360		
I na orhnestzin (In Him all nations)	360		X
Hymn Harevelitz (Hymn of the Sunrise)	361	X	
Proclamation Harevelitz (From the east)	362		X
Prayer Harevelitz (From the east)	363	X	
Psalm 99 Aghaghagetzek (All lands cry out)	364	X	
Hymn Jknavork (Hermits for God)	365-366	X	
Petition Aghachemk (We pray)	367		
Proclamation Soorp Juknavorok (Holy hermits)	367	X	
Prayer Soorp yes der (Holy are You)	367	X	
Recitation of Sargavak Vartabed, Hisha Der (Remember Lord Your ministers)	368		X
continuation to end Hisha Der yev voghormya (Remember Lord and have mercy)	368	X	
Psalm 62 Asdvadz Asdvadz im (God, my God)	369-371		X
Hymn Looys, ararich looso (Light, maker of light)	371-372		X
Petition Loosovt ko (With Your light)	373		
Proclamation Parravorestzook (May we glorify)	373	X	
Prayer Zarravodoo aghots (Prayers of the morning)	374		X
Psalm 22 Der hovestze zis (Lord is my shepherd)	375-378	X	
Hymn Janabarh (Christ the way)	379	X	
Petition Der ooghya (Lord straighten)	379		
Proclamation Aghachestzook (Let us request)	380		X
Prayers Arrachnort genatz (Leader of lives)	380	X	
or Orhnyal yes Der (Blessed are You)	381	X	
Lord's Prayer	381		
THIRD HOUR			
Lord's Prayer	383		
Orhnyal hokit soorp (Oh blessed Holy Spirit)	383		
Psalm 50 Voghormya intz Asdvadz (Have mercy upon me, God)	383-385		X
Hymn of the Third Hour Orhnemk uzkez (We bless)	386	X	
Petition Hamenayn zham (In every hour)	387		
Proclamation Miapan amenekyan (In unison let us all)	387-388	X	
Prayer Vor i krovpeagan (Who in cherubic)	389-390		X
Psalm Der Asdvadz Orhnyal (Lord God be blessed)	390		X
Proclamation Khuntrestzook (Let us request)	391		X
Prayer Arrachnortya mez (Lead us)	391	X	
Recitation of Sargavak Vartabed, Hisha Der (Remember Lord Your ministers)	392		X
continuation to end Hisha Der yev voghormya (Remember Lord and have mercy)	392	X	
Psalm 22 Der hovestze zis (Lord is my shepherd)	393-394	X	
Proclamation Kohapanelov (With thanksgiving)	394	X	
Prayer Khaghaghootyamp kov (Through Your Peace)	395		X
Lord's Prayer	395		

TABLE OF CONTENTS

	PAGE	SENIOR CHANCEL	STUDENT CHANCEL
SIXTH HOUR			
Lord's Prayer	396		
Orhnyal Hayr soorp (Blessed Holy Father)	396		
Psalm 50 Voghormya intz Asdvadz	396(383-385)		X
(Have mercy upon me, God)			
Hymn of the Sixth Hour Khavaretzav	397		X
(Light of the sun darkened)			
Petition Hamenayn zham (In every hour)	398		
Proclamation Artoon mdok (With awake minds)	398-400		X
Prayer Uzketzo mez (Clothe us)	400-401	X	
Psalm 78 Der mi hisher (Lord, do not remember)	401	X	
Proclamation Vasn hivantatz	401-402	X	
(For the sake of the infirmed)			
Prayer Paradya uztzavs (Remove the pains)	402		X
Recitation of Sargavak Vartabed, Hisha Der	403		X
(Remember Lord Your ministers)			
continuation to end Hisha Der yev voghormya	403	X	
(Remember Lord and have mercy)			
Psalm 40 Yerani vor khorhi (Fortunate is he)	404-405		X
Proclamation Khuntrestzook havadov	406		X
(Let us request in faith)			
Prayer Hayr ktootyantz (Father of compassions)	406	X	
Lord's Prayer	407		
NINTH HOUR			
Lord's Prayer	409		
Orhnyal Vortit soorp (Oh blessed Holy Son)	409		
Psalm 50 Voghormya intz Asdvadz	409(383-385)		X
(Have mercy upon me, God)			
Hymn of the Ninth Hour Charcharagtzyal	410	X	
(For You having suffered)			
Petition Hamenayn zham (In every hour)	411		
Proclamation Soorp srdiv (With holy heart)	411-413	X	
Prayer Der zorootyantz (Lord of hosts)	413-415		X
Psalm Dan. 3 Der mi madner (Lord, do not betray)	415		X
Hymn Nahabedatzn Aprahamoo	416	X	
(Forefather Abraham)			
Proclamation Aghachestzook (Let us pray)	416		X
Prayer Angyal arrachi	416	X	
(Having fallen down before You)			
Recitation of Sargavak Vartabed, Hisha Der	417		X
(Remember Lord Your ministers)			
continuation to end Hisha Der yev voghormya	417	X	
(Remember Lord and have mercy)			
Psalm 114 Siretzi (I loved)	418-419	X	

TABLE OF CONTENTS

	PAGE	SENIOR CHANCEL	STUDENT CHANCEL
NINTH HOUR (CONTINUED)			
Hanksdyan Sharagan (Hymns of Rest)	420-426	X	
Petition Hokvotzn hankootzelotz	426		
(For the souls of those who are at rest)			
Proclamation Vasn hankootzyal	426		X
(For the sake of the souls who are resting)			
Prayer Krisdos Vorti Asdoodzo (Christ Son of God)	427	X	
Lord's Prayer	427		
Petition Uzsaghmosyerkootyoons	428		
(Receive these singing of the Psalms and prayers)			
MIDDAY VARIABLES (JASHOO ZHAM)			
Zhamamood (Introit)	429-452		X
Proclamation Yev yevs khaghaghootyan	452		X
(And again in peace)			
Jashoo Pokh (Midday Anthem)	453-455	X	
Jashoo Sharagan (Midday Hymn)	456-470	X	
Soorp Asdvadz (Thrice Holy or Holy God)	471(305-306)	X	
Proclamation Yev yevs khaghaghootyan	471-472		X
(And again in peace)			
Petition Zi voghormadz (You God are merciful)	472		
Midday Psalm before Prophetic or Epistle Reading	473-479		X
Prophetic Reading or Epistle Reading	480-481		X
Jashoo Meseti (Middle Midday Psalm)	482-491		X
(Before the Prophetic or Epistle Reading)			
Prophetic Reading or Epistle Reading	492		X
Jashoo Alleluia (Midday Alleluia)	493-511	X	
Jashoo Avedaran **Midday Gospel**	511-515	X	
Nicene Creed	515-517	X	
Isk mek (The Glorification/Doxology by St. Gregory)	517		
Proclamation Yev yevs havadov	518-519		X
(And again in faith)			
Prayer Der mer prgich (Our Lord and savior)	519-520	X	
Jashoo Closing litanies (Midday Closing litanies)	521-522		
BLESSING OF THE TABLE	523-530		
EVENING HOUR			
Lord's Prayer	533		
Yes arr Asdvadz gartatzi (I cried out to God)	533		
Usbasei Asdoodzo imo (I waited for my God)	533		X
First Psalm and **Gospel Reading**	533	X	
(During the Fifty Days after Easter)			
Psalm 85 Khonarhetzo (Descend Your ear)	534-535	X	
Petition Parrk Kez (Glory to You)	536		
Psalm 139 Abretzo zis (Deliver me)	536-540		X
Hymn Looys zvart (Glad light)	540		X
Petition Orhnyal Der (Blessed Lord)	541		
Proclamation Hasyalks (Having arrived)	542		X

TABLE OF CONTENTS

	PAGE	SENIOR CHANCEL	STUDENT CHANCEL
EVENING HOUR (CONTINUED)			
Petition Hasyalks (Having arrived)	542		
Messeti (Evening Psalm Anthems)	543-552	X	
Old Testament and Epistle Readings during Lent	552	X	
Order of the Ooghigh yeghitzin	553	X	
(Let my prayers be upright)			
Proclamation Asastzook (Let us all say in unison)	553-556		X
Petition Parekhos oonimk (We have as advocates)	555		
or Proclamation Aghachestzook (Let us request)	557-558		X
or Proclamation Mayr soorp (Mother Holy)	299-301		X
Prayer Loor tzaynitz merotz (Hear our voices)	558-559	X	
Soorp Asdvadz (Thrice holy)	559(305-306)	X	X
Petition Prgel uzmez (To save us)	560		
Proclamation Vasn lseli (For the sake of the voice)	560	X	
Psalm 120 Hampartzi zachs im (I lifted up my eyes)	561	X	
Hampartzi Sharagan (Lifted up Hymn) and variables	561-566	X	
Proclamation Vasn khaghaghootyan	567	X	
(For the sake of peace)			
Prayer Hayr Ktadz (Compassionate Father)	567		X
Nakhadonag Sharagan (Feast Eve Hymn)	567		
Prayer of Manasseh (Lent)	568(334-337)		X
Proclamation (Lent) Yegyalks i khosdovanootyoon	568(337-338)		X
(Having come in confession)			
Prayer Der Asdvadz (Lord God)	568(338-339)	X	X
(The above Proclamation and Prayer are connected to the Prayer of Manasseh)			
Psalm 90 Anthem of Dismissal Vor pnagyaln	568-571		X
(He Who dwells) *Fasting and Martyr's Days*			
Petition Uzpartzryaln Krisdos (Uplifted Christ)	572		
Proclamation Yev mek mipan (And we in unison)	572		X
Prayer Hooys genatz (Hope of life)	572	X	
Recitation of Sargavak Vartabed, Hisha Der	573		X
(Remember Lord Your ministers)			
continuation to end Hisha Der yev voghormya	573	X	
(Remember Lord and have mercy)			
Lord's Prayer	573		
Psalm 133 Anthem for Sunday Eve Asd orhnetzek	574-575		X
(Bless the Lord here)			
Gospel of Dismissal *(During the 50 days after Easter)*	575		X

TABLE OF CONTENTS

	PAGE	SENIOR CHANCEL	STUDENT CHANCEL
EVENING HOUR (CONTINUED)			
Proclamation Khuntrestzook (Let us request)	575		X
and Prayer Takavor Khaghaghootyan	576	X	
(King of peace)			
or Prayer Koom amenazor (Your most powerful)	576(316)	X X	
or Proclamation Soorp yegeghetzyavs	576(578)		X
(Through the Holy Church)			
and Prayer i mech dajarris (In this temple)	576(580)	X	
or Proclamation Soorp zasdvadzadzinun	576(241)		X
(Holy God-Bearer)			
and Prayer Ungal Der (Receive, Lord)	576(242)	X X	
or Proclamation Soorp Khachivs	576		X
(Through the Holy Cross)			
and Prayer Bahbanya (Protect us)	576	X	
INSTRUCTION FOR WORSHIP			
Psalm 121 Oorakh yeghe (I became joyful)	577-578		
Proclamation Soorp Yegeghetzyavs	578		X
(Through the Holy Church)			
Prayer Arr tran srpo (Beside the door)	579	X	
Psalm 99 Anthem Aghaghagetzek (All lands cry out)	579	X	
Proclamation Orhnestzook zamenagaln	580		X
(Let us bless the almightyGod)			
Prayer i mech dajarris (In this temple)	580	X	
or Prayer i hargi srpootyan (In this dwelling)	581	X	
PEACE HOUR			
Lord's Prayer	583		
Psalm 33 Orhnetzitz uzDer (I shall bless the Lord)	583		
continued I Der bardzestzi (My being shall boast)	583-584	X	
Psalm 119-130 Yerk asdijanatz (Song of Ascents)	584		
Psalm 87 Der Asdvadz prgootyan imo	584-585		
(Lord God of my salvation)			
Psalm 4 i gartal imoom (While I cry out)	585-593	X	
Hymn Shorhya mez Der (Grace unto us Lord)	594-596	X	
Petition i mertzenal (While approaching)	596		
Proclamation Kohatzarook (Let us be thankful)	597-598	X	
Prayer Der parerar (Kind Lord)	598-599		X
Psalm 26 Der looys im (Lord my light)	600-602	X	
Hymn Nayatz sirov (Look with love)	602-605	X	
Petition Der, mi tartzootzaner (Lord, do not turn)	605		
Proclamation Aghachestzook zamenagaln	606		X
(Let us pray to almighty God)			
Prayer Shnorhadoo paryatz (He Who graces good)	606	X	
Lord's Prayer *for ordinary days*	606		
Psalm 118 *for Salt and Bread days*	607-625		X
Hymn i ken haytzemk (From You we request)	625-627		X
Modulated Chants *Wed Thurs Fri Mon Tue*	628-632		X

TABLE OF CONTENTS

	PAGE	SENIOR CHANCEL	STUDENT CHANCEL
PEACE HOUR (CONTINUED)			
Petition Hokvotzn Hankootzelotz	633		
(For the souls of those who are at rest)			
Proclamation Vasn hankootzyal	633		X
(For the sake of the souls who are resting)			
Prayer Krisdos Vorti Asdoodzo (Christ Son of God)	634	X	
Lord's Prayer	634		
REST HOUR			
Lord's Prayer	637		
Psalm 42 Arrakya Der uzlooys	637		
(Lord send Your light)			
continued Mditz arrachi (I shall enter)	637		X
Psalm 118 Yegestze (May Your mercy come)	638-648		X
Petition Antzn im (My being)	648		
Proclamation Aghachestzook zamenagaln	648-649		X
(Let us pray to almighty God)			
Prayer Der Asdvadz mer (Lord our God)	649-650	X	
Psalm 4 Khaghaghootyamp hays (With peace in this)	651	X	
Gospel of Rest	652	X	
Proclamation Soorp khachivs	653		X
(Through the Holy Cross)			
Prayer Bahbanya (Protect us)	653	X	
Lord's Prayer	654		
Petition Anganimk arrachi (We fall before You)	654		
Four Prayers of St. Gregory of Narek as Follows			
#12 Ungal kaghtzrootyamp (Accept Kindly)	655-656		X
#41 Vorti Asdoodzo (Son of the living God)	657-658	X	
#94 Asdvadz havidenagan (Eternal God)	659-660	X	
#80 Yev art i vera (And now, after so much)	661-664	X	
Prayer Havadov khosdovanim	666-673	X	
(With Faith I Confess)			
Petition Vasn srpoohvo asdvadzadznin	673		
(For the sake of the holy God-Bearer)			
Proclamation Soorp zasdvadzadzinn	674		X
(Holy God-Bearer)			
Prayer Ungal Der zaghachans (Receive Lord)	674	X	
Lord's Prayer	674		
Petition Parrk kez, Der Asdvadz mer	675-676		
(Glory to You, Lord our God)			
APPENDIX			
Lord's Prayer Translation	678		
References	679-680		

LOCATING THE HYMNS

The hardest aspect regarding the Common Hours of Prayer is to find the correct page in the Hymnal (Sharagan Book) as to which hymns should be sung on which days once we know which songs are to be sung according to the Church Calendar. Generally speaking one should look in the index, of a republished version of the Hymnal Etchmiadzin 1888 edition, according to the particular season or feast. If the particular Hymn is not listed in the index, then look under the Hartz Sharagan (Hymn of the Fathers) for that particular season or feast and the day's remaining hymns usually follow, however, the exceptions are frequent. The Hymns in this edition are not organized on a day to day basis but are grouped according to season or major feasts. The only real way to learn the eight tones of the Hymns and to learn the operation of the Hymnal (Sharagan Book) is to study in a monastery or attend a church which performs the hours and hymns on a daily basis, such as exist in the Middle East or Armenia. The rest of the text is very straight forward as to locating items in the table of contents. Every student must realize, however, that there is no substitute to daily recitation of the Common Hours of Prayer, when it comes to learning them. The student will also learn better when the Hours are performed in their entirety rather than when they are cut and abbreviated.

GLOSSARY

Aghotk- Prayer

Avedaran- Gospel

Change-When appears in margin means a change in melody

Jashoo- Midday

Jashotz- Lectionary Book

Karoz- Proclamation

Maghtank- Petition

Messeti- Anthem

Oratzooytz- Calendar

Saghmosaran- Psalter, Book of Psalms which are divided into 8 canons, containing both Prayers and Proclamations. This was the ancient form of the Common Hours of Prayer.

Salt and Bread- Days in which fasting is most strict. This includes all days of Great Lent except Sundays.

Sargavak- Deacon

Sharagan- Hymn specifically found in the Hymnal (ex. Orhnootyoon, Hartz, Hampartzi etc...)

Tas- Chancel of the church in which the Tubirs sing. Left or Right.

Tubir- Singers, students, acolytes, or scribes

Vartabed- Unmarried priest who has obtained a doctorate degree of the church. (modern day masters in divinity or theology)

Yerk- Song or Hymn but not found in the Hymnal

Zham- Hour

RENUNCIATION

We renounce of Satan and all his deceit,
his seductions, his thoughts,
his paths, his evil wills,
his evil angels, his evil officers,
his evil complacency,
and all of his evil power, through renouncing,
we renounce.

Repeat this three times facing west
with palms facing outward from body.
Then turn towards the east and
begin the Profession of the Orthodox Faith.
The Veghar (cowl) should not be worn
and hands should be held together in front of the body.

PROFESSION OF ORTHODOX FAITH
BY SAINT GREGORY OF DATEV

We confess and believe, with most perfect heart, in God the Father,
not created, not born, and without beginning,
and also who gives birth to the Son and
the emanator of the Holy Spirit.

We believe in God the Word, not created, born and having
begun from the Father before the eternities, not after and
not inferior, but as much as the Father is Father,
and with the same, the Son is Son.

We believe in God the Holy Spirit, not created,
timeless, not born, but emanating from the Father,
from the existence of the Father and of the
glories of the Son.

6

We believe in the Holy Trinity, in one nature,
in one Godly being, not three Gods, but one God,
in one will, in one kingdom, in one Lordship,
maker of that which is visible and invisible.

We believe in the Holy Church, in the forgiveness of sins,
with the communion of the saints.

We believe: in the one of the Three Persons,
God the Word, having been born of the Father before the eternities,
in time having descended into the birth-giver of God, the Virgin Mary,
having taken from her blood, having united her to the Godly being,
in the nine month waiting patiently in the womb of the pure virgin,
and He became perfect God, perfect man, in spirit, in mind and
in body, one person, one face, and having been united, one nature.
God having become man without change and without alteration,
with a seedless impregnation and incorruptible birth,
as there was no beginning to His Godly being, and no end to His
humanity. (For Jesus Christ is the same yesterday, and today and
unto eternity).

We believe that our Lord Jesus Christ walked upon the earth,
after thirty years He came to baptism. The Father from above
gave witness, "This is My beloved Son," and the Holy Spirit
in a dovelike manner descended upon Him. He was tempted
by Satan and defeated him. He preached salvation for
mankind.

He labored in body, became fatigued, became hungered and thirsty. Then came willingly to the suffering passions, became crucified and died in body, and alive with the Godly Being. The body was placed in the grave united with the Godly Being, and with the Spirit, having descended into the hells*, with the inseparable Godly Being. Having preached unto the souls, having destroyed the hells*, and freeing the souls. After three days He arose from the dead and appeared to the disciples.

* *Hades*

We believe that our Lord Jesus Christ, with the same body ascended into the heavens and is sitting at the right hand of the Father.
And also is to come with the same body and glory of the Father to judge the living and the dead. And which is the resurrection of all mankind.

And we believe in the recompense of deeds, eternal life for the just, and eternal torment for the sinners.

THE ORDER OF CONFESSION AND ACQUITTAL

(Depending on when the Confessional occurs, the Lord's Prayer may or may not be recited. Because the KJV of the Lord's Prayer is very close to the Armenian meaning, and because it is universally familiar, for practical purposes, this will be used throughout the book. See the Appendix for an exact translation.)

Priest: Blessed be our Lord Jesus Christ. Amen.

Priest and Those Confessing collectively:
Our Father Who art in heaven, Hallowed be Thy name. Thy kingdom come, Thy will be done on earth as it is in heaven. Give us this day our daily bread. And forgive us our debts, as we forgive our debtors. And lead us not into temptation, but deliver us from evil.

Priest: For Thine is the Kingdom, and the power, and the glory forever and ever. Amen.

In the Name of the Father, the Son, and the Holy Spirit. Amen.

Those Confessing: I have sinned against the All Holy Trinity, the Father, the Son, and the Holy Spirit. I Have sinned against God. I confess before God, before the Holy Bearer of God, and before you Reverend Father, all of the sins for which I have committed. For I have sinned in thought, in word, and in deed, willingly and unwillingly, knowingly and unknowingly; I have sinned against God.

Priest: May God grant you forgiveness.

8

Those Confessing: I have sinned by my spirit and its power, in mind and its actions, in body and its sensations. I have sinned by the power of the spirit: in deceit, in wickedness, in arrogance and in cowardliness, in extravagance and in stinginess, in debauchery and by injustice, in liking evil, in hopelessness and in mistrustfulness; I have sinned against God.

Priest: May God grant you forgiveness.

Those Confessing: I have sinned by thinking evil thoughts, by fraud, by hatred , by scowling upon others with dislike, by holding grudges, by witchcraft or charms, by slacking, with the having of pornographic thoughts: with men, with women, with beasts, with work animals and other beastly creatures, both during the night and during the day; with having impure dreams and visions of lewd obscene filth; I have sinned against God.

Priest: May God grant you forgiveness.

Those Confessing: I have sinned by desires of the flesh; by convenience, by idleness, by yawning from sleepiness, by bodily movements, by lewd and lascivious behavior leading to various diseases, by listening inattentively, by watching inattentively, by desires of the heart, by effeminization of the nostrils, by seductive behavior of the mouth, by insobriety, in all excesses and drunkenness; I have sinned against God.

Priest: May God grant you forgiveness.

Those Confessing: I have sinned by wickedness of the tongue, by lying, by taking false oaths, by perjury, by contradictions, by quarreling, by slander, by spreading malicious reports, by spreading secret accusations, by speaking in vain, and by laughter; by idle talk, by double talk, and by cursing; by murmuring up trouble, by spreading discontentment, by gossiping and blasphemy; I have sinned against God.

Priest: May God grant you forgiveness.

Those Confessing: I have sinned by thievery with my own hands: by greed, by deprivation, by compulsion, by murder, and by the trailing of others; I have sinned against God.

Priest: May God grant you forgiveness.

Those Confessing: I have sinned by every joint of which I am made and by every member of my body, by the five senses, by the six movements; by the kicking up of my feet, by slacking decadently, by misleading others to both the right and left, by committing the original sin, and by the final evil mark of existence; I have sinned against God.

Priest: May God grant you forgiveness.

Those Confessing: I have also sinned by the seven offences of the deadly sins: namely by pride and all its forms, by envy and all its forms, by anger and all its forms, by sloth and all its forms, by greed and all its forms, by gluttony and all its forms, and by lust and all its forms; I have sinned against God.

Priest: May God grant you forgiveness.

Those Confessing: I have also sinned against all of the commandments of God, both those which were commissioned and those which are prohibitory; for I have neither performed the commissioned commandments nor have I kept away from those things which are prohibitory. I accepted the laws but was derelict in keeping them; I was invited to the order of Christianity and was found unworthy of it by my deeds; while knowing the evil, I willingly gave way to it and from good deeds I kept myself away; woe to me, woe to me, woe to me. Which shall I recite? Or, which shall I confess? For my sins are innumerable, my iniquities are unspeakable, my afflictions are inexcusable, and my wounds are incurable. I have sinned against God.

Priest: May God grant you forgiveness.

Those Confessing: Reverend Father, I hold you as my mediator of reconciliation and advocate with the Only Begotten Son of God, that by the authority which has been granted unto you, you may release me of the bonds of my sins, I request of you.

Priest: Lord have mercy, Lord have mercy, Lord have mercy.

ACQUITTAL

Priest: May God, the lover of humanity, have mercy upon you and grant you forgiveness of all your offenses, both those confessed and those forgotten. And by the order of my priestly authority and by divine commandment, that, whatever you shall release on earth shall be released in heaven. By the same word, I release you from all participation of your sins committed in thought, in word, and in deed. In the name of the Father, of the Son, and of the Holy Spirit, I in turn give to you the Sacraments of the Holy Church, that whatever good works you may do, may be considered as good works for you and for the glory of the life to come. Amen.

PROCEDURAL INSTRUCTIONS

The instructions of how to begin and recite the prayers in the House of Prayer according to the Eastern rites as requested by Hagop Vartabed (Doctor of the Church) of Kharim from the Arch Bishop Krikor Khlatetzi were included in the original edition of the Armenian hand held edition of the Book of Hours, however, for a beginner a mere translation of the instructions would be completely inadequate and incomplete because much of the material was omitted. Below is a more detailed and understandable explanation.

The Common Hours of the Armenian Apostolic Church comprise of nine separate hours of prayer:

<u>*Approximate ancient traditional times of reciting*</u>

Kisherayin (Night Hour)	*Midnight*
Arravodyan Zham (Morning Hour)	*4:00 a.m. (Dawn)*
Arevakayl Zham (Sunrise Hour)	*6:00 a.m.*
Jashoo Zham (Third Midday Hour)	*9:00 a.m.*
Jashoo Zham (Sixth Midday Hour)	*Noon*
Jashoo Zham (Ninth Midday Hour)	*3:00 p.m.*
Jashoo (Midday) Creed and Lectionary Readings	
Yeregoyan Zham (Evening Hour)	*4:00 p.m.*
Khaghaghagan Zham (Peace Hour)	*6:00 p.m.*
Hanksdyan Zham (Rest Hour)	*8:00 p.m. (Bedtime)*

* *The term Jashoo is exclusive to the Armenian Church. It literally means meal. It refers not only to the Liturgical Meal but also to the Communal Meal at the Dining Table. A loose translation is "Midday"*

PROCEDURAL INSTRUCTIONS, CONTINUED

According to ancient traditions all of the hours should be performed on a daily basis. This was done during the middle ages in the monasteries. Present day tradition has changed. Only Night, Morning, Midday Creed and Lectionary portions, and Evening hours are performed year round. The other hours: Sunrise, (Midday Third, Sixth, and Ninth hours), Peace, and Rest are now only performed during Great Lent. In addition when all services are performed in present day, parts are always skipped, especially many verses of the day's Hymns. In addition, the times of performing the services have been changed to fit the conveniences of modern lifestyles. Frequently three or more services will be combined back to back.

The church is divided into two chancels Right and Left from the perspective of one's back being to the altar. One chancel is called the Senior Chancel and the other is called the Student Chancel. The determinant of which chancel of the church is named Senior or Student is the church calendar. The church uses the 8 tonal system to determine the tone of the day. The tone of the day tells us much more than the musical melody which will be sung, it tells us which chancel of the church will begin or perform a particular prayer, hymn, psalm, etc... If it is a piece that must be said in alternation, the opposite chancel will recite the next line or phrase, then the first chancel again etc. etc... until the piece is completed. Chancel assignments are notated in the Table of Contents and throughout this text.

The eight tones which the Armenian Church uses which will be abbreviated as the following for this text:

A Tz,   A G,   P Tz,   P G,   K Tz,   K G,   T Tz,   T G

The principal tones are always A Tz, P Tz, K Tz, and T Tz. The church calendar will state which chancel of the church is assigned to the principal tones for the entire year. By default the opposite chancel is assigned the remaining secondary tones A G, P G, K G, and T G for the entire year. The tone of the day alternates daily in sequence A Tz, A G, P Tz, P G etc... as shown in the calendar. The Senior Chancel is always given by the tone of the day. Therefore, the designation of Senior Chancel and Student Chancel flip flops back and forth each day. In this book's table of contents the letter "X" denotes which item is to either be started or performed by the appropriate chancel (Senior or Student). The only time of the year when the principal tones and secondary tones change chancel side in the church is the Feast Day of Poon Paregentan "Natural Goodliving"(Better known as Carnival or the Sunday eve before Great Lent.) On this day the tone of the day is always T G by definition. The sequence then resumes for the rest of the days with chancel sides being reversed from the year before.

First Authentic Tone	"Arrachin Tzayn"	"Ayp-Tza"	A Tz
First Variant Tone	"Arrachin Goghm"	"Ayp-Gen"	A G
Second Authentic Tone	"Yergrort Tzayn"	"Pen-Tza"	P Tz
Second Variant Tone	"Yergrort Goghm"	"Pen-Gen"	P G
Third Authentic Tone	"Yerrort Tzayn"	"Kim-Tza"	K Tz
Third Variant Tone	"Yerrort Goghm"	"Kim-Gen"	K G
Fourth Authentic Tone	"Chorrort Tzayn"	"Ta-Tza"	T Tz
Fourth Variant Tone	"Chorrort Goghm"	"Ta-Gen"	T G

Another way to determine which side should receive which tones for the year is the following: When the year according to the Armenian Calendar is odd, the principal tones belong to the right chancel which is the closest to the Baptismal Font. When the year is even according to the Armenian Calendar, the principal tones belong to the left chancel which is farthest from the Baptismal Font.

And for the prayers not assigned by the daily tone or by chancel side, they are to be performed by the most senior priest or by a priest who may be an honored guest.

The tones also represent musical melodies. There are actually more than eight tonal melodies because some of the tones have a secondary melody associated with them known as a modulated melody. When the tone of a hymn is given either in the calendar or in the Hymnal book, it is not specifically stated that the hymn should be sung with a modulated melody. Therefore the singer must "just know" that the particular hymn uses a modulated melody.

Even though the tone of the day is listed in the calendar, that does not mean that all Hymns are to be sung with that particular melody. Each day may contain several Hymns not belonging to that tone of the day. There may even be cases where none of the Hymns prescribed for the day belong to the same musical melody as the daily tone. The warning is not to confuse the tone of the day with the tone of musical melody of a particular Hymn; they do not have to correspond.

* Notes regarding the Psalms: The Common Hours of Prayer are based entirely upon the Book of Psalms (Psalter) or (Saghmosaran). At the time of this publishing the Book of Psalms (Saghmosaran) has not been translated from Classical Armenian. The author recommends the "Douay-Rheims Bible" for the closest translation of the Psalms to the Classical Armenian. When the Psalms are listed by chapter and verse in the text, they are numbered according to both the Armenian Church's numbering system, which is the same as the Greek Septuagint and Latin Vulgate versions, and the corresponding King James numbering system cited to the right.

Begin each service with the Lord's Prayer (Hayr Mer) by one of the following leaders in the manner described below:

Zhamorhnogh *(literally, the one who blesses the Hour of Prayer)* The most senior Cleric (Elder or "Yeretz") in attendance who presides over but does not necessarily officiate the services. The Zhamorhnogh is, by definition, always either of a higher clerical rank or of more seniority than the Zhamarar. A Zhamorhnogh is designated when there is more than one cleric present at a service. The Zhamorhnogh has the privilege of beginning the services by reciting the Lord's Prayer. If the Zhamorhnogh is a Bishop, then the participants gather around him in the center of the church, which may be either in the Chancel (Adyan) and/or in the Nave of the church, depending on how many participants there are, and he recites the Lord's Prayer from the center. If the Zhamorhnogh is a Vartabed (Celibate Priest) or Der Hayr (Married Priest), he then recites the Lord's Prayer (Hayr Mer) from his appointed place in the Chancel.

Zhamarar *(literally, the one who performs the Hour of Prayer)* The designated clerical officiant of the day regardless of rank or seniority. The Zhamarar recites the beginning Lord's Prayer (Hayr Mer) from his appointed place in the Chancel (Adyan) only if there is no Zhamorhnogh.

In cases in which there is no Bishop or Priest (Elder or "Yeretz") present or available, it is appropriate for a non-priest (elder or"yeretz) to lead the faithful in the Common Hours of Prayer. This non-priest (elder or yeretz) would usually be a Deacon (Sargavak) or Singer/Acolyte but may even be a lay-person as long as he knows the services and the accepted liturgical parameters. At home, families should be encouraged to collectively pray and observe the Common Hours of Prayer led by the Head of the Household (Dan Yeretz.)

Tasaklookh *(literally, the Chief of the Chancel Clerks)* Very often, the Tasaklookh is the Choirmaster of the church. The Choirmaster may recite the beginning Lord's Prayer (Hayr Mer) from his appointed place in the Chancel (Adyan) if the Zhamorhnogh or Zhamarar has not yet arrived in the church. The Choirmaster need not be a cleric.

All Prayers and Petitions are offered by a Priest or Bishop if they are present. All Proclamations are offered by a Deacon if one is present. Through the entire book, these shall be the rules by default, as not every section may show the assigned part belonging to which cleric. Psalms are generally read in alternation by two clerks, one from each chancel if they are present. Hymns and other songs are usually sung in alternating verses in alternation with the left and right chancels. Non-Gospel readings are generally read by the Clerks. Gospel readings are reserved for Deacons, Priests, or Bishops.

The Hours of Prayer which are according to the canons of the Eastern Rite Patriarchate are performed for the glory of God.

«Տէր, եթէ գտքուան իմ բանաս...»

The order of the Common Prayers of the Armenian Church which are performed during the Midnight Hour before God the Father

Blessed be our Lord Jesus Christ. Amen.

Our Father Who art in heaven, Hallowed be Thy name.
Thy kingdom come, Thy will be done on earth as it is in heaven.
Give us this day our daily bread.
And forgive us our debts, as we forgive our debtors.
And lead us not into temptation, but deliver us from evil.

For Thine is the Kingdom, and the power,
and the glory forever and ever. Amen.

<u>Priest Ps 50:17 KJV 51:15</u>
Lord, if You open my lips, my mouth will sing Your praises.

<u>Deacon</u>
Blessed be God.

<u>Priest</u>
Lord, if You open my lips, my mouth will sing Your praises.

<u>Deacon</u>
God is praised.

<u>Priest</u>
Blessed be the coexisting, united, and inseparable
Holy Trinity, Father, Son, and Holy Spirit. Now and always
and unto the eternity of eternities. Amen.

(While presenting the censer and incense to the Priest)

<u>Deacon</u>
And again in peace let us request of the Lord. Receive, save, and have mercy.

(Priest blesses and fills the censer with incense while saying)

<u>Priest</u>
Blessing and glory to the Father and to the Son and to the Holy Spirit.
Now and always and unto the eternity of eternities. Amen.

(Priest censes the entire Church)
Psalms read in alternation

<u>Ps 3:2-9 KJV 3:1-8</u> **Student Chancel**
Lord, for my oppressors are many, and many are rising against me.
Many were saying regarding me that there is no salvation in his God.

But You, Lord are my helper, my glory, and the uplifter of my head.
With my voice I cried unto the Lord, and He listens to me from His holy mountain.

NIGHT HOUR

I laid down and was in sleep, I awoke and the
Lord was accepting of me.
I will not have fear of their numerous soldiers, which
were keeping me encircled, surrounded, and besieged.

Arise, Lord, my God and save me, for you struck those
who groundlessly had enmity with me, and may You
break to pieces the teeth of the sinful.
Salvation is of the Lord, Your blessing upon your people:

<u>Ps 87:2-19 KJV 88:1-18</u>
Lord God of my salvation, from the day unto the
night I cried out before You.
May my prayers enter before You, may Your ear
descend upon my request.

For my being is filled with torments, and my life
is drawing near to hells*, and I am numbered
amongst those who are descending into the pit.
I became as a man without a helper, and
free unto the dead.

Hades

NIGHT HOUR

As the wounded, who sleep in the grave.
Those who You did not remember, those who
from Your hand are rejected.

They put me inside the interior of the pit in the
darkness and in the shadow of death.
Upon me Your passion was asserted,
all of Your amusements are brought upon me.

You have made those that I know far away from me,
and they placed me as their target.
I was betrayed and could not arise,
my eyes weakened from poverty.

I cried out unto the Lord daily,
and lifted my hands to You.
Is it possible that you make Your wonders
for the dead, or doctor them to arising,
that they will be made to confess to You.

Is it possible that in the grave one will ever
tell of Your mercies or Your truths in destruction.
Is it possible that in darkness they recognize
Your wonders, or justice to the
forgotten land.

NIGHT HOUR

To You, Lord, I cried out, my prayers
of the morning may reach to You.
Why, Lord, do You reject my being,
or turn Your faces from me.

I have been indigent and hard working
from my childhood, from highness I bowed
down and was amazed.
Your anger was asserted upon me,
Your terrors troubled me.

They encircled me as water, in which
together they all besieged me.
You made my friends and those I know far
away from me, for the sake of my misery.

<u>Ps 102:1-22 KJV 103:1-22</u>

May my being, and all of my bones
bless the Lord and His Holy Name.
May my being bless the Lord, and not
forget all of His gifts.

Who atones your sins, and heals
all of your illnesses.
Who saves your life from corruption, and
crowns you with mercy and compassion.

Who from kindness overfills your desires,
your youth may be renewed as the eagles.
The Lord makes mercies, and rights for
all those who are deprived.

The Lord showed His paths to Moses,
and His wills to the sons of Israel.
Compassionate and merciful is the Lord,
patient and abundantly merciful.

The Lord does not entirely get angry at us,
and does not hold a grudge eternally.
The Lord did not make us according to our
sins, and did not cut us down according to
our unrighteousness.

NIGHT HOUR

But as high as the heavens are from the earth,
in that manner the Lord strengthened His mercy
upon those who fear in Him.
As far as the east is from the west,
He made our unrighteousness that far from us.

As a father has compassion upon his sons,
in that same manner the Lord has compassion
upon those who fear in Him.
For He knew what we are created of,
and remembered that we are soil.

The days of man are, as of grass, as a wild flower,
in that manner he blossoms.
The wind blows from within it, and then it is no more,
and its place is no longer visible.

But the mercy of the Lord stays through the eternity
of eternities upon those who fear in Him, and His justice
from sons unto their sons.
Those who keep His covenants remember
His covenants and do them.

Lord in the heavens prepared His throne,
His kingdom reigns over all.
Bless the Lord, all of his angels, with mighty strength,
those who do His words while hearing the voice of His
messages.

Bless the Lord, all of His hosts,
and those who do His will.
Bless the Lord, all His works,
for through all places is His Lordship,
may my being bless the Lord.

Ps 142:1-12 KJV 143:1-12
Lord, hear my prayers, place Your ear upon my
requests with Your truth.
Hear me with Your justice, and do not enter
into a lawsuit with Your servant, for nobody
amongst all those alive is righteous before You.

The enemy persecuted my being, he has made my
life reduced into the ground, and sat me in the
dark as one dead unto eternity.
My soul within me became wearied, and my
heart within me became agitated.

NIGHT HOUR

I remembered the first days, I pondered upon
all Your works, I pondered upon
all of the things that Your hands have made,
and I lifted my hands up to You.
My being thirsts for You as a thirsty land,
quickly hear me, Lord, for of me,
my spirit has become faint.

Do not turn Your faces from me,
lest I resemble those who descend into the pit.
Make Your morning mercies audible to me,
for Lord I hoped in You.

Show me the path to which I should go,
for to you Lord, I lifted up my being.
Save me from my enemies, Lord,
for I made You my refuge.

Teach me to do Your wills,
for You are my God.
Your good spirit shall lead me into
upright land.

NIGHT HOUR

For the sake of Your Name, Lord, may You give me life,
with Your righteousness may You take my being
out of difficulty.
With Your mercy exterminate my enemies, and
destroy all the oppressors of my being, for I am
Your servant.

Glory to the Father and to the Son and to the Holy Spirit.

Now and always and unto the eternity of eternities. Amen.

*Hymn written by His Holiness Nerses Catholicos of the Armenians
which is sung for the night hour of worship.*

Senior Chancel

Let us remember Your name in the night, Lord.

May our hearts outpour the good word
and may our tongues tell Your works of
the heavenly King.

Having arisen in the middle of the night,
may we confess You Lord.

May we give our prayers to You Lord
in your courts in the New Jerusalem.

NIGHT HOUR

In the night may we lift our hands up
in holiness to You Lord.

In a voice of thanks
every soul bless the Lord.

<u>Melody Change</u>

Awake my glory, awake, and I shall
awake in this morning. Alleluia.

Awake with the joyful servants of Zion above. Alleluia.

Awake sons of light in blessing of the Father of Light. Alleluia.

Awake those having been saved by blood and
give glories to the One who saves. Alleluia.

Awake new people having made new songs to the Renewer. Alleluia.

Awake brides with spirit, having waited
for the coming of the Holy Bridegroom. Alleluia.

Awake, burning with light as the wise holy virgins. Alleluia.

Awake, prepare oil of warm tears for the lamps. Alleluia.

NIGHT HOUR

Awake and do not slumber as the foolish virgins. Alleluia.

Awake, let us bow down in worship with tears saying this. Alleluia.

<u>Melody Change</u>

Wake up, why do you sleep. Lord do not reject us unto the end.

Arise, Lord help us, may we give glories to Your Name.

Now and evermore, to the Father, and to the Son,
and to the Holy Spirit. Amen.

<u>Melody Change</u>

Upon our awakening from being occupied with the rest
of the nighttime.

May the Lord, lover of mankind grace us with
consolation and into the comfort of the Church.

Trembling with fear, let us stand in prayer.

Having come, let us confess our offences.

And let us find from Christ atonement
and the great mercy.

Unto the eternity of eternities amen.
Alleluia, alleluia, alleluia.

Amen. Alleluia, alleluia, alleluia.

NIGHT HOUR

<u>Accompanying Chant</u>

Inseparable and of the same being of the Trinity,
having one voice with the heavenly hosts,
we offer glories.

Glory to You: Which upon the simple throne
You rest, Holy God and mighty Who does
wondrous works.

Glory to You: Who from nothing gave existence
to all of Your creations. Holy God, inexpressible
Son who was not created of the Father.

Glory to You: Who by overseeing, takes care of all of
Your creations, Holy God, overflowing spring
without end.

Lord: From You, leaders of the congregation of the
Church shall request by saying, good shepherd have
mercy upon your spoken flock.

Amen. Alleluia, alleluia, alleluia.

Amen. Alleluia, alleluia, alleluia.

NIGHT HOUR

Proclamation

*Nighttime proclamation composed
by Hovhan Mantagouni (478-490 A.D.)*

Student Chancel

The awakening of all from the rest of sleep, God
the lover of mankind, while in our weakness, graced
unto us consolation and comfort. And having come
in unison with spiritual song in glorification
and in honor of the most Holy Name of our
Lord and savior Jesus Christ. Trembling with fear
let us stand before You in prayer. And
let us be satisfied from Him in this hour
of the night, for the sake of his righteousness
and justice. Who has chosen us with His
mercy, and has graced unto us bringing likeness
of the heavenly angels, in which we shall become,
glorifying the Lord God of all.
And we from this time forward, having
cleansed our beings from our conscious
and from evil deeds.

NIGHT HOUR

Let us raise our hands in holiness without
anger and without doubt.
With faith let us ask from Him
atonement* and forgiveness of our offences.
By confessing the secrets in our hearts
to God the knower of secrets. So that
by receiving our requests with prayer and
with the advocation of all of the saints.
May God the lover of mankind grace us
with living in virtue and conducting ourselves
purely according to His wills in this world.
And by being worthy of the eternal and
heavenly altars.
Which He promised to His beloved, the
true God Jesus Christ, Our Lord give life
and have mercy.

<u>Choir</u>
Give life Lord.

<u>Deacon</u>
For passing the remainder of this night in
peace. With faith let us ask from the Lord.

<u>Choir</u>
Grace unto us Lord.

---

* *The Armenian word is Kavootyoon in which the root is Kav. The actual meaning is: to prevent or to forbid.* **When used we are actually asking God to prevent us from sinning.** *Atone is a secondary meaning which has taken precedence in usage. Throughout this text Atone will be used because of its familiarity of already being in use and it is less problematic with regards to English syntax than the above choices. It is very important that the reader understands the nuances of this word!*

NIGHT HOUR

The angel of peace to be guardian
of our beings. Let us ask from the Lord.

Grace unto us Lord.

For atonement and forgiveness of our offences.
Let us ask from the Lord.

Grace unto us Lord.

For the great Holy Cross and able
strength for assistance of our beings.
Let us ask from the Lord.

Grace unto us Lord.

And again in one voice for the sake of
our true and holy faith.
Let us pray to the Lord.

Lord have mercy.

Let us make ourselves and one another as
the person of the Lord God almighty.

Let us become as Your Person Lord.

NIGHT HOUR

Lord our God be merciful to us,
according to Your great mercy,
let us all say in unison.

Lord have mercy. Lord have mercy. Lord have mercy.

"Lord Have Mercy" is recited according to the appropriate day. For Sundays and for Feasts of the Lord, "Lord Have Mercy" is repeated three times. For Feast Days of the Saints, "Lord Have Mercy" is repeated fifty times. For Days of Fasting, "Lord Have Mercy" is repeated one hundred times.

"Ashkharh Amenayn (All of the World)." A lamentful hymn of self repentance sung on Feast Days of the Saints and Fasting Days, composed by His Holiness Nerses Catholicos of the Armenians, in which all people should speak their objections to one another in a confession like manner. (Each verse begins with a successive letter of the Armenian alphabet.)

Senior Chancel

All of the world, having looked at me, let us share afflictions.
I open my lips, I speak with my tongue, I protest my being.
Lord have mercy. Lord have mercy. Lord have mercy.

NIGHT HOUR

I became a thief of sins, a finder of damnation, I dug a pit for myself.
I cheated myself, I betrayed myself, I built a snare for myself.
Lord have mercy. Lord have mercy. Lord have mercy.

Sometimes I was light, at this time I am darkness, and the shadow of death.
How shall I recount, the number of my sins, for they are innumerable.
Lord have mercy. Lord have mercy. Lord have mercy.

Heaven and earth, come and lament, my being is deplorable.
I chose the evil, I accepted it willingly, the multitudes of sin.
Lord have mercy. Lord have mercy. Lord have mercy.

I plunge into the mud. I wallow in sins, I am not able to shake away.
Being filled with pestilent illness, I became an infectious stench,
for long periods of time.
Lord have mercy. Lord have mercy. Lord have mercy.

Into the open I departed, away from holy thoughts, away from good deeds.
My being with a good reputation, going away from the light,
being along the way of darkness.
Lord have mercy. Lord have mercy. Lord have mercy.

NIGHT HOUR

Thoughts of evil, deceive the souls, they make an abyss.
They conceal with abysses, while falling they are mocked,
they make me contemptible.
Lord have mercy. Lord have mercy. Lord have mercy.

Willingly I became lost, with the bending of myself,
I cannot be stood up.
The one who burns fire for sins, set fire to me, for my spiritual good.
Lord have mercy. Lord have mercy. Lord have mercy.

I was whipped by sins, the onlookers whipped, my soul became wearied.
Bile of bitterness, being concealed in my heart, my torch was extinguished.
Lord have mercy. Lord have mercy. Lord have mercy.

Through the tasting of sins, I tasted death, from opulence I became poor.
I am dead in spirit, my thoughts are wandering, I exist only in body.
 Lord have mercy. Lord have mercy. Lord have mercy.

In the trap of death, I fell to the hunter, I was conquered by disease.
Of the arrows of the enemy, I became a target,
recently I am always pierced.
Lord have mercy. Lord have mercy. Lord have mercy.

NIGHT HOUR

Encircling and surrounding me, they were many dogs,
I became soiled with my blood.
I became prey to evil, with the net of sins, my being became hunted.
Lord have mercy. Lord have mercy. Lord have mercy.

Cruelly with affliction, my being became tortured, I have no cessation of it.
I found the debtor, of the debts of offences, having indebtedness in sins.
Lord have mercy. Lord have mercy. Lord have mercy.

I attempt to repent, I became warm again, I burn with the fire of sins.
I was called Rabbi, I was named insane, for my vulgar conduct.
Lord have mercy. Lord have mercy. Lord have mercy.

With love of desire, in extreme passion, my heart became pierced.
With wounds of offences, my soul became afflicted, I roam perplexed.
Lord have mercy. Lord have mercy. Lord have mercy.

Evil ones ruled over me, they displaced me into exile,
into despotic open arms.
Of the good Rabbi, in the rejoiceful sound, in my lowliness I was not heard.
Lord have mercy. Lord have mercy. Lord have mercy.

Desire of the evil ones, with desirable faces, my eyes became hurt.
Of each person, having mats and a crowd of disease,
my soul is exhausted.
Lord have mercy. Lord have mercy. Lord have mercy.

NIGHT HOUR

My being hastened, fleeing from evil, desiring good.
I always perceived You near, the sleep of death having come,
fault finding judge.
Lord have mercy. Lord have mercy. Lord have mercy.

With the advocation of the God-Bearer.
Remember, Lord, and have mercy.

---

*"Arravod Loosoh (Morning of Light)." A prayerful hymn for
Feast Days of the Lord sung to the Holy Trinity,
by His Holiness Nerses the Graceful Catholicos of the Armenians. Each
individual should sing in a prayerful manner to the Holy Trinity.
(Each verse begins with a successive letter of the Armenian alphabet.)*

Senior Chancel

Morning of light, just sun, shine light upon me.
Emanation from the Father, emanate from my soul,
words that please You.

Treasure of mercy, of the hidden treasure, make me the finder.
The door of mercy, open to me who professes the faith,
rank me amongst the heavenly hosts.

Three in union, will become caretaker, and have mercy upon me.
Awake, Lord, to help, awaken the lethargic, resembling angelic joy.

NIGHT HOUR

He that exists Father without beginning,
of the same existence of the Son, existence of the ever Holy Spirit.
Receive me compassionately, receive mercifully,
receive lover of mankind.

King of glories, giver of forgiveness, forgive me for my offences.
Gatherer of the good, and gather me, into the assembly of the first.

From You Lord I request, from Your lovingness of mankind,
healing for me.
Be life to the dead, light to the darkening, dissolver of pains.

Knower of thoughts, grace unto me in darkness, bright thoughts.
Birth in the bosom of the Father, of covering with a shadowy ghost,
shine light of glories.

Life giving savior, give life to those who are dead,
lift up those who have sunken.
Establish with faith, affirm with hope, build with love.

With my voice I pray, with my hands I request,
grace unto me the gift of glories.
With the torch of light, skillful director, fortify me in hiding.

NIGHT HOUR

Ray of glories, show me the road, to hasten into heaven.
Only begotten of the Father,
lead me to enter the curtained bridal chamber, pure for the nuptials.

At which time You come in glory, on the tremendous day,
remember me Christ.
Renewer of old, and renew me, decorate newly.

Grace giver of good, grace unto me atonement, grace unto me forgiveness.
Lord gladden me, unto my spirit with salvation,
for the sake of whose I am in sorrow.

Of the evil cultivator, of his evil seeds, dry up his fruit.
Gifter of good, gift unto me, pardon of my debts.

Grace water unto my eyes, warm pouring tears, cancel my offences.
Eraser of hunger, make my vulgar soul drink, show me the path of light.

Love, the name of Jesus, with Your love be compressed,
upon my heart of stone.
For the sake of compassion, for the sake of mercy, give life again.

NIGHT HOUR

Of desiring with sight, give to me so that I become satiated,
Lord Jesus Christ.
Heavenly Rabbi, gather the disciples, into the troops of heavenly hosts.

Dew of Your blood, Lord, sprinkle into my soul, may my being rejoice.
Exhausted with sin, exhaustedly I request, weave me into good.

Savior of all, hasten to save me, from the temptations of sin.
Atoner of offences, atone those singing blessings, glories to You.

With the advocation of the God-Bearer.
Remember, Lord, and have mercy.

Following this, the Nighttime prayer by Hovhan Mantagouni is said.

Senior Chancel

<u>Priest</u>
From You we are satisfied, Lord our God,
who has graced upon us in peace the
rest of sleep. And having awakened, You made
us to arrive early to worship Your awesome
praised, Holy Name.

NIGHT HOUR

Grant unto us, Lord,
we request of You, that we pass the
remainder of this night in peace, and at
all times during the pilgrimage of our lives,
in Your fear fortify and keep us.
So that with caution and pure behavior, we
that have become religious in this world may
arrive in the safe and peaceful harbor of
Your eternal life. With grace and
lovingness of mankind of our Lord and Savior
Jesus Christ. With whom You, the Father and
Holy Spirit enjoy glory, Lordship, and honor.
Now and always and unto the
eternity of eternities. Amen.

Peace unto all.

<u>Choir</u>
And with Your spirit.

<u>Deacon</u>
Let us bow down in worship of God.

<u>Choir</u>
Before You Lord.

<u>Priest</u>
Look, benevolent Lord, with mercy
upon Your worshippers and upon the
ones who give praise to Your Holy Name.

NIGHT HOUR

Lord of hosts, give peace to our
beings from every satanic agitation
and from worldly amusements.
Send unto us Your angel of peace,
who has come to keep us tranquil
from the day and into the night,
in wakefulness and in our rest.
So that through piety and worthiness
through serving You Lord in this life,
let us reach Your eternal heavenly
kingdom, which was prepared
from the beginning of the world for
Your saints. And with them, with
satisfaction let us glorify the Father
and the Son and the Holy Spirit,
now and always and unto the
eternity of eternities.

Blessed be our Lord Jesus Christ. Amen.
Alleluia. Alleluia.

NIGHT HOUR 41

At this point recite the Canonical Psalms according to the proper tone of the day. This refers to the entire order of Psalms and Prayers found in the Book of Psalms and Prayer which is found in the first section of the Chancel Book of Hours and is placed on the Bema lectern. The Book of Psalms consists of eight separate canons which are named by the same eight tones which the church uses (A Tz, A G, P Tz, P G etc...) Each Canon is comprised of seven subsections known as Koopgha(s) (originating from the Greek "kephalaion" meaning chapter or boundary). The separate Canons and the Koopgha(s) do not contain the same number of Psalms and verses amongst themselves. When the Canonical Psalms and Prayers are read, the entire eight canons are actually read, not only that of the daily tone. After the Canonic Psalms, sing the "Ganonaklookh," Canonhead (Primary Canon Psalm), which is derived from verses of the seventh Koopgha of the appropriate tone, according to the proper tone of the day.

Senior Chancel

<u>A Tz</u>
<u>Ps 34:1-7 KJV 35:1-7</u>

Lord judge, those who judge me. Alleluia.
Fight against those who fight against me. Alleluia.

Take your weapon and shield, and rise up to help me,
draw your sword against my persecutors, oppose them,
and say to my being that I am your salvation. Alleluia.

May those who were demanding my being become
humiliated and shamed, for those who were thinking
evil towards me, may they be turned back and be
humiliated. Alleluia.

May they become as dust before the wind,
and may the angel of the Lord trouble them. Alleluia.

May their roads become dark and slippery,
and may the angel of God persecute them. Alleluia.

In their corruption they fruitlessly hid a snare for me,
and in vain they insulted my being. Alleluia.

<u>Melody Change</u>
<u>Ps 35:6-13 KJV 36:5-12</u>

Lord, Your mercy is in the heavens,
Your truth unto the skies. Alleluia. Alleluia.

Your justice is as the mountains,
Your righteousness is as a great depth,
You Lord give life to man and animal. Alleluia. Alleluia.

So that You made many of Your mercies,
God, but the sons of man shall have hope
in the shadow of Your wings. Alleluia. Alleluia.

They become drunk feasting from the abundant fat
of Your house, and You give to them the delicacy of
Your stream to drink. Alleluia. Alleluia.

From You Lord is the fountain of life,
and with the light of Your faces we see
the light. Alleluia. Alleluia.

May Your mercies spring forth, upon those
who know You, Your justice upon those
who are upright in their heart. Alleluia. Alleluia.

NIGHT HOUR

Do not let the foot of arrogances come upon us,
nor let the hand of sinners cause us to tremble.
Alleluia. Alleluia.

Over there all those whom commit unrighteousness
have fallen, may they be cast down and be made not
able to recover. Alleluia. Alleluia.

Glory to the Father, and to the Son, and to the Holy Spirit.
Now and always and unto the eternity of eternities.
Amen. Alleluia. Alleluia.

A G
Ps 52:1-5 KJV 53:1-4

The senseless one says in his
heart that God does not exist. Alleluia.
They corrupted and defiled in
their unrighteousness, and there is
no one that makes pleasantness. Alleluia.

God looked from heaven upon all of
the sons of man, seeing, is there
anyone wise that will search for God?
Alleluia.

Together they all went astray
and became useless. Alleluia.

There is no one that does good, no one,
not even one. Alleluia.

Those who were eating my people as
a meal of bread, and they did not call
upon God. Alleluia.

Melody Change
Ps 54:20-24 KJV 55:19-23

For change does not exist in them, and they
have no fear of God. Alleluia. Alleluia.

He extended his hands out while cutting them down,
and they defiled their laws. Alleluia. Alleluia.

They became divided from the rage of His faces,
and it came into their hearts. Alleluia. Alleluia.

Their words were more smooth than olive oil,
and they themselves are as arrows. Alleluia. Alleluia.

Cast your soul unto the Lord, and He will
nourish you, and He does not give eternal trembling
to the just. Alleluia. Alleluia.

NIGHT HOUR

You, God, will cast them down into the
pit of destruction, blood shedding
and deceitful men shall live out half of their
days, but I Lord hoped in You. Alleluia. Alleluia.

Glory to the Father, and to the Son, and to the Holy Spirit.
Now and always and unto the eternity of eternities.
Amen. Alleluia. Alleluia.

P Tz
Ps 70:2-6 KJV 71:1-6

In You, Lord, I hoped, unto eternity
I will not be ashamed. Alleluia.
Save and give me life in Your justice. Alleluia.

May Your ear descend upon me, and give
me life. Alleluia.

My God be my refuge, my place's fortress for
giving me life, for You are my firmness and refuge.
Alleluia.

My God, save me from the hands of the sinner,
from the hands of the lawless and unrighteous.
Alleluia.

NIGHT HOUR

You are my patience Lord, Lord
my hope from my childhood. Alleluia.

I became firm in You from the womb,
from my mother's belly You have been my refuge,
and from You is my help at all times. Alleluia.

Melody Change
Ps 71:11-19 KJV 72:11-19

May all the kings of the earth bow down and
worship Him, and may all nations serve Him.
Alleluia. Alleluia.

For he saved the poor from the hands of the
powerful, the poor and the impoverished who
have no helper. Alleluia. Alleluia.

He spares the poor and the impoverished, and unto
those, beings of the impoverished, may He give life,
may He save those beings from the usury of the
wicked. Alleluia. Alleluia.

His name is honorable before them, may he live and
give unto him the gold of Arabia. Alleluia. Alleluia.

They shall say prayers to Him at all times,
and they shall bless Him during the entire day always.

NIGHT HOUR

May there be stability in all the lands,
and upon the mountain tops. Alleluia. Alleluia

May its fruit rise up as Lebanon, and may it blossom
in the city of the Lord as grass on the earth.
Alleluia. Alleluia.

May the name of the Lord be blessed
unto eternity, for His Name is before the sun.
Alleluia. Alleluia.

In Him all nations of the earth will be blessed,
and all nations shall be fortunate in Him.
Alleluia. Alleluia.

Blessed be the Lord God of Israel Who is the
only One Who does wonders, and blessed be His Holy
Name of glories unto eternity, may all of the
earth be filled with His glories.
Let it be, let it be. Alleluia. Alleluia.

Glory to the Father, and to the Son, and to the Holy Spirit.
Now and always and unto the eternity of eternities.
Amen. Alleluia. Alleluia.

NIGHT HOUR

<u>P G</u>
<u>Ps 88:2-7   KJV 89:1-6</u>

Your mercies Lord, I will bless unto eternity. Alleluia.
With my mouth I will tell of Your truths
from generation unto generation. Alleluia.

You said that this world shall be made with mercy,
in the heavens Your truth shall be prepared. Alleluia.

I made a covenant to my chosen one, I swore unto
David my servant. Alleluia.

Unto eternity I shall establish Your descendants,
and from generation to generation I shall build
Your throne. Alleluia.

May the heavens confess of Your wonders, Lord,
and Your truth in the assemblies of the saints. Alleluia.

Who is in the clouds that is equal to You,
or who of the sons of God can resemble the Lord. Alleluia.

<u>Melody Change</u>
<u>Ps 88:44-53 KJV 89:43-52</u>

You turned back the help of his sword, and
did not uphold him in war. Alleluia. Alleluia.

You had contempt upon his holiness,
and destroyed his throne to the ground. Alleluia. Alleluia.

NIGHT HOUR

You have made the time of his days lessened, and
You poured shame upon him. Alleluia. Alleluia.

Until when, will the turning back of Your faces end,
Your anger shall become inflamed as fire. Alleluia. Alleluia.

But now remember and see, who is it that
is my rest, is it possible that You created
all of the sons of man in vain. Alleluia. Alleluia.

Who is man that shall live and not see death,
or who shall save his being from the hands of hells*.
Alleluia. Alleluia.

Where are Your first mercies, Lord, which You
swore unto David with Your truth. Alleluia. Alleluia.

Remember the insults to Your servant, that I have
received into my bosom from many nations. Alleluia. Alleluia.

Who, which Your enemies have insulted, Lord, they instead
insulted Your anointed one. Alleluia. Alleluia.

Blessed be Lord God unto the eternity of eternities.
Let it be. Let it be. Alleluia. Alleluia.

Glory to the Father, and to the Son, and to the Holy Spirit.
Now and always and unto the eternity of eternities.
Amen. Alleluia. Alleluia.

---

* *Hades*

NIGHT HOUR

K Tz
Ps 105:1-6 KJV 106:1-6

May you all profess to the Lord that He is sweet. Alleluia.
That His mercy is eternal. Alleluia.

Who can speak the powers of the Lord, make heard all
of His blessings. Alleluia.

Fortunate are those who keep the laws, and
do justice at all times. Alleluia.

Remember us, Lord, with the pleasure of Your people,
and make visit to us in Your salvation. Alleluia.

May we see the sweetness of Your chosen ones,
may we rejoice in the joy of Your nation,
and may we give praise in your inheritance. Alleluia.

Melody Change
Ps 105:41-48 KJV 106:41-48

He gave them over to the hands of the heathens, and
they ruled over them with their hatred, and their enemies
troubled them, and they became submissive under their hands.
Alleluia. Alleluia.

NIGHT HOUR

He saved them many times, and they
converted him to their way of thought, and they
sunk down into their unlawfulness. Alleluia. Alleluia.

The Lord observed their troubles,
while hearing the sound of their prayers. Alleluia. Alleluia.

He remembered his covenant, and repented according
to His mercies, and gave them compassion
before all of their captive takers. Alleluia. Alleluia.

Save us, Lord our God, and gather us from
among the heathen. Alleluia. Alleluia.

May we profess Your Holy Name, and
may we boast in Your blessings. Alleluia. Alleluia.

Blessed be the Lord God of Israel, unto the
eternity of eternities. Alleluia. Alleluia.

And let all the people say; Let it be. Let it be.
Alleluia. Alleluia.

Glory to the Father, and to the Son, and to the Holy Spirit.
Now and always and unto the eternity of eternities.
Amen. Alleluia. Alleluia.

NIGHT HOUR

<u>K G</u>
<u>Ps 118: 121-126 KJV 119: 121-126</u>

I have done righteousness and justice. Alleluia.
Do not hand me over to the hands of my oppressors. Alleluia.

Receive Your servant in goodness, do not let
the arrogant disgust me. Alleluia.

My eyes awaited for Your salvation, Lord, and for
the word of Your justice. Alleluia.

Make with Your servant, Lord, according to
Your mercy, teach me Your justice. Alleluia.

I am Your servant, make me wise, and
I may know Your testimonies. Alleluia.

It is time to give adoration to the Lord,
they have annulled Your laws. Alleluia.

<u>Melody Change</u>
<u>Ps 118: 169-176 KJV 119: 169-176</u>

May my requests draw near before You, Lord, according
to Your word make me wise. Alleluia. Alleluia.

May my prayers enter before You, Lord, and through
Your word save me. Alleluia. Alleluia.

May Your blessings spring forth from my lips,
at which time You will teach me Your justice. Alleluia. Alleluia.

NIGHT HOUR

My tongue shall speak Your words, for all of
Your commandments are with justice. Alleluia. Alleluia.

Let it be Your hand which is giving me
life, for I chose Your commandments. Alleluia. Alleluia.

I became desirous of Your salvation, Lord,
and Your laws were my word. Alleluia. Alleluia.

May my being live, may it bless You,
and Your laws shall help me. Alleluia. Alleluia.

I was wandering as a lost sheep, search for this
Your servant, for I have not forgotten
Your commandments. Alleluia. Alleluia.

Glory to the Father, and to the Son, and to the Holy Spirit.
Now and always and unto the eternity of eternities.
Amen. Alleluia. Alleluia.

T Tz
Ps 145:2-7 KJV 146:1-7

May my being bless the Lord, I shall bless the Lord
throughout all of my life. Alleluia.
I shall say psalms to my God until I am no more. Alleluia.

Do not trust in princes, in sons of man
for whom salvation does not exist in them. Alleluia.

NIGHT HOUR

The spirit goes forth from them and from
there they return to the earth, and in that
day all of their thoughts will be destroyed. Alleluia.

Fortunate is the nation who has the Lord God
of Jacob as its helper, and whose hope is
in the Lord God. Alleluia.

Who made the heavens and the earth, the
sea and everything that is in them. Alleluia.

Who keeps the truth eternally, and
gives rights to those deprived. Alleluia.

Melody Change
Ps 147:12-20 KJV 147:12-20

Praise the Lord Jerusalem. Alleluia.

And bless your God, Zion. Alleluia.

He strengthened the bolts on your gates, and
blessed your sons within you. Alleluia.

Who put your borders in peace,
with the fat of the wheat He filled you. Alleluia.

He sends His word to the earth,
His messages run quickly. Alleluia.

He places down snow as wool, and scattered
mist as dust. Alleluia.

NIGHT HOUR

He throws out ice as morsels, who is
able to stand before His cold. Alleluia.

He sends out His word and melts them,
the winds shall blow and the waters shall flow. Alleluia.

He tells His word unto Jacob, justice
and righteousness unto Israel. Alleluia.

He has not done this for all nations Lord,
and He has not revealed His judgments to them. Alleluia.

Glory to the Father, and to the Son, and to the Holy Spirit.
Now and always and unto the eternity of eternities.
Amen. Alleluia. Alleluia.

T G
Ps 17:2-7 KJV 18:1-6

I shall love You Lord my strength. Alleluia.
Provider of my affirmation, my refuge and my salvation.
Alleluia.

God my helper and I hope in Him, He is
my refuge, my horn of salvation, and He is
acceptable to me. Alleluia.

With blessings I shall call upon the Lord, and from my
enemies I shall be kept alive. Alleluia.

The pangs of death have surrounded me, and
torrential floods of unrighteousness troubled me. Alleluia.

The afflictions of hells* besieged me, and
made me to arrive at the snares of death. Alleluia.

In my oppression I called upon You Lord,
and to my God I cried. Alleluia.

<u>Melody Change</u>
<u>Ps 17:40-51 KJV 18:39-50</u>

You clothed me with strength for war, and
those who have risen up against me, You subdued
under me. Alleluia. Alleluia.

You drove away my enemies, and You
slayed those who hated me. Alleluia. Alleluia.

They cried out but there was no one
to save them, they called upon the Lord
and He did not hear them. Alleluia. Alleluia.

I shall pulverize them as dust before the
wind, and I shall trample upon them
as clay in the streets. Alleluia. Alleluia.

He will save me from the adversity of the peoples,
and He will establish me the head of
the gentiles. Alleluia. Alleluia.

* *Hades*

NIGHT HOUR

People of whom I did not know served me,
and hearing with their own ears, they listened
to me. Alleluia. Alleluia.

Sons of foreigners lied to me, sons of
foreigners became worn out and lame
from their paths. Alleluia. Alleluia.

The Lord is alive and blessed is God, and
God shall be elevated on high for my salvation.
Alleluia. Alleluia.

It is God who demands my revenge,
and He makes the people submissive
under me. Alleluia. Alleluia.

My savior from passionate enemies of mine,
from those who were raised up against me, You
raised me up on high, and You raised me up from
the unrighteous and saved me. Alleluia. Alleluia.

For this I shall confess of You unto the gentiles,
and to Your Name I shall say psalms. Alleluia. Alleluia.

You made great the salvation of his king, making
mercy with his anointed David, and with
his children from generation unto generation.
Alleluia. Alleluia.

Glory to the Father, and to the Son, and to the Holy Spirit.
Now and always and unto the eternity of eternities.
Amen. Alleluia. Alleluia.

NIGHT HOUR

It is at this point that the order of the Canonical Psalms is performed. The order of Canonical Psalms is found in the Book of Psalms and Prayers, in the first section of the Chancel Book of Hours. The order is divided into eight sets, which are each assigned one of the eight tones (A Tz, A G, P Tz, etc...). Interestingly enough, T G begins as the first set of Canonical Psalms, not A Tz. The entire Canon contains the first 147 Psalms omitting the last three. Each Canon is comprised of seven subsections known as Koopgha(s) (originating from the Greek "kephalaion" meaning chapter or boundary). The "Ganonaklookh" Canonhead (Primary Canon Psalm) originates from the set of Psalms beginning the seventh Koopgha of each set. Following the Psalms of the seventh Koopgha are Canticles (Hymns of the Prophets), Petitions, Prayers, and Proclamations. The ancient form of the Common Hour of Prayers consisted of the entire order of Canonic Psalms in which all eight sets were performed throughout the day at their appropriate hours. If the Ganonaklookh with the Psalms are recited, the last Koopgha containing the Hymns of the Prophets is also said. If the Ganonaklookh is said without the Psalms, as is the custom for some, the following is said after the Ganonaklookh:

"And again in peace let us request of the Lord. Receive, save, and have mercy."
"Blessing and glory to the Father and to the Son and to the Holy Spirit.
Now always and unto the eternity of eternities. Amen."

Then the Order of Rest of the Souls (Hanksdyan Bashdon) is performed according to the proper tone of the day in which the Gospel of Rest is read. However if it is a pompous day or a Feast of the Cross, "Aysor anjarr (Today the Inexpressible Dawn)" is sung and the Gospel of the Crucifixion is read, which is found in the Chancel Gospel. After the gospel, "Norokogh diezeratz (Regenerator of the Universes)" is sung and then the Petition "Hokvotzn hankootzelotz (For the souls of those who are at rest...)" is recited.

Some prefer to sing the Orhnootyoon* (Hymns of the Prophets) connecting to the Order of Rest of the Souls and then the Gospel of the Rest is read followed by the Petition "Hokvotzn hankootzelotz (For the souls of those who are at rest...)" and Prayer "Krisdos vorti asdoodzo (Christ Son of God...)".

* *Ten, Hymns of the Prophets which are sung before, and not to be confused with, the Avak Orhnootyoon Sharagan found on and described in detail on Pg. 127. The term Orhnootyoon translates as Blessing.*

NIGHT HOUR 59

"Ganonaklookh" Canonhead (Primary Canon Psalm) for Poon Paregentan "Natural Goodliving" (Better known as Carnival or the Sunday Eve before Great Lent. The Armenian Church equivalent of Fat Tuesday. For the remainder of this book the term shall be referred to as "Carnival" for convenience only.) This is also the Canonhead for New Sunday (The First Sunday After Easter.)

<u>Ps 145:2-10 KJV 146:1-10</u>

May my being bless the Lord, I shall bless the Lord throughout all of my life.
I shall say psalms to my God until I am no more.

Do not trust in princes, in sons of man
for whom salvation does not exist in them.

The spirit goes forth from them and from there they return to the earth, and in that day all of their thoughts will be destroyed.

Fortunate is the nation who has the Lord God of Jacob as its helper, and whose hope is in the Lord God.

Who made the heavens and the earth, the sea and everything that is in them.

Who keeps the truth eternally, and gives rights to those deprived.

He gives bread to those that hunger and the Lord releases those in bondage.

The Lord opens the eyes of the blind, and the Lord lifts up those who have sunken.

The Lord loves the just, the Lord takes care of the emigrants, the Lord receives the orphans and widows, and He destroys the paths of those who are extremely wicked.

The Lord shall reign for eternity, Your God, Zion, from generation unto generation.

NIGHT HOUR

<u>Melody Change</u>
<u>(Sing verse 3 times)</u>

I shall bless the Lord with thanksgiving
throughout my life, I shall say Psalms to
You Christ the triumphant king with
new songs of blessing.

<u>Ps 146:1-11 KJV 147:1-11</u>

Bless the Lord for psalms are good, to our God,
let them be a sweet blessing.

The Lord builds Jerusalem, and those scattered
of the people of Israel, He gathers.

He heals the broken hearts,
and closes up all their wounds.

He Who counts the multitude of the stars,
and He calls each of them by name.

Great is our Lord and great is His power,
no limit exists to His wisdom.

The Lord receives the meek, and He makes the
arrogant lowered down to the ground.

Bless the Lord by professing,
say psalms to Him with blessing.

He Who adorned the heavens with clouds,
prepared the rain for its earth.

NIGHT HOUR

He caused grass to sprout up upon the mountains,
the green vegetation in the servitude of mankind.

He Who gives food to the beastly animals, to the
chicks of ravens which cry out to Him.

It was not through the strength of a horse that the
Lord had willed, and with the body of a giant man
He was not pleased.

But the Lord was pleased by fearing in Him,
and in those who hope in His mercy.

<u>Melody Change</u>
<u>(Sing verse 3 times)</u>

They will become sweet to You Christ,
the thanksgiving of those who are in awe of Your name,
of whom You made hopeful with Your mercy in the
mystery of Your life giving coming.

<u>Ps 147: 12-20 KJV 147: 12-20</u>

Praise the Lord Jerusalem.

And bless your God, Zion.

He strengthened the bolts on your gates, and
blessed your sons within you.

Who put your borders in peace,
with the fat of the wheat He filled you.

He sends His word to the earth,
His messages run quickly.

He places down snow as wool, and scattered
mist as dust.

He throws out ice as morsels, who is
able to stand before His cold.

He sends out His word and melts them,
the winds shall blow and the waters shall flow.

He tells His word unto Jacob, justice
and righteousness unto Israel.

He has not done this for all nations Lord,
and He has not revealed His judgments to them.

<u>Melody Change</u>
<u>(Sing verse 3 times)</u>

May Your Holy Church which having been saved
praise You Christ, rejoicing in seeing You,
the One Who saves, having come with Fatherly
authority during the wedding of Your saints.

NIGHT HOUR

"Ganonaklookh" Canonhead (Primary Canon Psalm) for Holy Friday*

<u>Ps 118:161-168 KJV 119:161-168</u>

Princes persecuted me in vain. Alleluia.
And my heart feared from Your words. Alleluia.

I rejoiced in Your word,
as one who finds many spoils. Alleluia. Alleluia.

I hated and despised sins,
and I loved Your laws. Alleluia. Alleluia.

I shall bless You seven times a day, for the
sake of Your righteousness and judgment. Alleluia. Alleluia.

Much peace is for those who love Your laws, and
for them there exists nothing that can make them stumble.
Alleluia. Alleluia.

I awaited for Your salvation Lord, and I
loved Your commandments. Alleluia. Alleluia.

My being kept Your testimonies,
and loved them greatly. Alleluia. Alleluia.

I shall keep Your commandments and testimonies,
for all of my roads are before You. Alleluia. Alleluia.

---

* *For practicality purposes only this is performed on the night of Holy Thursday*

NIGHT HOUR

__Melody Change__
__Ps 118: 169-176 KJV 119: 169-176__

May my requests draw near before You, Lord, according
to Your word make me wise. Alleluia. Alleluia.

May my prayers enter before You, Lord, and through
Your word save me. Alleluia. Alleluia.

May Your blessings spring forth from my lips,
as You will teach me Your justice. Alleluia. Alleluia.

My tongue shall speak Your words, for all of
Your commandments are with justice. Alleluia. Alleluia.

Let it be Your hand which is giving me
life, for I chose Your commandments. Alleluia. Alleluia.

I became desirous of Your salvation, Lord,
and Your laws were my word. Alleluia. Alleluia.

May my being live, may it bless You,
and Your laws shall help me. Alleluia. Alleluia.

I was wandering as a lost sheep, search for this
Your servant, for I have not forgotten
Your commandments. Alleluia. Alleluia.

Glory to the Father, and to the Son, and to the Holy Spirit.
Now and always and unto the eternity of eternities.
Amen. Alleluia. Alleluia.

NIGHT HOUR

Senior Chancel

 The Hymn of Rest (Hanksdyan Sharagan) is sung at this point (see p. 86 for explanation) or the Hymn below depending on the Church Calendar.

Senior Chancel
Place the Gospel and the Book of Psalms on the bookstand.
The two priests chant in alternation three psalms from the
first set of Canonical Psalms which are Psalms Ch. 2 through 4.
Ps 2:1 KJV 2:1, Ps 3:2, KJV3:1 , Ps 4:2 KJV 4:1
Others may sing the connecting psalms:

T G *Senior Chancel*

The princes assembled all together for the
sake of the Lord and for the sake of His anointing.

Sing this above verse three times with the third verse being sung on a higher note.

Hymn "Aysor anjarr (Today the Inexpressible Dawn)" by His Holiness Nerses Catholicos of the Armenians which is sung with regards to the Gospel readings of Holy Friday, Night Hour*. It is also sung during Great Lent and Feasts of the Cross.

Senior Chancel

Today the inexpressible dawn of the light
fulfillment in our salvation,
came down into the upper room
in the completion of the shadowy feast,
before the meal of mystery the One Who
emits light wrapped a towel around Himself,
and having taken water in a servant like
manner, He was washing the feet of
His disciples.

* *For practicality purposes only this is performed on the night of Holy Thursday.*

NIGHT HOUR

To the Word of the Father of the glory of the light
Peter having approached, he excused himself, "not my feet,"
those hands for which they do works of the heavens, heaven
and earthly, by which the blind opened their
eyes and the deaf and dumb became delivered from
their condition, which brought Him up from out of
the sea, stilled the waves and they became silent.

Chosen of the head of the small flock, He
denounced the mystery of ignorance, by which
he was turning and became obedient wishing for his
feet and head to be washed, regarding the head
He said it is not necessary to be washed of water
for it is already washed, it is necessary for
your feet to be of cleanliness, joined to your
head with holiness.

Of the lessons of the disciples which He taught at first
by word, today with extreme work He Himself
showed humility, having served those on the
earth, that which is unseen of the fiery angels, having
taken His position of servants, those who are
adored by the Seraphim.

If the Lord of existence and master of all says
to His disciples and servants He washed the
feet of the old filth, and you, with each
other, show in the same nature the same
humility, the raising up from devastation
and casting down your mannerisms of superiority.

NIGHT HOUR

Those whose feet you washed with clean
hands in the basin, you taught with
humility to be victorious in conquering
evil pride, and wash the mud of my sins with the
request of the regiment of holy soldiers,
and lead straight the journeys of the
feet with humility ascending into heaven.

<u>Deacon</u>
Stand

<u>Priest</u>
Peace unto all.

<u>Choir</u>
And with Your spirit.

<u>Deacon</u>
May you listen with awe.

<u>Reader (*priest or deacon*)</u> **Senior Chancel**
The Holy Gospel of Jesus Christ According to John 13:16-18:1

<u>Choir</u>
Glory to You Lord our God.

<u>Deacon</u>
Attention

<u>Choir</u>
God says.

The Reader then chants the Gospel. This paradigm above is used for all Gospel readings in all services.

<u>Reader (*priest or deacon*)</u>
Kneeling with prayers we request of the Lord. *(recite three times)*
And again in peace let us request of the Lord.

<u>Priest</u>
Blessing and glory to the Father and to the Son and to the Holy Spirit. Now always and unto the eternity of eternities. Amen.

NIGHT HOUR

The two priests chant in alternation three psalms from the second set of Canonical Psalms which are Psalm 40 through 42. Ps 40:2 KJV 41:1, Ps 41:2 KJV 42:1, Ps 42:1 KJV 43:1

They placed upon me the word of
unlawfulness Lord, Lord do not leave me.

Sing this above verse three times with the third verse being sung on a higher note.

The laws of the Exodus which were spoken to
Moses in the Sinai, he ate the lamb in precedent
with unleavened bread and bitter herbs*,
by exchanging the old into the new, by verifying the
shadow into the light, in place of the lamb, Him through
His existence by offering the Lamb of God.

Instead of the unleavened bread without yeast
He gave His heavenly Body, born of the
Virgin, seedless, incorruptible, and spiritual,
instead of the covenant of the lamb's
blood He gave us His Blood of the covenant
anew, and they exchanged the very bitter herb
of endive for a Godly way of life.

The King of all creation gave the Bread of Life to
those that hunger, and joyfully the cup to
those who had been filled with sorrow in
Adam, this is the new covenant of my blood in place
of the old covenant of bloods, that you shall do
in remembrance of Me until I will come once again.

---

* Endive and Succory

NIGHT HOUR

Having assembled we request from You
with the assembly of the eleven, to whom
Your life giving Body having been distributed
You gave with the cup, and grace unto
us Lord to be in the same company of those
who are in communion at Your table, Your Bread
of Life in which we desire and of Your drink
of which we thirst.

Of the disciples which were chosen, Judas
separated from the holy lambs, he
betrayed unto death the uplifter of sins,
the Lamb of God in exchange for silver,
with the approaching of the spiritual meal,
the insolent and deceitful one eating with the
Master resorts to deception.

The Light was speaking having requested
of the darkened for the sake of returning
back, brothers, one amongst you shall betray
Me unto death, Peter having
heard that became frightened and made
signs with his eyes to John, asking
who is the betrayer of the Master.

NIGHT HOUR

Deacon	Stand
Priest	Peace unto all.
Choir	And with Your spirit.
Deacon	May you listen with awe.
Reader (*priest or deacon*)	The Holy Gospel of Jesus Christ According to Luke 22:1-65
Choir	Glory to You Lord our God.
Deacon	Attention
Choir	God says.

Reader (*priest or deacon*)
Kneeling with prayers we request of the Lord. *(recite three times)*
And again in peace let us request of the Lord.

Priest
Blessing and glory to the Father and to the Son and to the Holy Spirit. Now always and unto the eternity of eternities. Amen.

The two priests chant in alternation three psalms from the third set of Canonical Psalms which are Psalm 58 through 60.
Ps 58:2 KJV 59:1, Ps 59:3 KJV 60:1, Ps 60:2 KJV 61:1

Save me from my enemies God, and
grant me life from those who persecute me.

Sing this above verse three times with the third verse being sung on a higher note.

With care of love He did away with the
sorrow of His beloved, the dipped piece of bread He
gave to Judas exposing the betraying thief, and which
having taken unveiled the Godly graces of the
spirit, he betrayed himself to the first evil one*
with the betrayal of the Master.

* *Satan*

NIGHT HOUR

Of the supreme light being deprived, the
lover of darkness got up and went outside, the
Lord revealed light onto disciples, what is to be,
of being offended in the night, Peter was speaking
with excitement and condemnation of the
crowing rooster, He told of being transformed
from His world and told of the coming of the Spirit.

On the other side of the Kidron Valley
in the upper room of mystery He arose,
He went into the garden instead of
Adam entering the garden vineyard of
paradise, and Lord have us enter with
the same one of which was taken out
as the very first, in order to inherit from
our Father, make us worthy anew.

He was sorrowfully caring about His painful
passions to come, with three disciples,
He became separated alone, to save the
world, My Spirit is willing but
the nature of My Body is weak,
not that one is strong and powerful and
the other one is weak and in danger, but
existing united one and the same, willingly the
passions are borne.

NIGHT HOUR

He was praying with a prayerful voice
for His sake to His Father that
exists, He was kneeling down, to
Whom all shall kneel anew, if it is
possible for mankind to be saved
without My death, as it is written,
may this cup of death pass from Me
not by My will but may it be Your will.

Having hidden in fear sweating round droplets
of blood with a gushing flow, to
strengthen Him an angel came near in
fulfilling the written laws, that in
fulfillment, the Word of God took the nature
of mankind, fear and sorrow were
necessary to be in Him in order to bear iniquity.

<u>Deacon</u>	Stand
<u>Priest</u>	Peace unto all.
<u>Choir</u>	And with Your spirit.
<u>Deacon</u>	May you listen with awe.
<u>Reader (priest or deacon)</u>	The Holy Gospel of Jesus Christ According to Mark 14:27-72
<u>Choir</u>	Glory to You Lord our God.
<u>Deacon</u>	Attention
<u>Choir</u>	God says.

<u>Reader (priest or deacon)</u>
Kneeling with prayers we request of the Lord. *(recite three times)*
And again in peace let us request of the Lord.

<u>Priest</u>
Blessing and glory to the Father and to the Son and to the Holy Spirit.
Now always and unto the eternity of eternities. Amen.

NIGHT HOUR

The two priests chant in alternation three psalms from the fourth set of Canonical Psalms which are Psalm 78 through 80. Ps 78:1 KJV 79:1, Ps 79:2 KJV 80:1, Ps 80:2 KJV 81:1

They were expelled from Your hand,
we people and flock of Your pasture.

Sing this above verse three times with the third verse being sung on a higher note.

Ray of glory, Who in accordance with
the nature of mankind, You became anguished
in the night, You prayed to the Father
in heaven, shine the heavenly light upon us
and eliminate the fear of the evil one,
part of our spirit and body in Your Holy
fear they shall nail.

Having approached, Judas who will betray
along with the order of Pharisees, they fell
as did the fallen angels who through eternity
will not rise up, Judas with the opportunity
of a deceitful kiss was giving the signal for
death, instead of love, by betraying Him, evil
in exchange for good through payment.

NIGHT HOUR

At that time Peter with the compassion of love,
cut off with a sword the right ear of the servant
whose name was Malchus, who would not hear his
Lord, but our Lord approaching quickly
to the ear as a physician, healed
it in a God like manner, the
blind ones did see that event.

Of the new little flock having been scattered
because of the brave shepherd having been
beaten, only Peter went with Him, Peter the
rock was shaken by the girl, the designated
crowing of the rooster having occurred, the Lord
looked at Peter giving him a message with His eyes,
he remembered His words and bitterly
wept to the ground and then again stood up.

Having given grace upon the Rock of the Church
after having run away, and having stood him back
up after his falling down for the sake
of the crying of his heart, stand me up
Lord in the same company as those who have fallen
from being unsteady, my eyes giving forth
tears, and water as like the ocean upon my head.

NIGHT HOUR

Who willed that the One Who could not be bound,
the hands of the releaser having been bound,
they lead Him away to the palace of Caiaphas
and Annas, the servant slapped that face of
Whom the Seraphim were protecting, they spat with
their filthy mouths upon Him who with His own
spit emanated light unto the blind.

Deacon	Stand
Priest	Peace unto all.
Choir	And with Your spirit.
Deacon	May you listen with awe.
Reader (*priest or deacon*)	The Holy Gospel of Jesus Christ According to Matthew 26:31-56
Choir	Glory to You Lord our God.
Deacon	Attention
Choir	God says.

Reader (*priest or deacon*)
Kneeling with prayers we request of the Lord. *(recite three times)*
And again in peace let us request of the Lord.

Priest
Blessing and glory to the Father and to the Son and to the Holy Spirit.
Now always and unto the eternity of eternities. Amen.

The two priests chant in alternation three psalms from the fifth set of Canonical Psalms which are Psalm 108 through 110. Ps 108:2 KJV 109:1, Ps 109:1 KJV 110:1, Ps 110:1 KJV 111:1

They spoke of me with a deceitful tongue,
and with words of hate they besieged me.

Sing this above verse three times with the third verse being sung on a higher note.

NIGHT HOUR

The one who unties the evil binding of man that You were
bound in exchange for the bound, release me
from my self-inflicted binds of sins bound
of hell*, that under sins of the condemned
He stood without sin in the court, at
the time of the coming of the glories of
the Father, may You not judge me with those.

With respect to the Adam of old who You
were mocked for his sake, erase the shame of
sins of the abusive of which my face was covered,
which You forgave the evil servant who brought
forth his hands to slap You, strike with much
strength the face of the evil one in same manner
that he struck me with much force.

The torch of light on Friday morning
of the old Passover, He was standing before the judge,
the servant was sitting in the court,
to the questioning of Pilate the Lord did not
give a reply, for as foretold that the writings shall
be fulfilled, He became a man which could not speak.

Hades

NIGHT HOUR

The rank of the common soldiers having
dressed in clothes of dishonor, He whose
clothes are light of glories as like a robe
that He himself clothed, kneeling down in
jest they were hitting His head with reeds,
they encircled His head with a crown of thorns,
the One Who takes out the thorn of sins.

The frightfulness of the Cherubim, He Himself
was lifting the wood of the cross, up to
the place of Golgotha in which the first
man has been placed*, they gave Him wine to
drink mixed with myrrh, and food mixed
in with bitterness, by which the bitter taste of the
fruit He changed for us to be sweet and appetizing.

The heavenly hosts having been terrified saw
the Lord having been naked, and His clothes
having been divided, the robe having cast
dice for, they pierced His hands and feet
visibly according to the prophecy of the voice
of David, upon the wood cross they nailed the
fingers that wrote on the stone tablets.

---

* *By Church tradition (Orthodox, Catholic, and Armenian) the burial place of Adam is directly under Golgotha symbolizing that the crucifixion of Christ conquered the original sin.*

NIGHT HOUR

<u>Deacon</u> Stand

<u>Priest</u> Peace unto all.

<u>Choir</u> And with Your spirit.

<u>Deacon</u> May you listen with awe.

<u>Reader (*priest or deacon*)</u> The Holy Gospel of Jesus Christ According to Matthew 26:57-75

<u>Choir</u> Glory to You Lord our God.

<u>Deacon</u> Attention

<u>Choir</u> God says.

<u>Reader (*priest or deacon*)</u>
Kneeling with prayers we request of the Lord. (*recite three times*)
And again in peace let us request of the Lord.

<u>Priest</u>
Blessing and glory to the Father and to the Son and to the Holy Spirit. Now always and unto the eternity of eternities. Amen.

The two priests chant in alternation psalms from the sixth set of Canonical Psalms which are Psalm 117:1-19 KJV 118:1-19

May you all profess to the Lord that
He is good, that His mercy is eternal.

Sing this above verse three times with the third verse being sung on a higher note.

His hands having been stretched out for the
hands (of Adam), His feet for the feet of those
who went near the bitter fruit, the wood of death,
the cross was changed into the tree of life, in between
two criminals, You having been stripped naked,
the giver of laws, of whom no one in the
generation of the blind saw except for one thief.

NIGHT HOUR

In seconds the day's sun became night,
the shadow cast a veil upon His nakedness,
that the eye of the unworthy ones shall not see it,
the midday became dark and gloomy at which
time Adam died in sin, in the ninth hour it
returned to light at which time death dissolved death.

With dewed tears grievously the mother of the
Lord who was standing near the cross, at which time she
heard the crying out with thirst of her only begotten, they
gave Him vinegar mixed with bitter flavoring,
the One Who made the rivers flow in Eden and the
stream of good water flow from the rock, He drank
for the lineage of the one made bitter.

As the third hour came to a close, the ideas of
the snake came to our foremother Eve, during
the sixth hour the first man had fallen most
probably by her words, for at that same hour the Lord
on the cross would atone for their sins, at which time
the Adam of old left paradise, He placed the thief in
paradise.

In a sweet sounding voice to me, He cried out
to His Father "Eli Eli," by the will of the Father
He rendered His spirit, in same He offered the
souls of mankind, the earth shook from its
foundation and the curtain tore in two, the grave
stones split apart and the graves of the dead
opened up.

NIGHT HOUR

His wonders having been proclaimed, God in body
was crucified for me, having our nature
He died, having been proclaimed God immortal,
having two streams flowing from His side His
Church became established, having been purified
with water, the Church drinks the blood, the Son
with the Father are given glory.

<u>Deacon</u>	Stand
<u>Priest</u>	Peace unto all.
<u>Choir</u>	And with Your spirit.
<u>Deacon</u>	May you listen with awe.
<u>Reader (priest or deacon)</u>	The Holy Gospel of Jesus Christ According to John 18:2-27
<u>Choir</u>	Glory to You Lord our God.
<u>Deacon</u>	Attention
<u>Choir</u>	God says.

<u>Reader (priest or deacon)</u>
Kneeling with prayers we request of the Lord. *(recite three times)*
And again in peace let us request of the Lord.

<u>Priest</u>
Blessing and glory to the Father and to the Son and to the Holy Spirit.
Now always and unto the eternity of eternities. Amen.

"Ganonaklookh" Canonhead (Primary Canon Psalm) for
Holy Saturday (Easter Eve)

The following is sung. (See Pg. 41 Tone A Tz)

Lord judge, those who judge me...

NIGHT HOUR 81

Hymns by His Holiness Nerses Catholicos of the Armenians which are sung during the day on Holy Friday, Great Lent, and Feasts of the Cross. All four Hymns are sung in which a gospel reading follows each.

Senior Chancel

$\overline{\text{P G}}$
$\overline{\text{T G}}$

Regenerator of the universes Who clothed us with the light of glories, mockingly having been cast to You, the red robe by the soldiers, make me naked of the burlap clothes of sins, the sorrowful painted with blood, and clothe me with the first joy of the robe.

Unto the Heavenly King they knelt down on their knees and made fun of Him, covering Your head they were beating You and they were striking You with reeds, and I having fallen to the ground in obedience to the wills of the evil one, may You not allow me to make fun in the same but may You stand me up again.

Everyone having gathered to Your body after the judges sentence, He took severe beatings of the cane for the sake of the canings of the first created, me who from feet to head is afflicted with impossible pain, make me well again, a second time as with the grace of the baptismal font.

Shining in holiness instead of having adorned ornaments which were worn by Aaron, a crown of thorns was placed upon Him by the Israeli vineyard cultivators, remove the thorn of sins from me by which my enemy beat me, and heal the bitten wound that the scar of sins may be erased.

NIGHT HOUR

<u>Deacon</u>	Stand
<u>Priest</u>	Peace unto all.
<u>Choir</u>	And with Your spirit.
<u>Deacon</u>	May you listen with awe.
<u>Reader (priest or deacon)</u>	The Holy Gospel of Jesus Christ According to Matthew 27:1-56
<u>Choir</u>	Glory to You Lord our God.
<u>Deacon</u>	Attention
<u>Choir</u>	God says.

<u>P Tz</u>
<u>T Tz</u>

In thirst they gave to You bitter and vinegar to drink, You willingly drank, that the taste of very bitter fruit would become sweetened, the bitterness of the poison one* which had been cast into pieces upon my soul, remove far away with the same and Your love shall become sweet in the same.

In place of the death bearing tree having been planted and that which sprouted up in the middle of paradise, You carried the wooden cross to its place in Golgotha, take my spirit which has fallen into sins and You are a carrier of a very heavy burden, carry it upon Your shoulders as a lamb and bring it to the place in heaven in which it was pledged.

* *Satan*

NIGHT HOUR

On Friday at the third hour the Lord was nailed to the cross, the bindings of the first created were removed and You bound up the enemy, strengthen me with the protection of Your life giving sign, and with the sunrise in the east illuminate me the same light.

Fortunate is the thief for You opened the door for him to the paradise of Eden, according to the faith of his heart in same You fulfilled his request, and Lord give that I may be in his company to hear the same response, today you will be with Me in Eden, in your first fatherland.

Deacon	Stand
Priest	Peace unto all.
Choir	And with Your spirit.
Deacon	May you listen with awe.
Reader (priest or deacon)	The Holy Gospel of Jesus Christ According to Mark 17:1-41
Choir	Glory to You Lord our God.
Deacon	Attention
Choir	God says.

NIGHT HOUR

<u>A G</u>
<u>K G</u>

Crying out "Eli Eli" the foundations of the earth
were shaking, and the curtain of the old
law was ripped from top to the ground,
now, with the stones that were shaking,
move my unmovable heart to what
is good, with the ripping of the curtain
rip up the record of my debt.

Having cast a veil upon the light of the sun the
midday was darkened, and the tombs were opened
and the bodies of the saints arose, with the darkening
of those who were illuminated, cleanse from me
the deeds of darkness, with those who have died yet
were risen, raise up my soul having died in sin.

The word in deed became the fulfiller of the new
commandment of love, by praying to the Father in heaven
to forgive the sins while upon the cross, me who believing
with my spirit I bow down and worship You the
Only Begotten, give the order of dissolution,
may the first sins not be remembered.

In the rendering of Your Spirit unto the Father,
the pits in the abyss shook, which into the interior
of the hells* You descended, into the prison of
death and darkness, having bound the death
bearing prince, You pulled out the souls which
were in prison, and Lord may You pull me out
with them also from the gloomy prison of sins.

* *Hades*

NIGHT HOUR

<u>Deacon</u>	Stand
<u>Priest</u>	Peace unto all.
<u>Choir</u>	And with Your spirit.
<u>Deacon</u>	May you listen with awe.
<u>Reader (*priest or deacon*)</u>	The Holy Gospel of Jesus Christ According to Luke 22:66-23:49
<u>Choir</u>	Glory to You Lord our God.
<u>Deacon</u>	Attention
<u>Choir</u>	God says.

<u>A Tz</u>
<u>K Tz</u>

Unpolluted springs which after the death were immortal, springing out from You a double stream for the renewing of the one born of the rib, open my mouth to drink of Your life giving blood, wash me again in the front not only with grace but with tears.

In Your immortal death grant life to my dead spirit, with burial in a new tomb raise me up from being buried in my sins, by descending into the interior of the pit, raise me up from the pit of sins, by Your dwelling in the shadow of death, and illuminate me with spirit.

My heart cries out unto You the Word Who was with the Father from the beginning, Who willingly for the sake of mankind suffered bodily all of these things, make me hear the voice of the calling into Your kingdom, with the assembly of the first born to bless You always and unto eternity.

NIGHT HOUR

Deacon	Stand
Priest	Peace unto all.
Choir	And with Your spirit.
Deacon	May you listen with awe.
Reader (*priest or deacon*)	The Holy Gospel of Jesus Christ According to John 19:17-37
Choir	Glory to You Lord our God.
Deacon	Attention
Choir	God says.

For Feasts of the Lord or of the Cross, after Hymn "Aysor anjarr (Today the Inexpressible Dawn)"recite the connecting Psalm 4:7 KJV 4:6 alternating with Psalm 4:2 KJV 4:1. Then the Gospel of Crucifixion is read according to the tone of the day as found in the Lectionary or Chancel Gospel, followed by the Hymn "Norokogh Diezeratz (Regenerator of the universes) Pg. 81. Some sing the first verse of the Hymn whereas others sing all verses. The decision is that of the Senior. But when the Hymn of Rest (Hanksdyan Sharagan) is sung, the Psalms and Gospel of Rest according to the proper tone of the day are then read. After the gospel, sing "Asdvadz Anegh (God uncreated)" Pg. 109 without alternating. Then recite the Petition "For the souls of those who are at rest" Pg. 126. However, after "Asdvadz Anegh (God uncreated)" some at times sing as the connection one verse of the Hymn "Ararich yev martaser (Maker and lover of mankind)" Pg. 119 or in the same manner may sing as the connection one verse of "Yes Asatzi (I said arising) Pg. 123. The decision is that of the Senior. After the Petition "For the souls of those who are at rest", the Prayer "Christ Son of God" Pg. 126 is said followed by the Lord's Prayer.

Senior Chancel

 *The **Hymn of Rest (Hanksdyan Sharagan)** is inserted here. To find the proper Hymn, we must turn to the Hymnal Book index Pg. 532-533 and look under the **Hymn of Rest (Hanksdyan Sharagan)** heading for the appropriate day and tone.*

NIGHT HOUR

Psalms according to the eight tones which proceed the Gospel of Rest

Senior Chancel

<u>A Tz</u>
<u>Ps 6:2-11   KJV 6:1-10</u>

Lord do not reprimand me in Your passion
and do not discipline me in Your anger.

Have mercy upon me Lord, for I am sick,
heal my being, for my bones are troubled.

My being is greatly troubled, and You, Lord, until when?

Turn, Lord, and save my being, grant me life,
Lord according to Your mercy.

For there is no one in death who remembers You,
nor in hells* who will confess of You.

* *Hades*

I became fatigued in my groanful lamentations,
I washed my mattress every night, and with my
tears I wet my bed.

My eye became disturbed from anger, I am worn
out by all my enemies above.

Stay far away from me, all you who commit
unlawfulness.

The Lord heard the sound of my weeping, the Lord
heard my prayers, and the Lord received my requests.

May all of my enemies become very ashamed and troubled,
may they turn back and become shamed and troubled
very quickly.

*The following psalm is said for Feast Days of the Lord
in which the tone of the day is A Tz*

A Tz
Ps 14:1-5 KJV 15:1-5

Lord, who shall stay in Your tabernacle, or who
shall dwell upon Your Holy mountain.

NIGHT HOUR

He who walks spotlessly works justice,
he speaks the truth in his heart.

Who with his tongue is not of the deceitful,
and does not do evil to his friend.

He does not take up insults upon those near to him,
he despises those who do evil works before him.

He glorifies those who fear of the Lord,
who make oath to their friend and does not lie.

He does not lend his silver out with interest,
and does not take bribes against the righteous,
he who does these things, unto eternity he
shall not be shaken.

A G
Ps 29:1-13 KJV 29:1-12

I lift You up on high, Lord, for You
received me, and You did not make
my enemy to rejoice over me.

Lord my God, I called upon You and
You healed me, Lord, You pulled my being
out from the hells,* You saved me from
amongst those who descend into the pit.

Hades

NIGHT HOUR

Say psalms unto the Lord, His saints, may
you confess the remembrance of His Holiness.

Passion is in His anger, and life is in His will.

Those weeping will be extinguished during
the evenings, in the morning let there be rejoicing.

I said in my prosperity, that I shall never be
shaken unto eternity.

Lord, in Your wills You gave strength to my
beauty, You turned Your faces away from me,
and I became troubled.

To You, Lord, I called upon, and to my
God I cried out, what use is it to You for
my blood, that I descend into destruction.

Is it possible that dirt will confess to You, or will
tell of Your truths.

NIGHT HOUR

The Lord heard me and had mercy upon me,
and the Lord became my helper.

He turned my mourning into joyfulness, He freed
me of the burlap cloths of mourning and
clothed me with joyfulness.

My glory shall recite as psalms to You, and moreover
I shall not become repenting again, Lord
my God, unto eternity I shall confess of You.

<u>P Tz</u>
<u>Ps 53:3-9 KJV 54:1-7</u>

God, in Your Name grant me life, and in
Your power make me just.

God, hear my prayers, place Your ear upon the
words of my mouth.

Foreigners rose up over me, and the mighty ones
demanded my being, and they did not regard
You as God before them.

Behold God my helper, and Lord receiver of my soul.

While returning the evil unto my enemies,
destroy them with Your truth.

Of my will I shall offer sacrifices to You,
I shall confess of Your Name, Lord, for it is good.

You saved me from all troubles, and
my eye has seen my enemies.

P G
Ps 66: 2-8 KJV 67:1-7

God, have mercy upon us and bless us, make
Your faces appear unto us and have mercy upon us.

To know Your ways upon the earth,
Your salvation unto all nations.

May the people confess unto You, God,
may all of the people confess unto You.

May the nations be happy and rejoice,
for You judge the people with uprightness,
and You lead the nations on earth.

May the people confess unto You, God,
all people from You shall be satisfied.

The land gave its fruit, and God
our God blessed us.

Bless us our God, and all ends
of the earth shall fear Him.

K Tz
Ps. 84:2-14 KJV 85:1-13

You were pleased, Lord, throughout Your land,
and You have overturned the captivity of Jacob.

You forgave the unrighteousness of Your people,
and You covered all their sins.

You silenced all of Your rage, and You
turned from Your anger of rage.

Turn to us, God our savior, and
turn Your rage from us.

Do not be angry at us unto eternity, Lord,
and do not cast Your anger from
generation unto generation.

God, You give us life again, and
may Your people rejoice in You.

Show us, Lord, Your mercies,
and grant us Your salvation.

We heard what God our Lord speaks, the peace of
His people is spoken to His saints and unto those
who turn towards Him with their heart.

But His salvation is near to those who
fear in Him, living for His glory in our land.

Mercy and truthfulness shall occur,
justice and peace shall kiss.

Truth sprouted up from the land,
justice appeared from the heavens.

Lord give peace and may our land give Your
fruit, may justice go before Him, place His
footsteps in the pathway.

NIGHT HOUR

<u>K G</u>
<u>Ps 101: 2-14 KJV 102:1-13</u>

Lord, hear my prayers, may my cry come
unto You, and do not turn Your faces
from me.

In the day of my distress may Your ear
descend upon me, of which in the day
I cry unto You, quickly hear me.

My days are consumed as smoke,
and my bones have dried out as dry bushes.

I was beaten as grass and my heart
withered away, I forgot to eat my bread
because of the sound of my groaning.

My bone is bound to my body, I
resembled a pelican in the desert.

I became as an owl among the ruins, I was
kept awake and became as the only sparrow
upon the rooftop.

My enemies abused me daily, and those who
praise me were sworn against me.

I ate ashes as bread, and I mixed my drink
with tears.

From the faces of the anger of Your passion,
for You lifted me up and brought me down
into humility.

NIGHT HOUR

My days have passed as a shadow, and
I have withered away as grass.

You, Lord, eternally exist, and Your remembrance
is from generation unto generation.

You having risen up shall have compassion upon Zion,
it is time for her compassion, her time has arrived.

T Tz
Ps 118: 169-179 KJV 119:169-176

May my requests draw near before You, Lord, according
to Your word make me wise.

May my prayers enter before You, Lord, and through
Your word save me.

May Your blessings spring forth from my lips,
as You will teach me Your justice.

My tongue shall speak Your words, for all of
Your commandments are with justice.

NIGHT HOUR

Let it be Your hand which is giving me
life, for I chose Your commandments.

I became desirous of Your salvation, Lord,
and Your laws were my word.

May my being live, may it bless You,
and Your laws shall help me.

I was wandering as a lost sheep, search for this
Your servant, for I have not forgotten
Your commandments.

T G
Ps 142:1-12 KJV 143:1-12

Lord hear my prayers, place Your ear upon my
requests with Your truth.

Hear me with Your justice, and do not enter
into a lawsuit with Your servant, for nobody
amongst all those alive is righteous before You.

The enemy persecuted my being, he has made my
life reduced into the ground, and sat me in the
dark as one dead unto eternity.

NIGHT HOUR

My soul within me became wearied, and my
heart within me became agitated.

I remembered the first days, I pondered upon
all Your works, I pondered upon
all of the things that Your hands have made,
and I lifted my hands up to You.

My being thirsts for You as a thirsty land,
quickly hear me, Lord, for of me,
my spirit has become faint.

Do not turn Your faces from me,
lest I resemble those who descend into the pit.

Make Your morning mercies audible to me,
for Lord I hoped in You.

Show me the path to which I should go,
for to you Lord, I lifted up my being.

Save me from my enemies, Lord,
for I made You my refuge.

Teach me to do Your wills, for You are my God.

Your good spirit shall lead me into upright land.

NIGHT HOUR

For the sake of Your Name, Lord, may You give me life,
with Your righteousness may You take my being
out of difficulty.

With Your mercy exterminate my enemies, and
destroy the oppressors of my being, for I am
Your servant.

---

*The following psalm is said for Feast Days of the Lord
in which the tone of the day is T G.*

T G
Ps 129:2-8 KJV 130:1-8

From the depths I cried out to You, Lord, Lord,
hear my voice.

May Your ears be hearing the voice of my prayers.

That You examine my injustices, Lord, Lord,
but who can stand before You, for
from You is atonement.

For Your name's sake I patiently awaited,
Lord, my being awaits patiently for Your Word,
my being hoped in the Lord.

More than watchmen from the morning
until the evening, more than watchmen of the
morning, Israel hoped in the Lord.

NIGHT HOUR

From the Lord mercy is abundant,
from Him is salvation, and He saved
Israel from all their oppressions.

---

*Following the psalms, the Gospel of Rest (Hanksdyan)
is read according to the tone of the day.
(Use the paradigm found on Pg. 67 to announce all gospel readings.)*

Senior Chancel

The Holy Gospel according to Matthew 13:36-52

$\overline{\text{P G}}$
$\overline{\text{T G}}$

Of our Lord Jesus Christ.

At that time Jesus having left the people,
He came home, the disciples approached
to Him and said, "Explain to us the
parable of the weeds of the field."
He gave reply and says to
them, "He who sows good seed is the
Son of Man, and the field is the world,
the good seed are those, who are
sons of the kingdom, but the
weeds are the sons of the evil one, and

the enemy who cultivated them is
Satan, and the harvest is the
end of this world, and the harvesters
are the angels. As the weeds are
gathered and burned in the fire, in
that manner it shall be at the end
of this world, the Son of Man shall
send His angels, and they shall gather
from His kingdom all of the stumbling blocks,
and those who commit injustices, and they
will throw them into the furnace of fire,
where there will be weeping and gnashing
of teeth. At that time the just shall
shine forth as the sun in the kingdom
of the heavens, whoever will have ears
for hearing, he shall hear. Again, the
kingdom of the heavens is resembling to a
treasure hidden in a field, that having
been found by a man, he then hid it, and
from his cheerfulness, from there he goes
and sells everything that he has, and
buys that field. Again, the kingdom of
the heavens is resembling to a merchant man,
who is in search for beautiful pearls, and

having found one precious pearl, having gone,
he sold all of which he had, and bought that
pearl. Again, the kingdom of heavens is
resembling to the throwing of a net into
the sea, and gathering all species, in which
it was nearly filled, having pulled it onto the
land, and having sat down they gathered
the good into the containers for the good ones, and
the worthless they cast away. It shall
be as such at the end of this world,
the angels will go forth, and
separate the evil from amongst the
just, and they shall cast them into
the furnace of fire, where there will
be weeping and gnashing of teeth."
Jesus says unto them, "Do you
understand all of these things?" They
say unto Him, "Yes Lord." And He
says unto them, "For the sake of
this all of the scribes who have
been discipled for the kingdom of
the heavens, are resembling to a man
who is a home owner who brings out
from his treasure the new and the old."

NIGHT HOUR

The Holy Gospel according to Mark 4:26-34

<u>P Tz</u>
<u>T Tz</u>

Our Lord Jesus Christ

And He was saying, "The kingdom of God
is as such, so that a man should
throw seeds upon the land, and
should he sleep and arise night and
day, and should the seeds sprout
and grow, and he does not know this,
whether the land brings forth fruit by itself,
first the shoot, then the head, and then the
head filled with wheat kernels, but at which
time it shall give fruit, quickly the
sickle is sent forth, for the harvests
have arrived." And He said, "To whom
will the kingdom of God resemble, or with
which parable shall we illustrate it? As
a seed of mustard, that at which time
when it is sown into the earth, it
is smaller than all other seeds which are
upon the earth, and at which time it
is sown, it grows and becomes larger
than all herbs and gives out very
large branches, until being capable so that

under its shade the birds of the skies inhabit."
And through these types of parables
He was speaking the Word with them,
such as they were able to hear, and
He would speak nothing with them
without a parable, but privately to
His own disciples, He was explaining everything.

The Holy Gospel according to Luke 12:32-48

A G
KG

Our Lord Jesus Christ Says

Do not fear little flock, for your Father
was pleased to give you the kingdom. Sell
your belongings and give charitable alms, and
make for yourselves money purses that do not
become old, inexhaustible treasure in the heavens,
where no thief comes near, and no moth corrupts.
For where your treasure is, and there your hearts will
be. Let your belts be tightened along your mid
sections, and your lamps having been lighted,
and you who resemble men who expected

NIGHT HOUR

their master, that when he shall return
from the wedding, that at which time he shall
come and knock, quickly they shall open for
him. Fortunate may those servants be,
in which upon arriving the master will
find them awake, so be it I say unto
you, that he shall bring the belt along
his mid section, and have them recline,
and passing forth shall serve them, and if
at the second or third watch he shall
come and find as such, fortunate are
those servants. But know that, if the
master of the house knew at which hour
the thief comes, he would keep watch
and not allow his home to be dug through
and you, be those who are ready, for at which
hour you do not think the Son of Man
comes. Peter says, "Lord, why were You saying
that parable to us or was it to everyone
also?" And the Lord says, "Who shall be the
faithful and wise manager, in which
his master placed over his household to
give the food in time. Fortunate it shall be

for that servant in which upon the
coming of his master he shall find
doing as such. Indeed I say to you,
that he will be placed over all of his possessions.
However, if that servant shall say in his heart,
my master is delayed in coming, and
he shall begin to beat the servants and the
maidservants, eating and drinking and getting
drunk, the master of the servant will
come on that day in which he
will not expect and at the hour in
which he will not know, he will
cut him in the middle, and his
portion will be placed with the
unbelievers. And a servant who shall
know the wills of his master and
does not prepare according to his
wills, he will be beaten many times
with a cane. And he who does not
know, and would conduct himself which
is deserving of the cane, he will
be beaten with the cane fewer times,
for everyone to whom much was given,
much shall be required from him, and to
whom much has been entrusted, even more so
will they demand from him."

NIGHT HOUR

The Holy Gospel according to John 5:19-30

A Tz
K Tz

Our Lord Jesus Christ

Jesus gave reply and says to them,
"Amen Amen* I say unto you, and the Son
of Man cannot do anything of Himself,
if He would not see what the Father does, that
which He does, the same and of the same likewise
is done by the Son. For the Father loves the
Son and He shows Him everything, which
He is doing, and even greater works than
these He will show Him, by which you
all may be astonished. For as the Father
raises those who have died, makes them
alive, and likewise the Son those whom He wills,
He makes them alive. And not that the
Father judges anyone, but all judgment
has been given to His Son, that all shall
honor the Son, as they honor the Father,
he who does not honor the Son, does not
honor the Father, the sender of Him. Amen Amen
I say unto you, for he who hears my word, and

---

* *"Amen" is actually Hebrew. The exact translation is "Let it be, Let it be" As a side note, the original translators of the Armenian Bible, St. Mesrob et al. decided to use the Hebrew "Amen" rather than the authentic Armenian "Yeghitzi" throughout scripture and to conclude prayers with, in the Armenian language.*

believes in He who sent me,
receives the life eternal, and does
not enter into judgment but transformed
from death into life. Amen Amen* I say
unto you, that time comes, and is
already indeed, at which time the dead
shall hear the voice of the Son of God,
and those who shall hear shall be
given life. For as the Father has this
life in Himself, and He likewise gave unto
the Son to have this life in Himself. And He gave
authority to Him to do judgment, and
because He is the Son of Man, why
are you amazed by that? For the
time shall come in which all of those
who shall be in the graves shall hear His
voice, and they shall come out, of those
whom have done good works, to the
resurrection of life, and of those
whom have done evil, to the resurrection
of judgment. I am not able to do
anything of myself, but as I listen,
I am judged, and my judgment is just, for
I do not seek my own will, but of Him
who sent me."

NIGHT HOUR

*Hymns written by Catholicos Nerses which
are sung for those resting in Christ.*

Senior Chancel

P G
T G

God uncreated without time Father
without beginning and immeasurable,
the cause of the birth of the Son is
with the unexplainable flowing out of the
Holy Spirit boundlessly, we request of You
being compassionate, considerate, and merciful,
Have mercy upon those You created who are
at rest with hope in You.

The Word Who in the bosom of the Father
only begotten and of original appearance,
through Whom heavens gave existence to
the earth and completely established it,
we request from you most merciful
life giving Lord and savior,
Have mercy upon those You created who are
at rest with hope in You.

Supreme distributor of graces to heavenly beings
and earthly beings, life giver and giver of life
spirit of the Father and of the Son co-creator,
we request from You the spring of goodness,
the giver of drink to the thirsty.
Have mercy upon those You created who are
at rest with hope in You.

NIGHT HOUR

We profess in place of the Seraphim of Your life giving
in its entirety, thrice holy one Lordship,
the Father, and the Son, and the Holy Spirit
in which those who are resting having
been baptized and with faith having confessed,
Have mercy upon those You created who are
at rest with hope in You.

The perfect number three having been
divided into three persons, with the
trinity having been united equally in
one nature, from whose bindings
we become released and again become
bound with unbreakable bonds.
Have mercy upon those You created who are
at rest with hope in You.

Of the persons of the Father, we glorify
the Son unceasingly, who descended
into the womb of the virgin and
gave form to the Adamic body, with
requests to the pure God-Bearer,
Your birth giver,
Have mercy upon those You created who are
at rest with hope in You.

You appeared with body upon the
earth from the Father, which was unexplainable,
You lived with the earthly having come
from the fiery angelic worshiping,
with the requests of the heavenly beings'
glorifications, of Your angels,
Have mercy upon those You created who are
at rest with hope in You.

NIGHT HOUR

According to the laws of Moses You
were presented to the temple, that
You will present human nature of the
Father in heaven, with the requests of
the Holy Elder (Simeon), from You the
releasing from binds.
Have mercy upon those You created who are
at rest with hope in You.

The King of fiery angels who with human
earthliness, was turned upside down
unjustly, bore the human sufferings,
Who for us, all of this You took to
Yourself with humility.
Have mercy upon those You created who are
at rest with hope in You.

$\overline{\text{P Tz}}$
$\overline{\text{T Tz}}$

The assemblings of this world
to the renunciation of Your
servant, by weeping we request
from You and plead by saying this,
the road went out through You
for those asleep, may You be their
fellow traveler,
In the Father's houses of rest, of Your light
give rest to those of ours who are asleep.

For our salvation, in the beginning
You were baptized in the Jordan,
which You granted a new basin
in the cleansing of human sins,
by pleading again to the great Forerunner
(John The Baptist) in this birth of the Baptist.
In the Father's houses of rest, of Your light
give rest to those of ours who are asleep.

With illuminated voice from the heavens,
the Father with the same existence
proclaimed of You, in the form of
a dove the Spirit having descended
and rested upon Your same existence,
those baptized by the same Spirit,
to adoption of the Father by faith.
In the Father's houses of rest, of Your light
give rest to those of ours who are asleep.

The darkness of sins was expelled
by the light of knowledge which
irradiated forth from You, the bite
of the snake was healed, our illness
was cured, Your giving of life to the
dead and Your giving of light to
those in darkness.
In the Father's houses of rest, of Your light
give rest to those of ours who are asleep.

The origin, name from the Father
which You chose from the world,
illuminator of the universes, the
chosen disciples, with the prayers
of the apostles, the trumpet of our
resurrection which is to be.
In the Father's houses of rest, of Your light
give rest to those of ours who are asleep.

NIGHT HOUR

Life from lives, light from
light who You created us from
earth, You renewed again once more
by birth of the Holy baptismal
font, that to the first one to
whom from death, with
Your grace You gave life.
In the Father's houses of rest, of Your light
give rest to those of ours who are asleep.

The first man You filled with spirit
who having become stray by the deceit of
the evil one, the same Spirit through Your
Word poured into our souls anew, with
the same Holy and good Spirit lead
of the same Spirit.
In the Father's houses of rest, of Your light
give rest to those of ours who are asleep.

You called out to Lazarus through
whom You gave hope to the dead,
with lifefulness in the four days, they
gave life again, those in Adam,
with the sound of life of the final
trumpet, call this at this time for those
buried in the earth.
In the Father's houses of rest, of Your light
give rest to those of ours who are asleep.

NIGHT HOUR

The keeper of death shook hiding
from the sound of the life giving
news, quickly a couple in company
with the Word gave the dead
according to the command, princes
will shake to the air, do not
impede their spirit.
In the Father's houses of rest, of Your light
give rest to those of ours who are asleep.

$$\frac{A\ G}{K\ G}$$

The path for those who wander astray
and the ray of light for those in
darkness, You invited the Son of Light
to Your heavenly wedding, in the
company of merry, there they shall
be gathered, make them worthy of being
in the heavenly order,
With filled lanterns enter the curtained
bridal chamber in the company of the wise
Holy Virgins.

With our (human) nature that You
wore, You were nailed to the wooden
cross, by unbinding us from the
binds of sins of the forefather (Adam), and unbind
them from their offences for the
sake of Your Holy torture,
With filled lanterns enter the curtained
bridal chamber in the company of the wise
Holy Virgins.

NIGHT HOUR

After volunteering to death of the
cross, You were placed in a new tomb,
with the burial of three days in the
earth, You created us new alive, the
descending of You through the earth of death
call again with the sound of the trumpet.
With filled lanterns enter the curtained
bridal chamber in the company of the wise
Holy Virgins.

The oil bearing women having sat
and with tearful lamentation, as the
hopeless dead, alive eternally, for
the sake of the same Holy tears,
cleanse them of their offences.
With filled lanterns enter the curtained
bridal chamber in the company of the wise
Holy Virgins.

The shaking of the foundations of
hells* seeing You in the internals
of hells*, You pulled out the souls
who were in the prison, binding the
prince of the dead, in the company
of the resting souls of the saints,
give rest to the souls who are sleeping.
With filled lanterns enter the curtained
bridal chamber in the company of the wise
Holy Virgins.

With joyfulness the heavenly soldiers
were descending from heaven to the
earth, at which time You raised
from the dead, You shined light
upon Your creatures, with
Your life giving resurrection raise them
into life immortal.
With filled lanterns enter the curtained
bridal chamber in the company of the wise
Holy Virgins.

Hades

NIGHT HOUR

Without suffering of the guards from
fear of the heavenly angels, who gave
good news to the women that death
dissolved mortality, this Who of
death, planted with You shall
become Your living communicants.
With filled lanterns enter the curtained
bridal chamber in the company of the wise
Holy Virgins.

The angels intertwined in fellowship
beside the life giving Holy tomb,
they give the good news to the
nations of man, for the sake of life
eternal, rank in order
their choirs and in the same those
sleeping on the last day.
With filled lanterns enter the curtained
bridal chamber in the company of the wise
Holy Virgins.

Enlightened with torches in the sign
of the Cross having shone arising
from the east, the believers will
rejoice in You and the deniers will lament,
in the same make the worshippers of the
Holy Cross shine with light.
With filled lanterns enter the curtained
bridal chamber in the company of the wise
Holy Virgins.

NIGHT HOUR

<u>A Tz</u>
<u>K Tz</u>

The road having been used by the
heavenly angels who came before
Your predecessors, with the
assembling of Your chosen ones they bring
before You in the clouds, in the
company of the doves, those flying
in the air, intermix them in
the Holy flock,
Rank them in order of those above singing
the glories along with those who will rejoice.

The elements of the earth tremble
at the time that You come in
the Fatherly glories, sun light
becomes darkened, the moon and
stars fade away, this, this
eternal day, illuminate with
Your light,
 Rank them in order of those above singing
the glories along with those who will rejoice.

From the celestial angels' army
commander's trumpet the sound
of good news, arise those who
have died, those since Adam, for behold
the groom has arrived, having married
with those who are clean in spirit,
Rank them in order of those above singing
the glories along with those who will rejoice.

NIGHT HOUR

You sit in the Lordly throne,
You are bowed down to in worship
by Your creatures, with justice
You judge the world, You compensate
rewards according to deeds,
at that time grant mercy, to those
of ours who are sleeping grant forgiveness.
Rank them in order of those above singing
the glories along with those who will rejoice.

Having assembled mankind, nations
gather who have been born from Adam,
and of the rank of the fiery heavenly
angels all together descend, in that
frightful spot remember them on that
terrifying day.
 Rank them in order of those above singing
the glories along with those who will rejoice.

They were shown the secrets of all
mankind, each one which they did,
those doers of good to the wedding,
the doers of evil are delivered up
to the unextinguishable fire,
at that time remember them, the good deeds
for the sins of those who will be sleeping.
Rank them in order of those above singing
the glories along with those who will rejoice.

Wedding fabrics of various colors and
garments shining with light have been
placed upon heads of the Holy Martyrs
and the just having been adorned,
make this communion with the same
request, those in the same light of glory.
Rank them in order of those above singing
the glories along with those who will rejoice.

NIGHT HOUR

Unto the glories of glories they raise up, those
on the right side rise up, at which time they
hear the fortunate voice of Your calling,
for those of us that are sleeping, make
them hear Your Godly voice.
Rank them in order of those above singing
the glories along with those who will rejoice.

Priests and people we request from You
compassionate Lord, with those sleeping
in faith receive us with the same hope,
in the Jerusalem city above in which
the just will be assembled, singing glories
loudly always in the company of the
same trinity, of three persons.

The following verses are all sung with the T G Melody.
The tonal listing below A Tz, A G, ...etc through T G
refer to the Calendar "Tone of the Day" not melody.

P G

Maker and lover of mankind, unvengeful
and compassionate, who of Your
praises from the seraphim, Lord judge
of justice, with the company of the Holy
Apostles, Lord crown in Your marriage
those of ours that are sleeping,
Merciful Lord, have mercy upon the
souls of those of ours who are sleeping.

NIGHT HOUR

<u>P Tz</u>
At which time the writings are fulfilled,
of which that day they told us,
the words of the prophets are honored,
the apostles paid the price,
Merciful Lord, have mercy upon the
souls of those of ours who are sleeping.

<u>A Tz</u>
In the Jerusalem above, in the dwellings
of the angels, where Enoch and Elijah reside
having reached old age in dovelike form,
in the Edenly paradise having brightly
shone worthily,
Merciful Lord, have mercy upon the
souls of those of ours who are sleeping.

<u>A G</u>
Christ, king of glories, having arrived
You come from heavens on wings of winds
with Your native appearance, and You do
test with fire the examination of the sons
of mankind,
Merciful Lord, have mercy upon the
souls of those of ours who are sleeping.

<u>K Tz</u>
Placing the bridegroom, He sits upon the
Bema* and the curtained bridal chamber
is adorned, the trumpet of Gabriel calls out
all of the holy ones to assemble over there,
the ranks of the just become joyful but the
sin loving become saddened with desire.
Merciful Lord, have mercy upon the
souls of those of ours who are sleeping.

---

* *The raised platform in a synagogue where services are performed or the platform which a church altar sits upon.*

NIGHT HOUR

K̄ G

At which time is the sound of the trumpet
and the Levitical writing becomes revealed,
the bright rays of the Holy Cross shining
having arisen from the east,
the extensive regiments of angels,
the archangels are surrounded.
Merciful Lord, have mercy upon the
souls of those of ours who are sleeping.

T̄ G

The frightful thought, of the Priest
Who is with open arms on the Bema*
before the Holy Table, the flame is
extinguished, darkness is expelled, the
sorrowful souls rejoice for there is
forgiveness of sins,
Merciful Lord, have mercy upon the
souls of those of ours who are sleeping.

T̄ Tz

Moses the speaker to God and Aaron the
Levite, prophets of Israel and priests of
the old law, beforehand they announced
to us the coming of the Holy Only
Begotten, they revealed to us salvation when
they were giving food to eat in the desert.
Merciful Lord, have mercy upon the
souls of those of ours who are sleeping.

---

* *The raised platform in a synagogue where services are performed or the platform which a church altar sits upon.*

Great Lent Sundays 2, 4, & 6

Participant full of grief with suffering, You took
unto Yourself death upon the cross, and
You made the one who ascended to the
wood, for the sake of Adam the first created,
Merciful Lord, have mercy upon the
souls of those of ours who are sleeping.

Great Lent Sundays 1, 3, & 5

The heavenly soldiers became terrified
at which time they see the Lord upon the
cross, sunlight having cast a
veil and light of the moon became faint,
in frightful glories for the Son of God
darkness became throughout the universes,
 Merciful Lord, have mercy upon the
souls of those of ours who are sleeping.

For the Resurrection & the Fifty Days following Easter

The nations of mankind rejoiced at which
time they heard of Your resurrection,
they grew new feathers *(became rejuvenated)*
in the resurrection of Your Holy Only Begotten,
Merciful Lord, have mercy upon the
souls of those of ours who are sleeping.

NIGHT HOUR

With requests of the Holy Cross and speechlessly
they advocate*, of the Holy God-Bearer, and of
John the Forerunner (Baptist), of St. Stephen the
first martyr, of St. Illuminator patriarch of the
Armenians, of the Holy Apostles, and all of
the martyrs,
Merciful Lord, have mercy upon the
souls of those of ours who are sleeping.

I said arising of my days, to whom shall
I go, and I today, before the dwelling
which I did not know, help me Christ
today, in front of the road, and in Your
second coming,
Help me.

My day of end arrived and came,
weeping lamentation and groaning,
my heart upset me, and my bones
dried and withered away,
Help me.

---

* *Most translate the word "parekhos" as intercede, however, "advocate" is much more accurate. It corrects Roman Catholic influence upon the Armenian Church's theology. "Parekhos" literally means "speak good." We ask members of the Church to pray for us. Those of the earthly church "Church Militant" and those in Paradise of the "Church Victorious." We believe that all are alive in Christ.*

NIGHT HOUR

They woke me up in my bed,
the demanders of my soul, they
were taking me on a distant road
in which I did not know,
Help me.

I looked and there was no one who
was helping me, I trusted in God
for my salvation, my soul will
rejoice for Your kingdom,
Help me.

I was written in the Book of Life, I
was left departed to go to the maker of
heaven and earth,
Help me.

To the shadowless and uncreated light,
I was removed far away by the deception of
darkness, I tasted the deadly fruit,
it reduces to dirt the one who in the likeness
of the kind creator,
Help me.

To the separation of my soul from
my body, in the decomposing
of my beautiful building (body), I become
terrified from the threats of the king,
that demands from me attainment of
the commandment,
Help me.

NIGHT HOUR

My God Jesus born of a virgin,
having become man, to that frightful
day of tribunal, do not condemn
this price of Your blood,
Help me.

Dreadful is the day of end, and
frightful day of judgment, to that
frightful day of tribunal, do not make
this price of Your blood invisible, for
I am the likeness of the kind creator,
Help me.

I saw the fearful judgment of the
judge, and I was terrified that without
preparation He knew me, from the orders
of the King of eternities,
Help me.

God-Bearer pure mother of the Lord
and Holy Virgin, advocate* to your
Only Begotten Son, that He will save
us from the threats of hell, and grant
us the kingdom of heavens, grant
rest upon those of ours who are sleeping,
Help me.

---

* *Most translate the word "parekhos" as intercede, however, "advocate" is much more accurate. It corrects Roman Catholic influence upon the Armenian Church's theology. "Parekhos" literally means "speak good." We ask members of the Church to pray for us. Those of the earthly church "Church Militant" and those in Paradise of the "Church Victorious." We believe that all are alive in Christ.*

NIGHT HOUR

Petition

<u>Priest</u>

For the souls of those who are at rest, Christ God, make them rest and have mercy, and for we sinners grace upon us the forgiveness of offences.

Proclamation

Student Chancel
<u>Deacon</u>

And again in peace let us request of the Lord.

For the sake of the souls who are resting we request, Christ our savior, that He rank them amongst the just, and give life to us with the grace of His mercy. Our almighty Lord God, give life and have mercy.

Lord have mercy, Lord have mercy, Lord have mercy.

Prayer

Student Chancel
<u>Priest</u>

Christ Son of God, unvengeful and compassionate, have compassion with Your love as creator upon the souls of Your servants who are resting. Remember them on the day of the great coming of Your kingdom. Make them worthy of mercy, atonement, and forgiveness of sins. Make them shine brightly placing them in the order of saints in the rank at Your right side. For You are Lord and creator of all, judge of the living and of the dead. And to You is befitting glory, Lordship, and honor, now and always and through the eternity of eternities, amen.

NIGHT HOUR

Priest: Blessed be our Lord Jesus Christ. Amen.
Our Father Who art in heaven...

Petition

Priest
Christ our God, inexpressible lover of
humanity, with grace and with advocation
of the pure blessed birther the holy, ever
virgin God-Bearer. Having been illuminated,
make the souls of all of the sleeping faithful
shine brightly in Your hope, and to those who are
resting under the protection of this Holy House of God.

(While presenting the censer and incense to the Priest)

Deacon
And again in peace let us request of the Lord. Receive, save, and have mercy.

(Priest blesses and fills the censer with incense while saying)

Priest
Blessing and glory to the Father and to the Son and to the Holy Spirit.
Now always and unto the eternity of eternities. Amen

Ex 15:1
Let us bless the Lord, for with glory He is glorified.

Student Chancel

 The **Blessing Hymn [Orhnootyoon Sharagan** also known as **Avak Orhnootyoon (Great Blessing)]** according to the proper day and tone is sung at this point. To find the proper Hymn (Sharagan) we must turn to the Hymnal Book index on page 532-533, under the following headings and sing the hymn appropriate for the tone of the day: **Resurrection** (Avak Orhnootyoonk Harootyan), **Feasts of the Lord** (Deroonagan Donitz), **Saint's Days** (Srpotz), **Martyr's Days** (Orhnootyoonk Mardirosatz), and **Days of Repentance or Fasting** (Orhnootyoonk Abashkharootyoon).

* Deacon censes the entire church

+ In the margins of the Hymnal on the pages of the Blessing Hymn, various abbreviations will be seen. These give a cross reference to verse of origin found in the Canticles (Hymns of the Prophets) of the Canonic Psalms. Thus the Blessing Hymns are derived from these Canticles.

NIGHT HOUR

Petition for Feasts of the Lord

<u>Priest</u>

Glory to Your majestic *(Insert appropriate Feast Name)* Lord, Your blessed and glorified, miraculous and victorious Holy *(Insert appropriate Feast Name)* we bless and glorify.

Lord, lover of humanity, for the sake of Your Holy, pure, and virgin mother, and for the sake of Your revered cross, receive our requests and give us life.

The following are the names of the various Feast Days of the Lord which are to be inserted in the appropriate place as designated by parentheses above: Birth, Revelation, Coming (of Palm Sunday), Administration*, Betrayal, Crucifixion, Burial, Resurrection, Ascension, Coming of the Holy Spirit (Pentecost), and Transfiguration.

For Feasts of the Holy Cross or Holy Church: "Glory to Your Lordship"

For Coming of the Holy Spirit (Pentecost), "Lord, lover of humanity" is recited as following:

Lord, lover of humanity, for the sake of the Holy, pure, and virgin mother, and for the sake of the revered cross, receive our requests and give us life.

Those who recite it directed to the Holy Spirit using, "Your Mother," or "Your Cross" are incorrect.

---

* *Theologians use the term "Redeeming Economy" In fulfillment of the law of the House of God.*

NIGHT HOUR

Petition for Feast Days of the Saints

<u>Priest</u>
With the advocation of the Holy God-Bearer,
and John the Baptist, St. Stephen the first martyr,
and our Gregory the Illuminator. With remembrance
and prayers of the Saints *(Insert Name)*, of whom
today is their remembrance. And for the sake of
Your revered cross, Lord, receiving our requests,
and give us life.

Petition for Fasting Days

<u>Priest</u>
<u>T G</u>

Christ is my God, and I give Him glory,
God of my father, and I shall elevate Him
on high.
Lord, lover of humanity, for the sake of the Holy,
pure, and virgin mother, and for the sake of the
revered cross, receive our requests and give us life.

<u>A Tz</u>

Give glories to God, give blessing
to the lover of mankind, the King
of eternities, who saves His
servants and gives life.
Lord, lover of humanity, for the sake of the Holy,
pure, and virgin mother, and for the sake of the
revered cross, receive our requests and give us life.

<u>A G</u>

You are our Lord God, You are Christ
our Savior, our beings bless You.
Lord, lover of humanity, for the sake of the Holy,
pure, and virgin mother, and for the sake of the
revered cross, receive our requests and give us life.

NIGHT HOUR

__P Tz__
My horn was raised up to God,
my savior, my heart took root
in the Lord, with the Lord and with faith.
Lord, lover of humanity, for the sake of the Holy,
pure, and virgin mother, and for the sake of the
revered cross, receive our requests and give us life.

__P G__
Christ giver of peaces, gift
Your peace and heavenly mercy
unto those whom You have created.
Lord, lover of humanity, for the sake of the Holy,
pure, and virgin mother, and for the sake of the
revered cross, receive our requests and give us life.

__K Tz__
Hope of life, hope and refuge of
salvation, savior Lord Jesus, save
and eliminate the pains of my being.
Lord, lover of humanity, for the sake of the Holy,
pure, and virgin mother, and for the sake of the
revered cross, receive our requests and give us life.

__K G__
Our prayers will come to Your
Holy Temple, Your ear will descend
upon our petitions.
Lord, lover of humanity, for the sake of the Holy,
pure, and virgin mother, and for the sake of the
revered cross, receive our requests and give us life.

__T Tz__
Hear us, Lord, hear us, with
Godly mercy, and with Your compassion
spare those whom You have created.
Lord, lover of humanity, for the sake of the Holy,
pure, and virgin mother, and for the sake of the
revered cross, receive our requests and give us life.

NIGHT HOUR

Proclamation, Prayer, and Petition which are according to the tone of the day. They originate from the Psalm Book found in the Canonic Psalm beginning with Ps 1:1 and in the Canonic Psalm beginning with Ps 72:1 KJV 73:1

P G

T G

<u>Deacon</u> **Student Chancel**
And again in peace let us request of the Lord.

<u>Choir</u>
Lord have mercy.

For the sake of peace from above and for salvation of
our beings, let us pray to the Lord.

Lord have mercy.

For the sake of the Lord God listening to the voice of our
prayers, let us pray to the Lord.

Lord have mercy.

For the sake of God being atoner and pardoner over our
sins, let us pray to the Lord.

Lord have mercy.

For the sake of forgiving us for all of our offences,
both willingly and unwillingly, let us pray to the Lord.

Lord have mercy.

For the sake of us that we shall not be found with those
who are vile on the day of accountability, let us pray to the Lord.

Lord have mercy.

For the sake of the souls who are at rest, who with true and
right faith are sleeping in Christ, let us pray to the Lord.

Remember Lord and have mercy.

And again in one voice for the sake of our true and
holy faith, let us pray to the Lord.

Lord have mercy.

NIGHT HOUR

Let us make ourselves and one another as the Person of the Lord God Almighty.

Let us become as Your Person Lord.

Lord our God be merciful to us, according to Your great mercy, let us all say in unison.

Lord have mercy. Lord have mercy. Lord have mercy.

Prayer

Senior Chancel

Lord of the day and giver of existence to the night, Who made the day in the occupation of good works for the salvation of our beings, and made the night for the rest of sleep for our feeble nature. But now having awakened us You opened our mouth to blessing Your fearful and glorious Holy Name. And now receiving our requests, make us prosper in the right faith and in virtuous works always arriving early at this same service of Yours, and of the same canons unceasingly glorifying the Father, the Son and the Holy Spirit, now and always and unto the eternity of eternities. Amen.

NIGHT HOUR

Priest: Peace unto all.

Choir: And with Your Spirit.

Priest: Let us bow down in worship of God.

Choir: Before You Lord.

We continuously pray to You, for You
are Lord compassionate to all lover of
mankind, for You will strengthen us
day by day sustaining us in the
order of our religious life. Lord
lighten Your sweet yoke which
You placed upon us, that we will
be able to hold to Your commandment,
and make pleasures before You
at all hours in the day and at night.
With the angelic accompaniment
in song blessing You, praising
You, and offering to You thanks and glories
to Your almighty Lordship, now and always
and unto the eternity of eternities. Amen.

NIGHT HOUR

Petition

With psalms, blessing, and spiritual
songs unceasingly we glorify the Father
and the Son, and the Holy Spirit, now and always
and unto the eternity of eternities. Amen.

Priest: Blessed be our Lord Jesus Christ. Amen.

Our Father Who art in heaven...

---

*Proclamation, Prayer, and Petition which are according
to the tone of the day. They originate from the Psalm Book
found in the Canonic Psalm beginning with Ps 18:2 KJV 19:1
and in the Canonic Psalm beginning with Ps 89:1 KJV 90:1*

A Tz

K Tz

Deacon **Student Chancel**
And again in peace let us request of the Lord.

Choir
Lord have mercy.

For the sake of the night and of the day and of every hour
that we speak the word of the Lord, let us pray to the Lord.

Lord have mercy.

For the sake of us not falling into temptation,
of which we cannot resist, let us pray to the Lord.

Lord have mercy.

For the sake of holding us pure and uncondemned
before the frightful court of Christ, let us pray to the Lord.

Lord have mercy.

For the sake of leading us to the harbor of life without
ending, let us pray to the Lord.

Lord have mercy.

NIGHT HOUR

For the sake of us being worthy of the call of above
and the kingdom of the heavens, let us pray to the Lord.

Lord have mercy.

For the sake of the souls who are at rest, who with true and
right faith are sleeping in Christ, let us pray to the Lord.

Remember Lord and have mercy.

And again in one voice for the sake of our true and
holy faith, let us pray to the Lord.

Lord have mercy.

Let us make ourselves and one another as the Person
of the Lord God Almighty.

Let us become as Your Person Lord.

Lord our God, be merciful to us, according to
Your great mercy. Let us all say in unison.

Lord have mercy. Lord have mercy. Lord have mercy.

Prayer

<u>Priest</u>
Senior Chancel

In the night and the day and at every hour we
pray to You, and we request from You Lord lover
of mankind. Hear us, God our savior, may Your ear
descend upon our requests, that the labors of Your
servants will not be in vain,

also count our labors as works of justice and to
the fruit of Godly adoration. Receiving, Lord,
our prayers and our bowing down in worship,
and cut us Your generous mercy, cover us
with the protection of Your almighty right
hand, strengthen us, Lord, with the power
of Your Holy Spirit, keep us as pupils*
of the eye, and make us a good sign
to the praise and glorification of Your
Holy Name. That unto You glories are
accomplished of all of whom You have
created, perpetual glorification in the highest
to the Father, and to the Son, and to
the Holy Spirit now and always and unto the
eternity of eternities. Amen.

Priest: Peace unto all.

Choir: And with Your Spirit.

Priest: Let us bow down in worship of God.

Choir: Before You Lord.

Brave shepherd, good shepherd and eternal,
look upon and make visit to the flock of Your
word, which You have gathered unto You with
Your compassion.

---

*Apple of the eye

NIGHT HOUR

For we stand before You, Lord,
and from You we expect in wait of
Your mercies and compassions. Bless
us all, make us all wise, and
gift unto all Your kingdom of the heavens.
For that You are Lord of life
and God of mercy, and unto You
is befitting glory, Lordship, and
Honor, now and always and unto
the eternity of eternities. Amen.

Petition

<u>Priest</u>
In the night and in the day and
at every hour we unceasingly
glorify the Father, and the Son,
and the Holy Spirit, now and
always, and unto the eternity
of eternities. Amen.

NIGHT HOUR

Proclamation, Prayer, and Petition which are according to the tone of the day. They originate from the Psalm Book found in the Canonic Psalm beginning with Ps 36:1 KJV 37:1 and in the Canonic Psalm beginning with Ps 106:1 KJV 107:1

Proclamation

<u>A Tz</u>
<u>K Tz</u>
<u>Deacon</u> **Student Chancel**
And again in peace let us request of the Lord.

<u>Choir</u>
Lord have mercy.

For the sake of leading our steps to the paths of peace, let us pray to the Lord.

Lord have mercy.

For the sake of dispersing from us all thoughts of the evil one, let us pray to the Lord.

Lord have mercy.

For the sake of granting to us healthy thoughts and virtuous behaviors, let us pray to the Lord.

Lord have mercy.

For the sake of keeping us covered with the protection of His almighty right hand, let us pray to the Lord.

Lord have mercy.

For the sake of crushing the enemy quickly under our feet, let us pray to the Lord.

Lord have mercy.

For the sake of the souls who are at rest, who with true and right faith are sleeping in Christ, let us pray to the Lord.

Remember Lord and have mercy.

NIGHT HOUR

And again in one voice for the sake of our true and holy faith, let us pray to the Lord.

Lord have mercy.

Let us make ourselves and one another as the Person of the Lord God Almighty.

Let us become as Your Person Lord.

Lord our God, be merciful to us, according to Your great mercy. Let us all say in unison.

Lord have mercy. Lord have mercy. Lord have mercy.

Prayer

<u>Priest</u> **Senior Chancel**

Lord of heaven and earth, creator of all creatures, visible and invisible. To You we call upon at every hour, for throughout all places is Your Lordship, and Your kingdom governs all. With fear grant us to always arrive early to Your service, to love You with all of our hearts and our entire minds, and with all of our strength to keep Your commandments. Having lifted up our hands unto You in holiness, without anger and without doubt, and finding from You the graces and mercy, and in virtuous works, success.
For that You are Lord of life and God of mercies, and unto You is befitting glory, Lordship, and Honor, now and always and unto
the eternity of eternities. Amen.

NIGHT HOUR

Priest: Peace unto all.

Choir: And with Your Spirit.

Priest: Let us bow down in worship of God.

Choir: Before You Lord.

To Your almighty and victorious Lordship
again every knee is kneeling in worship,
and Your kingship is glorified by all.
Look upon our bowings down in worship,
and teach us to do Your justice of truth.
For that You are God of peace, who lifted
out animosity from within, and made peace
in the heavens and on earth. To those far
away and to those near, You proclaimed the
good news, the new gifts of Your goodness.
And whom of Your great graces will make
us worthy, ranking us with those who truly
bow in worship to You, our God and our Lord
and savior Jesus Christ. Whom You are blessed
with the Father and with the Holy Spirit,
now and always and unto the
eternity of eternities. Amen.

Petition

<u>Priest</u>
In songs of blessing and in voice of
Psalms we unceasingly glorify the
Father and the Son and the Holy Spirit,
now and always and unto the
eternity of eternities. Amen.

NIGHT HOUR

Proclamation, Prayer, and Petition which are according to the tone of the day. They originate from the Psalm Book found in the Canonic Psalm beginning with Ps 55:2 KJV 56:1 and in the Canonic Psalm beginning with Ps 119:1 KJV 120:1

Proclamation

<u>P Tz</u>
<u>T Tz</u>
<u>Deacon</u> **Student Chancel**
And again in peace let us request of the Lord.

<u>Choir</u>
Lord have mercy.

For the sake of our finding the graces and
mercy from our kind Lord,
let us pray to the Lord.

Lord have mercy.

For the sake of saving us from the defamation
of man and from the traps of Satan,
let us pray to the Lord.

Lord have mercy.

For the sake of all persons who are Christians
and for the homes of the faithful,
let us pray to the Lord.

Lord have mercy.

For the sake of those who are living in
the caves of mountains and in the caverns
whom are our holy fathers, let us pray to the Lord.

Lord have mercy.

For the sake of those who fulfill all of the time
of their lives with Psalms and blessing,
let us pray to the Lord.

Lord have mercy.

NIGHT HOUR

For the sake of the souls who are at rest, who with true and right faith are sleeping in Christ, let us pray to the Lord.

Remember Lord and have mercy.

And again in one voice for the sake of our true and holy faith, let us pray to the Lord.

Lord have mercy.

Let us make ourselves and one another as the Person of the Lord God Almighty.

Let us become as Your Person Lord.

Lord our God, be merciful to us, according to Your great mercy. Let us all say in unison.

Lord have mercy. Lord have mercy. Lord have mercy.

Prayer

Priest **Senior Chancel**

From You we are satisfied, Lord our God, who awakened us from the rest of sleep with Your grace of mercy. Awaken our minds to You with justice, Lord our God, that our eyes will see Your salvation. Your Godliness will come and abide in us, and Your mercy will be a shield and guardian over Your ministers.
And make us, Your servants worthy in the day and in the night and at every hour, and to always meditate in the love of Your commandments. And with thanksgiving glorifying the Father and the Son, and the Holy Spirit, now and always and unto the eternity of eternities. Amen.

NIGHT HOUR

Priest: Peace unto all.

Choir: And with Your Spirit.

Priest: Let us bow down in worship of God.

Choir: Before You Lord.

You are life giving strength and fountain of immortality, Christ God our savior. Who graced us to arise in the middle of the night and to confess unto You for the sake of Your righteousness and of Your justice, and now we request of You, Lord our God, to make us awake and prepared in the morning hour in the company of Your saints. And in the same company with satisfaction glorifying You with the Father and with the Holy Spirit, now and always and through the eternity of eternities. Amen.

144 NIGHT HOUR

Petition

<u>Priest</u>
With satisfaction and true confession
we unceasingly glorify the Father and the
Son and the Holy Spirit, now and always
and through the eternity of eternities.
Amen.

ETERNAL KING (TAKAVORK)

These are sung verses directing glory to God. The liturgical term is "Ascription" because it ascribes or attributes glory to "God Eternal King." These are not classified as hymns nor songs but as odes (sung poetry). They are based on the Psalms but are not pure Psalms but are mixed with prose. They are not chanted but sung to their own unique melody. The "Eternal Kings" are sung throughout the year on Monday through Saturday according to the tone of the day. They are sung for the following category of days: Repentance or Fasting Days, Martyrs, Apostles and Prophets, and St. Stephen. On Sundays and the fifty days from Easter until Pentecost they are not sung because these are Resurrection Days. An Alleluia is sung in its place. The Church Calendar must be used to determine the correct variable.

Senior Chancel

Eternal King for Repentance or Fasting Days

Monday

Eternal King. Hear us God our savior, and
give us life, which You are capable of everything.

Ps 64:5-6 KJV 65:5-6
Hear us God our savior, hope of all
ends of the earth, and that of the distant sea.
Who prepares the mountains
with His strength, and is clothed with
might, and give us life, which You are
capable of everything.

Melody Change
Hear our requests,
and Lord, lover of mankind, have compassion upon us.

Eternal King
Do not make me unseen, but help me
lover of mankind.

Ps 50:11-12 KJV 51:11-12
Do not cast me away, Lord, from Your faces,
and do not take Your Holy Spirit from me.
Also give me the joyfulness of salvation,
and with the spirit of Your government affirm me,
but help me lover of mankind.

NIGHT HOUR

<u>Melody Change</u>
Do not neglect me, Lord God
my savior, but grace unto me
forgiveness, very compassionate lover of
mankind, and give life.

<u>Eternal King</u>
Heavens and earth are satisfied
from You Lord, all whom have
been created bow in worship to You,
and the angels on high cry out and say,
have mercy, You created, do not destroy.

<u>Ps 148:4-5 KJV 148:4-5</u>
Heavens of heavens, waters which are above
the heavens, bless the Name of the Lord.
For He said and they became,
He commanded and they became established,
and the angels on high cry out and say,
have mercy, You created, do not destroy.

<u>Melody Change</u>
The heavens and earth continually
praise You, King of glories, the Seraphim
and Cherubim below facing each other,
and in unison shouting out
with cries and saying, Holy Holy Holy
Lord of hosts.

NIGHT HOUR

Tuesday

Eternal King.
You are patient Lord towards everything,
and have compassion upon us Lord,
and as the savior of the thief,
and give life.

Ps 85:15-16 KJV 86:15-16
Patient, abundantly merciful and true,
look upon me, and have mercy upon me.
Give strength to Your servant,
give life to the son of Your maid,
and make unto me the sign of goodness,
and have compassion upon us Lord,
and as the savior of the thief,
and give life.

Melody Change
Lord, who had compassion upon
the thief being crucified with You,
and You cleansed the impurity of
his offences with the flowing stream
from Your side, and have compassion
upon me who is of the sinners,
which I am of thirst for You,
and I desire of Your courtyards in the
same manner as one of the deer for
the spring of water.

NIGHT HOUR

<u>Eternal King</u>
The enemy battled against me,
continually willing to destroy me,
but You my Lord, make visit unto this
wandering sheep and give life.

<u>Ps 108:4-5 KJV 109:4-5</u>
They battled against me groundlessly,
and instead of my love they betrayed
me, but I stayed in prayer.
They relinquish to me evil instead of good,
hatred instead of my love,
but You my Lord, make visit unto this
wandering sheep and give life.

<u>Melody Change</u>
You whom are the shepherd of the
flock of the spoken word of the
living, give me hope of life in
repentance, and return the wanderers
into Your flock Christ, and give life.

<u>Eternal King</u>
I sinned and request of You,
grant forgiveness for my sins, with
Your compassion be my atoner,
who only You are savior, and give life.

NIGHT HOUR

<u>Prayer of Manasseh 12-13</u>
I have sinned Lord I have sinned,
and I know of my unrighteousness.
I pray and request from You,
forgive me Lord, forgive me, and
do not destroy me according to my
unrighteousness, be my atoner.

<u>Melody Change</u>
I have sinned against You Lord,
I have sinned against You Lord,
I have sinned, and more than the
sands of the sea, my offences are
many, deceptions of this world
deceived me, and I have been
unfruitful in life to Your hope,
but You humane and unvengeful
savior, spare this servant who
has sinned, and give life.

NIGHT HOUR

Wednesday

Eternal King.
My Lord, much is the
unrighteousness of my being,
I did not remember Your frightful judgments,
now being unfortunate I pray to You, grant me
repentance, Lord, and have mercy.

<u>Ps 37:4-5 KJV 38:4-5</u>
My unrighteousness has risen above my head,
and as a heavy load weighted over me.
Because of my foolish insensitivity,
the sores on my face festered and putrefied,
I did not remember Your frightful judgments,
now being unfortunate I pray to You, grant me
repentance, Lord, and have mercy.

<u>Melody Change</u>
We offer prayers to You heavenly
Father, do not neglect our prayers,
but make Your wrath pass
us over, and remember that we are
in the likeness of Your kindness.

<u>Eternal King</u>
My Lord, Your compassions are very many,
make unto me Your kindnesses, and as to the
tax collector, and to me, have mercy.

NIGHT HOUR

<u>Ps 118:156-157 KJV 119:156-157</u>
Your compassions are many, Lord,
and according to Your laws give me life.
Many are those who persecute and
oppress me, I have not gone astray
from Your testimonies,
make unto me Your kindnesses, and as to the
tax collector, and to me, have mercy.

<u>Melody Change</u>
Humane and unvengeful Lord, Who
with compassion upon us sinners
granted repentance, and now have
compassion upon me, Lord, this
Your servant who has sinned and
broken the laws, transform the laborers
of evil into the remorse of repentance,
and give life.

<u>Eternal King</u>
In Your temple of holiness, glorifying
You, You have Lordship, have mercy upon us.

<u>Ps 5:7-8 KJV 5:7-8</u>
But me according to Your
many mercies, I shall enter
into Your house, and I shall bow
in worship into Your Holy Temple with
Your fear. Lord, lead me in Your
righteousness for the sake of my enemies,
and make Your roads straight before me,
You, You have Lordship, have mercy upon us.

<u>Melody Change</u>
In Your Temple of Holiness we continually
praise You, King of glories, Who has Lordship
of life and salvation, have mercy upon us.

NIGHT HOUR

Thursday

Eternal King.
From repentance tears become a basin, and
multitudes of sins are washed,
with that grant before death atonement
and Your great mercy.

Ps 41:2-3 KJV 42:2-3

My being is thirsty to You almighty
and living God, when shall I come
appear to the faces of God.
Tears have become to me my food
in the day and in the night, and
that which they were saying to me
daily, where is your God?
with that grant before death atonement
and Your great mercy.

NIGHT HOUR

Melody Change

At which time You come in
glories of the Father on that
frightful day to judge the world,
and they tremble in Your terror, all
those who were born of this earth,
from fear of sitting in Your court
frightful judge, and regarding those
whom You have created, and
remember me of multitudes of sins,
in which I am submerged with offences
of the deceiver of trickery, and I
request for the thief, Lord, and
remember me, that You only are savior.

Eternal King

I who am in the ship of the world
am being engulfed by waves of my sins,
abundantly merciful one grant unto me the harbor
of repentance, and give life.

Ps 68:2 KJV 69:1

Give me life God, for the waters
have come unto my person, I
have sunk into the depths of
the abysses where rest does not exist for me,
abundantly merciful one grant unto me the harbor
of repentance, and give life.

NIGHT HOUR

Melody Change
Compassionate captain in You
I take refuge, give me a hand
as on occasion You gave to Peter
upon the waves, for my floating
is having been engulfed by the waves
of the offences of sins, and give life.

Eternal King
You are Christ the fountain of life,
the springing forth of mercy,
savior, grace upon our beings
the forgiving of our sins.

Ps 35:9-10 KJV 36:9-10
From You Lord is the fountain of
life and with the light of Your faces we see the light.
Shine out Your mercies,
upon those who know You, Your justices upon
those who are upright in heart,
savior, grace upon our beings
the forgiving of our sins.

Melody Change
You who are the fountain
of those who thirst, and rest to
those who labor, the road to those who
wander, and spiritual shepherd to
flock of the spoken word, of those
who desire of You Christ, be the harbor
and make those of us who thirst drink
Your cup of sweetness from Your
never ending fountain.

NIGHT HOUR 155

Friday

Eternal King.
In Your Temple of Holiness hear Lord my voice,
and my prayers shall arrive to Your ears Lord.

Ps 17:7b-c KJV 18:6b-c

He heard me, the sound of my prayers,
from His Holy Temple, and my cry
before Him will enter His ears,
and my prayers shall arrive to Your ears Lord.

Melody Change
*Salt and Bread Days**

You who are luminescent to the
universes Christ God, enlighten my
dark thoughts, and give life.

Melody Change
Days of Remembrance of those at Rest

Blessed are You Lord, and glorified is
Your unlimited love of mankind, we offer
our prayers to You, whom You are King
of eternity, make those of ours who
are at rest worthy Lord to receive into
Your life of eternity.

---

* *Salt and Bread Days are the strictest Fasting Days of the Church calendar. The faithful would eat only salt and bread on those days. These are weekdays during the Fast of Great Lent.*

NIGHT HOUR

<u>Eternal King</u>
Grant me tears unto repentance Lord,
that I shall wash the sins of my being,
in the same manner as the prostitute I pray,
and give life.

<u>Ps 6:6a-b KJV 6:6a-b</u>
I became fatigued in my groanful lamentations,
I washed my mattress every night, and with my
tears I wet my bed, that I shall wash the sins of my being,
in the same manner as the prostitute I pray,
and give life.

<u>Melody Change</u>
You who are the pure fountain
Christ, God, heal Lord my being, having been
wounded from sins, with the springing forth
of tears, and give life.

<u>Eternal King</u>
Search Lord for this Your wandering servant,
and lover of mankind do not condemn me
on the day of Your visitation.*

<u>Ps 118:175-176 KJV 119:175-176</u>
Salt and Bread Days**
My being shall live and shall bless You
and Your laws shall help me.
I was wandering as a lost sheep, search for this Your
servant for I have not forgotten Your commandments,
and lover of mankind do not condemn me
on the day of Your visitation.*
I who wandered from Your flock Good Shepherd,
search for me who is wandering,
and make me worthy to become mixed into
Your flock Christ, and give life.

---

*   *Second Coming*
** *Salt and Bread Days are the strictest Fasting Days of the Church calendar. The faithful would eat only salt and bread on those days. These are weekdays during the Fast of Great Lent.*

NIGHT HOUR

Eternal King for Days of Martyrs

<u>A Tz</u>

Eternal King.
With the advocation of the saints
(Insert name of Saint whose feast day is being celebrated),
we request that You,
grace unto us forgiveness for our offences,
kind Christ.

<u>Ps 33:19-21 KJV 34:18-20</u>

The Lord is near to those who
are with worn out hearts, and
to those meek in spirit He gives life.
The oppressions to the just ones are many,
The Lord saves them from all of them, and He
 keeps all of their bones, and not one of them
shall be destroyed,
grace unto us forgiveness for our offences,
kind Christ.

NIGHT HOUR

<u>Melody Change</u>
Who with victorious strength in the
hermetic solemnity, You kept Your
witnesses who confess of You pure Christ
God, give us strength in our oppression, with
the advocation of the Holy Martyrs,
and give life.

<u>A G</u>
Eternal King.
Make Your mercy upon us Lord,
and with the advocation of the saints
(Insert name of Saint whose feast day is being celebrated),
do not destroy us, the Holy Trinity have mercy upon us.

NIGHT HOUR

<u>Ps 36:39-40 KJV 37:39-40</u>
The salvation of the just is from the
Lord, He is their guardian in times of distress.
The Lord will help them and save them,
He will deliver them from sinners, and
will give life to those who believed in Him,
and with the advocation of the saints
(Insert name of Saint whose feast day is being celebrated),
do not destroy us, the Holy Trinity have mercy upon us.

<u>Melody Change</u>
Those who undertook tortures and death for
Your sake, and they shed their blood for
the sake of Your Holy Name, with
their advocation do not destroy us,
the Holy Trinity have mercy upon us.

<u>P Tz</u>
Eternal King.
With the advocation of the saints
(Insert name of Saint whose feast day is being celebrated),
gift us Lord,
to take part and portion in the company of
those having been invited to the call of the
kingdom of heavens.

<u>Ps 67:36a-b KJV 68:35a-b</u>
God is wonderful over His saints God of Israel.
He shall give strength
of foundation to His people, blessed is God,
to take part and share in the company of
those having been invited to the call of the
kingdom of heavens.

NIGHT HOUR

<u>Melody Change</u>

Martyrs fortunate and glorified,
of whom multitudes of tortures
were enumerated, you are clothed with
the light of life, and advocate to
Christ for our sake.

<u>P G</u>

Eternal King.
You are Christ the fountain of life,
the springing forth of mercy,
You graced upon the saints
(Insert name of Saint whose feast day is being celebrated),
victorious martyrdom, to drive away
the darkness and illuminate our beings.

<u>Ps 88:7-8 KJV 89:7-8</u>

God is glorified in the council of
His saints, great and feared, over all
those who are around Him. Lord God
of (*heavenly*) hosts, who is like You?
You are mighty Lord, and Your truth is
around You, You granted unto us the saints
(Insert name of Saint whose feast day is being celebrated),
victorious martyrdom, to drive away
the darkness and illuminate our beings.

NIGHT HOUR

<u>Melody Change</u>

That with the graces of the Holy Spirit
You conquered the enemy, fortunate are the
Holy witnesses of Christ, for the sake of Your
celebrations request from God forgiveness of sins.

<u>Melody Change</u>

Whom You crowned in splendor all of those
of virtue, Forerunner* and leader of
eternal life, whom holy martyrs, and for our sake
advocate to the One Who crown the saints,
with gracing mercy from the never
ending eternal fountain of life.

<u>K Tz</u>
<u>K G</u>

Eternal King.
The suffering of the saints
(Insert name of Saint whose feast day is being celebrated),
advocation we have to You Christ,
and we pray with them, grant us
forgiveness of our sins, and in Your
life of eternity, renew and give life.

* *John the Baptist*

NIGHT HOUR

K Tz
Ps 96:11-12 KJV 97:11-12
He shined light upon the just,
those upright in heart became joyful.
Those just in the Lord be joyful, and confess to
the memory of His Holiness,
and we pray with them, grant us
forgiveness of our sins, and in Your
life of eternity, renew and give life.

K G
Ps 115: 15-17 KJV 116:15-17
Death of His saints is honorable
before the Lord, O Lord I am Your
servant, servant and son of Your maid servant.
You have cut my binds, to You I shall bring forth
an offering of blessing, and I shall call upon the
Name of the Lord and we pray with them, grant us
forgiveness of our sins, and in Your
life of eternity, renew and give life.

Melody Change
Having fought in the battles of war
we were found victorious Holy
Martyrs, for you paved the road
for us to the heavenly city of Jerusalem,
in the company of the order of angels
glorifying the Holy Trinity.

NIGHT HOUR

<u>T Tz</u>
Eternal King.
Those who are at the altar of holiness
having assembled to bless You, Christ,
with the prayers of the saints
(Insert name of Saint whose feast day is being celebrated),
do not make our requests unseen, who
only You are the abundantly merciful King of Glories, Christ.

<u>Ps144:18-19 KJV 145:18-19</u>
The Lord is near to all of those
who call upon Him in truth.
The Lord does fulfill the wills of those who
fear in Him, He hears their prayers,
and gives them life,
with the prayers of the saints
(Insert name of Saint whose feast day is being celebrated),
do not neglect our requests, Who
only You are the abundantly merciful King of Glories, Christ.

Eternal King for Feast Days of the
Apostles and Prophets

<u>Ps 18:4-5 KJV 19:3-4a</u>
Eternal King.
There are no words and there
is no speech, of those whom
their voices are not heard.
Their speech went forth into all lands, and
their words unto all ends of the world,
with the prayers of the saints
(Insert name of Saint whose feast day is being celebrated),
do not make our requests unseen, who
only You are very merciful King of Glories, Christ.

NIGHT HOUR

<u>Melody Change</u>

Martyrs and witnesses of Christ God,
sermons of salvation for the
universes, those of you who presented
yourselves as offering, and the sacrifice for
God the Father of sweet fragrances,
of this assembling to carry out the
remembrance of your names, advocate
to the Lord for the sake of atonement
for our sins.

<u>T G</u>

Eternal King.
To Your thrice Holy Lordship
in unison we pray, hear Lord,
with the prayers of the saints
(Insert name of Saint whose feast day is being celebrated),
spare us and give life.

<u>Ps 5:11-12 KJV 5:11-12</u>

Let all of those who have hoped in You
be joyful, they shall eternally
rejoice, and You shall dwell in them.
The beloved of Your Name shall splendor in You,
for You shall bless the just, Lord, as of
armament with Your pleasure you
crowned them,
with the prayers of the saints
(Insert name of Saint whose feast day is being celebrated),
spare us and give life.

NIGHT HOUR

<u>Melody Change</u>
Church, celebrate today the holy
remembrances of your holy
witnesses, who with the power of the
Holy Spirit, you witnessed the war
of evil, and governed in the arches of
angelic lights, to bless the Holy Trinity.

Eternal King for Feast Day of St.Stephen

(For a detailed liturgical description as to how and when to perform this order, see "A Dictionary of the Armenian Church" by M. Ormanian ed. 1984 Pg 141-142)

Eternal King.

Today the ranks of angels rejoice
in the company of the hardship of
St. Stephen the first martyr.

For Your Church Christ calls out the
victorious battle of His flowing blood
upon Your great Name Lord.

There is much courage of him before God,
in the hand of his holy outpouring blood.

For with willingness he delivered himself
up to cruel and bitter tortures for the
sake of the great Name of the Lord.

For with contempt he despised traveling
in the life of this world, and desired
eternal life, and always and forevermore
he rejoices in the company of His Lord,
in unceasing joyfulness.

For Your Church Christ calls out the
victorious battle of His flowing blood
upon Your great Name Lord.

Glory, to the Father that exists, to the
Only Begotten Son, and to the deliverer of
the Holy Spirit, is befitting.

NIGHT HOUR

Glory, honor, and Lordship now and
always and through the
eternity of eternities. Amen.

And at which time the heavens and the
earth shook from fear of the glories of the
Word of the Lord God.

In that time He seats the
beloved of His name at His right side in the
bright angelic paired altars.

The Bishop or Priest who is censing repeats the first verse only in recitation, without melody, beginning with verse "Today the ranks of Angels" (Aysor task hreshdagatz) through verse 3 ending with "His Holy outpouring Blood" (Soorp aryan yiuro.)

ALLELUIAS

The Alleluias are sung throughout the year on Sundays and during the Fifty Days of Pentecost which are Resurrection Days. It would be sung in place of "Eternal King"(Takavor Havidyan). The Church calendar must be used to determine the correct Alleluia of the day.

Senior Chancel

Alleluias for Feasts of the Lord

Alleluia for the Lighting of the Lamps of the Eve of the Holy Birth of Christ

Alleluia
Ps 106:20-21 KJV 107:20-21

Alleluia, Alleluia, Alleluia.
He sent forth His word, and healed
them, and saved them from their own corruption.
They shall confess to the Lord for
His mercies and for His wonders to
the sons of man.

Melody Change

Ps 71:6-7 KJV 72:6-7
Alleluia. Alleluia. Alleluia.
He will descend as rain upon
fleece, as dew that sprinkles upon the land.
Justice shall spring forth in His days,
much peace until the moon expires.

Glory and bowing down in worship of the
Father and of the Son and of the Holy Spirit,
now and always and unto the eternity of
eternities. Amen. Alleluia. Alleluia. Alleluia.

NIGHT HOUR

Alleluias for the Holy Birth of the Lord Jesus Christ

<u>A Tz</u>
<u>Ps 22:1-2 KJV 23:1-2</u>

Alleluia, Alleluia, Alleluia.
The Lord will shepherd me,
and for me, I shall lack nothing.
He made me dwell in a plain of green field,
and by the waters of rest He nourished me.

<u>Melody Change</u>

Alleluia, Alleluia, Alleluia.
He will descend as rain upon
fleece, as dew that sprinkles upon the land.
Justice shall spring forth in His days,
much peace until the moon expires.

Glory and bowing down in worship of the
Father and of the Son and of the Holy Spirit,
now and always and unto the eternity of
eternities. Amen. Alleluia. Alleluia. Alleluia.

---

*After each Feast of the Lord in which the
Alleluia is performed according to the tone
A Tz only, the following must also be sung.*

The order of angels bless You, Christ,
alleluia, the nations of mankind sing
psalms to You. Alleluia. Alleluia. Alleluia.

NIGHT HOUR

A G
Ps 44:10-13 KJV 45:9-12

Alleluia, Alleluia, Alleluia.
Hear daughter and see, may your ear
descend, forget your people and the house
of your father, because the king desired for your beauty.
He himself is your Lord,
you shall bow down in worship to Him,
and daughter of Tyre bow down in worship
to Him, and with offerings the very important
among the people will give adoration to
His faces.

Melody Change
Ps 88:27-28 KJV 89:26-27

Alleluia, Alleluia, Alleluia.
He will cry out unto me, You are
my Father, God receiver of my salvation.
I shall make Him the first born son,
and higher than all of the kings of the earth.

Glory and bowing down in worship of the
Father and of the Son and of the Holy Spirit,
now and always and unto the eternity of
eternities. Amen. Alleluia. Alleluia. Alleluia.

NIGHT HOUR

<u>P Tz</u>
<u>Ps 71:6-7 KJV 72:6-7</u>

Alleluia, Alleluia, Alleluia.
He will descend as rain upon
fleece, as dew that sprinkles upon the land.
Justice shall spring forth in His days,
much peace until the moon expires.

<u>Melody Change</u>
<u>Ps 97:2-3 KJV 98:2-3</u>

Alleluia, Alleluia, Alleluia.
The Lord showed His salvation, before
the nations He revealed His justice.
With His mercy He remembered Jacob, with His
truth the house of Israel, and all ends
of the earth saw the salvation of our God.

Glory and bowing down in worship of the
Father and of the Son and of the Holy Spirit,
now and always and unto the eternity of
eternities. Amen. Alleluia. Alleluia. Alleluia.

<u>P G</u>
<u>Ps 88:27-28 KJV 89:26-27</u>

Alleluia, Alleluia, Alleluia.
He will cry out unto me, You are
my Father, God receiver of my salvation.
I shall make Him the first born son,
and higher than all of the kings of the earth.

NIGHT HOUR

<u>Melody Change</u>
<u>Ps 109:3-5a KJV 110 3-5a</u>

Alleluia, Alleluia, Alleluia.
Through You is the beginning day of
power, in splendor of Your saints
from the womb before the morning star*
I gave birth to You.
The Lord gave oath and never again shall regret,
that You are priest eternally according to the
order of Melchizedek, and the Lord is at Your
right hand.

Glory and bowing down in worship of the
Father and of the Son and of the Holy Spirit,
now and always and unto the eternity of
eternities. Amen. Alleluia. Alleluia. Alleluia.

<u>K Tz</u>
<u>Ps 97:2-3 KJV 98:2-3</u>

Alleluia, Alleluia, Alleluia.
The Lord showed His salvation, before
the nations He revealed His justice.
With His mercy He remembered Jacob, with His
truth the house of Israel, and all ends
of the earth saw the salvation of our God.

<u>Melody Change</u>
<u>Ps 131: 1-2 KJV 132:1-2</u>

Alleluia, Alleluia, Alleluia.
Remember Lord, David, and all of his meekness.
As he gave oath to the Lord
and made vows to the God of Jacob.

* Morning Star has a double meaning. It is another term for Lucifer (Satan).

NIGHT HOUR

Glory and bowing down in worship of the
Father and of the Son and of the Holy Spirit,
now and always and unto the eternity of
eternities. Amen. Alleluia. Alleluia. Alleluia.

<u>K G</u>
<u>Ps 109:3-5a KJV 110 3-5a</u>
Alleluia, Alleluia, Alleluia.
Through You is the beginning day of
power, in splendor of Your saints
from the womb before the morning star*
I gave birth to You.
The Lord gave oath and never again shall regret,
that You are priest eternally according to the
order of Melchizedek, and the Lord is at Your
right hand.

<u>Melody Change</u>
<u>Ps 2:7b-8 KJV 2:7b-8</u>
The Lord said to me, You are
my Son, and today I have begotten you**.
Ask from me, and I shall give you the heathens as
inheritance, and Lordship unto You through all ends of the earth.

Glory and bowing down in worship of the
Father and of the Son and of the Holy Spirit,
now and always and unto the eternity of
eternities. Amen. Alleluia. Alleluia. Alleluia.

---

* *Morning Star has a double meaning. It is another term for Lucifer (Satan).*
** *Literally- Have given birth to You.*

NIGHT HOUR

<u>T Tz</u>
<u>Ps 131: 1-2 KJV 132:1-2</u>

Alleluia, Alleluia, Alleluia.
Remember Lord, David, and all of his meekness.
As he gave oath to the Lord
and made vows to the God of Jacob.

<u>Melody Change</u>
<u>Ps 22:1-2 KJV 23:1-2</u>

Alleluia, Alleluia, Alleluia.
The Lord will shepherd me,
and for me, I shall lack nothing.
He made me dwell in a plain of green field,
and by the waters of rest He nourished me.

Glory and bowing down in worship of the
Father and of the Son and of the Holy Spirit,
now and always and unto the eternity of
eternities. Amen. Alleluia. Alleluia. Alleluia.

<u>T G</u>
<u>Ps 2:7b-8 KJV 2:7b-8</u>

Alleluia, Alleluia, Alleluia.
The Lord said to me, You are
my Son, and today I have begotten you**.
Ask from me, and I shall give you the heathens as
inheritance, and Lordship unto You
through all ends of the earth.

** *Literally- Have given birth to You.*

NIGHT HOUR

<u>Melody Change</u>
<u>Ps 44:10-13 KJV 45:9-12</u>

Alleluia, Alleluia, Alleluia.
Hear daughter and see, may your ear
descend, forget your people and the house
of your father, because the king desired for your beauty.
He himself is your Lord,
you shall bow down in worship to Him,
and daughter of Tyre bow down in worship
to Him, and with offerings the very important
among the people will give adoration to His faces.

Glory and bowing down in worship of the
Father and of the Son and of the Holy Spirit,
now and always and unto the eternity of
eternities. Amen. Alleluia. Alleluia. Alleluia.

Alleluia for the Feast of the Presentation of
Christ to the Temple Forty Days After His Birth

<u>Alleluia</u>
<u>Ps 117:26-27 KJV 118:26-27</u>

Alleluia, Alleluia, Alleluia.
Blessed is he who comes in the
Name of the Lord, blessed are You Who are to come.
Lord our God appeared to us, make feasts of rejoicing
beforehand up to the corners of the altar table.

NIGHT HOUR

<u>Melody Change</u>
<u>Ps 10:5 KJV 11:4</u>

Alleluia, Alleluia, Alleluia.
The Lord in His Holy Temple,
the Lord in His throne in the heavens.
His eyes look upon the impoverished,
and His eyelids examine the sons of man.

Glory and bowing down in worship of the
Father and of the Son and of the Holy Spirit,
now and always and unto the eternity of
eternities. Amen. Alleluia. Alleluia. Alleluia.

Alleluias for the Resurrection of Christ

<u>A Tz</u>
<u>Ps 32:5b-6 KJV 33:5b-6</u>

Alleluia, Alleluia, Alleluia.
The earth has been filled with
the mercy of the Lord, and through
the word of the Lord the heavens became established.
And through the spirit of His mouth, all of their hosts.

<u>Melody Change</u>
<u>Ps 67:2 KJV 68:1a-1b</u>

Alleluia, Alleluia, Alleluia.
God arose and all of His enemies scattered.
Those who hate Him fled from His faces.

Glory and bowing down in worship of the
Father and of the Son and of the Holy Spirit,
now and always and unto the eternity of
eternities. Amen. Alleluia. Alleluia. Alleluia.

NIGHT HOUR

<u>A G</u>
<u>Ps 46:2-3 KJV 47:1-2</u>

Alleluia, Alleluia, Alleluia.
Clap your hands, all you heathens, cry
out unto God in a voice of joyfulness.
Lord on high and is fearsome, great
king over the entire earth.

<u>Melody Change</u>
<u>Ps 84:2-3 KJV 85:1-2</u>

Alleluia, Alleluia, Alleluia.
You were pleased, Lord, throughout Your land,
and You have overturned the captivity of Jacob.
You forgave the unrighteousness of Your people,
and You covered all their sins.

Glory and bowing down in worship of the
Father and of the Son and of the Holy Spirit,
now and always and unto the eternity of
eternities. Amen. Alleluia. Alleluia. Alleluia.

<u>P Tz</u>
<u>Ps 67:2 KJV 68:1a-1b</u>

Alleluia, Alleluia, Alleluia.
God arose and all of His enemies scattered.
Those who hate Him fled from His faces.

<u>Melody Change</u>
<u>Ps 92:1 KJV 93:1</u>

Alleluia, Alleluia, Alleluia.

The Lord ruled as king, He was clothed
in splendor. He was clothed with
strength brought forth from within Him.

NIGHT HOUR

Glory and bowing down in worship of the Father and of the Son and of the Holy Spirit, now and always and unto the eternity of eternities. Amen. Alleluia. Alleluia. Alleluia.

P G
Ps 84:2-3 KJV 85:1-2

Alleluia, Alleluia, Alleluia.
You were pleased, Lord, throughout Your land,
and You have overturned the captivity of Jacob.
You forgave the unrighteousness of Your people,
and You covered all their sins.

Melody Change
Ps 112:1-2 KJV 113:1-2

Alleluia, Alleluia, Alleluia.
Children serving the Lord, bless the Lord
and bless the name of the Lord,
Blessed be the Name of the Lord,
from this time forth unto eternity.

Glory and bowing down in worship of the Father and of the Son and of the Holy Spirit, now and always and unto the eternity of eternities. Amen. Alleluia. Alleluia. Alleluia.

NIGHT HOUR

<u>K Tz</u>
<u>Ps 92:1 KJV 93:1</u>

Alleluia, Alleluia, Alleluia.
The Lord ruled as king, He was clothed in splendor.
He was clothed with strength brought forth
from within Him.

<u>Melody Change</u>
<u>Ps 147:12-13 KJV 147:12-13</u>

Alleluia, Alleluia, Alleluia.
Jerusalem, praise the Lord
and Zion bless your God.
For He has strengthened the bars of your
gates, and within you has blessed your sons.

Glory and bowing down in worship of the
Father and of the Son and of the Holy Spirit,
now and always and unto the eternity of
eternities. Amen. Alleluia. Alleluia. Alleluia.

<u>K G</u>
<u>Ps 112:1-2 KJV 113:1-2</u>

Alleluia, Alleluia, Alleluia.
Children serving the Lord, bless the Lord
and bless the name of the Lord,
Blessed be the Name of the Lord,
from this time forth unto eternity.

<u>Melody Change</u>
<u>Ps 17:47-48 KJV 18:46-47</u>

The Lord is alive and blessed is God, and
God shall be elevated on high for my salvation.
It is God who demands my revenge,
and He makes the people submissive
under me.

Glory and bowing down in worship of the
Father and of the Son and of the Holy Spirit,
now and always and unto the eternity of
eternities. Amen. Alleluia. Alleluia. Alleluia.

<u>T Tz</u>
<u>Ps 147:12-13 KJV 147:12-13</u>

Alleluia, Alleluia, Alleluia.
Jerusalem, praise the Lord
and Zion bless your God.
For He has strengthened the bars of your
gates, and within you has blessed your sons.

<u>Melody Change</u>
<u>Ps 32:5b-6 KJV 33:5b-6</u>
Alleluia, Alleluia, Alleluia.
The earth has been filled with
the mercy of the Lord, and through
the word of the Lord the heavens became established.
And through the spirit of His mouth, all of their hosts.

Glory and bowing down in worship of the
Father and of the Son and of the Holy Spirit,
now and always and unto the eternity of
eternities. Amen. Alleluia. Alleluia. Alleluia.

<u>T G</u>
<u>Ps 17:47-48 KJV 18:46-47</u>

Alleluia, Alleluia, Alleluia.
The Lord is alive and blessed is God, and
God shall be elevated on high for my salvation.
It is God who demands my revenge,
and He makes the people submissive
under me.

NIGHT HOUR

<u>Melody Change</u>
<u>Ps 46: 2-3 KJV 47:1-2</u>

Alleluia, Alleluia, Alleluia.
Clap your hands, all you heathens, cry
out unto God in a voice of joyfulness.
Lord on high and is fearsome, great
king over the entire earth.

Glory and bowing down in worship of the
Father and of the Son and of the Holy Spirit,
now and always and unto the eternity of
eternities. Amen. Alleluia. Alleluia. Alleluia.

Alleluias for the Ascension of Christ

<u>A Tz</u>
<u>Ps 23: 7-8 KJV 24:7-8</u>

Alleluia, Alleluia, Alleluia.
Princes, lift up your gates,
the gates of eternity shall be lifted
up and the King of Glories shall enter.
Who is this, the King of Glories,
Lord almighty with His strength, the
Lord powerful in war.

NIGHT HOUR

<u>Melody Change</u>
<u>Ps 67:18-19a KJV 68:17-18a</u>

Alleluia, Alleluia, Alleluia.
The chariots of God are
tens of thousands, the chariot drivers
are thousands, and the Lord
is in them from Sinai in His holiness.
He ascended to the heights
and He took captive of captivity, He took
pillage, He divided the gifts, and gave
them to the sons of man.

Glory and bowing down in worship of the
Father and of the Son and of the Holy Spirit,
now and always and unto the eternity of
eternities. Amen. Alleluia. Alleluia. Alleluia.

The order of angels bless You, Christ,
alleluia, the nations of mankind sing
psalms to You. Alleluia. Alleluia. Alleluia.

<u>A G</u>
<u>Ps 46:6-7 KJV 47:5-6</u>

Alleluia, Alleluia, Alleluia.
God ascended with blessing,
and our Lord with the sound of the trumpet.
Say psalms to our God,
say psalms to our king, say psalms.

<u>Melody Change</u>
<u>Ps 79:2-3a KJV 80:1-2a</u>
Alleluia, Alleluia, Alleluia.
You Who shepherd Israel, look, You
Who leads Joseph as a flock.
You Who sit among the Cherubim, having become
revealed before Ephraim, Benjamin, and Manasseh.

NIGHT HOUR

Glory and bowing down in worship of the
Father and of the Son and of the Holy Spirit,
now and always and unto the eternity of
eternities. Amen. Alleluia. Alleluia. Alleluia.

<u>P Tz</u>
<u>Ps 67:18-19a KJV 68:17-18a</u>

Alleluia, Alleluia, Alleluia.
The chariots of God are
tens of thousands, the chariot drivers
are thousands, and the Lord
is in them from Sinai in His holiness.
He ascended to the heights
and He took captive of captivity, He took
pillage, He divided the gifts, and gave
them to the sons of man.

<u>Melody Change</u>
<u>Ps 103:3, 1b, 2, 3a KJV 104:3, 1b, 2, 3a</u>

Alleluia, Alleluia, Alleluia.
Who puts His departure into the clouds,
and He walks upon the wings of the winds.
You are clothed with confession
and great splendor, You dressed Yourself
in light as with a blanket, You
stretched out the heavens as a tent,
and You cast its upper floor upon the waters.

Glory and bowing down in worship of the
Father and of the Son and of the Holy Spirit,
now and always and unto the eternity of
eternities. Amen. Alleluia. Alleluia. Alleluia.

NIGHT HOUR

P G
Ps 79:2-3a KJV 80:1-2a

Alleluia, Alleluia, Alleluia.
You Who shepherd Israel, look, You
Who leads Joseph as a flock.
You Who sit among the Cherubim, having become
revealed before Ephraim, Benjamin, and Manasseh.

Melody Change
Ps 56:11-12 KJV 57:10-11

Your mercy has become great
unto the heavens, and Your
truth unto the clouds.
You are on high unto the heavens,
and unto all of the earth are Your glories.

Glory and bowing down in worship of the
Father and of the Son and of the Holy Spirit,
now and always and unto the eternity of
eternities. Amen. Alleluia. Alleluia. Alleluia.

K Tz
Ps 103:3, 1b, 2, 3a KJV 104:3, 1b, 2, 3a

Alleluia, Alleluia, Alleluia.
Who puts His departure into the clouds,
and He walks upon the wings of the winds.
You are clothed with confession
and great splendor, You dressed Yourself
in light as with a blanket, You
stretched out the heavens as a tent,
and You cast its upper floor upon the waters.

NIGHT HOUR

<u>Melody Change</u>
<u>Ps 143:5-6 KJV 144:5-6</u>

Alleluia, Alleluia, Alleluia.
Lord, make the heavens descend and
come down, come near to the mountains
and they shall smoke.
Make Your lightening shine, and upset them,
send Your arrows and scatter them.

Glory and bowing down in worship of the
Father and of the Son and of the Holy Spirit,
now and always and unto the eternity of
eternities. Amen. Alleluia. Alleluia. Alleluia.

<u>K G</u>
<u>Ps 56:11-12 KJV 57:10-11</u>

Alleluia, Alleluia, Alleluia.
Your mercy has become great
unto the heavens, and Your
truth unto the clouds.
You are on high unto the heavens,
and unto all of the earth are Your glories.

<u>Melody Change</u>
<u>Ps 17:10-11 KJV 18:9-10</u>

Alleluia, Alleluia, Alleluia.
He made the heavens descend and came down,
and fog under His feet.
He ascended upon Cherubim and flew,
He soared on the wings of the wind.

Glory and bowing down in worship of the
Father and of the Son and of the Holy Spirit,
now and always and unto the eternity of
eternities. Amen. Alleluia. Alleluia. Alleluia.

NIGHT HOUR

<u>T Tz</u>
<u>*Hab 3:5-6</u>

Alleluia, Alleluia, Alleluia.
Beatings shall come up to His faces,
and from the bird the great men
shall go in the paths of His footprints.
The mountains shall melt and the
forests waste away, the roads which
were from the beginning shall become
blind, and from Him the entire earth shall
tremble.

<u>Melody Change</u>
<u>Ps 23:7-8 KJV 24:7-8</u>

Alleluia, Alleluia, Alleluia.
Princes, lift up your gates, the gates of eternity
shall be lifted up and the King of Glories shall enter.
Who is this, the King of Glories, Lord
of Hosts, He Himself is the King of Glories.

Glory and bowing down in worship of the
Father and of the Son and of the Holy Spirit,
now and always and unto the eternity of
eternities. Amen. Alleluia. Alleluia. Alleluia.

---

* *This text of Habakkuk 3 is very different from the text in the Armenian Bible. This text used in the Alleluia section is based upon the liturgical version of the canticle found at the conclusion of the Seventh Canon of the Book of Psalms (Psalter). The origin is unclear and an English version whether canonical or apocryphal was not able to be found. If a Biblical Scholar can place the origins of this, please contact the author at Holy Trinity Armenian Church of Fresno, Ca.*

NIGHT HOUR

T G
Ps 17:10-11 KJV 18:9-10

Alleluia, Alleluia, Alleluia.
He made the heavens descend and came down,
and fog under His feet.
He ascended upon Cherubim and flew,
He soared on the wings of the wind.

Melody Change
Ps 46:6-7 KJV 47:5-6

Alleluia, Alleluia, Alleluia.
God ascended with blessing,
and our Lord with the sound of the trumpet.
Say psalms to our God,
say psalms to our king, say psalms.

Glory and bowing down in worship of the
Father and of the Son and of the Holy Spirit,
now and always and unto the eternity of
eternities. Amen. Alleluia. Alleluia. Alleluia.

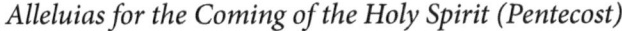

Alleluias for the Coming of the Holy Spirit (Pentecost)

A Tz
Ps 18:11-12 KJV 19:10-11

Alleluia, Alleluia, Alleluia.
It is more desirable than gold and
more than many precious gems, it is
sweeter than of honey from the honeycomb.
For Your servant shall keep this, in keeping,
to him shall be an abundant reward.

NIGHT HOUR

<u>Melody Change</u>
<u>Ps 67:14b-15 KJV 68:13b-14</u>
Silver plated wings of a dove, and
its back in the color of gold.
When the heavenly kings were assembled
upon it, they shall be as snow on Mt. Zalmon.

Glory and bowing down in worship of the
Father and of the Son and of the Holy Spirit,
now and always and unto the eternity of
eternities. Amen. Alleluia. Alleluia. Alleluia.

The order of angels bless You, Christ,
alleluia, the nations of mankind sing
psalms to You. Alleluia. Alleluia. Alleluia.

<u>A G</u>
<u>Ps 50:12-13 KJV 51:11-12</u>
Alleluia, Alleluia, Alleluia.
Establish unto me a holy heart, God,
and renew an upright spirit within my belly.
Do not cast me away, Lord, from Your faces,
and do not take Your Holy Spirit from me.

<u>Melody Change</u>
<u>Ps 88:21-22 KJV 89:20-21</u>
Alleluia, Alleluia, Alleluia.
I have found David my servant,
and with my holy oil I have anointed him.
My hand shall receive
him and my forearm shall strengthen him.

Glory and bowing down in worship of the
Father and of the Son and of the Holy Spirit,
now and always and unto the eternity of
eternities. Amen. Alleluia. Alleluia. Alleluia.

NIGHT HOUR

<u>P Tz</u>
<u>Ps 67:14b-15 KJV 68:13b-14</u>

Alleluia, Alleluia, Alleluia.
Silver plated wings of a dove, and
its back in the color of gold.
When the heavenly kings were assembled
upon it, they shall be as snow on Mr. Zalmon.

<u>Melody Change</u>
<u>Ps 103:30-31</u>

Alleluia, Alleluia, Alleluia.
You send Your soul and You receive
them, and You renew the faces of the earth.
The glories of the Lord shall be
made eternal, and the Lord shall
be joyful in what He has made.

Glory and bowing down in worship of the
Father and of the Son and of the Holy Spirit,
now and always and unto the eternity of
eternities. Amen. Alleluia. Alleluia. Alleluia.

<u>P G</u>
<u>Ps 88:21-22 KJV 89:20-21</u>

Alleluia, Alleluia, Alleluia.
I have found David my servant,
and with my holy oil I have anointed him.
 My hand shall receive
him and my forearm shall strengthen him.

NIGHT HOUR

<u>Melody Change</u>
<u>Ps 118:130-131 KJV 119:130-131</u>
Alleluia, Alleluia, Alleluia.
The revelation of Your words is
enlightening and makes the boys knowledgeable.
I opened my mouth and took the spirit,
my being desired for Your commandments.

Glory and bowing down in worship of the
Father and of the Son and of the Holy Spirit,
now and always and unto the eternity of
eternities. Amen. Alleluia. Alleluia. Alleluia.

<u>K Tz</u>
<u>Ps 103:30-31</u>
Alleluia, Alleluia, Alleluia.
You send Your soul and You receive
them, and You renew the faces of the earth.
The glories of the Lord shall be
made eternal, and the Lord shall
be joyful in what He has made.

<u>Melody Change</u>
<u>Ps 142:10c-11 KJV 143:10c-11</u>
Alleluia, Alleluia, Alleluia.
Your good and Holy Spirit shall
lead me into upright land.
For the sake of Your Name, Lord, may You give me life,
with Your righteousness may You take my being
out of difficulty.

Glory and bowing down in worship of the
Father and of the Son and of the Holy Spirit,
now and always and unto the eternity of
eternities. Amen. Alleluia. Alleluia. Alleluia.

NIGHT HOUR

<u>K G</u>
<u>Ps118:131-132 KJV 119:131-132</u>
Alleluia, Alleluia, Alleluia.
I opened my mouth and took
the spirit, my being desired for
Your commandments.
Look upon me and be merciful unto
me according to the righteousness
of those who love Your name.

<u>Melody Change</u>
<u>Ps 17:16b-17 KJV 18:15b-16</u>
From Your strong reprimand, Lord, and
from the breathing of the spirit of Your anger.
He sent from the heights and received me, He received me
by taking me out of many waters.

Glory and bowing down in worship of the
Father and of the Son and of the Holy Spirit,
now and always and unto the eternity of
eternities. Amen. Alleluia. Alleluia. Alleluia.

<u>T Tz</u>
<u>Ps 132:2-3a KVJ 133:2-3a</u>
Alleluia, Alleluia, Alleluia.
It is as oil that descends upon
the head and upon the beard of
Aaron, and from the beard it
descends to the hems of his garment.

<u>Melody Change</u>
<u>Ps 22:2-3 KJV 23:2-3</u>
He made me dwell in a plain of
greenfield, and by the waters of
rest He nourished me.
He returned my being back to me and led me to
paths of justice for the sake of His name.

NIGHT HOUR

Glory and bowing down in worship of the
Father and of the Son and of the Holy Spirit,
now and always and unto the eternity of
eternities. Amen. Alleluia. Alleluia. Alleluia.

<u>T G</u>
<u>Ps 17:16b-17 KJV 18:15b-16</u>

Alleluia, Alleluia, Alleluia.
From Your strong reprimand, Lord, and
from the breathing of the spirit of Your anger.
He sent from the heights and received me,
He received me by taking me out of many waters.

<u>Melody Change</u>
<u>Ps 50:12-13 KJV 51:11-12</u>

Establish unto me a holy heart, God,
and renew an upright spirit within my belly.
Do not cast me away, Lord, from Your faces,
and do not take Your Holy Spirit from me.

Glory and bowing down in worship of the
Father and of the Son and of the Holy Spirit,
now and always and unto the eternity of
eternities. Amen. Alleluia. Alleluia. Alleluia.

NIGHT HOUR

Alleluias for Feasts of the Holy Cross

A Tz
Ps 22:4d-5a KJV 23:4d-5a
Alleluia, Alleluia, Alleluia.
Your rod and staff, they will comfort me.
You have prepared the table before me, before
the eyes of my oppressors.

Melody Change
Ps 59:6-7 KJV 60:4-5
Alleluia, Alleluia, Alleluia.
You gave a sign to those who fear
You, that they shall live in the faces of the bow.
As they saved Your beloved,
give life with Your right hand and hear us.

Glory and bowing down in worship of the
Father and of the Son and of the Holy Spirit,
now and always and unto the eternity of
eternities. Amen. Alleluia. Alleluia. Alleluia.

The order of angels bless You, Christ,
alleluia, the nations of mankind sing
psalms to You. Alleluia. Alleluia. Alleluia.

A G
Ps 44:6-7 KJV 45:5-6

Alleluia, Alleluia, Alleluia.
Your arrows have been sharpened,
mighty, and peoples shall fall beneath
You, in the hearts of the enemies of the king.
Your throne, God, unto the eternity
of eternities, staff of uprightness, staff of
Your kingdom.

NIGHT HOUR

<u>Melody Change</u>
<u>Ps 85:16b-17 KJV 86:16b-17</u>
Alleluia, Alleluia, Alleluia.
Give strength to Your servant,
give life to the son of Your maid,
and make unto me the sign of goodness.
Those that hate me shall see and shall
be ashamed, for You, Lord, helped me
and comforted me.

Glory and bowing down in worship of the
Father and of the Son and of the Holy Spirit,
now and always and unto the eternity of
eternities. Amen. Alleluia. Alleluia. Alleluia.

<u>P Tz</u>
<u>Ps 59:6-7 KJV 60:4-5</u>
Alleluia, Alleluia, Alleluia.
You gave a sign to those who fear
You, that they shall live in the faces of the bow.
As they saved Your beloved,
give life with Your right hand and hear us.

<u>Melody Change</u>
<u>Ps 98:4b-5 KJV 99:4b-5</u>
Alleluia, Alleluia, Alleluia.
You prepared integrity and righteousness,
and You made justice unto Jacob.
You make our Lord God elevated on high, you
bow down in worship to the stool of His
feet for it is holy.

Glory and bowing down in worship of the
Father and of the Son and of the Holy Spirit,
now and always and unto the eternity of
eternities. Amen. Alleluia. Alleluia. Alleluia.

NIGHT HOUR

<u>P G</u>
Ps 85:16b-17 KJV 86:16b-17
Alleluia, Alleluia, Alleluia.
Give strength to Your servant,
give life to the son of Your maid,
and make unto me the sign of goodness.
Those that hate me shall see and shall
be ashamed, for You, Lord, helped me
and comforted me.

<u>Melody Change</u>
Ps 109:1-2 KJV 110:1-2
The Lord said unto my lord,
sit under my right hand, until
I shall put your enemies at the stool of your feet.
The Lord from Zion shall
send to you the staff of strength, and you
shall rule in the midst of your enemies.

Glory and bowing down in worship of the
Father and of the Son and of the Holy Spirit,
now and always and unto the eternity of
eternities. Amen. Alleluia. Alleluia. Alleluia.

NIGHT HOUR

T Tz
Ps 98:4b-5 KJV 99:4b-5

Alleluia, Alleluia, Alleluia.
You prepared integrity and righteousness,
and You made justice unto Jacob.
You make our Lord God elevated on high, you
bow down in worship to the stool of His
feet for it is holy.

Melody Change
Hab 3:3b-4*

Alleluia, Alleluia, Alleluia.
The heavens will reveal the elegance
of His glories, and with His
blessing the universes were filled.
As rays of light having been cut from Him,
and horns were found from His hand,
and there the power of His glories
became established.

Glory and bowing down in worship of the
Father and of the Son and of the Holy Spirit,
now and always and unto the eternity of
eternities. Amen. Alleluia. Alleluia. Alleluia.

---

* *This text of Habakkuk 3 is very different from the text in the Armenian Bible. This text used in the Alleluia section is based upon the liturgical version of the canticle found at the conclusion of the Seventh Canon of the Book of Psalms (Psalter). The origin is unclear and an English version whether canonical or apocryphal was not able to be found. If a Biblical Scholar can place the origins of this, please contact the author at Holy Trinity Armenian Church of Fresno, Ca.*

NIGHT HOUR

__K G__
__Ps 109:1-2 KJV 110:1-2__

Alleluia, Alleluia, Alleluia.
The Lord said unto my lord,
sit under my right hand, until
I shall put your enemies at the stool of your feet.
The Lord from Zion shall
send to you the staff of strength, and you
shall rule in the midst of your enemies.

__Melody Change__
__Ps 4:7b-8 KJV 4:6b-7__

Alleluia, Alleluia, Alleluia.
A sign of the light of Your faces was placed
before us, and You gave joy to our hearts.
More than from the fruit of grain,
wine, and olive oil You filled it (my heart).

Glory and bowing down in worship of the
Father and of the Son and of the Holy Spirit,
now and always and unto the eternity of
eternities. Amen. Alleluia. Alleluia. Alleluia.

__T Tz__
__Hab 3:3b-4*__

Alleluia, Alleluia, Alleluia.
The heavens will reveal the elegance
of His glories, and with His
blessing the universes were filled.
As rays of light having been cut from Him,
and horns were found from His hand,
and there the power of His glories
became established.

Melody Change
Ps 22:4d-5a KJV 23:4d-5a

Alleluia, Alleluia, Alleluia.
Your rod and staff, they will comfort me.
You have prepared the table before me, before the eyes of my oppressors.

Glory and bowing down in worship of the Father and of the Son and of the Holy Spirit, now and always and unto the eternity of eternities. Amen. Alleluia. Alleluia. Alleluia.

T G
Ps 4:7b-8 KJV 4:6b-7

Alleluia, Alleluia, Alleluia.
A sign of the light of Your faces was placed before us, and You gave joy to our hearts.
More than from the fruit of grain,
wine, and olive oil You filled it (my heart).

Melody Change
Ps 44:6-7 KJV 45:5-6

Your arrows have been sharpened,
mighty, and peoples shall fall beneath
You, in the hearts of the enemies of the king.
Your throne, God, unto the eternity
of eternities, staff of uprightness, staff of
Your kingdom.

Glory and bowing down in worship of the Father and of the Son and of the Holy Spirit, now and always and unto the eternity of eternities. Amen. Alleluia. Alleluia. Alleluia.

NIGHT HOUR

Alleluia for Feasts of the Church

<u>A Tz</u>
<u>Ps 25:7-8 KJV 26:7-8</u>

Alleluia, Alleluia, Alleluia.
We hearing the sound of Your blessing,
and telling of all of Your wonders.
Lord, I loved the elegance of Your
house, and the dwelling place of Your glories.

<u>Melody Change</u>
<u>Ps 64:5 KJV 65:4</u>

Alleluia, Alleluia, Alleluia.
Fortunate is he who You chose
and received, and they may dwell in Your courts.
We will be filled from the goodness of Your house,
Your temple is Holy with wonderful righteousness.

Glory and bowing down in worship of the
Father and of the Son and of the Holy Spirit,
now and always and unto the eternity of
eternities. Amen. Alleluia. Alleluia. Alleluia.

<u>A G</u>
<u>Ps 47:2-3 KJV 48:1-2</u>

Alleluia, Alleluia, Alleluia.
The Lord is great and is greatly blessed,
in the city of our God, in His Holy mountain.
With solid joyfulness the entire earth shall rejoice,
the mountains of Zion, on the north sides, in the city of
the Great King.

NIGHT HOUR

<u>Melody Change</u>
<u>Ps 86:2-3 KJV 87:1-3</u>

Alleluia, Alleluia, Alleluia.
His foundation is in His holy
mountain, the Lord loves the
gates of Zion more than all
of the dwellings of Jacob.
Glorification was spoken regarding
You, behold the City of God.

Glory and bowing down in worship of the
Father and of the Son and of the Holy Spirit,
now and always and unto the eternity of
eternities. Amen. Alleluia. Alleluia. Alleluia.

<u>P Tz</u>
<u>Ps 64:5 KJV 65:4</u>

Alleluia, Alleluia, Alleluia.
Fortunate is he who You chose
and received, and they may dwell in Your courts.
We will be filled from
the goodness of Your house, Your temple
is Holy with wonderful righteousness.

<u>Melody Change</u>
<u>Ps 101:13-14 KJV: 12-13</u>

Alleluia, Alleluia, Alleluia.
You Lord are eternal, and Your
memory shall be from generation unto generation.
You having risen up shall have compassion upon
Zion, time for compassion upon
her, the time has arrived.

NIGHT HOUR

Glory and bowing down in worship of the Father and of the Son and of the Holy Spirit, now and always and unto the eternity of eternities. Amen. Alleluia. Alleluia. Alleluia.

P G
Ps 86:2-3 KJV 87:1-3

Alleluia, Alleluia, Alleluia.
His foundation is in His holy
mountain, the Lord loves the
gates of Zion more than all
of the dwellings of Jacob.
Glorification was spoken regarding
You, behold the City of God.

Melody Change
Ps 117:24, 23 KJV 118:24,23

Alleluia, Alleluia, Alleluia.
This day is which the Lord has made,
let us rejoice and let us be glad in it.
From the Lord this was done, and
it is wonderful before our eyes.

Glory and bowing down in worship of the Father and of the Son and of the Holy Spirit, now and always and unto the eternity of eternities. Amen. Alleluia. Alleluia. Alleluia.

NIGHT HOUR

K Tz
Ps 101:13-14 KJV: 12-13

Alleluia, Alleluia, Alleluia.
You Lord are eternal, and Your
memory shall be from generation unto generation.
You having risen up shall have compassion upon
Zion, time for compassion upon
her, the time has arrived.

Melody Change
Ps 137:1-2 KJV 138:1-2

Alleluia, Alleluia, Alleluia.
I shall confess You, Lord, with
all of my heart, before the angels I
shall say psalms unto You.
For You heard the words of my mouth,
I shall bow down in worship to Your
Holy Temple, and I shall confess of
Your Name for the sake of Your
mercy and truth.

Glory and bowing down in worship of the
Father and of the Son and of the Holy Spirit,
now and always and unto the eternity of
eternities. Amen. Alleluia. Alleluia. Alleluia.

K G
Ps 117:24, 23 KJV 118:24,23

Alleluia, Alleluia, Alleluia.
This day is which the Lord has made,
let us rejoice and let us be glad in it.
From the Lord this was done, and
it is wonderful before our eyes.

NIGHT HOUR

<u>Melody Change</u>
<u>PS 14:1-2 KJV 15:1-2</u>

Alleluia, Alleluia, Alleluia.
Lord, who shall dwell in Your tent,
or who shall live on Your Holy mountain.
Who goes without blemish, who performs
works of justice, who speaks truth in their hearts.

Glory and bowing down in worship of the
Father and of the Son and of the Holy Spirit,
now and always and unto the eternity of
eternities. Amen. Alleluia. Alleluia. Alleluia.

<u>T Tz</u>
<u>Ps 121:1-2 KJV 122:1-2</u>

Alleluia, Alleluia, Alleluia.
I became joyful, those who were
saying to me, let us go to the house of the Lord.
Having arrived, our feet
were standing at your gates, Jerusalem.

<u>Melody Change</u>
<u>Ps 25:7-8 KJV 26:7-8</u>

Alleluia, Alleluia, Alleluia.
For me, hearing the voice of Your
blessing, and telling of all of Your wonders
Lord, I loved the elegance of Your house, and
the dwelling place of Your glories.

Glory and bowing down in worship of the
Father and of the Son and of the Holy Spirit,
now and always and unto the eternity of
eternities. Amen. Alleluia. Alleluia. Alleluia.

NIGHT HOUR

<u>T G</u>
<u>Ps 14:1-2 KJV 15:1-2</u>

Alleluia, Alleluia, Alleluia.
Lord, who shall dwell in Your tent,
or who shall live on Your Holy mountain.
Who goes without blemish, who performs
works of justice, who speaks truth in
their hearts.

<u>Melody Change</u>
<u>Ps 47:2-3 KJV 48:1-2</u>

Alleluia, Alleluia, Alleluia.
The Lord is great and is greatly blessed,
in the city of our God, in His Holy mountain.
With solid joyfulness the entire earth shall rejoice,
the mountains of Zion, on the north sides, in the city of
the Great King.

Glory and bowing down in worship of the
Father and of the Son and of the Holy Spirit,
now and always and unto the eternity of
eternities. Amen. Alleluia. Alleluia. Alleluia.

NIGHT HOUR

*Alleluia and Eternal King for
Feast of the Archangels*

Ps 103:4-5 KJV 104:4-5

Alleluia, Alleluia, Alleluia.
Who made His angels in the spirits,
and His ministers from burning flames.
He established the earth upon its foundation,
that it shall not be shaken throughout eternity.

Melody Change
Ps 148:1-2 KJV 148:1-2

Alleluia, Alleluia, Alleluia.
Bless the Lord from the heavens, Bless Him on high.
Let all of His angels bless Him,
let all of His hosts bless Him.

Glory and bowing down in worship of the
Father and of the Son and of the Holy Spirit,
now and always and unto the eternity of
eternities. Amen. Alleluia. Alleluia. Alleluia.

The order of angels bless You, Christ,
alleluia, the nations of mankind sing
psalms to You. Alleluia. Alleluia. Alleluia.

Eternal King

Heavens and earth are satisfied
from You Lord, all whom have
been created bow in worship to You,
and the angels on high cry out and say,
have mercy, You created, do not destroy.

NIGHT HOUR

Heavens of heavens, waters which
are above the heavens, bless the name of the Lord.
For He said and they became,
He commanded and they became established,
and the angels on high cry out and say,
have mercy, You created, do not destroy.

<u>Melody Change</u>

The heavens and earth continually
praise You, King of glories, the Seraphim
and Cherubim below facing each other,
and in unison shouting out
with cries and saying, Holy Holy Holy
Lord of hosts.

Alleluia for the Resurrection of Lazarus
(The Saturday before Palm Sunday)

<u>Ps 29:1-3 KJV 29:1-3</u>

Alleluia, Alleluia, Alleluia.
I lift You up on high, Lord, for You
received me, and You did not make
my enemy to rejoice over me.
Lord my God, I called upon You and
You healed me, Lord, You pulled my being
out from the hells,* You saved me from
amongst those who descend into the pit.

---

* *Hades*

NIGHT HOUR

<u>Melody Change</u>
<u>Ps 39:3 KJV 40:2</u>

He pulled me from the pit of
misery, from the clay and from the mud.
He firmly propped my feet upon a rock,
and straightened my path.

Glory and bowing down in worship of the
Father and of the Son and of the Holy Spirit,
now and always and unto the eternity of
eternities. Amen. Alleluia. Alleluia. Alleluia.

Alleluia for Palm Sunday

<u>Ps 117:27-28 KJV 118:27-28</u>

Alleluia, Alleluia, Alleluia.
Lord our God had appeared to us, make
feasts of rejoicing beforehand up to
the corners of the altar table.
You are my God, and I shall confess of You,
You are my God, and I shall place
You on high.

<u>Melody Change</u>
<u>Ps 97:8b-9 KJV 98:8b-9</u>

The mountains shall rejoice before
the Lord, for the Lord comes and
has arrived to judge the earth.
Judge this world with justice and its people with equity.

NIGHT HOUR

Glory and bowing down in worship of the Father and of the Son and of the Holy Spirit, now and always and unto the eternity of eternities. Amen. Alleluia. Alleluia. Alleluia.

Alleluias for Holy Week

Holy Monday

<u>Ps 148:5b-6</u>

Alleluia, Alleluia, Alleluia.
For He said and they became, He commanded and they became established.
He ranked them unto eternity, and placed a border which no one shall pass.

<u>Melody Change</u>
<u>Ps 101:26-27a KJV 102:25-26a</u>

Alleluia, Alleluia, Alleluia.
Lord from the beginning You established the foundations of the earth, and the heavens are the works of Your hands.
They will perish, and You stand and remain eternal.

Glory and bowing down in worship of the Father and of the Son and of the Holy Spirit, now and always and unto the eternity of eternities. Amen. Alleluia. Alleluia. Alleluia.

NIGHT HOUR

Holy Tuesday

<u>Ps 44:10-12a KJV 45:9-11a</u>

Alleluia, Alleluia, Alleluia.
The princess shall stand at Your right hand,
in dresses fashioned and adorned with woven gold.
Hear daughter and see, may your ear
descend, forget your people and the house
of your father, because the king desired
for your beauty.

<u>Melody Change</u>
<u>Ps 44:15b-17a KJV 45:14b-16a</u>

Alleluia, Alleluia, Alleluia.
The virgins shall be brought to the
king with her, and her friends
shall be brought to him.
They shall be brought in with
joyfulness and gladness, and they shall
be brought to the temple of the king,
and instead of your fathers, let be
your sons.

Glory and bowing down in worship of the
Father and of the Son and of the Holy Spirit,
now and always and unto the eternity of
eternities. Amen. Alleluia. Alleluia. Alleluia.

NIGHT HOUR

Holy Wednesday

Ps 40:10-11 KJV 41:9-10

Alleluia, Alleluia, Alleluia.
He who was eating my bread,
he visited me frequently, committing deceit towards me.
But You Lord have mercy
upon me, and lift me up, and I shall repay them.

Melody Change
Ps 72:8-9 KJV 72:8-9

Alleluia, Alleluia, Alleluia.
They thought and spoke evil, and on
high they thought malice.
They placed their mouths in the heavens, and their
tongues were walking about the earth.

Glory and bowing down in worship of the
Father and of the Son and of the Holy Spirit,
now and always and unto the eternity of
eternities. Amen. Alleluia. Alleluia. Alleluia.

Holy Thursday

Ps 25:6,8 KJV 26:6,8

Alleluia, Alleluia, Alleluia.
I will wash my hands with holiness, and
I shall go around Your altar Lord.
Lord, I loved the elegance of Your house, and
the dwelling place of Your glories.

NIGHT HOUR

<u>Melody Change</u>
<u>Ps 22:5a-b KJV 23:5a-b</u>

Alleluia, Alleluia, Alleluia.
You have prepared the table before me,
before the eyes of my oppressors, You
anointed my head with oil, as Your
pure cup gave drink to me.

Glory and bowing down in worship of the
Father and of the Son and of the Holy Spirit,
now and always and unto the eternity of
eternities. Amen. Alleluia. Alleluia. Alleluia.

Holy Friday

<u>Hab 3:9-11a</u>

Alleluia, Alleluia, Alleluia.
The long bow arose, You made them drink Your quivering arrows, You
dispersed the rivers, You shook the earth from the
intenseness of rain, which passes through it.
The abysses cried out greatly, light of
the sun rays were obstructed, and the rising of the moon ceased.

<u>Melody Change</u>
<u>Ps 87:9c-10 KJV 88:8c-9</u>

Alleluia, Alleluia, Alleluia.
I was betrayed and could not arise, my eyes weakened from poverty.
I daily cried out unto the Lord and lifted my hands to You.

Glory and bowing down in worship of the Father and of the Son and
of the Holy Spirit, now and always and unto the eternity of
eternities. Amen. Alleluia. Alleluia. Alleluia.

NIGHT HOUR

Holy Saturday

<u>Ps 87:7-8 KJV 88:6-7</u>

Alleluia, Alleluia, Alleluia.
They placed me inside the interior
of the pit, in the darkness and in the
shadow of death. Upon me Your
indignation was asserted, all of Your
amusements are brought upon me.

<u>Melody Change</u>
<u>Ps 87:5b-6a KJV 88:4b-5a</u>

Alleluia, Alleluia, Alleluia.
I became as a man without a helper,
and free unto the dead.
As the wounded who sleep in the grave.

Glory and bowing down in worship of the
Father and of the Son and of the Holy Spirit,
now and always and unto the eternity of
eternities. Amen. Alleluia. Alleluia. Alleluia.

Holy Saturday Alternate Version

<u>Job 21:32-33</u>

He went into the grave and
a vigil was kept at the tomb.
The gravel of the ravine became sweet
to him, in his footsteps all men shall go.

Glory and bowing down in worship of the
Father and of the Son and of the Holy Spirit,
now and always and unto the eternity of
eternities. Amen. Alleluia. Alleluia. Alleluia.

NIGHT HOUR

*Alleluia for the Transfiguration of Christ
(Known as Vartavarr*)*

<u>Sunday</u>
<u>Ps 88:12-13 KJV 89:11-12</u>

Alleluia, Alleluia, Alleluia.
The heavens are Yours, and the earth is
Yours, You established the world in its entirety.
You made the north and the south,
Tabor and Hermon will rejoice in Your Name.

<u>Melody Change</u>
<u>Ps 94:4b-6 KJV 95:4b-6</u>

Alleluia, Alleluia, Alleluia.
The heights of the mountains are His,
the sea is His and He made it, and His
hands created the dry land.
Come we shall bow in worship to Him,
we shall fall and weep before the Lord our maker.

Glory and bowing down in worship of the
Father and of the Son and of the Holy Spirit,
now and always and unto the eternity of
eternities. Amen. Alleluia. Alleluia. Alleluia.

---

* *Loosely translated as "Festival of Roses." For more information research keywords: Vartavar, Vardavar, and Water Festival.*

NIGHT HOUR

Monday
Ps 94:4b-6   KJV 95:4b-6

Alleluia, Alleluia, Alleluia.
The heights of the mountains are His,
the sea is His and He made it, and His
hands created the dry land.
Let us be His Moses and Aaron, Samuel in that company
of those who call upon His name.

Melody Change
Ps 97:8b-9   KJV 98:8b-9

The mountains shall rejoice before
the Lord, for the Lord comes and has
arrived to judge the earth. Judge this
world with justice, and it people
with equity.

Glory and bowing down in worship of the
Father and of the Son and of the Holy Spirit,
now and always and unto the eternity of
eternities. Amen. Alleluia. Alleluia. Alleluia.

Tuesday
Ps 94:4-5 KJV 95:4-5

Alleluia, Alleluia, Alleluia.
In His hands are all of the
(cosmoses or macrocosms) of the earth,
and the heights of the mountains are His.
The sea is His and He made it,
and His hands created the dry land.

Melody Change
Ps 96:5-6 KJV:97:5-6

The mountains shall melt like wax
before the faces of the Lord, from the
faces of the Lord, the entire earth.
The heavens shall tell of His
justice, and all peoples shall see His
glories.

Glory and bowing down in worship of the
Father and of the Son and of the Holy Spirit,
now and always and unto the eternity of
eternities. Amen. Alleluia. Alleluia. Alleluia.

Յարեաւ Աստուած եւ զուեցան
ամենայն թշնամիք նորա։

The order of the common prayers of the Armenian Church which are performed during the Morning Hour (Dawn) before the Son of God, who appeared before the Oil Bearing Women

Blessed be our Lord Jesus Christ. Amen.

Our Father Who art in heaven, Hallowed be Thy name.
Thy kingdom come, Thy will be done on earth as it is in heaven.
Give us this day our daily bread.
And forgive us our debts, as we forgive our debtors.
And lead us not into temptation, but deliver us from evil.

For Thine is the Kingdom, and the power,
and the glory forever and ever. Amen.

Priest
Ps 89:14-17 KJV 90:14-17

In the morning we were filled with
Your mercy, we rejoiced and became
glad all of the days of our lives.

Deacon **Student Chancel**

We became glad in return for the days
in which You made us humble, and for
the years in which we have seen suffering.

Look, Lord, upon Your servants and
upon the works of Your hands,
lead their sons, let the light of the
Lord be upon us.

Make the works of our hands straight unto us,
Lord, and make the works of our hands
successful for us.

MORNING HOUR

<u>Priest</u>

Glory to the Father and to the Son and to the Holy Spirit.

<u>Deacon</u>

Now and always and unto the eternity of eternities. Amen.
And again in peace let us request of the Lord. Receive, save, and have mercy.

<u>Priest</u>

Blessing and glory to the Father and to the Son and to the Holy Spirit, now and always and unto the eternity of eternities. Amen.

Blessing of the Three Young Men in the Furnace

A Canticle, Song from the Prophet Daniel 3:26-45 and 52-86

Student Chancel

Blessed are You Lord, God of our fathers, Your name
is praised and glorified unto eternity.

Unto Your righteousness You made all of these things
pass through us, You are just Lord, and
all of Your works are true.

Your paths are straight and all of Your
judgments are just.

You brought judgment of justice upon us
according to all, which You brought upon us,
and to the holy city of our fathers Jerusalem.

With justice and of rights You brought these
things upon us for the sake of our sins.

We broke the laws and committed offences with
rebellion to You, we sinned against all, and of
Your commandments we have not become unshaken.

We have not kept and have not done as You
commanded to us, that we may find good from You.

So, all which You made and that which You brought
upon us, You made with just judgment.

You betrayed us into the hands of our enemies,
to the lawless, to the harsh, and to the
rebellious.

You betrayed us into the hands of the lawless and
evil king, more than of all the lands.

And now, time does not exist for us to open our mouths,
for we Your servants and ministers have become
shamed and insulted.

But do not betray us unto the end for the sake of Your name,
do not disperse Your vows, and do not take away
Your mercy from us.

For the sake of Your beloved Abraham,
Your servant Isaac, and Your holy Israel.

You promised to them and said, "I shall multiply your children as the multitudes of stars in the heavens, and as sand upon the seashore."

And now, Lord, we have become diminished more than all other nations and we have suffered today in all lands for the sake of our sins.

There does not exist at this time prince, prophet, or leader, no burnt offerings of sacrifices, no incenses of the laws, no place to offer sacrifices before You, to find mercy from You.

But we ourselves having become humbled and with spirit of torments we shall be acceptable as burnt offerings of rams and bulls and as thousands of fattened lambs.

In that manner they shall be today our acceptable sacrifices before You, that we shall be found perfect after You, that there is no shame to those who place their hope in You.

MORNING HOUR

And now, we come in Your footsteps with
all of our hearts, we fear in You, and we
search for Your faces, Lord, do not make us
shamed.

But make unto us according to Your gentleness,
and according to Your multitude of mercy,
save us for the sake of Your wonders, Lord,
and Your Name shall be glorified unto eternity.

They all shall be shamed, those who torture Your
servant, their violence shall be shamed, and
all of their forces shall be crushed.

And they shall know that You only are Lord God,
that You are glorified over all of the universes.

Blessed are You, Lord God of our fathers,
being praised and most elevated on high
unto eternity.

And blessed be Your Holy Name of glories,
being praised and most elevated on high
unto eternity.

Blessed be You in the temple of Your
glories of holiness, being praised and
most elevated on high unto eternity.

Blessed be You upon the throne of
Your kingdom, being praised and
most elevated on high unto eternity.

Blessed be You which You sit upon
the cherubim and look into the abysses,
being praised and most elevated on high
unto eternity.

Blessed be You upon the establishment
of the heavens, being praised and
most elevated on high unto eternity.

Bless the Lord, all of the works of the Lord,
bless and make Him elevated on high
unto eternity.   *(k) * see pg 224 for definition*

Bless the Lord, heavens, bless and make
Him elevated on high unto eternity.

Bless the Lord, angels of the Lord, and
waters which are upon the heavens,
bless and make Him elevated on high
unto eternity.

Bless the Lord, forces of the Lord,
the sun and the moon,
bless and make Him elevated on high
unto eternity.

Bless the Lord, all of the stars of the heavens,
the rains and the dew, bless and make Him
elevated on high unto eternity.

Bless the Lord, all of the winds, fire and heat,
bless and make Him elevated on high
unto eternity.

Bless the Lord, cold and heat,
dew and snowfall, bless and make
Him elevated on high unto eternity.

MORNING HOUR

Bless the Lord, ice and clear weather, the frost and snow,
bless and make Him elevated on high unto eternity.

Bless the Lord, days and the nights light and darkness,
bless and make Him elevated on high unto eternity.

Bless the Lord, clouds and lightening and the earth,
bless and make Him elevated on high unto eternity.

Bless the Lord, mountains and hills and
all plants of the earth,
bless and make Him elevated on high unto eternity.

Bless the Lord, springs, seas, and rivers,
bless and make Him elevated on high unto eternity.

Bless the Lord, whales and all things that
are lively in the waters, and the birds of the skies,
bless and make Him elevated on high unto eternity.

Bless the Lord, beasts and cattle, and sons of man,
bless and make Him elevated on high unto eternity.

Israel shall bless the Lord, it shall bless and make
Him elevated on high unto eternity.

Bless the Lord, priests,
bless and make Him elevated on high unto eternity.

Bless the Lord, servants of the Lord,
bless and make Him elevated on high unto eternity.

Bless the Lord, persons and spirits of the just,
bless and make Him elevated on high unto eternity.

MORNING HOUR

Bless the Lord, holy ones and those humble in heart,
bless and make Him elevated on high unto eternity.

Bless the Lord, Anania, Azaria, and Misael,
bless and make Him elevated on high unto eternity.

Glory to the Father and to the Son and to the Holy Spirit.

Now and always and unto the eternity of eternities. Amen.

Petition

<u>Priest</u>
All which are made bless the maker of all things made,
Lord of Lords, the King of Kings, the God of gods. Bless,
praise, speak well, for He is sweet, for His mercy is eternal.

Student Chancel

 The **Hymn of the Fathers (Hartz Sharagan)** *is sung at this point. To find the proper hymn we must turn to the Calendar (Oratzooytz Book) first to determine the type of day, the tone of the day, and which verses are to be sung. Then we must turn to the Hymnal Book's Index and look for the* **Hartz** *under the type of day; then we may find the correct tone and verse to be sung. (The following are only examples of various Hymns of the Fathers for various types of days e.g. Resurrection of Christ, Archangels, Prophets, Days of Repentance, Apostles, Those Resting in Christ, and Martyrs.) They may not be sung without first consulting the Calendar and Hymnal.*

---

* *In the Hymn of the Fathers (Hartz Sharagan) a "k" will appear in the middle of the hymn, an abbreviation for "Kordzadoon." (verse containing the word "work"). This is a reference to the (canticle) Prophetic Song of the Three Young Men in the Furnace, in which a verse from this (canticle) Prophetic Song is going to be sung in the Hymn of the Fathers.*

MORNING HOUR

Hymn of the Fathers
For the Holy Resurrection of Christ

A Tz

That You Christ king unto eternity
came to the salvation of the universes,
we glorify You God of our fathers.
You willingly took to Yourself tortures,
and You tasted death for our sake,
we glorify You God of our fathers.
You were sealed with a stone in the tomb,
and You dissolved the seals of the
offences of death,
we glorify You God of our fathers.

(k)

Bless the Lord, all of the works of the Lord,
bless and make Him elevated on high
unto eternity. Having been resurrected from
the dead Christ God, Who abolished
death through His resurrection,
make Him elevated on high unto eternity.
The wonderful resurrection of Christ God,
with the praising of all the people,
make Him elevated on high unto eternity.

MORNING HOUR

Hymn of the Fathers
For Feast Days of the Archangels

K̄ G

Father without beginning inexpressible first light,
Whom light of light having put the intelligent
beings into operation, we bless You God of our fathers.
Of Your same existence of the Father, Son emanating
light of light, Who You made to Your ministers of
Your glories soldiers of fiery angels,
we glorify You God of our fathers.
From the Father emanating the same glories
of the Son, Your uncreated spirit, which You
created unto the souls the order of perfect angels,
we glorify You God of our fathers.

(k)

Bless the Lord, all of the works of the Lord,
bless and make Him elevated on high
unto eternity. Heavenly angels, angels and
archangels, governments above, make the
heavenly Father most elevated on high.
Multitudes of bodiless heavenly beings,
authorities, forces, immortal lordships, make
Christ the King most elevated on high. Of the
six winged seraphim, of the four form cherubim,
of the uncreated thrones, make the true spirit
most elevated on high.

MORNING HOUR

Hymn of the Fathers
For Feast Days of the Holy Prophets

T̄ T̄z
Who with our earthly nature You blended
with rational souls, to have strength to
receive the Godly and spiritual graces
having descended from above,
blessed be the Lord God of our fathers.
Which You granted the spirit of prophecy
unto the pure souls of Israel, through whom
You knew beforehand with multiple examples
the inexpressible mystery of Your prophecy,
blessed be the Lord God of our fathers.
Which the uncreated origin of Your existence
they saw as having been, unto their leadership
minds being impressed, the figure object of
Your spirit, with the supreme wonders from
above, as much as the Word,
blessed be the Lord God of our fathers.

(k)
Bless the Lord, all of the works of the Lord,
bless and make Him elevated on high
unto eternity. Beforehand through the
bearers of good news of our salvation,
clap your hands churches of the
heathens* while crying out,
bless the Lord and make Him elevated
on high unto eternity. In the company
of the visionary prophets of the old
Israel, the servant priests of the new
covenant, bless the Lord and make Him
elevated on high unto eternity.

---

* Heathen is not an offensive term in this case. It means all peoples who are not believers in the God of Israel. The term "Gentiles" could be used but heathen is more precise.

MORNING HOUR

Hymn of the Fathers
For Days of Repentance

<u>A Tz</u>

God almighty which You look with
sweetness upon Your created beings,
blessed be You God of our fathers.
Which You were descending while
saving Your created beings,
Your only begotten Son,
blessed be You God of our fathers.
Which You care for Your created beings
with Your directorship, Your true spirit,
blessed be You God of our fathers.

(k)

Bless the Lord, all of the works of the Lord,
all of Your works bless You. Which from nothing
You gave existence to the heavens and the earth,
remember us Lord with Your love of humanity,
all of Your works bless You. Which You are
unceasingly glorified from Your created beings,
receive the prayers of Your Holy Church,
all of Your works bless You.

MORNING HOUR

Hymn of the Fathers
For Feast Days of all Apostles

<u>A Tz</u>

Of the same being Word of the Father and
of the Spirit, which descended from the
heavens in the salvation of the nations
of mankind, God of our fathers.
You Who kept victorious the hardships
of the Holy Apostles, today and we in the
company with the same, with joyfulness
we bless You, God of our fathers.
Which You are most elevated on high
unto eternity, today with the order of
Your martyrs we praise You,
God of our fathers.

(k)

Bless the Lord, all of the works of the Lord,
bless and make Him elevated on high
unto eternity. That He chose the fortunate
apostles and that through them fished for
those in the universes that have faith in Christ,
make Him elevated on high unto eternity.
Those who drove out the darkness of idol
worship and spread the light of knowledge
upon the entire earth, with those same ones
make Him elevated on high unto eternity.

MORNING HOUR

Hymn of the Fathers
For All of Those Resting in Christ

A Tz

Blessed be You Christ, which Your
having risen from the dead You are
merciful, and You trampled death,
Lord, God of our fathers. Which for this dead man
You are life, receive the souls of those of ours
that are sleeping, Lord, God of our fathers.
Those which You transformed from the world of
the living, make them worthy of rest,
Lord, God of our fathers.

(k)

Bless the Lord, all of the works of the Lord,
bless and make Him elevated on high
unto eternity. Nights bless the Lord, Who is
to come with much might, through the effect
of the voice He restores life to those asleep,
bless the Lord and make Him elevated on high
unto eternity. Israel shall bless the Lord, and
make Him elevated on high unto eternity. We
pray to You kind one, make the souls of Your
servants rest with Your saints, let us bless and
elevate Your name on high unto eternity.

MORNING HOUR

Hymn of the Fathers
For Feast Days of All Martyrs

<u>A Tz</u>

Just and right judge, You are praised amongst Your saints,
God of our fathers You are blessed unto eternity.
You are praised, You Who descended into the
furnace as refuge, having become humble in
the battalion of martyrs, God of our fathers
You are blessed unto eternity.
Today with the ranks of Your witnesses
we praise You, Who is the frightful king of eternities,

God of our fathers You are blessed unto eternity.

(k)

Bless the Lord, all of the works of the Lord,
bless and make Him elevated on high
unto eternity.
Immeasurable of the heavens and of the
fiery angels, He was pleased to choose His
soldiers from the earthly beings,
make Him elevated on high unto eternity.
From where and we believers in Christ God,
in the company of the same, by requesting
the forgiveness of our sins.
make Him elevated on high unto eternity.

MORNING HOUR

Proclamation After the Hymn of the Fathers

Student Chancel

<u>Deacon</u>

We all having come to the Holy catholic*
and Apostolic Church, we will pray to the
Only Begotten Son of God, our Lord and
Savior Jesus Christ. Who descended with
the glory of God in the middle of the furnace,
and saved the three children there from the
Chaldeans. May He keep our minds enlightened
and Holy, that we may never be deceived
by sins and of desires of the world.
And may we be worthy to keep His commandments,
to receive the crown of light and life unto our beings,
which He promised to His beloved,
true God Jesus Christ our Lord, give life
and have mercy.
Lord have mercy. Lord have mercy. Lord have mercy.

---

* *Catholic means universal in its Greek origin. It has no connection to the Roman Catholic Church in this context. The text above used the term "gatooghige" the Armenicized form of the Greek. Armenian has borrowed this term for unknown reasons as the Armenia language already has its own words for universal, "diezeragan" and general, "unthanoor" which is already used in many other liturgical phrases. Either one of these would be better choices.*

MORNING HOUR

Petition
For Sundays and Other Feasts of the Lord

(Resurrection, Lordship, Birth, Coming etc...
The Calendar must be consulted to determine
the type of Sunday or Feast Day.)

<u>Priest</u>

Powerful, victorious, worker of miracles, Your
great and Holy *(insert appropriate type of feast
day from above)* Christ our God, is befitting
glory, Lordship and honor, now and always
and unto the eternity of eternities, Amen.

Petition for Days of Martyrs

Lord, sprinkle as dew, Your
benevolent dew of mercy upon our
sinful beings, extinguish the flame of the
furnace of our offences, and save us
from the eternal fire. Make us worthy
in the company of the three holy children,
and in the company of the fortunate holy martyrs
to bless You, to praise and to offer thanksgiving
and glories to You, to the Father and to the
Son, and to the Holy Spirit, now and always
and unto the eternity of eternities, Amen.

MORNING HOUR

Petition for Fasting Days

Lord, sprinkle as dew, Your
benevolent dew of mercy upon our
sinful beings, extinguish the flame of the
furnace of our offences, and save us
from the eternal fire. Make us worthy
in the company of the three holy children,
and in the company of the fortunate holy martyrs
to bless You, to praise and to say,
God, make me atone, me this sinner,
God, make me atone, me this sinner,
God, make me atone, me this sinner,
for my sins, and give life.

MORNING HOUR

Song of Mary the God-Bearer

Senior Chancel

Lk 1:46-55

My soul shall magnify the Lord, and
my spirit shall rejoice with God my savior.

He paid visit upon the humility of His
maid servant, from now on all nations
shall regard me as fortunate.

The Mighty One has made very great
things through me, and Holy is His Name.

You made mercy from generation unto
generation upon those who fear in Him,
He made power with His right arm.

He scattered those who are arrogant in
thoughts of their hearts, and pulled down
the mighty ones from their thrones.

He uplifted the humble, He filled those who
are impoverished, with goodness, and He
sent the wealthy away empty.

He defended Israel His servant,
by remembering His mercy.

As He spoke unto our fathers, in the
company of Abraham and his child,
unto eternity.

MORNING HOUR

Song of Zechariah the Father of John the Baptist
(Canticle Blessing)

Senior Chancel
Lk 1:68-79

Blessed by the Lord God of Israel, Who
paid visit, and has made salvation for
His people.

He has raised the horn of salvation unto
us from the House of David, His servant,
as was spoken by the mouths of the holy
ones, whom from eternity were prophets.

Salvation from our enemies, and from
the hands of all those who hate us.

To make mercy unto our forefathers,
and to remember His Holy Testaments.

The vow which He vowed to Abraham
our father, to give us without fear the
salvation from our enemies.

To adore Him with holiness and justice
before Him all of the days of our lives.

And you child, shall be called prophet
on high, you will go before the Lord
to prepare His pathways.

MORNING HOUR

To give the knowledge of salvation to
His people, for the forgiveness of all
of our sins.

For the sake of compassion of mercy of the
Lord our God, through Whom the sun
appeared to us on high to make our
darkness enlightened.

To shine light upon those of us who
were sitting in darkness and in the
shadow of death, and to direct our
feet into the pathways of peace.

The Prayer of the Elderly Simeon
Senior Chancel
Lk 2:29-32

Now, release this Your servant in peace
Lord, according to Your Word, for my
eyes have seen Your salvation, which
You have prepared before all peoples.

Light has been revealed to the heathens,*
and glory to Your people of Israel.

Glory to the Father and to the Son and to the Holy Spirit.
Now and always and unto the eternity of eternities. Amen.

---

* *Heathen is not an offensive term in this case. It means all peoples who are not believers in the God of Israel. The term "Gentiles" could be used but heathen is more precise.*

MORNING HOUR

Senior Chancel

 The **Hymn of Magnification** *(Medzatzoostze Sharagan)* is inserted here. To find the proper hymn we must turn to the Calendar *(Oratzooytz Book)* first to determine the type of day and the tone of the day. Then we must turn to the Hymnal Book's Index to find which page to locate the day's hymn verses. There is a separate index of Hymns of the Magnification found on pages 46-48 of the hymnal. The following are only examples of various Hymns. They may not be sung without first consulting the Calendar and Hymnal.

A Tz

From the inexpressible glories You humbled
Yourself into our natures, God the Word and
You took human body from the Holy Virgin.
Glory to the Father and to the Son and to the Holy Spirit.
And You were born of the Holy Virgin with
uncorrupted body, unceasingly praising You
we magnify you.
Now and always and unto the eternity of eternities. Amen.
Today Your coming unto the salvation of
the nations of mankind, in one voice all
people magnify You.

K G

Mother and virgin, servant of Christ,
whom you are always an advocate for the world,
all nations are fortunate to you.
Glory to the Father and to the Son and to the Holy Spirit.
Pure dove and Mary the bride of the heavens,
temple and throne of God the Word,
all nations are fortunate to you.
Now and always and unto the eternity of eternities. Amen.
Through You the spiritual intelligences along
with the earthly beings are pleased, and through
You we come near to the wood (tree) of life.
all nations are fortunate to you.

MORNING HOUR

T Tz

Pure Virgin Mary the God-Bearer, holy
and mother of Christ, in your womb you
have taken away for everyone those
things that are intolerable,
God-Bearer with blessing we magnify you.
Glory to the Father and to the Son and to the Holy Spirit.
You the heavenly door which Ezekiel saw,
and the wool which Gideon knew,
Seraphim, earthly beings, and the highest of the
Cherubim, God-Bearer with blessing we magnify you.
Now and always and unto the eternity of eternities. Amen.
The three frightful mysteries are seen in you
God-Bearer, seedless conception,
pure birth, remaining with pure virginity
after birth, God-Bearer with blessing we magnify you.

A Tz

The door having appeared to You during the time
of Ezekiel the prophet, through which no one
had passed, if not God only, virgin God-Bearer,
with blessing we magnify.
Glory to the Father and to the Son and to the Holy Spirit.
You that during the time of Moses the prophet, from the
blackberry bush You revealed the new mystery of the
virgin for the nations of mankind,
with blessing we magnify.
Now and always and unto the eternity of eternities. Amen.
You Who from the Father eternally and from the
mother inexplicably, in time of birth for the
salvation of all, the Son was revealed on high,
with blessing we magnify.

MORNING HOUR

<u>A Tz</u>

Today new peoples, rejoice with the
coming of the Holy Spirit, with the
magnification of the One Who comes
out from the Father.
Glory to the Father and to the Son and to the Holy Spirit.
Today the apostles rejoice, those who
have been adorned in the graces of the Holy Spirit,
magnification of the One Who comes
out from the Father.
Now and always and unto the eternity of eternities. Amen.
Today those who He has made have rejoiced
with the true coming of the Holy Spirit,
magnification of the One Who comes
out from the Father.

<u>A Tz</u>

Of the One Who resurrected from the dead, His
dwelling, mother and virgin, which those
who are asleep from the time of Adam,
He gives them pure life again,
we magnify you which you are blessed amongst women.
Glory to the Father and to the Son and to the Holy Spirit.
To the maker of heaven and earth You became
temple and curtain, He that renews into fiery spirits
those of ours that are asleep,
we magnify you which you are blessed amongst women.
Now and always and unto the eternity of eternities. Amen.
The One Who feeds the universes* drank of your
holy milk, He that again renews those of ours
that are asleep,
we magnify you which you are blessed amongst women.

* *earth*

MORNING HOUR

<u>A Tz</u>

Which you received the good news of
the Spirit from the fiery angel, be you
joyful in your delight, the Lord is with
you Mary the unmarried one.
Glory to the Father and to the Son and to the Holy Spirit.
The Word without beginning was pleased to take
human nature beginning from the virgin,
Christ God king of the eternities.
Now and always and unto the eternity of eternities. Amen.
We request of you holy God-Bearer, to advocate to
Christ to save His people, which He bought with
His blood.

Proclamation after the Hymn of the Magnification

Senior Chancel

<u>Deacon</u>

Holy God-Bearer and all of the saints
make advocation to the Father in the
heavens, that having willed it He may
have mercy, and having compassion
He shall give life to those whom He has
made. Our Lord God almighty give
life and have mercy.

MORNING HOUR

Prayer

Senior Chancel

<u>Priest</u>

Receive, Lord, our requests with the advocation of the holy God-Bearer, pure bearer of Your Only Begotten Son, and with the requests of all of Your saints, and with the grace of this day.*

> * *The following substitution may be made in its place which is a mention of the Saint or Saints whose names are remembered on this particular day according to the Calendar.*

(Saints' name) of whom today are remembered:

Hear us, Lord, and have mercy, pardon, atone, and forgive our sins. Make us worthy with thanksgiving to glorify You with the Son and with the Holy Spirit, now and always and unto the eternity of eternities. Amen.

MORNING HOUR

Proclamation for Sundays

<u>Deacon</u> **Student Chancel**
And again in peace let us request of the Lord.

<u>Choir (*continue in alternation*)</u>
Lord have mercy.

For the sake of the building structure of this
holy place, and for its good order, let us pray to the Lord.

Lord have mercy.

For the sake of the people who enter through
the doors of the Holy Church, let us pray to the Lord.

Lord have mercy.

For the sake of His receiving their requests
according to His great mercy, let us pray to the Lord.

And again in one voice for the sake of
our true and holy faith, let us pray to the Lord.

Lord have mercy.

Let us make ourselves and one another
as the person of the Lord God almighty.

Let us become as Your person Lord.

Lord our God, be merciful to us, according to
Your great mercy. Let us all say in unison.

Lord have mercy. Lord have mercy. Lord have mercy.

Prayer

<u>Priest</u> **Senior Chancel**

You are king unto the eternity of eternities,
Christ our God, and You with the Father
and Holy Spirit are befitting glory, Lordship,
and honor, now and always and unto the
eternity of eternities. Amen.

MORNING HOUR

Song of the Gospel of the Oil Bearing Women (Yiughaperitz)
This order is performed on Sundays

<u>Ps 112:1-3 KJV 113:1-3</u> *Senior Chancel*

The Name of the Lord shall be blessed,
from this time forth unto eternity.
Children serving the Lord bless the Lord,
and bless the Name of the Lord. The Name
of the Lord shall be blessed,
from this time forth unto eternity. From
sunrise until sunset the Name of the Lord
is blessed, from this time forth unto eternity.

Glory and bowing down in worship of the
Father and of the Son and of the Holy Spirit,
now and always and unto the eternity of
eternities amen, from this time forth unto eternity.

<u>Ps 43:27 KJV 44:26</u>

Student Chancel
Rise Lord help us, and save us for
Your Name's sake.

Senior Chancel
Rise and do not
reject us entirely, for Your name's sake.

<u>Ps 145:10 KJV 146:10</u>

Student Chancel
The Lord shall rule as king unto eternity,
Your God Zion from generation to
generation.

Senior Chancel
My being, bless the Lord, I
shall bless the Lord throughout all of my life.

MORNING HOUR

*Gospels of The Oil Bearing Women (Yiughaperitz)
according to Tone of the Day*

<u>Deacon</u>　　　Stand

<u>Priest</u>　　　Peace unto all.

<u>Choir</u>　　　And with Your spirit.

<u>Deacon</u>　　　May you listen with awe.

<u>Reader (priest or deacon)</u> **Senior Chancel**
The Holy Gospel of Jesus Christ According to Matthew 28:1-20

<u>Choir</u>　　　Glory to You Lord our God.

<u>Deacon</u>　　　Attention

<u>Choir</u>　　　God says.

<u>P G</u>
<u>T G</u>

On account of the Resurrection of our Lord Jesus Christ

And of the evening of the Sabbath in which day break appeared on the first day of the week, Mary Magdalene and the other Mary came to see the tomb. And behold there had been a great earthquake, for an angel of the Lord having descended from the heavens, having approached, rolled away the stone there from the doors, and was sitting upon it. And his appearance was as lightening, and his clothes were white as snow. And there from fear the guards became agitated, and they became as the dead. The angel gave reply and says to the women, "Do not fear, I know that you are searching for Jesus the one Who has been crucified, He is not here, for He has risen as He had said, come and see the place where He remained. And quickly go say to His disciples that He has risen, and behold He will go before you to Galilee, there you shall see Him, behold I have said unto you." And having gone out quickly from the tomb, from there with fear and much cheerfulness they were running to tell the disciples. And behold Jesus met them and says, "Greetings to you.*" And they having approached they held on to His feet, and they worshiped Him.

---

* Literally- "you are alive" This is a traditional Armenian greeting

MORNING HOUR

At that time Jesus says to them, "Do not fear, go say to my brothers that they shall go to Galilee and there they will see me." As they went, behold some of the soldiers came into the city, and told the chief priests all that had happened. And they having gathered with the elders, and having taken counsel, they gave a large sum of silver to the soldiers and they said, "You will say that His disciples had come in the night and stole Him while we were asleep, and if that news shall be heard before the judge we will satisfy him and will make you free of worries." And they having taken the silver, they did as they were instructed, and this renown report has gone out from amongst the Jews to this day. But the eleven disciples went to Galilee, to the mountain, where Jesus had appointed for them, as they saw Him, they worshipped Him, and some of them doubted. And having come forth Jesus spoke with them and says,

"To me has been given all authority in the heavens and
upon the earth, in the same that the Father sent me,
I am sending you. Go from this time forth, make
disciples of all heathens,* baptize them in the name of the
Father, and of the Son, and of the Holy Spirit. Teach
them to keep all, that I have commanded you. And
behold, I am with you all of the days, until the
conclusion of the world.

---

* *Heathen is not an offensive term in this case. It means all peoples who are not believers in The God of Israel. The term "Gentiles" could be used but heathen is more precise.*

===

The Holy Gospel According to Mark 15:42-16:8

<u>P Tz</u>
<u>T Tz</u>

On account of the Burial and Resurrection of our Lord Jesus Christ

As it became evening, for it was Friday
which was entering into the Sabbath,
Joseph who was of Arimathea had come,
he was an honest man, a councilman, and
which he indeed was awaiting for the
Kingdom of God, he became emboldened

MORNING HOUR

and entered unto Pilate, and requested
for the body of Christ. And Pilate was
surprised, that He died so soon, and
having summoned the centurion to him, he
asked him and said, "Did He indeed die that
soon?" and from there as he verified with the
centurion, he granted the body to Joseph.
And Joseph bought a linen cloth, and having
taken Him down, he wrapped Him with the cloth,
and placed Him in the tomb, which had been
dug out from rock, and rolled a stone to the
door of the tomb. But Mary of Magdala*
and Mary of James and of Joses saw the
place where He was placed. And when the
Sabbath had passed, Mary of Magdala*
and Mary of James, and Salome went and
prepared incenses, in order that they may
come and anoint Him. And during the
morning of the first day of the week, they
come to the tomb during sunrise, and said
to each other, "Who will roll away the stone
for us from the doors of the tomb?"

Magdalene

And having looked upon, they saw that the stone had been rolled away from the tomb, for it was exceedingly large. And having entered inside of the tomb, they saw a young man, that was sitting on the right side, having been clothed in a white robe, and they were frightened. And he says to them, "Do not be afraid, you seek Jesus the Nazarene Who has been crucified, He has risen, He is not here, behold there the place where they had put Him. But go, say to His disciples and to Peter, that behold He goes before you to Galilee, there you shall see Him as He said to you. And as they heard this, they went out and fled from the tomb, for they were struck with terror, and they did not say anything to anybody, for they were afraid.

MORNING HOUR

The Holy Gospel According to Luke 23:50-24:12

A̅ G̅
K̅ G̅

On account of the Burial and Resurrection of our Lord Jesus Christ

And behold a man, whose name is Joseph,
who was a councilman, a man of good
deeds and just, he had not been in agreement
with the councils and with their deeds, he
was from the town of Arimathea of the Jews,
and that he indeed was awaiting for the kingdom
of God. He having approached to Pilate, he
requested the body of Christ, and having taken
Him down he wrapped Him in winding linen
and placed Him in a cut out tomb, where
no one had ever been placed. And the day was
Friday, and the Sabbath was dawning, and the
women were going with him (Joseph), the ones who had
come with Him (Jesus) from Galilee, they saw the
tomb, and how His body was placed. They returned
and prepared incenses and oils, and on the Sabbath
they rested for the sake of the commandment.

But on the first day of the week very early in the morning they came to the tomb, they brought the incenses which they prepared, and other women in company with them. And they found the stone which had been rolled away there from the tomb, and having entered inside, they did not find the body of the Lord Jesus. And it was with amazement to them on account of that, and behold two men came to them in bright clothes. And as they became struck with fear, and they bowed down their faces to the earth, they say to them, "Why do you seek the living amongst the dead, He is not here, but He has risen. Remember, as He spoke to you, while He was in Galilee, and He was saying, that it was necessary for the Son of Man to be delivered up unto the hands of sinful men, and to be raised upon the cross, and to rise on the third day." And they remembered His words. And they returned and told all of this to the eleven, and to all of the others. And they were Mary of Magdala and Joanna,

and Mary of James and others with them,
who told this to the apostles, and before them,
their words appeared nonsensical, and they
were not believing them. But Peter having
risen up ran to the tomb, and having looked
he sees the linens that were remaining alone,
and he went, in his mind having wondered,
what it was that happened.

The Holy Gospel According to John 19:38-20:18

A Tz
K Tz

On account of the Burial and Resurrection of our Lord Jesus Christ

After this Joseph, who was from Arimathea,
and was a disciple of Jesus in secret for fear
of the Jews, requested from Pilate that he
may lift the body of Jesus, and Pilate
gave the order, and he came and lifted Him off.
And Nicodemus came, who had come to
Jesus the previous night,

and he brought the mixture of myrrhs
with aloes, about one hundred litras.*
They took the body of Jesus, and wrapped it with
linens and with incenses, as it was the law of
the Jews to wrap. And there was a garden in the
place in which He was crucified, and there
in the garden was a new tomb, in which no
one had ever been placed. On account of it
being Friday** for the Jews, and that the tomb
was near, there they placed Him.
And on the first day of the week Mary of
Magdala comes there in the morning during
the daybreak to the tomb, and she sees the
stone has been taken up from the doors of
the tomb. She then runs and comes to
Simon Peter and to the other disciple who
Jesus loved and she says to them, "They
took the Lord up from the tomb there, and
I do not know where they placed Him."
Peter having arisen and also the other disciple,
they were coming to the tomb, they both were
running together.

---

* *1 Litra of Roman weights and measures was equal to 12 ounces. Therefore 100 Litras would equal 75 pounds.*

** *The Sabbath would begin on Friday evening sunset. Jewish law prohibited burial on the Sabbath.*

MORNING HOUR

And the other disciple ran and advanced
before Peter, and came to the tomb first,
and having leaned over he sees that the linens
were remaining there, but he did not enter
inside. And Simon Peter came, who was
coming following him, and he entered into
the tomb, and he sees the linens that were
remaining there, and the linen napkin
that was upon His head, which had not
remained in the place of the other linens, but
separately had been wrapped up and set to one
side. And at that time the other disciple
entered, who had come to the tomb first,
he saw and believed, that not until now,
they did not know the scriptures,
that it was necessary for Him to rise from
the dead. The disciples went away again
beside each other by themselves. But Mary
was standing outside of the tomb and was
crying, and while she was crying, she
leaned inside the tomb, and sees two angels
in white, that were sitting, one at the head
and one at the foot, where the body of
Jesus remained. And they say to her,
"You, woman, why do you cry?"
She says to them,

"Because they have taken away my Lord
from the tomb here and I do not
know where they put Him." As she said
this, she turned to her side shoulder, and sees
Jesus that was standing, and she did know
that it shall be Jesus. Jesus says to her,
"You woman, why do you cry? Who do you
seek?" She considered Him in this way that
He should be the gardener, she says to Him,
"Lord if you have taken Him away, say to
me where you put Him, for I shall get Him."
Jesus says to her, "Mary." And she turned
and says to Him in Hebrew, "Rabbi," which
translates as teacher. Jesus says to her,
"Do not touch me, for I have not yet arisen
unto my Father, but you go to my brothers,
and say to them, I arise unto my Father
and unto your Father, and my God and
your God." Mary of Magdala comes and
tells the disciples that she saw the Lord,
and He said these things to her.

MORNING HOUR

Hymn Following the Gospel of the Oil Bearing Women
For Resurrection Sundays

Student Chancel

Glory to Your Resurrection Lord,
I shall not cease, Christ, to bless You
all the days of my life.

Glory to Your Resurrection Lord,
I shall not cease, Jesus, to praise You
all the days of my life.

I shall not cease, savior, to glorify
You, all the days of my life.

Hymn for Salt and Bread (Lenten) Sundays

*(Sing this verse three times with the
third time being sung on a high note)*

Student Chancel

All the days of my life, I shall not cease to
bless You Christ Savior of the world.

<u>Ps 133: 2,1 KJV 134: 2,1</u>

In the night raise your hands to the
sanctuary, and bless the Lord.

All servants of the Lord bless the Lord here
in the sanctuary, and bless the Lord.

+ *For this order of service the term Hymn has been used. This is not considered an actual hymn both musically and according to its classification in the rubrics. The rubrics use the term "song" others have translated it as an "anthem." The term "chant" could also be used. For simplicity purposes only, the term "Hymn" is being used.*

MORNING HOUR

The last verse of the Hymn following the Gospel of the Oil Bearing Women depends on the occasion or season listed

Palm Sunday

The brilliant angelic orders were awaiting
for the great coming of the Lord.
And they were singing a new song,
blessed be Your holy coming.

Easter

The brilliant angel sitting at the
life giving tomb. And was telling the
good news to the women, God has risen.

Ascension
Ps 23:7 KJV 24:7

Princes lift up your gates.
And He comes entering with
glories unto glories.

Pentecost

The spirit having descended upon
the apostles, and the chosen were armed
with fire without burning in the holy upper
room. And through them rested unto the
nations of man with the distribution of
various languages.

MORNING HOUR

Transfiguration

Rejoice Mount Tabor with Mount Hermon, and
the apostles had become numb from the
Fatherly voice. And Moses and Elijah made
You known, Lord to the living and to the dead.

Feasts of the Cross

Today the Lord had come willingly to the
cross. And He spread His arms upon it.

Birth of Christ (Christmas)

Bands of angels with the company
of the shepherds were proclaiming
the Word having been reclined in the
manger of animals. And the magi,
with the star having foretold, they
offered gifts of mystery.

Presentation

The forty day old boy and Lord,
giver of the law, (in fulfillment of the
Law of the House of God)* came to the temple.
And Simeon was caressing Him in his chest,
he requested the dissolution of the bindings
of the laws into the life of good news.**

---

* *The Armenian term "Dnorinapar" derived from Greek "Oikonomia" give a loose translation for the term "Redeeming Economy" used by theologians. It may also be loosely translated as "Administrative."*

** *The Armenian term "Avedaran" translates to "Gospel" in modern English. It translates to "Good-Story" in old English. It translates to "Good News" in Latin and Greek.*

MORNING HOUR

Proclamation after the Gospel of the Oil Bearing Women and its hymns.

Student Chancel

<u>Deacon</u>

Having rejoiced with great gladness with the good news of the resurrection of our Lord and savior Jesus Christ. Who became fruit and first born of all those who are asleep, He crushed the gates of hells, and dissolved the force of death, and gave hope of confirmation again for the renewal of life to all mankind.

Let us ask from our Savior Jesus Christ with faith, that He will make us worthy of His resurrection, to conform our bodies to humility according to the likeness of His body of glories. Because He promised this, the great and the inexpressible graces to gift unto His beloved, true God Jesus Christ our Lord, save and have mercy.

Prayer

Senior Chancel

<u>Priest</u>

True most life giving, holy of the great resurrection of Christ our God, is befitting glory, Lordship and honor, now and always and unto the eternity of eternities. Amen.

MORNING HOUR

Psalm 50 (KJV 51)

Senior Chancel
  (read in entirety in alternation)

Have mercy upon me, God, according to
Your great mercy, according to Your many
compassions atone my unrighteousness.

Moreover wash me from my unrighteousness,
and from my sins, make me pure.

Of me I know my unrighteousness, and
my sins are before me at all times.

Against You only I have sinned, and
I have done evil before You.

As You will be just in Your words,
and victorious in Your judging.

With unrighteousness she became pregnant,
and my mother gave birth to me in sin.

You, Lord, loved the truth, with Your wisdom
You revealed to me things unknown and concealed.

Sprinkle me with hyssop and I shall
be purified, wash and I shall become
whiter than snow.

Make me to hear, Lord, the rejoicing and
gladness, and my bones which have
been afflicted will rejoice.

Turn Your faces from my sins, and
atone all of my unrighteousness
from me.

Establish in me a pure heart, God, and in my gut
renew my soul upright.

Do not cast me away, Lord, from Your faces,
and do not take Your Holy Spirit from me.

Give me the joyfulness of Your salvation,
and with the spirit of Your government affirm me.

I shall teach to the unrighteous Your
pathways, and the wicked will turn to You.

Save me from blood, God, God of my salvation,
my tongue will rejoice unto Your justice.

Lord, if You open my lips,
my mouth will sing Your praises.

MORNING HOUR

You had willed that we would present offerings,
but with the burnt sacrifices, in reality, You were
not pleased.

Offering to God, is a humble spirit, the pure
heart and the humble spirit God does not despise.

Make good, Lord, with your will of Zion,
and they will make the fortress walls of Jerusalem.

At that time You shall be pleased with the
offerings of justice, at which time of the vows,
the offerings of bulls will be placed up to Your
table.

Glory to the Father, and to the Son, and to the Holy Spirit.
Now and always and unto the eternity of eternities.
Amen.

Senior Chancel

 *The **Hymn of Mercy (Voghormya Sharagan)** according to the proper day and tone as shown by the Calendar is sung at this point. To find the proper hymn we will (most of the time) have to turn to the Hymnal Book's index under the **Hymn of the Fathers (Hartz Sharagan)** sections because the Hymnal does not separately list the Hymn of Mercy (Voghormya Sharagan) in its index. Immediately following the Hymn of the Fathers (Hartz Sharagan) are the correct Hymn of Mercy (Voghormya Sharagan) verses which are to be sung. "Hymns of the Fathers" will be grouped according to the following days: Resurrection, Fasting Days (Repentance), Saints and Martyrs, and For those Resting in Christ. For other special days look in either the index for Feasts of the Lord or in the index for Feasts of the Saints.*

MORNING HOUR

The following are only examples of various Hymns of Mercy (Voghormya Sharagan) verses. For the complete and exact verses follow the previous instructions.

Resurrection
A Tz

The Word Who had descended from the Father, You took bodily form from the virgin, with the will of the Father You were crucified for our sake and killed our sins, Holy God have mercy upon us. Whom to those that You have made You are incomprehensible, through nailing to the wooden cross You trampled down death, Holy God have mercy upon us. Who, in times past having fallen into servitude of death, with Your honorable body and blood, You freed, Holy God have mercy upon us.

Holy Archangels
T Tz

Which from the armies of fiery angels in the heavens, God, through whom pure heavenly Godly graces You poured upon the sons of Adam, with their requests have mercy upon us God. In bodily form those without having material bodies by appearing to these earthly beings, and those who made known to the prophets multiple times, the mystery of Your coming, through seeing by example, with their requests have mercy upon us God. Of Your inexpressible administration Gabriel and Michael, bearers of good news, were sent, their ranks of bodiless beings ministering upon the earth, with their requests have mercy upon us God.

Prophets
T Tz

Whom bearers of the good news of Your
coming, You sent the holy prophets to the
world, and having come in humbleness
with new manners, You fulfilled the
incompleteness in the writings of the laws
and prophets, with their advocation Christ,
have mercy upon us. That with the prophets
beforehand You called the heathens* to You,
new people, and the daughter of Zion the Church
of the heathens,* the beloved bride of the
immortal bridegroom, with their advocation
Christ, have mercy upon us. That the glories of
this temple which You built, Your builder of
existence upon the stone, higher than the first,
and richly ornamented with elegance the seers
made known with meaning of the spirit.
with their advocation Christ, have mercy upon us.

Repentance Days
A Tz

Abundantly merciful Father I confess to You
as the prodigal son, forgive me my sins,
and have mercy. Lord who had compassion
upon the Canaanite woman, and have compassion
upon me this sinner, and have mercy. Lord, Who
You turned the tax collector to the knowledge
of truth, and return me this wanderer, and
have mercy.

---

* Heathen is not an offensive term in this case. It means all peoples who are not believers in the God of Israel. The term "Gentiles" could be used but heathen is more precise.

Apostles
A Tz

Lord, which Your abundant compassion
You flowed from the heavens into the midst
of Your holy apostles,
with their requests have mercy.
Which by their means, graces of the Holy
Spirit were spread throughout the entire
earth, with their requests have mercy.
Which through them You illuminated
Your Church with baptism of the holy font,
with their requests have mercy.

Resting in Christ
A Tz

Who by creating according to Your image,
Lord You honored us, and receive now those
resting in You with right faith, according to
Your great mercy. Who with graces of the Holy
Spirit You illuminated, for their remembrance,
lover of mankind, receive their souls, according
to Your great mercy. Those who have been in
communion of Your body and blood Lord, make
rest their souls with Your saints Christ God,
because they are of Your holy blood.

MORNING HOUR

<u>Martyrs</u>
<u>A Tz</u>

We having assembled in memory of
Your saints Christ, we pray to You,
with their advocation, have mercy.
We bow down in worship before Your bema,*
Christ, receive our prayers with Your compassion.
With their advocation, have mercy.
Those who with spirit and body You will
keep as the pure bodiless beings unto Your
coming, savior, lover of mankind,
with their advocation, have mercy.

―――――

Proclamation following the Hymn of Mercy

Senior Chancel

We bow down in worship of You, Lord our God,
we having passed through the length of this night,
and we having arrived early to the place of
confession, we offer our prayers of the morning.
You Lord we bless and praise; and from You we are
satisfied, Who made worthy to pass this night in
peace and to arrive to this morning hour. Make us
worthy, Lord, of Your inexpressible promises, which
You promised to Your beloved, true God, Jesus
Christ our Lord, give life and have mercy. Be
merciful to us, Lord our God, according to Your great
mercy, let us all say in unison.
Lord have mercy. Lord have mercy. Lord have mercy.

---

* *The raised platform in a synagogue where services are performed or the platform which a church altar sits upon.*

MORNING HOUR

Petition for Feasts of the Lord

(Recited for all Sundays and other Feast Days of the Lord)

Merciful, compassionate, true, holy,
of the great *(Resurrection*)* of Christ
our God, Who is befitting glory,
Lordship, and honor now and always
and unto the eternity of eternities. Amen.

* *or other appropriate Feast Days of the Lord (example Birth, Coming, etc..)*

Petition for Fasting Days including Wednesdays and Fridays

With Your mercy and compassion,
hear us, Lord and have mercy, pardon,
atone, and forgive our sins.
Make us worthy with thanksgiving to
glorify the Father and the Son and the
Holy Spirit, now and always and unto
the eternity of eternities. Amen.

MORNING HOUR 269

Petition for Feast Days of the Saints

Recited on all Mondays, Tuesdays, Thursdays and Saturdays unless a Feast Day of the Lord or Fasting Day falls upon this day.

With advocation and prayers of the
holy martyrs *(* names)* who are remembered
today, and all of Your saints, hear us Lord and
have mercy, pardon, atone, and forgive our
sins. Make us worthy with thanksgiving to
glorify the Father and the Son and the
Holy Spirit, now and always and unto
the eternity of eternities. Amen.

* *insert the appropriate names of the saints or martyrs*

Psalm 148:1 through 150:6 read in alternation
KJV 148:1 through 150:6

Student Chancel

Bless the Lord from the heavens,
bless Him from the heights.

Bless Him all of His angels,
bless Him all of His hosts.

Bless Him sun and moon,
Bless Him all stars and lights.

Bless Him heavens of heavens,
and waters which are above the
heavens, bless the Name of the Lord.

For He said, and they became, He
commanded, and they became established.

He set them in place unto the eternity of
eternities, He placed a boundary, and
they do not pass.

Bless the Lord from the earth, dragons and
all of the depths.

Fire and hail, snow and ice, wind and storm,
those which do His word.

Mountains and all heights, fruit bearing
trees and all cedars.

Beasts and all livestock, reptiles and all
winged birds.

Kings of the earth and their armies,
princes and all judges of the earth.

Young men and virgins, aged men and
children, bless the name of the Lord.

Only His Name is lifted up on high,
professing of Him to the heavens and
to the earth.

The Lord lifted up on high the horn for
His people, blessing to Him to all of His saints,
to the assembly of the sons of Israel,
which is near to the Lord.

MORNING HOUR

Bless the Lord in a new song
blessing to Him in the assembly
of saints.

Israel shall become glad in their maker,
the sons of Zion shall rejoice in their king.

They shall bless His Name with song,
with harps and instruments* they shall
sing psalms to Him.

The Lord is pleased with His holy people, and
He lifts up on high the meek into salvation.

The saints shall become boastful with glory,
and will rejoice in their rest, and they
will lift up God on high with their mouths.

He gave a double edged sword into their hands,
to take vengeance upon the heathens, in
reprimand to all peoples.

To bind their kings with bindings, their generals
with iron handcuffs.

To make for them judgment according to what
is written, and these are glories to all of His saints.

tambourines and timbrels

MORNING HOUR

Bless God in His sanctuary, bless Him
in the expanse of the skies,* in His
power.

Bless Him in His power, bless Him in His
multitudes of greatness.

Bless Him in the sound of song, bless Him
with harps and instruments.**

Bless Him with rejoicing, praise Him
with cheerfulness.

Bless Him with sweet words, praise Him in
sound to hear.

Bless Him in a voice of thanksgiving,
every soul bless the Lord.

Glory to the Father and to the Son and to the Holy Spirit.
Now and always and unto the eternity of eternities. Amen.

---

* *firmament*

** *tambourines and timbrels*

MORNING HOUR

Student Chancel

 The Lord of the Heavens Hymn (Der Hergnitz Sharagan) *according to the proper day and tone, as shown by the calendar, is sung at this point. To find the proper hymn we will (most of the time) have to turn to the Hymnal's index under the* **Hymn of the Fathers (Hartz Sharagan)** *sections just as we did for the Hymn of Mercy (Voghormya Sharagan) because the hymnal does not separately list the Lord of the Heavens Hymn (Der Hergnitz Sharagan) in its index."Hymns of the Fathers" will be grouped according to the following days: Resurrection, Fasting Days (Repentance),Saints and Martyrs, and For those Resting in Christ. Immediately following the "Hymn of the Fathers" then the "Hymn of Mercy" in the Hymnal, are the correct verses of the "Lord of the Heavens Hymn" verses which are to be sung. For other special days look in either the index for Feasts of the Lord or in the index for Feasts of the Saints.*

*The following are only examples of various
"Lord of the Heavens Hymn" verses.
For the complete and exact verses, follow
the above instruction.*

<u>Resurrection</u>
<u>A Tz</u>

Along the way of daybreak of the first day of the week the women arrived early to the tomb, to anoint the pure uncorrupted body. And they found the stone had been taken up from the doors of the tomb, and having heard the speech from the angel, that Christ arose and abolished death. And your Lord having met the apostles and having given the life giving greeting, You sent them unto salvation of the whole world.

Holy Archangels
T Tz

The immortal king of simple thrones,
the multi-eyed cherubim, the seraphim with
a voice of holy blessing, chief priests
first in the heavens, be advocates for us
to the Lord for the sake of the Church.
Lordships lifted up on high to glories
lifted up on high, undefeatable armies,
supreme Lordship, chief priests of the
second order, be advocates for us
to the Lord for the sake of the Church.
They were supreme powers above,
heavenly archangels, militias of angels,
chief priests of the third (order) in the heavens,
being in unison with you we sing glories
in the highest.

Prophets
T Tz

Today those people of the heathens,*
those having been predestined through
the prophets, to come to the God of Abraham
to bow down in worship, bless the Lord in the
heavens in the company of the heavenly
beings. Today sons, daughter of the Zion
above, having built upon the foundation of
the apostles and prophets, and those of you
who drink of the abundant flowing stream of
the spirit from the spring of Israel in the churches
of the saints, bless the Lord in a new song. Today
the armies of above having been in unison, with
the ranks of the martyrs and prophets, sing
spiritual songs to God, and in their remembrance
we sing glories in the highest.

---

* *Heathen is not an offensive term in this case. It means all peoples who are not believers in the God of Israel. The term "Gentiles" could be used but heathen is more precise.*

MORNING HOUR

Repentance Days
A Tz

Lord Who above the glorifications of
the cherubim, having become humbled
with sweetness, receive our prayers.
Lord You Who graced mercy upon the
nation of mankind, having become humbled
with sweetness, receive our prayers. Lord You
Who taught us to give glories to Your Holy Name
at every hour having become humbled
with sweetness, receive our prayers.

Apostles
A Tz

Those who from the beginning have been
honored from all of the Father's love, with
the apostolic calling they invited the whole
world with hope to arrive in part, through their
teaching, let everyone bless the Lord. Those
eye witnesses and servants became embodied to
the Word, superior to the ranks of the bodiless
heavenly beings, through meeting of grace,
through their teaching, let everyone bless the Lord.

To those, stay the judicial seat of the
magnificent frightful court, to execute
judgment unto us according to what
has been written, let us fall down to them
with our beings having shown remorse
through begging with submission, through
them reconciling us with the fearful judge.

Apostles
A Tz

Apostles of God pillars of faith of the
catholic* church, disciples of Christ God the
heavenly teacher, advocate to grace peace unto the
entire world. Friends of Christ and lieutenants
of the Godly mysteries, receivers of the Word of
life and illuminators of the universes,
advocate to grace peace unto the entire world.
Fearful judges of the court and condemners of
Christ not those who confess of Him, we
request of you, advocate to grace peace unto the
entire world.

---

* *catholic means universal in its Greek origin. It has no connection to the Roman Catholic Church in this context. The text above used the term "gatooghige" the Armenicized form of the Greek. Armenian has borrowed this term for unknown reasons as the Armenia language already has its own words for universal, "diezeragan" and general, "unthanoor" which is already used in many other liturgical phrases. Either one of these would be better choices.*

MORNING HOUR

<u>Resting in Christ</u>
<u>A Tz</u>

To You God blessing is befitting,
in which You are the resurrection with the
voice unto the eternities for the ones that
are asleep, king and prince we bless You on
high. In Your second coming Christ, king of
glories, from the sound of the trumpet, the souls
of those at rest are renewed, and they rise from
the dead with pure uncorrupted bodies. And
for the sake of those for whom we pray to You heavenly
Father, judge those of ours who are at rest in
Your Jerusalem above, into the assemblies of
the first born to be written into the heavens.

<u>Resting in Christ</u>
<u>A Tz</u>

Voice with the life giving Godly cry
having been cast out, which says,
"come blessed ones of my Father, inherit
what has been prepared for you, lives in
the magnificent earth." To meet You
with faith in the air above, carrying God
with light having been brilliantly shining
by the ranks of the bodiless heavenly beings,
to hear the blissful call. Make them to dwell
at Your right side in the company of the wise
virgins, in the bright angelic bridal chamber having
been brilliantly shining by the ranks of the
bodiless heavenly beings, into the assemblies of
the first born to be written into the heavens.

<u>Martyrs</u>
<u>A Tz</u>

We having assembled in remembrance
of the holy martyrs by singing in unison,
blessing on high to the heavenly king.
Because with the flowing of His blood
the enemy was defeated, and having
received honor, Zion boasts with song,
blessing on high to the heavenly king.
Of their ranking in the company of armies
of angels above being delightful with
remembrance, let us sing to their holiness,
blessing on high to the heavenly king.

<u>Martyrs</u>
<u>A Tz</u>

Those who showed the demonstration of
violent martyrdom, and were victorious in
faith, on the occasion they became to us
three of light, with their requests give us life.
Those whom to expel the darkness of
idolatry, rejected it, and stood for us as a
sign of victory against the enemy,
with their requests give us life. And with
miraculous resistance having made wars on
the earth, having ascended up to the ranks of
the heavenly angels they became accompanist
singers, with their requests give us life.

MORNING HOUR

*After the Lord of the Heavens Hymn (Der Hergnitz Sharagan)
the morning blessing
"Glory to God in the Highest" (Parrk i partzoons Asdoodzo)
is sung by the angels and by the 150 church fathers who were present at the
Second Ecclesiastical Council of Constantinople 381 A.D.*

(While presenting the censer and incense to the Priest in the chancel)

Deacon

And again in peace let us request of the Lord. Receive, save, and have mercy.

(Priest blesses and fills the censer with incense while saying)

Priest

Blessing and glory to the Father and to the Son and to the Holy Spirit. Now and always and unto the eternity of eternities. Amen.

*(All shall proceed to the center of the church
facing the altar and sing the hymn.
The Deacon censes the entire Church during the hymn.)*

Glory to God in the Highest (Parrk i partzoons Asdoodzo)

Student Chancel

Lk 2:14

Glory to God in the highest, and peace on earth, goodwill to men.

And blessing to You in the highest,
blessed are You Lord our God, we bless You and
praise You. We confess You Lord and we bow down
in worship to You. We glorify You, from You we are
satisfied Lord for the sake of Your great glories.
Lord King, holy, heavenly, God and Father almighty.
Lord and only begotten Son of the Father Jesus Christ
and Holy Son.

MORNING HOUR

Lord God, Lamb of God and Son of the Father, who took our nature* from the virgin. Be merciful to us, You took up the sins of the world, and now receive our prayers. The Holy One, which You sit at the right hand of the Father, have mercy upon us. For You are holy, You only are elevated on high, You only are our Lord Jesus Christ. Lord and Holy Spirit Who are in glories God, with the Father. Amen.

(The following was recited at the Third Ecumenical Council of Ephesus)

Senior Chancel

And at all hours we bless You, Lord, and praise your Holy Name eternally and through the eternity of eternities. Lord make this day worthy with peace, and keep us without sins. You are blessed Lord God of our Fathers, Your Holy Name has been praised and glorified unto the eternities amen.

Ps 118:12 KJV 119:12
Blessed Lord teach me Your justices.
Blessed Lord teach me Your justices.
Blessed Lord teach me Your justices. **

---

* "nature" is implied. "took on as us" may be a closer but not the exact translation.

** The deacon censes the altar three times on each one of these verses. Then the senior priest in the middle of the church is censed three times and the censor chain is then extended out by the deacon with both hands, the priest places his right hand upon the chain and then the deacon bows to him while kissing his hand.

MORNING HOUR

Lord You became our refuge from generation unto generation. I pray Lord, have mercy upon me and heal my being, I have sinned against You. Show us Lord Your mercies, and give us Your salvations. Lord Your mercy is eternal, do not neglect the works of Your hands. My Lord I made You my refuge, teach me to do Your wills, for You are my God.

<u>Ps 35:10-11a KJV 36:9-10a</u>

From You is the fountain of life, and with the light of Your faces we see the light. Shine Your mercies upon those that know You Lord.

Petition

Glory, honor and bowing down in worship in the highest, to the Father and to the Son and to Holy Spirit, now and always and unto the eternity of eternities. Amen.

MORNING HOUR

MORNING SONGS

(These are anthems which are sung or chanted in alternation after Glory to God in the Highest, according to the proper tone of the day.)

Senior Chancel

Resurrection days of Christ*

<u>A Tz</u>
<u>A G</u>
<u>Ps 67:2a KJV:68:1a</u>

Let us bless the resurrection of the savior,
the resurrection of our savior let us bless.
God arose and all of His enemies scattered.

<u>P Tz</u>
<u>P G</u>

Let us bless the resurrection of the savior,
the resurrection of our savior let us bless.
Let us bless the resurrected Christ and let
us glorify His resurrection.

<u>K Tz</u>
<u>K G</u>
<u>Ps 67:19 KJV 68:18</u>

Let us bless the resurrection of the savior,
the resurrection of our savior let us bless.
Who ascended to the heights, and He took captive of captivity,
He took pillage, He divided the gifts, and gave them to the sons of man.

<u>T Tz</u>
<u>T G</u>

Let us bless the resurrection of the savior,
the resurrection of our savior let us bless.
Who endured of the cross and was laid in the newly dug out stone,
and with the Godly resurrection He raised up those who have
died, into life.

* *The assigned tone pairing shown is most likely a perpetuated typographical error. This is the only case in all of the Armenian Church's texts where this pairing exists. Traditional pairing is: (A Tz, K Tz) (P Tz, T Tz) (A G, K G) (P G, T G)*

MORNING HOUR

Ascension of Christ

<u>Ps 46:6 KJV 47:5</u>

Let us bless the resurrection of the savior,
the resurrection of our savior let us bless.
God ascended with blessing, and our Lord
with the sound of the trumpet.

Pentecost

<u>Ps 67:27 KJV 68:26</u>

Let us bless the coming of the Holy Spirit,
the coming of the Holy Spirit let us bless.
Praise God in His assemblies, and the Lord
from the fountains of Israel.

Bread and Salt Days
(Lenten days and other fasting days)

<u>Monday</u>
<u>Ps 12:4-5 KJV 13:3-4</u>

Give light, Lord, to my eyes that
I will never sleep unto death.
Do not let the enemy say, "I was
victorious over him," or that my
oppressors will rejoice if I am shaken.

<u>Tuesday</u>
<u>Ps 35:10-11 KJV 36:9-10</u>

From You is the fountain of life,
and with the light of Your faces we see the light.
Shine Your mercies upon those that know You Lord,
Your justices to those who are right in their hearts.

Wednesday
Ps 40:5, 2 KJV 41:4, 1

I said Lord have mercy upon me,
heal my being, I have sinned against You.
Fortunate is he who considers the poor and
the indigent, the Lord saves him on the day
of evil.

Thursday
Ps 87: 14-15 KJV 88:13-14

I cried unto You Lord, my prayers of
the morning will arrive unto You.
Why Lord do You reject my being, or
turn Your faces from me?

Friday
Ps 87: 3, 2 KJV 88: 2, 1

My prayers enter before You Lord,
may Your ear descend upon my requests.
Lord God of my salvation, from day I cried
out and in the night before You.

The Raising of Lazarus
Ps 29:3, 1 KJV 30:3, 1

Lord You pulled my being out from the hells,*
You saved me from amongst those who descend
into the pit.
I raise You up on high, Lord, because You received me,
and You did not make my enemy joyful over me.

Hades

MORNING HOUR

Palm Sunday

Today our King Christ enters into Jerusalem
the new City of David.
The aged went forth before him with branches
of olive trees, and they were glorifying the
Son of God.

Holy Monday
Ps 101:26-27a KJV 102:25-26a

From the beginning, Lord, You established
the earth, and the heavens are the works of
Your hands.
They perish and You exist and remain unto
eternity.

Holy Tuesday
Ps 44:15b-16 KJV 45:14-15

The virgins, following her, shall be taken to the king,
and her friends shall be taken to him.
They shall be brought in with joy and gladness, and
they shall be taken to the temple of the king.

Holy Wednesday
Ps 72:8-9 KJV 73:8-9

They thought and spoke evilness, and they
thought wickedness in the heights.
They set their mouths to the heavens, and they
were bringing their tongues around the earth.

MORNING HOUR

Holy Thursday
PS 93:21-22 KJV 94:21-22

They hunted for the person of the just,
and they were condemning innocent blood.
The Lord became my refuge, God helper
of my hope.

Holy Friday
Ps 87: 9c-10a KJV 88:8c-9

I was betrayed and could not come out,
my eyes became weakened from poverty.
I cried out unto the Lord daily,
and raised my hands up to You.

connection
Ps 108:4 KJV 109:4

In exchange for my love they betrayed me,
but I remained in prayer.

melody change
Ps 108:2 KJV 109:1

God do not be silent to my blessing,
because the mouth of the sinner,
the mouth of the deceitful was opened
upon me.

Recite Psalm 108 KJV 109 in its entirety in alternation.

Holy Saturday
Ps 87:7-8 KJV 88:6-7

They placed me inside the interior
of the pit, in the darkness and in the
shadow of death.
Upon me Your indignation was asserted,
all of Your amusements are brought upon me.

MORNING HOUR

<u>connection</u>
<u>Ps 87:7 KJV 88:6</u>

They placed me inside the interior
of the pit, in the darkness and in the
shadow of death.

<u>melody change</u>
<u>Ps 87:2 KJV 88:1</u>

Lord God of my salvation, from the day unto the
night I cried out before You.

Recite Psalm 87 KJV 88 in its entirety in alternation.

<u>For the Dead*</u>
<u>Ps 114:7 KJV 116:7</u>

Return my soul unto Your rest,
because the Lord has called you.

<u>melody change</u>
<u>Ps 114:1-2 KJV 116:1-2</u>

I loved that the Lord shall hear the voice
of my prayers for He descended His ear upon
me, and through all of my days I called out
unto Him.

Recite Psalm 114 KJV 115 in its entirety in alternation.

* This is chanted after the singing of Glory to God in the Highest (Parrk i partzoons Asdoodzo) during the burial service at the cemetery. Glory to God in the Highest is actually sung while the dirt is being shoveled onto the casket.

<u>Feasts of the Church</u>
<u>Ps 92: 5b, 1 KJV 93: 5b, 1</u>

Holiness is befitting to Your House Lord unto lengthy days.
The Lord ruled as king, He was clothed in splendor,
He was clothed with strength brought forth from within Him.

Ark of the Covenant
Assumption of Mary
Ps 131:8,1 KJV 132:8,1

Rise Lord to Your rest, You and the ark
of Your holy covenant.
Lord remember David and all his meekness.

Transfiguration
Ps 88:12-13 KJV 89:11-12

Yours are the heavens and Yours is the earth,
this world in its entirety You established.
You made the north and the south,
Mount Tabor and Mount Hermon will rejoice
in Your Name.

Annunciation to Mary
Feasts of Mary the God-Bearer
Ps 71:6, 2a KJV 72: 6, 1

He will descend as rain upon fleece,
as dew that sprinkles upon the land.
God give Your righteousness to the king,
and Your justices to the son of the king.

Feasts of the Cross
Ps 59:6-7 KJV 60:4-5

You gave a sign to those who fear
You, that they shall live in the faces
of the bow. As they saved Your beloved,
give life with Your right hand and hear us.

Holy Archangels
Ps 148:1-2 KJV 148:1-2

Bless the Lord from the heavens, Bless Him on high.
Let all of His angels bless Him,
let all of His hosts bless Him.

MORNING HOUR

Apostles
Ps 18:4-5 KJV 19:3-4a
There are no words and there is no speech,
of whom their voices are not heard.
Their speech went forth, into all lands,
and their words unto all ends of the world.

Prophets
Ps 18:4 Ps 67:27 KJV 19:3 68:26
There are no words and there is no speech,
of whom their voices are not heard.
Praise God in His assemblies, and the Lord
from the fountains of Israel.

Patriarchs
Ps 131:9, 1 KJV 132:9, 1
Your priests shall be clothed with justice,
and Your saints will rejoice with joy.
Lord remember David, and all his meekness.

Martyrs
Ps 149:5, 1 KJV 149:5, 1
The saints shall become boastful with glory,
and will rejoice in their rest.
Bless the Lord in a new song,
blessing to Him in the assemblies of the saints.

Martyrs A G
Ps 42:3a 84:8a 42:3b-4a KJV 43:3a 85:7a 43:3b-4a
Lord send Your light and Your truths,
Lord show us mercy, and be the helper to
Your servants, with the advocation of saints *(*Name)*,
whose remembrance is today.
That having been led by them we will ascend to
Your holy mountain and to Your dwellings, I shall
enter before the altar of God, to God who makes my
youth cheerful, Lord show us mercy,
and be the helper to Your servants.

* Insert the Name of the Martyr who is being remembered on this day.

MORNING HOUR

<u>Revelation or Birth of Christ</u>
<u>Presentation of Christ to the Temple</u>
<u>Ps 109:3b KJV 110:3b</u>

Sun of justice today You were revealed to
nations of mankind, having become man,
You purified the waters, we have been born
again through the baptism of the Holy Spirit.

In the splendor of glories of Your holiness,
from the womb before the morning star*
I gave birth to You, having become man,
You purified the waters, we have been born
again through the baptism of the Holy Spirit.

*Morning Star has a double meaning.
It is another term for Lucifer (Satan).*

---

*Proclamation for Saturday evenings during the Evening Hour,
Sundays, and during the entire Fifty Days after Easter.*

Student Chancel

<u>Deacon</u>

Let us all say in unison, Lord have mercy.

<u>Choir (continue in alternation)</u>

Lord have mercy.

For the sake of peace of the entire world and
for the stability of the holy church, let us
request of the Lord.

Lord have mercy.

MORNING HOUR

For the sake of all holy and orthodox bishops, let us request of the Lord.

Lord have mercy.

For the sake of the life of our patriarch Lord *(insert name)*, and for the salvation of his soul, let us request of the Lord.

Lord have mercy.

For the sake of doctors of the church, priests, deacons, choristers* and the order of all the children who are servants of the church,** let us request of the Lord.

Lord have mercy.

For the sake of pious kings and God loving princes, generals and their armies, let us request of the Lord.

Lord have mercy.

For the sake that the Lord almighty shall make obedient before them all of the wars of the enemies, let us request of the Lord.

Lord have mercy.

For the sake of our fathers and brothers who are in captivity and in evil servitude, let us request of the Lord.

Lord have mercy.

For the sake of travelers and passengers at sea, that they may arrive at the harbor of goodness, let us request of the Lord.

Lord have mercy.

---

* *Actual translation is "scribe or clerk"*

** *Even though "children" is used, this term includes those of all ages who serve the church whether they be adults or children.*

For the sake of those who are sick and all
of those who are afflicted, for their speedy
recovery, let us request of the Lord.

Lord have mercy.

For the sake of temperate weather, gentle
rains and abundance of fruits, let us request
of the Lord.

Lord have mercy.

For the sake of pilgrims and those who bring
fruit for the holy Church of God, let us
request of the Lord.

Lord have mercy.

And for the sake of those who are delivered up
into the hands of the unlawful for the sake of
the name of Christ, let us request of the Lord.

Free them Lord and have mercy.

For the sake of the souls of those who are at rest,
who sleep in Christ with the true and right faith,
let us request of the Lord.

Remember Lord and have mercy.

For the sake of the Lord God saving us from the
enemy, visible and invisible, let us request of
the Lord.

Lord have mercy.

Petition

<u>Priest</u>

We have as advocates St. Mary the God-Bearer,
the glorified and blessed ever Holy Virgin, St. John
the Baptist, St. Stephen the first martyr, the Holy Apostles
and Prophets, the brave and victorious Holy Martyrs, and
the great confessor of Christ our patriarch St. Gregory the
Illuminator of the land of the Armenias.

MORNING HOUR

<u>Deacon</u>

And remember all of the saints, and with them let us request of the Lord.

<u>Choir *(continue in alternation)*</u>

Lord have mercy.

To pass this morning of light and this coming day in peace, with faith let us ask from the Lord.

Grace unto us Lord.

The angel of peace to be guardian of our beings. Let us ask from the Lord.

Grace unto us Lord.

For atonement and forgiveness of our offences. Let us ask from the Lord.

Grace unto us Lord.

For the great Holy Cross and able strength for assistance of our beings. Let us ask from the Lord.

Grace unto us Lord.

And again in one voice for the sake of our true and holy faith. Let us pray to the Lord.

Lord have mercy.

Let us make ourselves and one another as the person of the Lord God almighty.

Let us become as Your Person Lord.

Lord our God be merciful to us, according to Your great mercy, let us all say in unison.

Lord have mercy. Lord have mercy. Lord have mercy.

MORNING HOUR

Proclamation of St. Gregory the Illuminator which is said on Days of the Apostles, Prophets, and for St. Hripsime and her followers. (This would be recited on a Monday, Tuesday, Thursday, or Saturday)

Student Chancel

<u>Deacon</u>
Great God mighty and glorified, enlightener of the saints and having rested in the saints, the torments of the holy *(* insert type of saint)* we have as an advocate** to You, we pray.

<u>Choir *(continue in alternation)*</u>
Hear Lord and have mercy

Whom You are blessed unceasingly from the ranks of heavenly spiritual joyful angels, make us worthy upright with glorification to You in the company of Your saints, to bow down in worship of Your great and fearful Lordship, we pray.

Hear Lord and have mercy.

We bless You in unison with love unto the remembrances of Your witnesses, who became followers of Your well lit paths Lord, Who for our sake You took to Yourself the sufferings of the cross and of death, we pray.

Hear Lord and have mercy.

Conductors of pleasure of the wills of Your Godly being, they offered sacrifice of their beings in witness of Your true love, and they aromatized the sweet fragrance of Your Lordship, we pray.

Hear Lord and have mercy.

---

* *(Insert the appropriate type: Apostle, Prophet or Saint, being remembered on this day.)*

** *Most translate the word "parekhos" as intercede, however, "advocate" is much more accurate. It corrects Roman Catholic influence upon the Armenian Church's theology. "Parekhos" literally means "speak good." We ask members of the Church to pray for us. Those of the earthly church "Church Militant" and those in Paradise of the "Church Victorious." We believe that all are alive in Christ.*

MORNING HOUR

They purified their beings to, a temple of Your Holy Name, having cleansed their minds, and their thoughts with Your holy fear, and they became of the same order of the heavenly spiritual beings of joyful angels, we pray.

Hear Lord and have mercy.

With the advocation of the holy God-Bearer, and John the Forerunner *(Baptist)*, and the holy apostles, prophets and martyrs, and St. Gregory our illuminator, with the advocation and prayers of the saints *(* insert name)* whose remembrance is today, and all of Your saints Lord, who are united in the love of Your Godliness, remember the souls of those of ours that are sleeping, and make visit to them at Your coming, we pray.

Remember Lord and have mercy.

---

* *(Insert the appropriate type: Apostle, Prophet or Saint, being remembered on this day.)*

And moreover especially the encouragement
of love, and to gift unto us to do works of good,
we request.

Give unto us Lord God.

Let us make ourselves and one another as the Person
of the Lord God Almighty.

Let us become as Your Person Lord.

Lord our God be merciful to us, according to Your
great mercy, let us all say in unison.

Lord have mercy. Lord have mercy.
Hear Lord and have mercy.

---

*Proclamation for Days of the Church Fathers and
Doctors of the Church*

Student Chancel

<u>Deacon</u>
They became leaders for us with goings, straight
to the paths of the kingdom of heavens, with the
brilliant torch of their faith and love, they shined
the light of the knowledge of God in our hearts,
we pray.

<u>Choir</u>
Hear Lord and have mercy.

MORNING HOUR

With the guarding of our thoughts, words, and deeds, with holiness to glorify the all Holy Trinity, the Father and the Son and the Holy Spirit unto eternity amen, we pray.

Hear Lord and have mercy.

With the prayers of the holy patriarchs, Lord, who resisted for the sake of Your Holy Name, look upon these having assembled bowing down in worship, and grace the forgiveness of sins, and take up part and portion with all of the saints, we pray.

Hear Lord and have mercy.

With the prayers of the holy patriarchs, Lord, of whom they cleansed their beings to, a temple of Your Holy Spirit, gift unto our land temperate weather, and delicious herbs, to fill all of our necessary needs, we pray.

Hear Lord and have mercy.

With the advocation of the holy God-Bearer, and John the Forerunner *(Baptist)*, and the holy apostles, prophets and martyrs, and St. Gregory our illuminator, with the advocation and prayers of the saints *(* insert name)* whose remembrance is today, and all of Your saints Lord, who are united in the love of Your Godliness, remember the souls of those of ours that are sleeping, and make visit to them at Your coming, we pray.

Remember Lord and have mercy.

And moreover especially the encouragement of love, and to gift unto us to do works of good, we request.

Give unto us Lord God.

Let us make ourselves and one another as the Person of the Lord God Almighty.

Let us become as Your Person Lord.

Lord our God be merciful to us, according to Your great mercy, let us all say in unison.

Lord have mercy. Lord have mercy.
Hear Lord and have mercy.

---

* (Insert the appropriate type: Apostle, Prophet or Saint, being remembered on this day.)

MORNING HOUR

Proclamation for Days of Martyrs and Hermits

Student Chancel

Deacon

The resistance of the holy martyrs we have
as advocates to the kind Son of God,
that You may grace upon the world
unshaken peace, and may You keep the Holy Church firm,
having been established upon the foundation of the apostles
and prophets, we pray.

Choir

Hear Lord and have mercy.

The resistance of the holy martyrs we have
as advocates to the kind Son of God,
that agitations may become calm, and that
the attacks of the enemies may be ceased, may
love and justice be planted in the earth, we pray.

Hear Lord and have mercy.

With the prayers of the holy martyrs,
Lord, those who resisted for the sake of Your Holy
Name, look upon the bowing down in
worship of those who are assembled,
and grace unto us the forgiveness of sins, and bring
us part and portion with all of the saints, we pray.

Hear Lord and have mercy.

With the requests of the holy witnesses through
the blood of those who have been martyred, Lord,
of whom they cleansed their beings to, a temple of
Your Holy Spirit, gift unto our land temperate weather,
and delicious herbs, to fill all of our necessary needs, we pray.

Hear Lord and have mercy.

MORNING HOUR

With the advocation of the holy God-Bearer, and John the Forerunner *(Baptist)*, and the holy apostles, prophets and martyrs, and St. Gregory our illuminator, with the advocation and prayers of the saints *(* insert name)* whose remembrance is today, and all of Your saints Lord, who are united in the love of Your Godliness, remember the souls of those of ours that are sleeping, and make visit to them at Your coming, we pray.

Remember Lord and have mercy.

And moreover especially the encouragement of love, and to gift unto us to do works of good, we request.

Give unto us Lord God.

Let us make ourselves and one another as the Person of the Lord God Almighty.

Let us become as Your Person Lord.

Lord our God be merciful to us, according to Your great mercy, let us all say in unison.

Lord have mercy. Lord have mercy.
Hear Lord and have mercy.

*(Insert the appropriate type: Apostle, Prophet or Saint, being remembered on this day.)

Proclamation for the Birth of Christ, Annunciation to Mary the God-Bearer, Assumption of Mary the God-Bearer, and The Presentation of the Lord to the Temple

<u>Deacon</u> **Student Chancel**
Mother Holy of wonderful light, who carried the God of all eternities in your womb, and you gave birth to God the Word, the joy of the world, we pray.

<u>Choir</u>
Mother holy, advocate.

Pray for our sake to God Who has taken bodily form
made from you, who lowered Himself from the
Fatherly bosom, He took body according to human
nature to make peace in the heavens and upon the earth,
we pray.

Mother holy, advocate.

Pray for our sake to God Who has taken bodily form
made from you, to pardon us by overlooking our offences,
and to give us assistance for resisting the adversaries
in war, we pray.

Mother holy, advocate.

Pray for our sake to God Who has taken bodily form
made from you, that wars shall be silenced, the attacks
of the enemies shall be halted, love and justice
shall be planted on the earth, we pray.

Mother holy, advocate.

Pray for our sake to God Who has taken bodily form
made from you, to increase upon our land the
gentile emanation of springs, abundant producing crops
of vegetation and plants, to be pleasing in all of our essential
needs, we pray.

Mother holy, advocate.

Pray for our sake to God Who has taken bodily form
made from you, that Your Holy Church may unite, having
been built upon the foundation of the apostles and
prophets, to keep it pure until the day of the appearing of His
coming, we pray.

Mother holy, advocate.

MORNING HOUR

Pray for our sake holy woman, to the
only begotten, your Son, and for the sake
of the souls which are at rest, to receive
them into the kingdom of the heavens, and
to give part and portion with all of the saints,
we pray.

Remember Lord and have mercy.

And moreover especially the encouragement of
love, and to gift unto us to do works of good
we request.

Give unto us Lord God.

Let us make ourselves and one another as the Person
of the Lord God Almighty.

Let us become as Your Person Lord.

Lord our God be merciful to us, according to Your
great mercy, let us all say in unison.

Lord have mercy. Lord have mercy. Lord have mercy.

MORNING HOUR

Proclamation for Days of Fasting

Student Chancel

<u>Deacon</u>
Let us glorify the almighty God the Father of our Lord Jesus Christ, by giving thanks unto Him, who kept us with peace in this night. And led us from darkness into light, from death into life, from impurity to purity, from ignorance to the knowledge of His truth. Let us pray and request from Him that He will make us to pass of this day in peace and with all diligent cheerfulness. And having defended His people may He guard them with His Godly power, Who with His kindness He has Lordship over all. Our Lord God almighty, give life and have mercy.

<u>Choir</u>
Give life Lord.

<u>Deacon</u>
To pass this morning of light and this upcoming day in peace, with faith we ask from the Lord.

<u>Choir</u>
Grace unto us Lord.

The angel of peace to be guardian of our beings. We ask from the Lord.

Grace unto us Lord.

For atonement and forgiveness of our offences. We ask from the Lord.

Grace unto us Lord.

For the great Holy Cross and able strength for assistance of our beings. We ask from the Lord.

Grace unto us Lord.

MORNING HOUR

And again in one voice for the sake of
our true and holy faith.
Let us pray to the Lord.

Lord have mercy.

Let us make ourselves and one another as
the person of the Lord God almighty.

Let us become as Your Person Lord.

Lord our God be merciful to us,
according to Your great mercy,
let us all say in unison.

Lord have mercy. Lord have mercy. Lord have mercy.

Prayer for All Days

Senior Chancel

<u>Priest</u>
From You we are satisfied, Lord our
God, Who with Your visible light You
delighted all of Your creatures, but with
the intelligent light of Your commandments,
You enlightened all of those who have believed
in You. And strengthen us Lord, in the keeping
of Your commandments, in this day and at all
times. That as with enlightened minds, we may
always do Your pleasures, and together with
Your saints we may arrive unto Your
goodness which has been prepared,

MORNING HOUR

with graces and love of mankind of
our Lord and savior Jesus Christ, to
Whom is befitting Lordship and honor,
now and always and unto the eternity
of eternities, Amen:

Peace unto all

<u>Choir</u>

And with Your Spirit.

<u>Deacon</u>

Let us bow down in worship of God

<u>Choir</u>

Before You Lord.

<u>Priest</u>

Our peace and life, which You were
sent from the Father, only begotten Son of
God, our Lord and savior Jesus Christ. Give us
Your peace, which You graced upon Your holy
apostles, by breathing upon them Your life giving
and almighty Holy Spirit. And in order that we who
have been at peace from all worldly slippings,*
may we become temple and dwelling of Your
Godly graces, and by giving thanks we
will glorify You with the Father and the
Holy Spirit, Christ our God, now and
always and unto the eternity of eternities, Amen.

---

* *Backsliding may be a more modern interpretation.*

MORNING HOUR 305

Sing the "Thrice Holy" also known as "Holy God" (Soorp Asdvadz)
according to the proper day or season.
The verse is sung three times.

Senior Chancel

For the Annunciation to Mary, the Birth of Christ,
and the Naming of Christ

Holy God, holy and mighty, holy and immortal,
You Who were revealed for our sake,
have mercy upon us.

For the Presentation of Christ to the Temple
and Palm Sunday

Holy God, holy and mighty, holy and immortal,
You Who came and are to come,
have mercy upon us.

For the Betrayal of Holy Friday Night

Holy God, holy and mighty, holy and immortal,
You Who were betrayed for our sake,
have mercy upon us.

For the Holy Friday Midday (Jashoo) Hour,
for all Days of the Saints, Feasts of the Cross,
Feasts of the Church, and for Fasting Days.*

Holy God, holy and mighty, holy and immortal,
You Who were crucified for our sake,
have mercy upon us.

For Holy Friday evening and for Holy Saturday Night

Holy God, holy and mighty, holy and immortal,
You Who were buried for our sake,
have mercy upon us.

---

* *This hymn is attributed to Nicodemus and Joseph of Arimathea having sung this for the first time when removing Christ's body from the cross.*

MORNING HOUR

For Easter and all Resurrection Sundays

Holy God, holy and mighty, holy and immortal,
You Who rose from the dead,
have mercy upon us.

For the Ascension

Holy God, holy and mighty, holy and immortal,
You Who ascended with glory to the Father,
have mercy upon us.

Pentecost

Holy God, holy and mighty, holy and immortal,
You Who came and rested upon the apostles,
have mercy upon us.

Transfiguration

Holy God, holy and mighty, holy and immortal,
You Who were revealed on Mount Tabor,
have mercy upon us.

For the Assumption of the Mother of God (God-Bearer)

Holy God, holy and mighty, holy and immortal,
You Who came to the assumption* of
Your mother and virgin, have mercy upon us.

The Ascription** of Thomas the Apostle

Glorified and blessed ever holy virgin
God-Bearer, Mary mother of Christ,
offer our prayers to your Son and to our God.

---

* Literally-changing from this world to the next
** Attributable composition of Thomas the Apostle

MORNING HOUR

Petition

<u>Priest</u>
To save us from temptation and from all of our dangers.

Proclamation

Senior Chancel

<u>Deacon</u>
And again in peace let us request of the Lord.

For the sake of the voice of our prayers being heard by the Lord God, with the advocation of the holy God-Bearer, and for mercy and compassion of the Lord God to descend upon us. Our Lord God almighty, give life and have mercy.

Petition

<u>Priest</u>
Blessing and glory to the Father and to the Son and to the Holy Spirit. Now and always and unto the eternity of eternities. Amen.

Psalm 112:1-9 KJV 113:1-9 is sung on Sundays only, just before the Gospel of Healing (Pzhshgootyan). It is not sung on Feasts of the Lord or Great Lent in which the Lectionary (Jashotz Kirk) or Calendar prescribes other Psalms which precede special Prophetic, Epistle, and Gospel readings.

Senior Chancel

The Name of the Lord shall be blessed, from this time forth unto eternity.

Children serving the Lord, bless the Lord and bless the Name of the Lord.

The name of the Lord shall be blessed, from this time forth unto eternity.

From sunrise to the setting of the sun, the Name of the Lord is blessed.

MORNING HOUR

The Lord is high above all nations
and His glories are above the heavens.

Who is as Lord our God, dwelling in the
heights and He sees the humble in the
heavens and upon the earth.

He raises up the poor from the earth,
and lifts up the afflicted from the garbage dump.

He makes them sit with princes,
with the princes of His people.

He makes the barren woman dwell joyfully
in her house, as a cheerful mother with sons.

Deacon	Alleluia Stand
Priest	Peace unto all.
Choir	And with Your spirit.
Deacon	May you listen with awe.

For regular Sundays only, read the appropriate one of the following Gospels of Healing (Pzhshgootyan) according to Tone of the Day. For Feasts of the Lord and Great Lent, read the special Psalms, Epistles, and/or Gospel according to the proper day as prescribed by the Lectionary (Jashotz Kirk) or Calendar.

Student Chancel

Reader (priest or deacon)	The Holy Gospel of Jesus Christ
P G	According to Matthew 15:21-28
T G	
Choir	Glory to You Lord our God.
Deacon	Attention
Choir	God says.

MORNING HOUR

Of our Lord Jesus Christ

And having gone out from there Jesus went to the districts of Tyre and Sidon. And behold a Canaanite woman having gone out from the borders there, was crying out and saying, be merciful to me, Lord, Son of David, my daughter is severely possessed by a demon. And He does not give an answer to her. And His disciples having approached, were begging Him and were saying,

"Let her go for she is crying after us." He gave answer and says, "I was not sent anywhere, except to the sheep of the lost House of Israel." And she having approached, bowing down in worship of Him and said, "Lord, help me." He gave answer to her and says, "It is not good to take the bread of children, and throw it to the dogs." And she says, "Yes, Lord, for the dogs also are fed from the crumbs that fall from the table of their master." Then Jesus gave answer to her, and says, "O` you woman, great are your faiths, may it be unto you and as you will." And her daughter was healed in that same hour.

Follow the paradigm on Page 308 for the introduction to all of the following Gospel readings.

The Holy Gospel According to Mark 7:31-37

P Tz

T Tz

Of our Lord Jesus Christ.

And once again having gone forth from the borders of Tyre and Sidon, and He came to the sea-shore of Galilee through the midst of the borders of Decapolis.

And they brought before Him one who was deaf and dumb,* and they begged, that He would put His hand upon him. And having taken him from there, alone, from the crowd, He put His fingers to his ears, and spat there, and had** of his tongue, He looked to the heavens, groaned and says, "Ephphatha" which is, be opened. And at that same time his hearing opened up, and the binds of his tongue were loosened, and he was speaking correctly, and He commanded him that they shall not say of this to anyone. And as much as He was commanding them, even more so they were proclaiming it, and more and more they were astonished and saying, "He has done all things well, for He gives hearing to the deaf and speech to the dumb."

———

* *a mute or speechless person*

** *touched*

MORNING HOUR

The Holy Gospel According to Luke 9:37-44

A G
K G

To our Lord Jesus Christ.

And it had been the next day, while they
were descending there from the mountain,
before Him there became a multitude of people.
And behold one of the men from the people
there cried out and says, "Teacher, I beg You,
look upon my son, for he is my only one,
and behold an evil spirit possesses him,
and suddenly he cries out and beats himself, and
rolls himself and foams, and it rarely departs from
him, having crushed him, and I begged Your
disciples, that they may remove it, and they
were not able." Jesus gave an answer
and says, "O faithless and perverse generation,
until when shall I be with you and submit
to you, bring your son forth here." And
while he was approaching, the demon struck
him and he shook. Jesus repulsed the unclean
spirit and healed the boy, and He gave him to
his father. And all were amazed over the
greatnesses of God.

MORNING HOUR

The Holy Gospel According to John 4:46-54

$\overline{\text{A Tz}}$
$\overline{\text{K Tz}}$

Our Lord Jesus Christ

He came again to Cana of Galilee, where
He made the water wine, and there was
a nobleman, of whom his son was ill and
was residing in Capernaum. As he heard,
that Jesus had come from Judea to
Galilee, he came to Him and begged that He
would come down and heal his son,
because he was close to dying. And He says
to him, "If you do not see signs and
miracles you do not believe." The nobleman
says to Him, "Lord, come down before
my child will have died." Jesus says
to him, "Go, your son is alive." And
the man believed in the words which Jesus
said to him, and he went. And while he
was going down, his servants met him, they
gave him the good news and say, that
the child of his is alive. He was asking
them regarding the time, at which he recovered,
and they say to him.

MORNING HOUR

"Yesterday at the seventh hour* the fever
left him." His father knew for at that time,
of which Jesus said to him that, "Your
son is alive," and he believed and his
entire household. This again was the second
sign that Jesus made, having come from Judea
to Galilee.

* *1:00 p.m.*

---

*Sunday's Hymn of Creation sung with respect to the First Day of the week,
to the Mystery of Creation, and to the Resurrection of Christ.
(In the original Armenian the first letter beginning each verse
spells out the composer's name, "Nerses."
His Holiness Nerses the Graceful Catholicos of the Armenians)*

Senior Chancel

From the beginning the Word having newly created
the heavens of the heavens from nothing, and the
intelligent bodiless joyful army of heavenly angels,
and the tangible four elements in opposition but in
agreement, by which the inexpressible Trinity is
eternally glorified.

Of the thrice Holy one Lordship with one Godly
nature, the light which was uncreated that creates,
He said there be light form, and which
shined upon the first, first day of the week
which was Sunday, by which the inexpressible Trinity is
eternally glorified.

Rabbinically let us explain and recognize the
hidden mystery, that the unseen intelligent
light is visible to pure souls, in the same shined
upon us the first day of the week of the
Holy radiant resurrection, come, those that have
been saved, with the joyful angels, give blessing
to the resurrected one.

Your love, through love You humbled Yourself
and You took bodily form, for our salvation,
with the same body You were crucified and
placed in the tomb of death, today You arose
Godlike and were proclaimed by the angels,
come, those that have been saved, with the
joyful angels, give blessing to the resurrected one.

You appeared to the ones bringing incense,
the greeting of lives filled with joy,
and upon the mountain of Galilee to
the eleven apostles, make us worthy
in the company of them to see You on
the last day, come, those that have
been saved, with the joyful angels, give blessing
to the resurrected one.

MORNING HOUR

Sons of Zion awake, give the good news
to the bride of light, that Your bridegroom
having defeated death through His Lordship,
He comes to crown you with glory, going
forth having been adorned with ornaments,
sing a new song to the resurrected One,
to the fruit of lives for those that are asleep.

Proclamation for Sundays and other Feasts of the Lord

<u>Deacon</u> **Student Chancel**

Let us request in unison with faith from
the Lord that He may make the graces
of His mercy be upon us. May the Lord
almighty give life and have mercy.

Proclamation for Sundays in which the Holy Mother of God
(God-Bearer) is remembered.*

Holy God-Bearer and all of the saints
make advocation to the Father in the
heavens, that having willed it He may
have mercy, and having compassion
He shall give life to those whom He has
made. Our Lord God almighty give
life and have mercy.

<u>Choir</u> **Senior Chancel**

Give life Lord.

(The Gospel is elevated while facing the altar and is then censed on all Sundays except for Sundays of Great Lent, when it is neither elevated nor censed)

Lord have mercy, Lord have mercy, Lord have mercy.

* *Some parishes recite this proclamation for Feasts of the Holy Mother of God. This is a local tradition as it is not in the rubrics, Church Calendar nor the Book of Feasts (Donatzooytz). Only the former is prescribed.*

MORNING HOUR

Prayer for all Sundays

Senior Chancel

To Your most powerful and wonderful *(resurrection*)* Christ our God, the armies of angels bow down in worship, that only You have immortality, You having dwelled in unapproachable light. And we created beings from soil, having become humbled, with fear bow down in worship, we bless and glorify Your Holy and wondrous, and victorious *(resurrection*)*. And in the company of the heavenly armies we offer blessing and glories, with the Father and the Holy Spirit, now and always and unto the eternity of eternities. Amen.

* *The name of the proper season according to the Church Calendar is inserted here. e.g. Birth, Revelation, Coming, Lordship etc...)*

** *Some parishes recite the prayer found on pg. 242 for Feasts of the Holy Mother of God in place of the above prayer. This also is a local tradition as it is not in the rubrics, Church Calendar nor the Book of Feasts (Donatzooytz). Only the above prayer is prescribed.*

Blessed be our Lord Jesus Christ. Amen.

Our Father Who art in heaven, Hallowed be Thy name. Thy kingdom come, Thy will be done on earth as it is in heaven. Give us this day our daily bread. And forgive us our debts, as we forgive our debtors. And lead us not into temptation, but deliver us from evil.

For Thine is the Kingdom, and the power, and the glory forever and ever. Amen.

(The Morning Hour is now complete if the day is a regular Sunday)

MORNING HOUR

*The Ritual of Blessing the Four Corners of the Earth
(Antasdan) as prescribed by the Church Calendar*

Begin Facing East

Proclamation

<u>Deacon</u>
And again in peace let us request of the Lord.

<u>Choir</u>
Lord have mercy.

<u>Deacon</u>
For the sake of peace from above and for the
salvation of our beings, we request of the Lord.

<u>Choir</u>
Lord have mercy.

<u>Deacon</u>
Lord our God be merciful to us according to
Your great mercy, let us all say in unison.

<u>Choir</u>
Lord have mercy. Lord have mercy. Lord have mercy.

<u>Priest</u>
Blessing and glory to the Father and to the Son,
and to the Holy Spirit, now and always and
unto the eternity of eternities.

<u>Choir</u>
Amen. Alleluia, alleluia, alleluia.

<u>Priest</u>
The eastern side of the world shall be blessed
and protected and shall be kept provided for,
and the Patriarchate of the Armenians,
by the sign of this Holy Cross and this Holy Gospel,
and by the grace of this day, in the name of the
Father and of the Son and of the Holy Spirit, now
and always and unto the eternity of eternities.

MORNING HOUR

Procession around facing the West

<u>Choir</u>
Amen. Alleluia, alleluia, alleluia.

<u>Priest</u>
The western side of the world and the kingdom of Christians
shall be blessed and protected and shall be kept provided for,
by the sign of this Holy Cross and this Holy Gospel,
and by the grace of this day, in the name of the
Father and of the Son and of the Holy Spirit, now
and always and unto the eternity of eternities.

Procession around facing the South

<u>Choir</u>
Amen. Alleluia, alleluia, alleluia.

<u>Priest</u>
The southern side of the world and the lands, fields, and crops of this
year shall be blessed and protected and shall be kept provided for,
by the sign of this Holy Cross and this Holy Gospel,
and by the grace of this day, in the name of the
Father and of the Son and of the Holy Spirit, now
and always and unto the eternity of eternities.

Procession around facing the North

<u>Choir</u>
Amen. Alleluia, alleluia, alleluia.

<u>Priest</u>
The northern side of the world, the monasteries, the desert
monasteries of hermit monks, cities, and villages and the people
dwelling in them shall be blessed and protected and shall be kept
provided for, by the sign of this Holy Cross and this Holy Gospel,
and by the grace of this day, in the name of the
Father and of the Son and of the Holy Spirit, now
and always and unto the eternity of eternities.

Procession around facing the Bema and recite the following while turning
<u>Priest</u>
Blessing and glory to the Father and to the Son and to the Holy Spirit
now and always and unto the eternity of eternities. Amen.

MORNING HOUR

Proclamation of the procession and of the Holy Cross

<u>Deacon</u>
Through the Holy Cross let us request of the Lord,
that through it He may save us from sins, and that
He may grant us life by the grace of His mercy.
Almighty Lord our God, give life and have mercy.

Prayer

<u>Priest</u>
Protect us, Christ our God, under the shadow of
Your Holy and revered Cross in peace,
save us from the visible and invisible enemy.
Make us worthy with thanksgiving to glorify
You with the Father and with the Holy Spirit, now
and always and unto the eternity of eternities. Amen.

Blessed be our Lord Jesus Christ. Amen.

Our Father Who art in heaven, Hallowed be Thy name.
Thy kingdom come, Thy will be done on earth as it is in heaven.
Give us this day our daily bread.
And forgive us our debts, as we forgive our debtors.
And lead us not into temptation, but deliver us from evil.
For Thine is the Kingdom, and the power,
and the glory forever and ever. Amen.

For days other than Sunday (Saints days and Fasting days), after the "Thrice Holy" (Soorp Asdvadz) and its proclamation, recite the following Introit Psalm 112:1-9 KJV 113:1-9 in alternating verse. It is not to be chanted for these days.

Senior Chancel

Children serving the Lord, bless the Lord
and bless the Name of the Lord.

The name of the Lord shall be blessed,
from this time forth unto eternity.

MORNING HOUR

From sunrise to the setting of the sun,
the Name of the Lord is blessed.

The Lord is high above all nations
and His glories are above the heavens.

Who is as Lord our God, dwelling in the
heights and He sees the humble in the
heavens and upon the earth.

He raises up the poor from the earth,
and lifts up the afflicted from the garbage dump.

He makes them sit with princes,
with the princes of His people.

He makes the barren woman dwell joyfully
in her house, as a cheerful mother with sons.

Glory to the Father and to the Son and to the Holy Spirit.

Now and always and unto the eternity of eternities. Amen.

MORNING HOUR 321

Senior Chancel

 *The Hymn of the Children Serving the Lord (Mangoonk Sharagan) according to the proper day and tone as instructed by the Church Calendar (Oratzooytz Book) is to be sung at this point. This hymn is sung on Monday through Saturday only after recitation of the previous psalm. It is not sung during the fifty days following Easter, on Feast Days of the Lord, or on Resurrection days. To find the proper hymn we must turn to the Hymnal Book's index under the The Hymn of the Fathers (Hartz Sharagan) headings under the same season and tone as the proper Mangoonk Sharagan, because the index does not list any Mangoonk Sharagans separately. Then we sing the appropriate verses for the day as determined by the particular tone of the day. Note that frequently the Mangoonk Sharagan will be of a different tone than the Hartz Sharagan which is sung on the same day and therefore, will not be found in pages immediately following the day's Hartz Sharagan. (The following are only examples of various **Hymns of the Children Serving the Lord (Mangoonk Sharagan)** for various types of days e.g. Archangels, Prophets, Days of Repentance, Apostles, and Martyrs.) They may not be sung without first consulting the Calendar and Hymnal.*

<u>Holy Archangels</u>
T G
Chosen heavenly flock, which the good-shepherd
has left to the heavens, and He has come in search
of us wanderers, by whom Your number of one hundred
has been completed, You made joyfulness to Your
heavenly beings in the heavens, we request of you to be
advocate to the Lord for the sake of atonement of our sins.

Those who see of the unseen, who shall ponder the
depth of God, those who have descended with the Only
Begotten to serve in administrating, announcers of the
Good News of the birth to the shepherds, and proclamations
of life of the living one to the oil bearing women,
we request of you to be advocate to the Lord for the sake
of atonement of our sins.

Protectors of the world, armies of the Lord all around those
with fear, friends of the nation of mankind, mediators of
death and resurrection, great ones Michael and Gabriel, you
who stand always before the most Holy Trinity, we request of
you to be advocate to the Lord for the sake of atonement of our sins.

Prophets
T G

Today the Church of the heathens* having been delighted rejoices, by celebrating the remembrance of the great patriarch and the father of faith Abraham, children servants of Zion bless the Father of light without being silenced.

Today New Israel having been called to God through the prophets, with joy celebrate the feast of the first shepherds of Israel, with praising the keystone of two symmetrical walls.

Today in the summits of the mountains the home of God has been established, and which always watering from the clouds of the spirit produced by God abundantly flowing with rains, praise the fountain of life, the one Who makes those of thirst drink.

---

* *Heathen is not an offensive term in this case. It means all peoples who are not believers in the God of Israel. The term "Gentiles" could be used but heathen is more precise.*

MORNING HOUR

Repentance Days
A Tz

King of glories receive with Your
love of mankind the morning songs of praise,
and keep Your children servants of the
Church in peace.
You are the seer of humanity from the
heavens to the earth, and giver of mercy
to the nations of man, keep Your children
servants of the Church in peace.
In the company of the seraphim having been
in unison we sing in holy reverence to You,
Lordship of the three Holies with sweetness
spare those which You have made and
keep Your children servants of the
Church in peace.

Apostles
AG

Disciples of Christ, and apostles to all of
the universes, advocate to the Lord for our sake.
Those who took the command to fearlessly proclaim
the Word of life to the world, advocate to
the Lord for our sake.
Those of you who were worthy to openly see the
Son of God in body, advocate to the Lord for
our sake.

MORNING HOUR

Martyrs
A Tz

The torment of Your saints Christ, celebrating today
in the company of the bodiless armies of heavenly
angels, we sing to You unceasingly hymns of praise.
Those who have become naked of the human
weakness of clothing, for faith having burned
with clothing, those having been victorious over
the opponent in war.
Those having been baptized with the flowing
blood of Christ to death, wonders existing with Godliness,
they having been built in elegance of the Holy Kingdom.

Proclamation after the Hymn of the Children
Serving the Lord

Senior Chancel

Deacon
For the sake of peace for the whole world, and
for the establishment of the Holy Church let us
pray to the Lord. Let us all say in unison.

Priest
Lord have mercy. Lord have mercy. Lord have mercy.

MORNING HOUR

*Prayer after the Hymn of the Children
Serving the Lord*

Student Chancel

Priest

You are holy, Lord our God, mighty and having been
glorified, who sits upon the Cherubic* chariots
and light shines upon those You have made.
Illuminate us, Lord, in the hour of this morning,
so that in the dawn of this day, Your compassion
for the love of mankind shall emanate upon us.
Remove from us the deceit of Satan, and crush
his tyranny through prayer and with advocation of
all of the saints. And make these lands fruitful
for the nourishment of Your servants, by whom,
being continually glorified Your most Holy Trinity
is praised, now and always and unto the eternity of
eternities. Amen.

---

*For Salt and Bread (Great Lenten) days, beginning the first Wednesday
of Great Lent through Holy Thursday, recite at this point the Prayer
of Manasseh the King (Der amenagal...) found on page 334, then
recite Psalm 5 (Panitz imotz...) found on page 339. However for all
other Fasting days, recite Psalm 5 only. Then continue on from the
appropriate Hymn of Creation (Ararchagan Yerk) page 344.*

Feasts of the Saints

Senior Chancel
Ps 114:1-9 KJV 115:1-9

I loved that the Lord shall hear the
voice of my prayers, for He descended His
ear upon me, and through all of my days
I called out unto Him.

* *Adjective of the noun Cherubim*

The pangs of death have me surrounded,
and the afflictions of hells* found me.

I found trouble and anguish, and called
upon the Name of the Lord.

O Lord, save my being, our merciful
God be merciful and Lord keep the
children.

I became humble and the Lord gave me life,
return my being to Your rest, for the Lord
helped me.

He saved my being from death, my eyes from tears,
and my feet from stumbling, I shall be pleasing
before the Lord in the land of the living.

<u>Ps115:10-19 KJV 116:10-19</u>

I believed and of that I spoke
I became exceedingly humbled.

I said in my amazement, that all men are false.

What repayment shall I give to the Lord,
in exchange for all that He gave me.

*Hades

MORNING HOUR

I shall receive the cup of salvation, and
shall call upon the Name of the Lord.

I shall give my prayers to the Lord,
before all of His people.

Death of His saints is honorable before the
Lord, O Lord, I am Your servant, servant
and son of Your maid-servant.

You have cut my binds, to You I shall bring
forth an offering of blessing, and I shall call
upon the Name of the Lord.

I shall give my prayers to the Lord, before all
of His people, in the courtyards of the House of
the Lord, and within you Jerusalem.

Ps 116:1-2 KJV 117:1-2

Bless the Lord all nations, praise Him,
all peoples.

His mercy shall become strengthened upon us,
the truth of the Lord will remain unto eternity.

Ps 53:3-9 KJV 54:1-7

God, in Your Name grant me life, and in
Your power make me just.

God, hear my prayers, place Your ear upon the
words of my mouth.

Foreigners rose up over me, and the mighty ones
demanded my being, and they did not regard
You as God before them.

Behold God my helper, and Lord receiver of my soul.

While returning the evil unto my enemies,
destroy them with Your truth.

Of my will I shall offer sacrifices to You,
I shall confess of Your Name, Lord, for it is good.

You saved me from all troubles, and
my eye has seen my enemies.

<u>Ps 85:16b-17 KJV 86:16b-17</u>

Give strength to Your servant,
give life to the son of Your maid,
and make unto me the sign of goodness.

Those that hate me shall see and shall
be ashamed, for You, Lord, helped me
and comforted me.

Glory to the Father and to the Son and to the Holy Spirit.

Now and always and unto the eternity of eternities. Amen.

---

* *Sing the Hymn of Creation (Ararchagan Yerk) for the appropriate day of the week beginning on page 344 then turn back to page 329 and recite the following Petition if it is a Saint's Day. If it is a Fasting Day then continue on from the Hymn of Creation.*

MORNING HOUR

Petition for Feasts of the Saints

Senior Chancel

(Performed on Mondays, Tuesdays, Thursdays, and Saturdays only)

<u>Priest</u>
Christ our God, for the sake of Your revered Holy Cross grant us Your peace Lord.

<u>Choir</u>
Grant us Lord.

<u>Priest</u>
For the sake of the holy God-Bearer, and for John the Forerunner, and for Saint Stephen the first martyr, grant us Your peace Lord.

<u>Choir</u>
Grant us Lord.

<u>Priest</u>
For the sake of Your holy apostles, prophets, doctors of the Church, martyrs, patriarchs, hermits, virgins, hermetic monks, and the heavenly angelic armies, grant us Your peace Lord.

<u>Choir</u>
Grant us Lord.

<u>Priest</u>
And for the sake of our previous illuminators Thaddeus and Bartholomew, and for Saints Jameses the happy apostles, and for Saint Gregory our illuminator, and for Saints: *(James the Patriarch of Nisibis, Marouge the hermit, Bishop Meletius, and George the captain.)* With advocation, remembrance, and prayers of the saints *(* insert name)* whose remembrance is today, gift Your peace and great mercy unto us Lord, lover of mankind.

* Insert the name of the appropriate Saint who is being remembered on this day.

MORNING HOUR

Proclamation

Student Chancel

Deacon

Through the holy hermits let us request
of the Lord, those who defeated the evil ones,
endured oppressions, and became worthy of
the bright and heavenly unfading crowns.
Through their prayers and advocation may
You be merciful to us. Almighty Lord
our God, give life and have mercy.

---

*Prayer for Feasts of the Apostles, Prophets, Church Fathers,
and Doctors of the Church (Vartabeds).
(Performed Monday, Tuesday, Thursday, and Saturday only)*

Senior Chancel

Priest

You Who chose and received Your fortunate
witness *(* insert name)*, Christ our God, and
You made them share in Your voluntary tortures.
Now we have as advocate to You, those who are
here and those throughout the entire world that
may be saints.

---

* *(Insert the name of the appropriate Apostle, Prophet, Church Father, or Doctor of the Church who is being remembered on this day).*

MORNING HOUR

So that by their prayers and advocation
You may make our conduct in life peaceful,
by serving us from the visible and invisible
enemy. Grace unto us, Lord, to live according
to their example and seal our death with the
orthodox confession in hope of lives unto eternities.
And that we shall become worthy to enter the
heavenly tents of light, and to inherit Your
kingdom which has been prepared from the
beginning of the world for Your saints. And in their
company by giving thanks we may glorify You
with the Father and with the Holy Spirit now and
always and unto the eternity of eternities. Amen.

Prayer for Feasts Days of Martyrs, Hermits, and Virgins
(Performed Monday, Tuesday, Thursday, and Saturday only)

Senior Chancel

Priest

Crowner of saints, Christ, You Who crown
Your saints, and does the wills of those who
have fear in You and You look with love and
gentleness upon those whom You have made.

Hear us from Your holiness in the heavens,
with the advocation of the holy God-Bearer,
and with the prayers of all of Your saints,
and of those whose remembrance is today.
Hear us, Lord, and have mercy, pardon,
atone and forgive our sins. Make us worthy
with thanksgiving to glorify You with
the Father and with the Holy Spirit,
now and always and unto the eternity
of eternities. Amen.

The Recitation of Sargavak Vartabed

The real first name of this 12th century theologian remains unknown. He was both an ordained Deacon "Sargavak" and was conferred with the degree Doctor of the Church "Vartabed." It was common for many Vartabeds not to be ordained as Priests, but it was imperative that they be ordained Deacons so they would be able to read and to preach the Holy Gospel.

Student Chancel

Deacon
Remember, Lord, Your ministers, our parents,
our teachers, our brothers, our friends, those
that feed us, those that have made vows,
travelers, those who give rest, those who are
laborers, those who are confessors and those
repentant, those who are forced captives,
those who are ill, those who are oppressed,
those who are princes, those who are doers of evil,
those who are doers of kindness, those who are enemies,
those who are hateful and those who have joined us
through faith.

Senior Chancel

Priest
Remember Lord and have mercy.

MORNING HOUR

<u>Priest</u>
Kind and abundantly merciful God,
with Your unforgetting knowledge and
unlimited love for mankind, remember all
of those who have faith in You, and have
mercy upon all. Help and save each one
from dangers and temptations. Make us
worthy with thanksgiving to glorify the
Father and the Son and the Holy Spirit,
now and always and unto the eternity
of eternities. Amen.

Blessed be our Lord Jesus Christ. Amen.

Our Father Who art in heaven, Hallowed be Thy name. Thy kingdom come, Thy will be done on earth as it is in heaven. Give us this day our daily bread. And forgive us our debts, as we forgive our debtors. And lead us not into temptation, but deliver us from evil.

For Thine is the Kingdom, and the power,
and the glory forever and ever. Amen.

(The Morning Hour is now complete if the day was a Saint's Day)

MORNING HOUR

Prayer of King Manasseh

By current practice this is recited only for Salt and Bread Days (Weekdays during the Fast of Great Lent). In older traditions it was recited throughout the year.

Student Chancel
Lord almighty God of Abraham, Isaac, Jacob
and of their just descendants, almighty Lord,
forgive my sins.

Who made the heavens and the earth,
and all of their ornaments,
almighty Lord, forgive my sins.

Who bound the sea by the order of Your Word,
You closed the depths, You sealed it by Your
fearful and glorified Holy Name,
almighty Lord, forgive my sins.

Which everything becomes shaken and trembles
at the fearful power of Your faces,
almighty Lord, forgive my sins.

The magnificence of Your holy glories is
unlimited, the anger of Your threats upon the
sinners is severe, the mercies of Your good news
are immeasurable and incomprehensible,
almighty Lord, forgive my sins.

You Lord, having been raised on high, compassionate,
patient, abundantly merciful, and You make repentance
over the evils of men, almighty Lord, forgive my sins.

You God, did not put in place repentance
for the sake of the just, for Abraham, for
Isaac and for Jacob, those who have not
sinned against You, almighty Lord, forgive my sins.

But You put in place repentance for
my sake of being a sinner, for I have
sinned more than the sands of the sea,
and my unrighteousness has multiplied,
almighty Lord, forgive my sins.

MORNING HOUR

I am unworthy to look upon and see the
heights of the heavens, from the multitudes of
my unrighteousness, almighty Lord, forgive my sins.

I have become bent down from the constraint
of my iron bindings, and rest does not exist
for me, almighty Lord, forgive my sins.

I caused You to anger passionately, and I
did evil before You, I erected idols and multiplied
the wrath, almighty Lord, forgive my sins.

And now, Lord, I bow the knee of my heart,
and I request of Your gentleness,
almighty Lord, forgive my sins.

I sinned, Lord, I sinned, and I know of
my unrighteousness, almighty Lord, forgive my sins.

I pray and request of You, forgive me, Lord,
forgive me, and do not destroy me according
to my unrighteousness, almighty Lord, forgive my sins.

Lord do not be angry at me unto eternity, and do not
remember my evil acts, and do not condemn me with those
who have descended with evilness into the inner parts of the
earth, almighty Lord, forgive my sins.

For You, God, You are God of those who repent,
and show to me Your goodness, for I am unworthy,
almighty Lord, forgive my sins.

Give me life according to Your many mercies,
and I shall bless You all of the days of my life,
almighty Lord, forgive my sins.

All of the angels of the heavens bless You, Lord,
and glories are Yours unto the eternities. Amen.

Glory to the Father and to the Son and to the
Holy Spirit.

Now and always and unto the eternity of eternities. Amen.

I pray and request from You, Lord, unto me forgive my sins.

Abundantly merciful, Lord, have mercy upon me.

God, atone me this sinner from sins and give me life.

God my maker and hope, have compassion upon
me this servant which has sinned, and have mercy
upon me this extensive sinner.

Most blessed holy woman, and ever virgin Mary
the God-Bearer, advocate to the Lord for my sake,
this sinner.

MORNING HOUR

All saints of God, advocate to the Father in
the heavens for the sake of us sinners.

Christ Son of God Who is unvengeful, receive our
prayers, for in You our beings have taken refuge.

Victorious through strength is Your Holy and life giving
and revered cross, Lord protect us.

Lord, send Your angel of peace, which having
come shall keep us undisturbed in the day and
in the night. And with Your love of humanity
remember us, Lord, remember us, at which time
You come with Your kingdom, and have mercy
upon us.

Proclamation by Hovhan Mantagouni (478-490 A.D.)

This continues for Salt and Bread Days
(Weekdays during the Fast of Great Lent).

(This proclamation in some local traditions is read by the deacon only,
not by a priest, during the Divine Liturgy when granting forgiveness to
the celebrant after he confesses his sins. There is no rubric for this.
It is a very new tradition having begun circa 1995.)

Student Chancel

Deacon

Having come in confession of repentance,
may we place upon our hearts with faith,
the hope in the only begotten Son of God,
requesting from Him the atonement
and the forgiveness of our offences.

Because He Himself is the provider God
eternal, Who came by the will of the
Father to save those who He had made, and
He declared He Himself to be: atoner for sinners,
hope for those repenting, by gracing rest
to those who labor, by receiving those
who are heavy burdened and weary with sins
unto repentance for atonement. Now come
everyone, with humbled beings, with
broken hearts, may we fall down and
cry before the Lord our maker, that through
His kindness He may pass, away from us,
the wrath of punishment for our offences.
Almighty Lord our God, give life and have mercy.

Prayer

Senior Chancel

<u>Priest</u>
Lord God of our salvation, You Who are
merciful and compassionate, patient, abundantly
merciful and You make repentance over the
evils of men, which You do not will death
to the sinner,

MORNING HOUR

but for his turning from evil paths
and turning to life. You Lord, with
Your abundant mercy comfort Your servants,
and give to them opportunity for repentance.
Reconcile with Your love of humanity, and
make them members of Your Holy Church. In
order that those having been healed in spirit,
through confession and repentance they may
enter into Your Holy Church. And in the company
of Your people, to You they may offer up blessings
and glories to the Father and to the Son, and to the
Holy Spirit, now and always and unto the
eternity of eternities. Amen.

---

*Psalms after the Hymn of the
Children Serving the Lord (Mangoonk Sharagan).*

*These are recited for all types of fasting days both Salt and Bread Days
(Weekdays during the Fast of Great Lent)
and Ordinary Fasting Days.*

Senior Chancel

Ps 5:2-13 KJV 5:1-12

Give ear to my words, Lord, and understand
my cry.

Look unto the voice of my prayers,
my King and my God.

MORNING HOUR

I pray to You, Lord, during the mornings You
shall hear my voice, during the mornings I shall
be prepared to appear before You.

Not that You God wills unrighteousness, evil ones
do not dwell in You, the unlawful shall not
dwell before Your eyes.

You hated those who perform deeds of unrighteousness,
You destroy all those who speak evil lies.

Lord, You make the blood shedding and deceitful man
impure, but I, according to Your multitude of mercies
may enter into Your house, I shall bow down in
worship in Your Holy Temple with Your fear.

Lord, lead me to Your justice, for the sake of
my enemies make straight Your paths before me.

For truth does not exist in their mouths, and
their hearts have become vain.

MORNING HOUR

Their throats are open as a grave, by
their tongues they became deceivers.

Judge them, God, that they may fall
by the counsels of their hearts, according to
the multitude of their wickedness, cast them
away, for they made You bitter.

All of those who have hoped in You shall
become joyful, they shall rejoice unto eternity,
and You shall dwell in them.

The beloved of Your name shall boast in You,
for You shall bless the just, Lord, with Your
pleasure You crowned them as armor.

<u>Ps 89:14-17 KJV 90:14-17</u>

In the morning we were filled with
Your mercy, we rejoiced and became
glad all of the days of our lives.

We became glad in return for the days
in which You made us humble, and for
the years in which we have seen suffering.

Look, Lord, upon Your servants and
upon the works of Your hands,
lead their sons, let the light of the
Lord be upon us.

Make the works of our hands straight unto us,
Lord, and make the works of our hands
successful for us.

MORNING HOUR

Ps. 129:2-8 KJV 130:1-8

From the depths I cried out to You, Lord, Lord,
hear my voice.

May Your ears be hearing the voice of my prayers.

That You examine my injustices, Lord, Lord,
but who can stand before You, for
from You is atonement.

For Your Name's sake I patiently awaited,
Lord, my being awaits patiently for Your Word,
my being hoped in the Lord.

More than watchmen from the morning
until the evening, more than watchmen of the
morning, Israel hoped in the Lord.

From the Lord mercy is abundant,
from Him is salvation, and He saved
Israel from all their oppressions.

MORNING HOUR

<u>Ps 142:8-12　KJV 143:8-12</u>

Make Your morning mercies audible to me,
for Lord I hoped in You.

Show me the path to which I should go,
for to you Lord, I lifted up my being.

Save me from my enemies, Lord,
for I made You my refuge.

Teach me to do Your wills,
for You are my God.

Your good spirit shall lead me into
upright land.

For the sake of Your Name, Lord, may You give me life,
with Your righteousness may You take my being
out of difficulty.

With Your mercy exterminate my enemies, and
destroy the oppressors of my being, for I am
Your servant.

<u>Ps 53:3-9 KJV 54:1-7</u>

God, in Your Name grant me life, and in
Your power make me just.

God, hear my prayers, place Your ear upon the
words of my mouth.

Foreigners rose up over me, and the mighty ones
demanded my being, and they did not regard
You as God before them.

MORNING HOUR

Behold God my helper, and Lord receiver of my soul.

While returning the evil unto my enemies,
destroy them with Your truth.

Of my will I shall offer sacrifices to You,
I shall confess of Your name, Lord, for it is good.

You saved me from all troubles, and
my eye has seen my enemies.

Of my will I shall offer sacrifices to You,
I shall confess of Your Name, Lord, for it is good.

You saved me from all troubles, and
my eye has seen my enemies.

Glory to the Father and to the Son and to the Holy Spirit.

Now and always and unto the eternity of eternities. Amen.

The following Hymns of Creation are sung on the appropriate day of the week, Monday through Saturday only. They were written by St. Nerses with respect to God's Creation of the Universe in the Seven Days. (Throughout the Monday through Saturday hymns, each verse begins with a successive letter of the Armenian alphabet.)

Senior Chancel

Monday's Hymn

(With respect to the Second Day of Creation and to the Heavenly Armies.)

The command of the Word of the Maker at the beginning of the second day, separated the waters from the waters and contained them with the firmament, through which He partitioned this world of earthly beings from the fiery angels, in the same company the sons of light, give blessing to the triad of light.

MORNING HOUR

The assembly of the multi eyed cherubim
and of the thrice holy seraphim, uncreated thrones
of the Godliness of the Trinity of the same existence,
be advocate to the Lord for the sake of
children servants of the Church,
in the same company the sons of light, give blessing
to the triad of light.

Supreme princedoms and always unchangeable
Lordship, unconquerable holy powers
glorification to the maker, pray to the
merciful Lord to not make unseen
the works of the hands,
in the same company the sons of light, give blessing
to the triad of light.

The ranks of the bodiless heavenly beings
governments, archangels of the heights, fiery souls
and ministering servants, armies of angels,
petition to the Lord of Lords for the sake
of earthly men, in the same company the sons of light,
give blessing to the triad of light.

The heavenly ranks of above
Your angels shall bless, they will
become sweet to You, being compassionate
which for the sake of the petitions of our
voice, and which You shall give us
guardians from this time forth until the end,
in the same company the sons of light, give blessing
to the triad of light.

Of powers and Lordships, princedoms and
governments, and through the requests of all
those who are named in the heavens,
Christ receive us with gladness in the day of
death and resurrection, to bless You in their
company with spirit, with the glorification
of the Father.

MORNING HOUR 347

Tuesday's Hymn

(With respect to the Third Day of Creation, to the Third Age, and to John the Baptist)

The Word that exists Who with the Father
is co-creator and equal in power, in the
third day He divided the waters, the vegetation
and plants spring forth, but in the third age
again of the waters flood He dried up, Noah
through his ark lived, the species of animals
increased, give blessing to the inexpressible
light of the Father and to the Son and to the
Holy Spirit.

Together He planted trees of the earth having senses
and plants having intelligence, the flood
of sins having diminished, the ranks of the just
having multiplied, and from whom, the great one,
from the births of women, mediator of graces and
the laws, give blessing to the inexpressible
light of the Father and to the Son and to the
Holy Spirit.

Of the King of the heavens, soldier of the
kingdom, bearer of good news, request
to place in our heart exits from this
valley of sadness, to the place of the
Lord's which He has vowed and has been
promised to the sons of man,
give blessing to the inexpressible
light of the Father and to the Son and to the
Holy Spirit.

MORNING HOUR

To the heir of the Father, minister
and worshipper from the womb,
forerunner and baptist to He Who
is atoner for our sins, be advocate
to the same compassionate One to erase
the written record of our offences,
give blessing to the inexpressible
light of the Father and to the Son and to the
Holy Spirit.

From the Father You shined forth light,
to our dying nature You gave life,
You sent the Forerunner Saint John
preaching of life, of the same through whose
request, almighty receive our requests,
give blessing to the inexpressible
light of the Father and to the Son and to the
Holy Spirit.

Enlightened path to the heavens arose,
for the earthen holy angel, make us
worthy for the same narrow and straight
road, that being followers of the same,
of Your Father in the abode above,
and let us sing in the company of
the happy sons of light, to You
songs of glories.

MORNING HOUR 349

Wednesday's Hymn

(With respect to the Fourth Day of Creation, to the Fourth Age, and to the Annunciation to the God-Bearer)

And the nonexistent darkness was dispersed in
the initial first day, that shining light
in the fourth day having gathered into solar
matter,* the moon having been created into a
type of light and clusters of stars having been
arranged, by which the Creator of beings
is blessed by rational ministers.

The mystery which had been hidden was
made known in the fourth age through
Isaac, again in the fourth day the angel
gave the good news to the virgin, that the
light which can not be completed, through you in
the body is contained, in whom you were blessed
generations born of the earth, give blessing to the
fruit of the virgin.

Of the virgin of our ancestors the mother Eve
from whom the old Adam becomes indebted,
the sorrowful curses were lifted through your
holy birth Virgin Mary, pray to your Only Begotten
to forgive the sins of their sons, in whom you were blessed
generations born of the earth, give blessing to the
fruit of the virgin.

---

* *This describes the physics of subatomic particles and energy as theorized by Einstein in his famous equation $E=MC^2$ one thousand years later. If there was a "Big Bang" during creation this would not oppose the theology of creation as understood by the Armenian Church.*

The bride having been presented from
the earth to the heavens, in which
we raise up our spirits to you, in the
day of your hearing the good news,
request to be for us to hear, the voice
of the good news of your only begotten,
that, Come! those blessed of my Father,
in whom you were blessed generations born
of the earth, give blessing to the
fruit of the virgin.

With voice to You Lord we request
and we fall before You, with requests
of the God-Bearer, extinguish from
within us the flame of the furnace,
with tears give erasure of our sins
and to renew us again,
in whom you were blessed generations born
of the earth, give blessing to the
fruit of the virgin.

Helmsman and master shipbuilder,
You passed through the trackless sea of
lives, raise us up in the company of Peter
from the waves of the sea of sins, through
the requests of Your uppermost pure mother.

MORNING HOUR

Thursday's Hymn

*(With respect to the Fifth Day of Creation, to the Fifth Age,
and to the Holy Apostles of Christ)*

The Word having radiated from the Father
is commanded in the fifth day, springing up
from the waters species of reptiles and winged
creatures of the air, but in the fifth age old
Israel was baptized in the cloud and in the sea,
let us give honor and glories to the uncreated
Word, conductor of wonders.

Cleanly of the example of apostles of Christ, who
were called from the Tiberian Sea to the heavenlies,
they passed through the worldly sea and in
the spirit they were baptized,
let us give honor and glories to the uncreated
Word, conductor of wonders.

To the infinite joys to the pure weddings,
the Father of glories sent You giving invitation
to the sorrowful, to the holy weddings
request that, for us to be partners in
Your company, let us give honor and glories
to the uncreated Word, conductor of wonders.

MORNING HOUR

Regenerator of the universes in the
offences of the forefather, You were
adorned with new feathers, the churches
of the gentiles,* request to the same
compassionate One to regenerate us from
the sins of old, let us give honor and glories
to the uncreated Word, conductor of wonders.

Constructor of all beings, of all creatures,
from inexistence, You the same built
the Church, the rock upon the rock of
the Word, through having placed the
foundations in the New Zion, in the same, join
us through building, let us give honor and glories
to the uncreated Word, conductor of wonders.

The city having been built by You Jesus
became joyful with the flowing of rivers,
from Whom brooks of grace flow, the souls
of man are watered, and make us drink
from the water of lives, through the
request of the cupbearers of the spirit,
for this Your intelligent land is fruit bearing
for Your glories.

---

* Heathen is not an offensive term in this case. It means all peoples who are not believers in the God of Israel. The term "Gentiles" could be used but heathen is more precise.

MORNING HOUR 353

Friday's Hymn

(With respect to the Sixth Day of Creation, to the Sixth Age, and to the Crucifixion of Christ)

Not having tolerated, with the nature of good,
to have only the inexpressible good, also the
man having been created in His image in the
morning of the sixth day, and in the third
hour He gave the one born of the rib as helper to
the one born of the earth, whom He placed
in paradise to enjoy, but to prohibit of the
fruit of death.

Having become silent beside the judge, after
the offences of the old Adam, having put
the woman as the cause for the deception,
and the woman put the serpent as betrayer,
through whom this earth was cursed, thorn
and thistle grew in it, the sentence of
death was given to man, to return to
earth from where he was created.

The Father of glories was hurrying to erase
the written record of the debts of our offences,
by whom the compassionate Son was clothed in
the body of sin in the sixth age, through the
pleasure of the Father, He willingly
came to death of the cross on Friday,
the Lamb was sacrificed on the old
Passover, instead of the original lambs.

Through the path of light of the
commandment, the road of justice,
through Your being raised upon the cross,
You raised us into the heavens, through Your
unspeakable humility and Your voluntary
crucifixion, be reconciled with us
Lord with compassion and forgive the sins
with mercy.

Your frightfulness to the seraphim and terror
to the cherubim, You became humble to
the tortures, to feel suffering in
the nature of man, upon the cross
You killed the sins, and You dismissed the
sentence of death, be reconciled with us
Lord with compassion and forgive the sins
with mercy.

You are supreme of the natures of the
beings and You are the maker of all,
at which time You emanate forth the sign
of Your cross at Your second coming, now
enlighten the worshipers in faith with its light,
that in unison with those who have endured the
cross we bless You unto eternity.

MORNING HOUR

Saturday's Hymn

(With respect to the Seventh Day of Creation, to the Seventh Age, and to the Mystery of Rest)

After the creation of creatures the Lord
rested from work in the seventh day, that
He Who is rest to those who labor and wills
that the beings work, for that reason to us He
gave firm hope through the rest of the Sabbath,
that here to perform the works of God, there is
rest with God.

Rabbinically we are instructed, from the example of
the Lord we were advised, that in the second
creation after fulfillment of the law of the House
of God,* in the seventh day of rest having descended
in body into the grave, He raised up the spirits
of those who had been bound, He prepared for them
rest.

---

* *The Armenian terms "Dnorenootyoon, Dnorinapar" derived from Greek "Oikonomia" give a loose translation for the term "Redeeming Economy" used by theologians. It may also be loosely translated as "Administrative."*

MORNING HOUR

Your dew which having shed from
Your side shall heal those who are at rest,
it shall descent onto the earth of their
death and they shall spring up on the last day,
with Your life giving voice call them into
Your life, and rank them with the just,
to sing unto You glories with the angels.

Our lean nature which holds our lives,
the offences turned into the earth of death, but of
Your immortal death again graced immortality,
those who having been buried with You,
by death in the font through baptism,
raise up with You to Your glories resembling
solar light.

MORNING HOUR

The just shine in the kingdom and
the hermits are in rest, the martyrs
are crowned and lamps of the virgins
are burning, Lord rank with the same,
those who confess You God, do not
be judged by justice but you all shall be
atoned through Your compassion.

Your untold humility in which You were
buried through death, and You raised from
the sons of man those in faith who
have fallen down to You, and raise us up with
justice and with mercy for those that are asleep,
for through the mouth of the living they gave to
You glories with the Father and with the Spirit.

Petition

*(Recited on Days of Fasting after the appropriate
Hymn of Creation)*

<u>**Senior Chancel**</u>
May Your cross be a refuge to us, Lord
Jesus, at which time You appear with glories
of the Father upon the luminous clouds.
At which time we shall not be ashamed having
hoped in You, but with Your great power
we shall become delighted in Your right hand
as the sons of light and sons of the day.

MORNING HOUR

Proclamation

Student Chancel
Deacon
Let us request of the almighty God,
that He shall protect His people in peace
under the shadow of His holy and revered
cross. Almighty Lord our God give life
and have mercy.

Prayer

(For Fasting Days)

Senior Chancel
Priest
Help us, Lord, help us, God our savior,
for the sake of the glories of Your Name,
Lord, save us and atone our sins for the
sake of Your Holy Name. Having fortified
them, keep Your people who have taken
refuge and have hoped in You, in peace
under the shadow of His holy and revered
cross. Save us from the visible and invisible enemy.
Make us worthy with thanksgiving to glorify
You with the Father and with the Holy Spirit, now
and always and unto the eternity of eternities. Amen.

MORNING HOUR

The Recitation of Sargavak Vartabed

The real first name of this 12th century theologian remains unknown. He was both an ordained Deacon "Sargavak" and was conferred with the degree Doctor of the Church "Vartabed." It was common for many Vartabeds not to be ordained as Priests, but it was imperative that they be ordained Deacons so they would be able to read and to preach the Holy Gospel.

Deacon **Student Chancel**

Remember, Lord, Your ministers, our parents,
our teachers, our brothers, our friends, those
that feed us, those that have made vows,
travelers, those who give rest, those who are
laborers, those who are confessors and those
repentant, those who are forced captives,
those who are ill, those who are oppressed,
those who are princes, those who are doers of evil,
those who are doers of kindness, those who are enemies,
those who are hateful and those who have joined us through faith.

Priest **Senior Chancel**

Remember Lord and have mercy.

Kind and abundantly merciful God, with Your unforgetting knowledge and unlimited love for mankind, remember all of those who have faith in You, and have mercy upon all. Help and save each one from dangers and temptations. Make us worthy with thanksgiving to glorify the Father and the Son and the Holy Spirit, now and always and unto the eternity of eternities. Amen.

Blessed be our Lord Jesus Christ. Amen.

Our Father Who art in heaven, Hallowed be Thy name.
Thy kingdom come, Thy will be done on earth as it is in heaven.
Give us this day our daily bread.
And forgive us our debts, as we forgive our debtors.
And lead us not into temptation, but deliver us from evil.

For Thine is the Kingdom, and the power,
and the glory forever and ever. Amen.

(The Morning Hour is now complete if the day was a Fasting Day)

The order of the common prayers of the Armenian Church which are performed during the Sunrise Hour before the Holy Spirit and before the Resurrection of Christ who appeared to his Disciples.

Blessed be our Lord Jesus Christ. Amen.

Our Father Who art in heaven, Hallowed be Thy name. Thy kingdom come, Thy will be done on earth as it is in heaven. Give us this day our daily bread. And forgive us our debts, as we forgive our debtors. And lead us not into temptation, but deliver us from evil.

For Thine is the Kingdom, and the power, and the glory forever and ever. Amen.

Priest
Ps 71:17-19 KJV 72:17-19

May the name of the Lord be blessed
unto eternity, for His name is before the sun.

Deacon *Student Chancel*
In Him all nations of the earth shall be blessed, and all nations shall be fortunate in Him.

Blessed be the Lord God of Israel Who is the only one who does wonders, and blessed be His Holy Name of glories unto eternity, may all of the earth be filled with His glories. Let it be, let it be.

Glory to the Father, and to the Son, and to the Holy Spirit.
Now and always and unto the eternity of eternities. Amen.

Deacon
And again in peace let us request of the Lord. Receive, save, and have mercy.

Priest
Blessing and glory to the Father and to the Son and to the Holy Spirit. Now and always and unto the eternity of eternities. Amen.

SUNRISE HOUR

Hymn of the Sunrise

Senior Chancel

T G

From the east to the west, from the
north and from the south, all nations and races,
in a new blessing bless the maker of all things
made, Who today shined forth the sun light
upon this world.

The churches of the just, those who glorify the
all Holy Trinity, in this morning of light praise the
morning of peace Christ with the Father and the Spirit,
Who shined forth the light of His knowledge unto us.

Sequential Verses (Hortorag)

From the east to the west children of Zion
always bless continually the one Who shines
forth of the light.

Churches of the just and those who glorify,
praise Him Who gave the knowledge of light.

Proclamation

<u>Deacon</u> **Student Chancel**
From the east to the west throughout all
places in Christendom, and where they
cry out to the Name of the Lord in holiness,
may the Lord with their prayers and advocation
be merciful to us. Let us pray to God with vows
that He will save us from sins and from
the desire of the world. May the vows
and requests of our hearts be accepted, and
may He make us worthy of His faiths and
commandments in the company of all His saints.
Almighty Lord our God give life and have mercy.

<u>Choir</u>
Give life Lord.

<u>Deacon</u>
To pass this morning of light and this upcoming day in peace,
with faith let us ask from the Lord.

<u>Choir</u>
Grace unto us Lord.

The angel of peace to be guardian
of our beings. Let us ask from the Lord.

Grace unto us Lord.

For atonement and forgiveness of our offences.
Let us ask from the Lord.

Grace unto us Lord.

For the great Holy Cross and able strength for
assistance of our beings. Let us ask from the Lord.

Grace unto us Lord.

And again in one voice for the sake of
our true and holy faith. Let us pray to the Lord.

Lord have mercy.

SUNRISE HOUR

Let us make ourselves and one another as
the person of the Lord God almighty.

Let us become as Your Person Lord.

Have mercy upon us Lord our God, according to
Your great mercy. Let everyone say in unison.

Lord have mercy. Lord have mercy. Lord have mercy.

Prayer

Senior Chancel
<u>Priest</u>
From the east to the west blessed are You, Lord, for You are a gentle king, and Your Name is fearful throughout all of the world. May our songs of Psalms become sweet before You, may righteousness rise up from Your justice to our weaknesses, and may Your most holy Name be glorified. And may we become worthy to live in Your commandment, and to sing blessing and glories to the Father and to the Son and to the Holy Spirit, now and always and unto the eternity of eternities. Amen.

<u>Priest</u>
Peace unto all.

<u>Choir</u>
And with Your spirit.

<u>Deacon</u>
Let us bow down in worship of God.

<u>Choir</u>
Before You Lord.

<u>Priest</u>
God everlasting, God eternal, You Who shined light into this lower world. Who for our sake You came in measure, immeasurable God, and having poured out You spread the graces of the Holy Spirit upon those whom You have made.
Now and unto the eternities of ages You are praised, most great God, in the company of the Father and most Holy Spirit, now and always and unto the eternity of eternities. Amen.

SUNRISE HOUR

Ps 99:2-5 KJV 100:1-5
(Chanted in Alternation)

Senior Chancel

All lands cry out unto the Lord,
serve unto the Lord with gladness.

Enter before Him with joy,
let us know that He is Lord our God.

He made us and we were not ourselves,
we the people and the flock of sheep of His pasture.

Enter through His gates with confession,
and with blessing to His dwellings.

Be confessing to the Lord, and bless His name.

The Lord is sweet, His mercy is eternal,
from generation to generation is His truth.

Glory to the Father, and to the Son, and to the Holy Spirit.
Now and always and unto the eternity of eternities. Amen.

SUNRISE HOUR

Hymn

Senior Chancel

T̄ Ḡ

Hermits for God, and inheritors of the kingdom of the
heavens, those who have exchanged transitional things,
took the good things that do not pass away,
advocate to the Lord for the sake of the
children servants of the Church.

The magnificent martyrs,
and those beloved from the heavenly Father,
those who were baptized by Your blood in the company
of Christ unto death on the cross,
advocate to the Lord for the sake of the
children servants of the Church.

Desirable martyrs, and dwellings of the spirit
of truths, those who with spirit defeated of
forces and of desire,
advocate to the Lord for the sake of the
children servants of the Church.

SUNRISE HOUR

Those of this world who are praised, and those desirable ones of the above government, those of you who arrived about to fortunateness as much as all of the sons of man, advocate to the Lord for the sake of the children servants of the Church.

Voluntary victims of sacrifice, children with age and perfect with wisdom, those who instead of milk drink the charming wine, advocate to the Lord for the sake of the children servants of the Church.

Sequential Verses (Hortorag)

True hermits witnesses of Christ, advocate
to the Lord for the sake of our beings.

Living martyrs lovers of Christ, those
who were tortured in body for the
sake of the Name of the Lord.

Desirable martyrs those desirable of men,
request of the Holy Spirit to
give us the good things.

Those who are praised of the ranks above,
boasts of the world, request to give
peace to the Church.

Voluntary holy victims of sacrifice, grown
children, and request for us to be
crowned together with You.

SUNRISE HOUR

Petition

We pray be merciful, kind Lord,
we pray be merciful, for the sake of
the prayers of the holy hermits, we pray
be merciful.

Proclamation

Senior Chancel

Deacon
Through the holy hermits let us pray to the Lord,
those who conquered the evil ones, of oppressions
they endured, they became worthy of the bright
and unfading heavenly crowns. With their prayers
and advocation may He have mercy upon us.
Almighty Lord our God, give life and have mercy.

Prayer

Senior Chancel

Priest
Holy are You Lord, and having rested in the
saints, and we with the holy witnesses pray to You,
with the advocation of the holy God-Bearer and
with the prayers of all of Your saints, do not
exclude us from Your mercy, but through
their prayers give us life, for You are abundantly
merciful God, and to You is befitting glory
Lordship and honor, now and always and unto the
eternity of eternities. Amen.

SUNRISE HOUR

The Recitation of Sargavak Vartabed

The real first name of this 12th century theologian remains unknown. He was both an ordained Deacon "Sargavak" and was conferred with the degree Doctor of the Church "Vartabed." It was common for many Vartabeds not to be ordained as Priests, but it was imperative that they be ordained Deacons so they would be able to read and to preach the Holy Gospel.

Student Chancel

<u>Deacon</u>
Remember, Lord, Your ministers, our parents,
our teachers, our brothers, our friends, those
that feed us, those that have made vows,
travelers, those who give rest, those who are
laborers, those who are confessors and those
repentant, those who are forced captives,
those who are ill, those who are oppressed,
those who are princes, those who are doers of evil,
those who are doers of kindness, those who are enemies,
those who are hateful and those who have joined us
through faith.

Senior Chancel

<u>Priest</u>
Remember Lord and have mercy.

Kind and abundantly merciful God,
with Your unforgetting knowledge and
unlimited love for mankind, remember all
of those who have faith in You, and have
mercy upon all. Help and save each one
from dangers and temptations. Make us
worthy with thanksgiving to glorify the
Father and the Son and the Holy Spirit,
now and always and unto the eternity
of eternities. Amen.

SUNRISE HOUR

Psalms
(read in alternation)

Student Chancel

Ps 62:2-12 KJV 63:1-11

God, my God, in the morning I commit to
You, my spirit thirsted for You many times
more than my body.

As a desert and waterless land, where no
road to it exists.

In this manner, in the holies I shall appear to You,
for me to see Your strength and Your glories.

Because for me your mercy is better than
my life, and my lips shall praise You.

In this manner I shall bless you during
my life, and unto Your name I shall
raise up my hands.

As with the oil of fatty abundance my
being shall be filled, with lips of joy my
mouth shall bless You.

For that upon my bed I was remembering You,
throughout the early mornings I was speaking with You.

For You became my helper, in the shadow
of Your wings I shall become joyful.

My being came after you, and Your right hand
received me, they sought my being in vain.

They shall enter into the interior of the
abysses of the earth, they shall be delivered
up to the hands of the sword, and they shall
be portions for foxes.

The king had hope in the Lord, all
those who take oaths by Him shall be
praised, the mouths of those who were
speaking unrighteousness shall be put to silence.

Ps 63:2-11 KJV 64:1-10
Hear, God, my prayers while me praying
to You, from fear of the enemy save my being.

May You hide me from the assemblies
of the evil ones, from the multitude of those
who commit unrighteousness.

Those who sharpened their tongues as swords,
they drew their bows into things of bitterness.

To shoot in secret those who are with an
honest heart, suddenly they will shoot at
them and they shall not be afraid.

Those who strengthened to their beings
the words of evil, they thought to conceal
for me a snare, and they said the Lord does
not see this.

They searched out for unrighteousness, they
became weary while searching.

SUNRISE HOUR

Man shall draw near to the depth of his heart,
and may God be on high.

Arrows of boys became their wounds,
their own tongues weakened them,
and all those who were looking with them
shall become troubled.

Every man became afraid while telling
the works of God, and they understood those
whom He has made.

The just shall be joyful in the Lord, and
shall hope in Him, through Him all those who are
with an honest heart shall be praised.

Glory to the Father, and to the Son, and to the Holy Spirit.
Now and always and unto the eternity of eternities. Amen.

Hymn

Student Chancel

T̄ T̄z

Light, maker of light, the first light,
that having dwelled in the unapproachable light,
heavenly Father, in the ranks of the bright angelic
beings You are blessed, while dawning of light
of this day, shine forth upon our spirits
Your intelligent light.

SUNRISE HOUR

Light, emanation from light, just sun, inexpressible birth Son of the Father, before the sun was, Your Name has been praised with the Father, while dawning of light of this day, shine forth upon our spirits Your intelligent light.

Light, emanation from the Father, source of goodness, that Holy Spirit of God, children servants of the Church praise You in the company of the angels, while dawning of light of this day, shine forth upon our spirits Your intelligent light.

Light, three in union and one inseparable Holy Trinity, we who are born of the earth always glorify You in the company of the heavenly angels, while dawning of light of this day, shine forth upon our spirits Your intelligent light.

Sequential Verses (Hortorag)

God that can not be created,
Father almighty, receive the prayers
of we Your ministers.

From the Father, inexpressible emanation,
just sun, shine forth upon our beings
the light of mercy.

The spirit having emanated from
the Father, source of goodness,
fill us with Your light in this morning.

Three persons and one nature,
one Godliness, Holy Trinity we eternally
confess of You.

SUNRISE HOUR

Petition

<u>Priest</u>
With Your light, Christ, we all have
become enlightened, and in Your holy cross,
savior, we believers took refuge. Hear us,
God our savior, give us Your peace, and make
unto us Your mercy, Lord lover of mankind.

Proclamation

Senior Chancel

<u>Deacon</u>

And again in peace let us request of the Lord.

May we glorify the almighty God, Who
shined the light of the morning upon those whom
He has made, and now may He shine forth
His abundant mercy upon those who glorify
His name. Almighty Lord our God, give life
and have mercy.

SUNRISE HOUR

Prayer

Student Chancel

<u>Priest</u>
Most great almighty God receive
our prayers of the morning and this reasonable
service, to Your incorruptible and heavenly altars.
Shine upon us Your light of justice and of
wisdom, make us sons of light and sons of
the day, so that in this coming day may we
conduct our lives with fear, and
may we complete it without stumbling.
For You are our helper and savior, and to
You is befitting glory, Lordship,
and honor, now and always and unto
the eternity of eternities. Amen.

SUNRISE HOUR

Psalms
(read in alternation)

Senior Chancel

Ps 22:2-6 KJV 23:1-6

The Lord will shepherd me,
and for me, I shall lack nothing.

He made me dwell in a plain of green field,
and by the waters of rest He nourished me.

He returned my being back to me
and led me to paths of justice for
the sake of His name.

And although I may walk in the midst
of the shadows of death, I will not fear from evil,
for You Lord are with me.

Your rod and staff, they will comfort me.

You have prepared the table before me,
before the eyes of my oppressors.

You anointed my head with oil,
as Your pure cup gave drink to me.

Your mercy, Lord, shall come after me all of the
days of my life, for me to dwell in the
House of the Lord throughout long days.

SUNRISE HOUR

Ps 142:8b-12 KJV 143:8b-12

Show me the path to which I should go,
for to you Lord, I lifted up my being.

Save me from my enemies, Lord,
for I made You my refuge.

Teach me to do Your wills,
for You are my God.

Your good spirit shall lead me into
upright land.

For the sake of Your Name, Lord, may You give me life,
with Your righteousness may You take my being
out of difficulty.

With Your mercy exterminate my enemies, and
destroy all the oppressors of my being, for I am
Your servant.

Ps 45:2-12 KJV 46:1-11

God our refuge and strength, helper over
troubles which have found us exceedingly.

For the sake of this we shall not fear during the
agitation of the earth, during the transformation
of the mountains to the heart of the sea.

Their waters roared and became agitated,
mountains became agitated from His strength.

The currents of the rivers make
the city of God joyful, and He made
holy His dwellings, the One elevated on high.

SUNRISE HOUR

God is in their midst, and they shall
not be shaken, God shall help for them
from morning until morning.

The heathens became troubled, and kingdoms
declined, the One elevated on high gave His
voice, and the earth became troubled.

Lord of hosts with us, acceptable is our
God of Jacob.

Come and see the works of God, Who made
signs and skillful art upon the earth.

He struck out the wars from one end
of the earth to the other, the bow
was pulverized, the weapons were broken
into pieces and the shields were burnt with fire.

Proceed and know that I am God, I shall
be elevated on high to the heathens and I shall
be raised on high upon the earth.

The Lord of hosts with us, acceptable
is our God of Jacob.

SUNRISE HOUR

<u>Ps 69:2-6 KJV 70:1-5</u>

God, look at me while helping,
and Lord hurry while assisting me.

May those who were demanding my being
become humiliated and shamed, for those who
were thinking evil towards me, may they
be turned back and be humiliated. *

May those who are shameful be turned back instantly,
who were saying to me woe, woe.

May everyone rejoice and be glad in You,
those who seek You, Lord.

May those who love Your salvation say at all
times, God is great.

I am poor and indigent, God, help me, You are my
helper and savior, and You my Lord, do not delay.

<u>Ps 85:16b-17 KJV 86:16b-17</u>

Give strength to Your servant,
give life to the son of Your maid,
and make unto me the sign of goodness.

Those that hate me shall see and shall
be ashamed, for You, Lord, helped me
and comforted me.

Glory to the Father and to the Son and to the Holy Spirit.

Now and always and unto the eternity of eternities. Amen.

---

* *This is also Ps 34:4 KJV 35:4*

SUNRISE HOUR

Hymn

Senior Chancel

T G

Christ the way and truth and life,
lead our spirits, to ascend from the earth
into the heavens.

Jesus the door of entrances of lives,
and lead us to enter unto Your Father and Spirit,
to always sing the glories.

Sequential Verses (Hortorag)

Christ, the good way and truth, leader of
our spirits from the earth into the heavens.

Jesus the door of entrances of lives,
true God, and lead us to enter
unto Your Father, through the Holy Spirit.

Petition

Priest

Lord, straighten our steps to the paths
of peace, Lord straighten and lead our spirits
and all of the faithful, to walk in the paths
of justice and into the lives of eternities.

SUNRISE HOUR

Proclamation

Student Chancel

<u>Deacon</u>

Let us request of the almighty God,
that having made prosper, He may straighten the
paths of His servants into good and peace.
Almighty Lord our God, give life and have mercy.

Prayer

Senior Chancel

<u>Priest</u>

Leader of lives and gift giver of peace,
Christ our God, lead us to walk in the paths
of Your justice, and to arrive in peace to the
harbor of lives and salvation, through the
grace of Your mercy, for You are our
helper and savior, and to You is befitting
glory, Lordship, and honor, now and always
and unto the eternity of eternities. Amen.

SUNRISE HOUR

Prayer
(For Days of Fasting, in which there is no Feast)

Senior Chancel

Priest

Blessed are You, Lord God our savior, Who
at all times You are with us, and not ever
letting go from Your hand those
who cry out to You with faith and truth.
We pray and request from you, Lord, be
co-traveler of Your servants with Your supervision
by keeping them in peace, and lead us
once more in peace and cheerfulness for each
one to arrive to their dwellings in Christ Jesus
our Lord.

To Whom is befitting glory, Lordship,
and honor, now and always and unto the
eternity of eternities. Amen.

Blessed be our Lord Jesus Christ. Amen.

Our Father Who art in heaven, Hallowed be Thy name. Thy kingdom come, Thy will be done on earth as it is in heaven. Give us this day our daily bread. And forgive us our debts, as we forgive our debtors. And lead us not into temptation, but deliver us from evil.

For Thine is the Kingdom, and the power,
and the glory forever and ever. Amen.

Այսօր զնման Առաքեալքն, զարդարեալք
՚ի շնորհաց Հոգւոյն Սրբոյ։

The order of the common prayers of the Third Hour, which are performed before the Holy Spirit which has descended, and before our foremother Eve, whose eating of the forbidden fruit gave us death, and before Christ through whom we were released of this death by His resurrection.

In practice, the three Midday (Jashoo) Hours should be performed in their entirety at their appropriate times on days in which the Divine Liturgy is not performed in the morning, for example most weekdays and Saturdays. However, if the Divine Liturgy is performed in the morning such as on Sunday or other Feast Days of the Lord, the Midday (Jashoo) Hours are not performed separately but are already incorporated into the Divine Liturgy. On these days only the petition named "The singing of the Psalms" (Uzsaghmosyerkootyoons) page 428, is recited and the Divine Liturgy is begun.

It must be noted that in ancient times the three Midday (Jashoo) Hours were performed separately at their assigned times on days when the Divine Liturgy was performed because the original starting time of the Divine Liturgy was approximately 4:00 p.m. The Divine Liturgy in the ancient era was substantially shorter. In the modern day we do see the remnant of this ancient practice only on Easter Eve "Lighting of the Lamps" (Jrakalooytz) where some parishes perform a very abbreviated version of the three Midday (Jashoo) Hours, followed by a very abbreviated Evening Hour, followed by the Divine Liturgy, then followed by the Communal Banquet. Note that the rubrics actually show the Evening Hour immediately following the Communal Banquet.

Blessed be our Lord Jesus Christ. Amen.

Our Father Who art in heaven, Hallowed be Thy name. Thy kingdom come, Thy will be done on earth as it is in heaven. Give us this day our daily bread. And forgive us our debts, as we forgive our debtors. And lead us not into temptation, but deliver us from evil. For Thine is the Kingdom, and the power, and the glory forever and ever. Amen.

O blessed Holy Spirit true God. Amen.

Psalm 50 (KJV 51) (read in entirety in alternation)
Student Chancel
Have mercy upon me, God, according to Your great mercy,
according to Your many compassions atone my unrighteousness.

Moreover wash me from my unrighteousness,
and from my sins, make me pure.

Of me I know my unrighteousness, and
my sins are before me at all times.

Against You only I have sinned, and I have done evil before You.

As You will be just in Your words, and victorious in Your judging.

With unrighteousness she became pregnant,
and my mother gave birth to me in sin.

You, Lord, loved the truth, with Your wisdom
You revealed to me things unknown and concealed.

Sprinkle me with hyssop and I shall
be purified, wash and I shall become
whiter than snow.

Make me to hear, Lord, the rejoicing and
gladness, and my bones which have
been afflicted will rejoice.

Turn Your faces from my sins, and
atone all of my unrighteousness
from me.

Establish in me a pure heart, God, and in my gut
renew my soul upright.

Do not cast me away, Lord, from Your faces,
and do not take Your Holy Spirit from me.

Give me the joyfulness of Your salvation,
and with the spirit of Your government affirm me.

THIRD HOUR

I shall teach to the unrighteous Your
pathways, and the wicked will turn to You.

Save me from blood, God, God of my salvation,
my tongue will rejoice unto Your justice.

Lord, if You open my lips,
my mouth will sing Your praises.

You had willed that we would present offerings,
but with the burnt sacrifices, in reality, You were
not pleased.

Offering to God, is a humble spirit, the pure
heart and the humble spirit God does not despise.

Make good, Lord, with your will of Zion,
and they will make the fortress walls of Jerusalem.

At that time You shall be pleased with the
offerings of justice, at which time of the vows,
the offerings of bulls will be placed up to Your
table.

Glory to the Father, and to the Son, and to the Holy Spirit.
Now and always and unto the eternity of eternities.
Amen.

If performing the Sixth Hour now return to page 397.
If performing the Ninth Hour now return to page 410.

THIRD HOUR

Hymn of the Third Hour of the Day

(This is sung after Psalm 50 KJV 51. In the original Armenian this is written acrostically with each verse beginning with sequential letters of the Armenian alphabet. The entirety of the acrostic verses are divided, continuing throughout the Sixth and Ninth Hours.

Senior Chancel

T̄ Ḡ

We bless You Father without beginning being of beings from nonexistence, with hands You raised matter from soil and created man in Your likeness, the head descended in humility to the feet because it forgot Your commandment, again we say that, according to the prodigal son, Father I have sinned against You unto the heavens.

To the heavenly beings You were incomprehensible, You became visible to man, You dressed Yourself in the image of the one from the soil, Your image of the unchangeable Father, at the third hour You rose up to the cross for the sake of Adam the first created one, in the company of the thief, Your companion in the crucifixion make us worthy of paradise.

King of kings free-flowing spirit of graces, to those who have gathered in the upper room to the twelve apostles, in tongues of fire You appeared, You sat upon their souls, hear those who are gathered in Your Name and descend upon us in this third hour.

THIRD HOUR

Petition

Priest

Ps 18:13b-14a KJV 19:12b-13a

In every hour my prayers are this, make me
pure from my sins, Lord, and keep Your servants
from the foreigner Lord lover of mankind.

Deacon

And again in peace let us request of the Lord. Receive, save, and have mercy.

Priest

Blessing and glory to the Father and to the Son and to the Holy Spirit. Now and always and unto the eternity of eternities. Amen.

Proclamation

(Composed by Hovhan Mantagouni 478-490 A.D. which is recited during Great Lent)

Senior Chancel

Deacon

In unison let us all be thankful from
God the lover of mankind and from our savior
Jesus Christ. Who freed the nations of man
from the condemnation of curses, and
He took up the sins of the world in this
hour through His cross, and He graced abundantly
the gifts of the Holy Spirit to the fortunate
apostles. Let us request with faith, that
we all may be made participants of those great
and Godly goodness through prayers and
advocation of all the saints, those here
and throughout the entire universes.
Because we have stood according to His wills
in this world with pure conduct and true

THIRD HOUR

virtue, we may receive the portion
and lot of inheritance in the company of
all His saints, in the dwelling place of the
eternal and heavenly altars. Which was
promised to His beloved true God
Jesus Christ, our Lord give life and have mercy.

<u>Choir</u>
Give life Lord.

<u>Deacon</u>
To pass this hour and this upcoming day in peace,
with faith let us ask from the Lord.

<u>Choir</u>
Grace unto us Lord.

The angel of peace to be guardian of our beings. Let us ask from the Lord.

Grace unto us Lord.

For atonement and forgiveness of our offences. Let us ask from the Lord.

Grace unto us Lord.

For the great Holy Cross and able strength for assistance of our beings. Let us ask from the Lord.

Grace unto us Lord.

And again in one voice for the sake of our true and holy faith.
Let us pray to the Lord.

Lord have mercy.

Let us make ourselves and one another as the person of the Lord God almighty.

Let us become as Your Person Lord.

Lord our God be merciful to us, according to Your
great mercy, let us all say in unison.

Lord have mercy. Lord have mercy. Lord have mercy.

THIRD HOUR

Prayer

Student Chancel

<u>Priest</u>

You Who in cherubic and indescribably have rested upon the throne, and always make visitations to those whom You have created. And You Who at this hour pour upon the fortunate apostles the graces of the Holy Spirit. You Lord, at this upcoming hour, and always until the completion of this life, having made impression, unite us with all encouragements of good doing, and make us worthy to be partakers of Your promised good things, our Lord and savior Jesus Christ. You Who are blessed with the Father and with the Holy Spirit, now and always and unto the eternity of eternities. Amen.

Peace unto all.

<u>Choir</u>

And with Your spirit.

<u>Deacon</u>

Let us bow down in worship of God.

<u>Choir</u>

Before You Lord.

<u>Priest</u>

You Who were existing before the eternities, the Word of God, of the same existence of the Father and co-creator with the Holy Spirit.

THIRD HOUR

And whom of the first created
committed the misdeed of the commandment
by tasting of the fruit, with the sign
of Your most victorious cross at
this hour having overcome, You transformed
into life, and our unrighteousness has
been nailed to it, to those who have
hope from You, You promised pure life and renewal of
lives. For those partaking and make us worthy,
our Lord Jesus Christ, You Who is blessed
with the Father and with the Holy Spirit,
now and always and unto the eternity of
eternities, Amen.

Psalm

Student Chancel

Ps   67:19c, 20a, 21a, 19c, 20a, 20b
KJV 68:19a, 19a', 20a, 19a, 19a', 19b

Lord God be blessed, blessed be the Lord daily.

Our God, life giving God, and He shall save us.

Lord God be blessed, blessed be the Lord daily.

He shall lead us God our savior.

THIRD HOUR

Proclamation

Student Chancel

<u>Deacon</u>

Let us request from the Lord with faith
for the sake of travelers, of our fathers and brothers,
those who will go by sea and by land, in
order that He may guide them, may He keep
them in peace, and having led them may the
Lord our God have them arrive to their individual places.
Because He Himself is leader of lives and hope
of salvation, who succeeds for His servants guiding
them in peace to the harbor of lives and of salvation.
Almighty Lord our God, give life and have mercy.

Prayer

Senior Chancel

<u>Priest</u>

Lead us, Lord our God, and teach us to walk
in Your paths with justice, keep our lives in peace,
and our footsteps in Your pleasure. Have the
spiritual and bodily journeys of Your servants arrive,
through Your pure path to Your eternal life,
through grace of Your only begotten our Lord and
savior Jesus Christ, Who became for us leader of
lives and hope of salvation. With whom
You are blessed, Father almighty, together with the
life giving liberator, the Holy Spirit, now
and always and unto the eternity of eternities.
Amen.

THIRD HOUR

The Recitation of Sargavak Vartabed

The real first name of this 12th century theologian remains unknown. He was both an ordained Deacon "Sargavak" and was conferred with the degree Doctor of the Church "Vartabed." It was common for many Vartabeds not to be ordained as Priests, but it was imperative that they be ordained Deacons so they would be able to read and to preach the Holy Gospel.

Student Chancel

Deacon

Remember, Lord, Your ministers, our parents, our teachers, our brothers, our friends, those that feed us, those that have made vows, travelers, those who give rest, those who are laborers, those who are confessors and those repentant, those who are forced captives, those who are ill, those who are oppressed, those who are princes, those who are doers of evil, those who are doers of kindness, those who are enemies, those who are hateful and those who have joined us through faith.

Senior Chancel

Priest

Remember Lord and have mercy.

Kind and abundantly merciful God, with Your unforgetting knowledge and unlimited love for mankind, remember all of those who have faith in You, and have mercy upon all. Help and save each one from dangers and temptations. Make us worthy with thanksgiving to glorify the Father and the Son and the Holy Spirit, now and always and unto the eternity of eternities. Amen.

THIRD HOUR

Psalms
(read in alternation)

Senior Chancel

<u>Ps 22:2-6 KJV 23:1-6</u>

The Lord will shepherd me,
and for me, I shall lack nothing.

He made me dwell in a plain of green field,
and by the waters of rest He nourished me.

He returned my being back to me
and led me to paths of justice for
the sake of His name.

And although I may walk in the midst
of the shadows of death, I will not fear from evil,
for You Lord are with me.

Your rod and staff, they will comfort me.

You have prepared the table before me,
before the eyes of my oppressors.

You anointed my head with oil,
as Your pure cup gave drink to me.

Your mercy, Lord, shall come after me all of the
days of my life, for me to dwell in the
House of the Lord throughout long days.

<u>Ps 142:8b-12 KJV 143:8b-12</u>

Show me the path to which I should go,
for to you Lord, I lifted up my being.

Save me from my enemies, Lord,
for I made You my refuge.

Teach me to do Your wills,
for You are my God.

THIRD HOUR

Your good spirit shall lead me into
upright land.

For the sake of Your Name, Lord, may You give me life,
with Your righteousness may You take my being
out of difficulty.

With Your mercy exterminate my enemies, and
destroy all the oppressors of my being, for I am
Your servant.

Glory to the Father and to the Son and to the Holy Spirit.

Now and always and unto the eternity of eternities. Amen.

Proclamation

Senior Chancel

<u>Deacon</u>

And again in peace let us request of the Lord.

With thanksgiving let us pray to the kind
spirit God, and let us request mercy from Him,
that through His kindness He may pass,
away from us, the wrath of punishment for our offences.
Almighty Lord our God, give life and have mercy.

THIRD HOUR

Prayer

Student Chancel

<u>Priest</u>

Through Your peace Spirit holy true God,
Who is above all intelligence and design, comfort the
beings of Your servants, by accepting our prayers,
that through His kindness He may pass, away from us,
the wrath of punishment for our offences.
Pardon and hear us, atone and forgive our sins,
make us worthy with thanksgiving to glorify You
with the Father and with the only begotten Son,
now and always and unto the eternity of eternities.
Amen.

Blessed be our Lord Jesus Christ. Amen.

Our Father Who art in heaven, Hallowed be Thy name.
Thy kingdom come, Thy will be done on earth as it is in heaven.
Give us this day our daily bread.
And forgive us our debts, as we forgive our debtors.
And lead us not into temptation, but deliver us from evil.

For Thine is the Kingdom, and the power,
and the glory forever and ever. Amen.

The order of the common prayers of the Sixth Hour which are performed before God the Father, and before the torture and crucifixion of the Son of God.

Blessed be our Lord Jesus Christ. Amen.

Our Father Who art in heaven, Hallowed be Thy name. Thy kingdom come, Thy will be done on earth as it is in heaven. Give us this day our daily bread. And forgive us our debts, as we forgive our debtors. And lead us not into temptation, but deliver us from evil.

For Thine is the Kingdom, and the power, and the glory forever and ever. Amen.

Blessed Holy Father true God. Amen.

Psalm 50 KJV 51

(Read entirely in alternation. See page 383-385 for the complete text of this Psalm.)

Student Chancel

Have mercy upon me, God, according to Your great mercy, according to Your many compassions atone my unrighteousness.

Moreover wash me from my unrighteousness, and from my sins, make me pure.

SIXTH HOUR

Hymn of the Sixth Hour

Student Chancel

Light of the sun darkened on the sixth
hour of Friday, He announced that the light
of creation darkened the created light, You
having been hung naked upon the cross
with a veil of shadow they covered Him,
from us reject the weight of the wandering
demon of the mid day.

Weary battle of the evil demon which at this
hour is at war, our spirits having hidden,
it shall be repulsed through the sign of the
holy cross, the ray of Your truth made from
the heavens, fallen lightning bolts having repelled it
it shall be expelled from us, and with Your light
You shall light us up.

In this noon hour of the day, to the elegant
eyes of this body with hidden arrows and
let not pierce from the darkness which is
in secret, encircled around, the armies of angels
shall encamp with us, those who being together with
us through the glorifying of You with the Father.

SIXTH HOUR

Petition

<u>Priest</u>

<u>Psalm 18:13b-14a KJV 19:12b-13a</u>

In every hour my prayers are this, make me pure from my sins, Lord, and keep Your servants from the foreigner Lord lover of mankind.

<u>Deacon</u>

And again in peace let us request of the Lord. Receive, save, and have mercy.

<u>Priest</u>

Blessing and glory to the Father and to the Son and to the Holy Spirit. Now and always and unto the eternity of eternities. Amen.

Proclamation for Great Lent

Student Chancel

<u>Deacon</u>

With awake minds and with undistracted thoughts in unison let us stand in prayer before our Lord and savior Jesus Christ. In faith let us ask from Him for the angel of peace, guardian of our beings, who has come and shall encamp around us, and fearlessly he shall guard us from all fiery arrows of Satan which fly in the day, of things going in the dark, from obstacles of the demon in ordinary days. From whom with precaution by keeping in prayer and with the advocation of all the saints, may God lover of mankind grace unto us to live with virtue unto the salvation of our beings, in honor and in glories of His life giving Name. May we receive the hope of communion

SIXTH HOUR

in the revelation of the only begotten Son
of God, in humbleness becoming similar to
our body, according to the resemblance of the body
of His glories, because this was promised
to His beloved true God, Jesus Christ
our Lord, give life and have mercy.

<u>Choir</u>

Give life Lord.

<u>Deacon</u>

To pass this hour and upcoming day in
peace, with faith let us ask from the Lord.

Grace unto us Lord.

The angel of peace to be guardian
of our beings. Let us ask from the Lord.

Grace unto us Lord.

For atonement and forgiveness of our offences.
Let us ask from the Lord.

Grace unto us Lord.

For the great Holy Cross and able
strength for assistance of our beings.
Let us ask from the Lord.

Grace unto us Lord.

And again in one voice for the sake of
our true and holy faith.
Let us pray to the Lord.

Lord have mercy.

Let us make ourselves and one another as
the person of the Lord God almighty.

Let us become as Your Person Lord.

Lord our God be merciful to us,
according to Your great mercy,
let us all say in unison.

Lord have mercy. Lord have mercy. Lord have mercy.

Prayer

Senior Chancel

<u>Priest</u>

Clothe us, Lord our God, with the
armament of justice, to be powerful and
victorious against satanic wars, and with
the extinguishing of all of his fiery arrows,
may we be doubtless of things going in the
dark, from obstacles of the demon in ordinary days.
And we having been vigilant through
this elegant day, may we stand in virtue
unto the salvation of our beings, to the
honor and to the glories of the Holy Trinity,
now and always and unto the eternity of eternities.
Amen.

Peace unto all.

<u>Choir</u>
And with Your spirit.

<u>Deacon</u>
Let us bow down in worship of God.

<u>Choir</u>
Before You Lord.

<u>Priest</u>
With Your heavenly peace having fortified, protect
our beings. Because You are God of peace,
and besides You we do not know any other,

SIXTH HOUR

and we call upon Your most powerful Name to the
assistance of our beings. Look upon our
bowings down in worship, and teach us to
do the justice of truth. And with satisfaction
let us glorify the Father and the Son and
the Holy Spirit, now and always and unto
the eternity of eternities. Amen.

Psalm 78:8-9 KJV 79:8-9

Senior Chancel

Lord, do not remember our previous sins,
send Your mercy to us quickly, Lord, for
we became greatly impoverished.

Help us, God our savior, for the sake of
the glories of Your Name.

Lord, save us and atone our sins
for the sake of Your Name.

Proclamation

Senior Chancel

Deacon

For the sake of the infirmed and those
afflicted let us pray to Christ our savior,
that He may have mercy according to
His great mercy and that He may
heal the diseases and illnesses

of the spirits and bodies of His
servants, and with perfect health He
may deliver all to eternal and disease
free lives. Who was sent from the Father
for the healing of the nations of mankind,
the only begotten Son of God, our Lord
and savior Jesus Christ give life and have mercy.

Prayer

Student Chancel

Priest

Remove the pains and heal the
illnesses from Your people, Lord our
God, and grace unto all perfect health
through the sign of Your most victorious
cross, by which You uplifted the weakness
of the nations of man, and You condemned the
enemy of our lives and salvation. You are
our life and salvation, kind and abundantly
merciful God, Who only You are able
to forgive sins and expel diseases and illnesses
from us, our wants of necessities are evident to You,
gift giver of good things, gift Your abundant
mercy upon those whom You have made, according
to each individual's needs, by Whom the most
Holy Trinity having been continually glorified is
praised, now and always and unto the
eternity of eternities. Amen.

SIXTH HOUR

The Recitation of Sargavak Vartabed

The real first name of this 12th century theologian remains unknown. He was both an ordained Deacon "Sargavak" and was conferred with the degree Doctor of the Church "Vartabed." It was common for many Vartabeds not to be ordained as Priests, but it was imperative that they be ordained Deacons so they would be able to read and to preach the Holy Gospel.

Student Chancel

Deacon

Remember, Lord, Your ministers, our parents, our teachers, our brothers, our friends, those that feed us, those that have made vows, travelers, those who give rest, those who are laborers, those who are confessors and those repentant, those who are forced captives, those who are ill, those who are oppressed, those who are princes, those who are doers of evil, those who are doers of kindness, those who are enemies, those who are hateful and those who have joined us through faith.

Senior Chancel

Priest

Remember Lord and have mercy.

Kind and abundantly merciful God, with Your unforgetting knowledge and unlimited love for mankind, remember all of those who have faith in You, and have mercy upon all. Help and save each one from dangers and temptations. Make us worthy with thanksgiving to glorify the Father and the Son and the Holy Spirit, now and always and unto the eternity of eternities. Amen.

SIXTH HOUR

Psalms
(Read in alternation)

Student Chancel

Ps 40:2-5 KJV 41:1-4

Fortunate is he who considers the poor and
the impoverished, in the day of evil the Lord saves him.

The Lord saves him and gives him life, He makes him fortunate
upon the earth, and does not deliver him up to the hands
of his enemies.

The Lord is an aid to him in the beds of
their pains, he restores all of his beds from his illness.

I said, Lord, have mercy upon me, heal my being,
I sinned against You.

Ps 90:1-16 KJV 91:1-16

He who dwells in aid of the One on
high, he shall rest under the
shadow of God in the heavens.

He shall say to the Lord, You are my
receiver, God is my refuge, and I hope in Him.

He shall save me from the snare of the
hunter, and from words of trouble.

Into His backbone you will be received,
in the shadow of His wings you shall have hope.

May His truth be as armor around you.

You shall not fear the fright of the night,
nor the arrow which flies in the day.

Nor from things that walk in the dark,
nor from obstacles of the demon at midday.

Thousands shall fall at Your side, and
tens of thousands at Your right hand, which
no one shall come near You.

SIXTH HOUR

But only with Your eyes You shall look,
and You shall see the restitution of the sinners,
because You, Lord, You are my hope.

The One on high made for you a refuge,
no evil shall come near to you, and plague
shall not approach to your dwelling.

He having commanded to His angels for your sake
while keeping you in all your ways.

They received you in their arms, that you
will never strike your foot upon a stone.

You shall walk over serpents and vipers, and
by the foot you shall trample the lion and
the dragon.

Because he hoped in Me and I shall save him,
I shall be a shield to him, for he knew My Name.

He shall cry out to Me, and to him I shall be heard,
and I shall be in him in trouble.

I shall save and glorify him, I shall fill him with
long days and I shall show him My salvation.

Glory to the Father and to the Son and to the Holy Spirit.

Now and always and unto the eternity of eternities. Amen.

SIXTH HOUR

Proclamation

Student Chancel

Deacon

And again in peace let us request of the Lord.

Let us request in faith from the
Father for the sake of atonement of sins
and for forgiveness of offences, for
saving us from sorrows and oppressions,
for descending upon us in mercy and
compassion of the Lord God almighty,
give life and have mercy.

Prayer

Senior Chancel

Priest

Father of compassions and God of all consolations,
You Who console us in all of our troubles,
and now listen to the voice of the requests
of Your servants, by receiving of our prayers,
through Your kindness, pass away from us the wrath
of punishment for our offences. Pardon
and hear us, atone and forgive our sins, make
us worthy with thanksgiving to glorify You with
the Son and with the Holy Spirit, now and
always and unto the eternity of eternities. Amen.

SIXTH HOUR

Blessed be our Lord Jesus Christ. Amen.

Our Father Who art in heaven, Hallowed be Thy name. Thy kingdom come, Thy will be done on earth as it is in heaven. Give us this day our daily bread. And forgive us our debts, as we forgive our debtors. And lead us not into temptation, but deliver us from evil.

For Thine is the Kingdom, and the power, and the glory forever and ever. Amen.

Մեկնէր զնոսա զամենայն գիրս։

The order of the common prayers of the Ninth Hour which are performed before the Son of God, His death, and the giving up of His rational spirit.

Blessed be our Lord Jesus Christ. Amen.

Our Father Who art in heaven, Hallowed be Thy name. Thy kingdom come, Thy will be done on earth as it is in heaven. Give us this day our daily bread. And forgive us our debts, as we forgive our debtors. And lead us not into temptation, but deliver us from evil.

For Thine is the Kingdom, and the power, and the glory forever and ever. Amen.

O blessed Holy Son true God. Amen.

Psalm 50 KJV 51

(Read entirely in alternation. See page 383-385 for the complete text of this Psalm.)

Student Chancel

Have mercy upon me, God, according to Your great mercy, according to Your many compassions atone my unrighteousness.

Moreover wash me from my unrighteousness, and from my sins, make me pure.

NINTH HOUR

Hymn of the Ninth Hour

Senior Chancel

For You having suffered, for three hours
the day of light was darkening, having
shined in the ninth hour in the image of the
fulfillment of the shadow of death, the
magnificent torch of light You gave up the spirit
to the Father, You, companion through the road
direct us to the heavens through Your Holy Spirit.

The deep abysses shook and released the
souls which have been bound, stones were
torn from stone, those who had died
arose from the tombs, elements of the
earth were swinging and the pillars of
the world quaked, we having flocked
to You let us request, that we may be
ranked in the company of the just.

At that time You showed the wonders and
now may You be merciful to us, our natures
having been wasted away, through You became
healed, and grace unto us to be
without pain, instead of Your life-giving
death give us life kind Lord, to You
we request as with the thief,
remember us on the awesome day.

NINTH HOUR

Petition

<u>Priest</u>
<u>Ps 18:13b-14a KJV 19:12b-13a</u>

In every hour my prayers are this, make me pure from my sins, Lord, and keep Your servants from the foreigner Lord lover of mankind.

<u>Deacon</u>

And again in peace let us request of the Lord. Receive, save, and have mercy.

<u>Priest</u>

Blessing and glory to the Father and to the Son and to the Holy Spirit. Now and always and unto the eternity of eternities. Amen.

Proclamation During Great Lent

Senior Chancel

<u>Deacon</u>

With holy heart and firm faith let us stand in unison in prayer before our Lord and savior Jesus Christ, by remembering His very great immeasurable graces, the endurance of the life giving cross, and the pouring out of His liberating blood, and of this same like which at this hour He bore for the sake of us sinners. And we, by bearing this all in mind let us become cleansed from thoughts, words,

and deeds of sins, through the fear of God
let us perfect the holiness of our beings. Let
us not delay to confess our sins to Him
and to request forgiveness of our sins, that we
shall not perish unrepentant into eternal damnation.
But during this time which is in hand, let
us perform good works in these lives, by
having for our example the manners of lives of all
the saints and the victorious martyrs, those who
at once from the beginning were
pleasing to the Lord and to the savior
of all. Through whose prayers
and advocation, may God the lover of
mankind grace unto us His good wills
and benefit for us to always think and
do, and to be found sharing of the unspeakable gifts.
Which He promised to His beloved, true
God Jesus Christ, our Lord give life and
have mercy.

Choir

Give life Lord.

Deacon

To pass this hour and upcoming day in
peace, with faith let us ask from the Lord.

Choir

Grace unto us Lord.

NINTH HOUR

The angel of peace to be guardian
of our beings. Let us ask from the Lord.

Grace unto us Lord.

For atonement and forgiveness of our offences.
Let us ask from the Lord.

Grace unto us Lord.

For the great Holy Cross and able
strength for assistance of our beings.
Let us ask from the Lord.

Grace unto us Lord.

And again in one voice for the sake of
our true and holy faith.
Let us pray to the Lord.

Lord have mercy.

Let us make ourselves and one another as
the person of the Lord God almighty.

Let us become as Your Person Lord.

Lord our God be merciful to us,
according to Your great mercy,
let us all say in unison.

Lord have mercy. Lord have mercy. Lord have mercy.

Prayer

Student Chancel

<u>Priest</u>

Lord of hosts, Who through Your voluntary death in this hour, from death of our sins You gave us life, and You nailed the seal of our damnation upon the cross, and You graced freedom to the nations of mankind from servitude of corruption to freedom of glories through the pouring out of Your holy blood. And now receive our prayers, and make us successful with upright faith and virtuous works to live in this world,

and to be made worthy for the eternal
and heavenly joys in the company of all
Your saints. And to glorify You with thanksgiving
with the Father and the Holy Spirit, now
and always and unto the eternities.

Peace unto all.

Choir

And with Your spirit.

Deacon

Let us bow down in worship of God.

Choir

Before You Lord.

Priest

Abundantly merciful God and establisher
of peace, affirm our beings through Your
peace, by which You have a rank to each
of all of Yours which You have made, by administering
with Your upright command because that
indeed is Your will, for us to remain with peaceful
and spiritual love towards each other, and to wait
with awake minds for the revelation of the only
begotten of God and for our savior Jesus Christ, for Whom
we may be worthy to meet the Lord
in the clouds in the air. May we stand
with cheerful face at Your right hand in the
company of the saints and those who

NINTH HOUR

love Your Holy Name, and may we
inherit that which has been prepared from
the beginning of the world for your saints,
    that being the kingdom.
And in the company of the same,
with thanks let us glorify You with the
Father and most Holy Spirit, now and
always and unto the eternity of eternities.
Amen.

Psalm

(This psalm is from Daniel 3:34, 35, 34 according to the Armenian Church Bible version. KJV lists this in its Apocrypha under the title "Prayer of Azariah" vs. 11, 12, 11. This is found in the "Blessing of the Three Young Men in the Furnace" reference to pg. 219)

Student Chancel

Lord, do not betray us unto the end for the sake of Your Name, do not disperse Your vows, and do not take away Your mercy from us.

For the sake of Your beloved Abraham,
Your servant Isaac, and Your holy Israel.

Lord, do not betray us unto the end for the sake of Your name, do not disperse Your vows, and do not take away Your mercy from us.

NINTH HOUR

Hymn written by Catholicos Nerses the Graceful.
(This hymn is also acrostic being that in the Armenian, the first letter in sequence of each verse spells the name Nerses)

P Tz *Senior Chancel*

Through the request of our forefather Abraham,
Lord receive our prayers, and through the
requests of your servant Sahag* have compassion
upon us, and through the love of the Holy One of Israel
who has seen God, spare us, of the thrice holy by
the three of the same, cleanse the spirit, the minds
and the body.

Proclamation

Deacon *Student Chancel*

Let us pray to Christ our life giving savior, Who voluntarily,
through His crucifixion saved those whom He has
created, and through the pouring out of His blood
He graced forgiveness to those who have hope in Him.
Almighty Lord our God, give life and have mercy.

Prayer

Priest *Senior Chancel*

Having fallen down before You, kind and
abundantly merciful God, we pray with all of our
hearts and we request forgiveness from You, as
You promised to Your servants and You said,
"Everything that which You shall ask for with
faith from the Father in the Name of the Son
shall be given to you."** And now grace unto those
who have faith in You, and fulfill in good our requests,
for in You we have taken refuge. And with
Your abundant mercy, console us in this
life, and having guided us, make us to arrive
to Your unspeakable kingdom of the heavens,
unto the glorification and honor of the all Holy
Trinity, now and always and unto the
eternity of eternities. Amen.

---

* *Isaac in Hebrew*
** *John 16:23*

NINTH HOUR

The Recitation of Sargavak Vartabed

The real first name of this 12th century theologian remains unknown. He was both an ordained Deacon "Sargavak" and was conferred with the degree Doctor of the Church "Vartabed." It was common for many Vartabeds not to be ordained as Priests, but it was imperative that they be ordained Deacons so they would be able to read and to preach the Holy Gospel.

Student Chancel

Deacon

Remember, Lord, Your ministers, our parents, our teachers, our brothers, our friends, those that feed us, those that have made vows, travelers, those who give rest, those who are laborers, those who are confessors and those repentant, those who are forced captives, those who are ill, those who are oppressed, those who are princes, those who are doers of evil, those who are doers of kindness, those who are enemies, those who are hateful and those who have joined us through faith.

Senior Chancel

Priest

Remember Lord and have mercy.

Kind and abundantly merciful God, with Your unforgetting knowledge and unlimited love for mankind, remember all of those who have faith in You, and have mercy upon all. Help and save each one from dangers and temptations. Make us worthy with thanksgiving to glorify the Father and the Son and the Holy Spirit, now and always and unto the eternity of eternities. Amen.

NINTH HOUR

Senior Chancel

Ps 114:1-9 KJV 116:1-8

I loved that the Lord shall hear the
voice of my prayers, for He descended His
ear upon me, and through all of my days
I called out unto Him.

The pangs of death have me surrounded,
and the afflictions of hells* found me.

I found trouble and anguish, and called
upon the Name of the Lord.

O Lord, save my being, our merciful
God be merciful and Lord keep the
children.

I became humble and the Lord gave me life,
return my being to Your rest, for the Lord
helped me.

He saved my being from death, my eyes from tears,
and my feet from stumbling, I shall be pleasing
before the Lord in the land of the living.

Hades

NINTH HOUR

<u>Ps 115:10-19 KJV 116:10-19</u>
I believed and of that I spoke
I became exceedingly humbled.

I said in my amazement, that all men are false.

What repayment shall I give to the Lord,
in exchange for all that He gave me.

I shall receive the cup of salvation, and
shall call upon the Name of the Lord.

I shall give my prayers to the Lord,
before all of His people.

Death of His saints is honorable before the
Lord, O Lord, I am Your servant, servant
and son of Your maid-servant.

You have cut my binds, to You I shall bring
forth an offering of blessing, and I shall call
upon the Name of the Lord.

I shall give my prayers to the Lord, before all
of His people, in the courtyards of the House of
the Lord, and within you Jerusalem.

<u>Ps 116:1-2 KJV 117:1-2</u>

Bless the Lord all nations, praise Him,
all peoples.

His mercy shall become strengthened upon us,
the truth of the Lord will remain unto eternity.

Glory to the Father and to the Son and to the Holy Spirit.

Now and always and unto the eternity of eternities. Amen.

NINTH HOUR

*Hymns of Rest (Hanksdyan Sharagan) for
Feast Days of the Lord and Days of Martyrs*

Senior Chancel

A Tz

Who by creating according to Your likeness
You honored us, and now receive those sleeping
in You with upright faith, according to Your great mercy.

Who through the graces of the Holy Spirit You
illuminated, lover of mankind in their remembrance
receive the souls, according to Your great mercy.

Those who partook Lord of Your body and blood,
make rest their souls in the company of Your
saints Christ God, for they are the prices of
Your holy blood.

Only you blessed amongst women,
mother and ever virgin and intelligible light,
bearer, unto our maker we unceasingly praise.

NINTH HOUR

A G

God maker and creator of the nations
of mankind do not abandon those of
ours who are sleeping but make rest
their souls in the company of Your saints.

O only begotten Son, resurrection
of the universes, do not abandon those of
ours who are sleeping but make rest
their souls in the company of Your saints.

Of the spirit, having been protected only through you
holy woman, you gave birth to God the Word
of the inexpressible birth for the Father,
and revealed the union of the Trinity.

P Tz

That You Lord called unto You all
of the universes, receive those of ours who
are sleeping in the bosom of the
forefather Abraham, merciful Lord and
kind savior.

You giver God Who ruled as king, forgive the
sins of those of ours who are sleeping,
capable of everything and mighty,
merciful Lord and kind savior.

You Who is giver of light to the universes,
and illuminate those of ours who are sleeping,
with the blissful light of angelic joy,
merciful Lord and kind savior.

NINTH HOUR

Our hope and assurance, mother of the Lord
and holy virgin, which the Godly flame did
not burn your holy womb, advocate to
the Lord for the sake of our salvation.

$\overline{\text{P G}}$

You Who are the Son and God the Word,
equal in existence with the Father, lover of
mankind unto You we call upon, make rest to the souls
of those of ours who are sleeping in the company of
Your saints.

You Who descended from the heavens for our sake,
You took away the first offences of Adam,
with our nature You ascended upon the
cross with spotless hands, make rest to the souls
of those of ours who are sleeping in the company of
Your saints.

You Who dissolved the ruling power of death
Christ through Your voluntary death,
we wish for the prayers of
reason having poured out before You,
make rest to the souls of those of ours who are
sleeping in the company of Your saints.

Ladylord pure mother of the Lord and virgin
Mary, on the earth we saw you in the cherubic
throne, advocate to the Lord for the sake of
our salvation.

NINTH HOUR

K̄ Tz

Compassionate Father Whom You had compassion
unto the nations of the sons of man, You
sent Your only begotten in salvation,
remember the souls of those of ours who are sleeping,
and make rest to them in the company of Your saints.

O only begotten Son You Who rose from
the dead, You promised to us resurrection
in Your second coming,
remember the souls of those of ours who are sleeping,
and make rest to them in the company of Your saints.

O true spirit consoler of mourners, through the
prayers of the holy God-Bearer and all of Your saints,
remember the souls of those of ours who are sleeping,
and make rest to them in the company of Your saints.

Holy God-Bearer hurry in advocation for us,
receive while saving the people from sins and
from corruption.

NINTH HOUR

K G

In the bosom of the Father without beginning the Word
having become humbled, You took human bodily form
from the virgin for the sake of our salvation,
we pray to You, Lord remember those of ours who are
sleeping with upright faith at which time You come with
Your kingdom.

Son of God unrevengeful with gentleness, You were pleased
to take up the sins of the world through Your crucifixion,
we pray to You, Lord remember those of ours who are
sleeping with upright faith at which time You come with
Your kingdom.

Through Your voluntary death You dissolved
the pangs of death, and You atoner made worthy
for forgiveness of offences through Your blood,
we pray to You, Lord remember those of ours who are
sleeping with upright faith at which time You come with
Your kingdom.

You Who in place of the dying of sinners
took to Yourself, by descending into the hells*
You saved the captives from the sinful prison,
we pray to You, Lord remember those of ours who are
sleeping with upright faith at which time You come with
Your kingdom.

We praise Your immeasurable love
for humanity, which of the third day
having resurrected You gifted life to the world,
we pray to You, Lord remember those of ours who are
sleeping with upright faith at which time You come with
Your kingdom.

Clean and pure, virgin after the birth, who
through body gave birth to the One Who releases the
binds of sin, be advocate for the sake of our
sins, to save us from the threats of Gehenna.

* *Hades*

NINTH HOUR

T Tz

Lord at which time Your horn of the
second coming is blown, at which
time those whom You have made, shake
from having been frightened from Your terror,
we pray to You savior, and make rest
to those of ours who are sleeping with
Your saints, Whom only You are
abundantly merciful.

Lord into Your terrifying emanating light,
the ranks of the virtuous rejoice upon
the bright angelic cloud,
we pray to You savior, and make rest
to those of ours who are sleeping with
Your saints, Whom only You are
abundantly merciful.

Unvengeful abundantly compassionate merciful
Lord, do not neglect those who have sinned,
on the tremendous day, Whom only You are
abundantly merciful.

You Who descended from the heavens and
You took bodily form from the holy
virgin through Your inexpressible birth,
and do not neglect me, but guard me with
Your honorable cross.

NINTH HOUR

T G

O You Who are king of the eternities
Christ God, receive Your servants in good,
and grace them to rank on Your right side.

You Who has Lordship of death and life, make
rest the souls of Your servants
and grace them to rank on Your right side.

At which time the throne of the rank of Your
Lordship, is established for the court of judgment,
at that time spare Your servants,
and grace them to rank on Your right side.

Most blessed Mary mother of God, the cherubic throne
of our maker for administration,
which all nations declare fortunate at all times.

Petition

Priest

For the souls of those who are at rest, Christ God, make them rest and have mercy, and for we sinners grace upon us the forgiveness of offences.

Proclamation

Student Chancel

Deacon

And again in peace let us request of the Lord, for the sake of the souls who are resting we request, Christ our savior, that He rank them amongst the just, and give life to us with the grace of His mercy. Our almighty Lord God, give life and have mercy.

Priest

Lord have mercy, Lord have mercy, Lord have mercy.

NINTH HOUR

Prayer

Senior Chancel

<u>Priest</u>

Christ Son of God, humane and compassionate, have compassion with Your love as creator upon the souls of Your servants who are resting. Remember them on the day of the great coming of Your kingdom. Make them worthy of mercy, atonement, and forgiveness of sins. Make them shine brightly placing them in the order of saints in the rank at Your right side. For You are Lord and creator of all, judge of the living and of the dead. And to You is befitting glory, Lordship and honor, now and always and through the eternity of eternities, amen.

Blessed be our Lord Jesus Christ. Amen.

Our Father Who art in heaven, Hallowed be Thy name.
Thy kingdom come, Thy will be done on earth as it is in heaven.
Give us this day our daily bread.
And forgive us our debts, as we forgive our debtors.
And lead us not into temptation, but deliver us from evil.

For Thine is the Kingdom, and the power,
and the glory forever and ever. Amen.

NINTH HOUR

Petition

<u>Priest</u>

May God the lover of humanity receive
these singing of the Psalms and prayers
in the pleasures of His kind wills, for our
sins and abundant offences may He grace
forgiveness, save us from evils, and keep us
from sins, and to Him glory unto the eternities.
Amen.

Blessed be the kingdom of the Father and
of the Son and of the Holy Spirit, now and
always and unto the eternity of the
eternities. Amen

This begins the Midday Service (Jashoo) which includes
the Creed and Lectionary readings for both on days in which the
Holy Offering "Divine Liturgy" (Soorp Badarak) is celebrated
and on days in which it is not celebrated.
This continues through the closing of the Midday Service (Jashoo).

This section contains all Midday Variables but always check the Church
Calendar (Oratzooytz) for the correct variables of the day.

Recite or chant the following Introits (Zhamamood-which literally means-
The Entrance into the Hour) according to the proper day as listed:

Student Chancel
Fasting Days
Monday, Tuesday, Thursday.
You savior Who were sent from the
Father, and took bodily form from the
holy virgin, Who for our sake You descended from
the heavens and illuminated the entire earth.
Give us Your peace, Lord, Whom You are the
king of peaces, the peace and mercy, which
in everything You are capable, lover of mankind

Fasting Days
Wednesday, Friday
Whom into all minds You shall pass,
God, give us Your peace continually,
to You we pray.

Sundays of Lent and most
Ordinary Resurrection Sundays
Only begotten Son and Word of God and
immortal existence, You took to Yourself
human bodily form from the holy woman
and ever virgin God-Bearer, unchangeable,
having become man, You were crucified, Christ
our God, through death You trampled down
death, You being one of the Holy Trinity
glorified together with the Father and Holy Spirit,
give us life.

MIDDAY INTROITS

Birth of Christ First Day

Unmarried God-Bearer, you conceived
The Word without beginning, and you gave birth to
the incomprehensible God, in your bosom
you lifted up the limitless One, advocate
to Him unceasingly for the sake of our beings.

Birth of Christ Second Day

The Church of the orthodox believers bows
down in worship having confessed You God-Bearer,
for where the multi-eyed cherubim and fiery
thrones and six winged seraphim
did not dare to look, you carried
the seedless incorruptible One in your womb
as a servant to the Lord, and gave birth as
man the God of all, the One having taken bodily
human form from you, the indescribable Word,
for salvation of the world and life to our beings.

Birth of Christ Third Day

We request from you, holy virgin Mary the
God-Bearer, having been protected by the
strength of the One Who is raised on high
and by the coming of the illuminating Holy
Spirit, Whom the Creator of everything which
exists having conceived, You gave birth
inexpressibly, advocate to the One Who has taken
bodily form from you to give life to our beings.

MIDDAY INTROITS

Presentation of the Lord to the Temple

Today the Elderly Simeon came
to the temple, by appearing as superior to the
cherubim, for whom having soared with
wings they did not dare to look upon the
awesome glories, having raised Him up in his
bosom he boldly kissed Him and caressed Him
as an infant child, and by praying he requested
to be delivered in peace.

Presentation of the Lord to the Temple

God the Word without beginning,
in this last day You took to
Yourself to become man from the
virgin, and O Maker from the eternities, and You
became enclosed for a time,* holy, Lord of
holiness and not in need of purifications,
You came to the temple for the fortieth day,
You fulfilled the righteous laws. Simeon requested
that You the limitless One, having been raised up in his bosom,
You Whom are the releaser of those who are bound,
"Deliver me into peace." ** For the sake of Whom, in
the company of the Elderly Simeon we
cry out to You Lord, Holy, Holy, Holy Lord
of heavenly hosts, the heavens and the earth
are filled with Your glories*** unto our
salvation Christ God, Glory to You.

---

*This describes Christ having been carried in the womb
for the gestation term of nine months.

** *Luke 2:29*

****Isaiah 6:3*

MIDDAY INTROITS

<u>Raising of Lazarus</u>

The sleep of Lazarus, as foreknowing before
You have said, and which You went
forth to Bethany, so that You may raise
Your beloved. Behold, and crying out we say,
blessed is He Who comes in tortures through the
will of the Father, unto the salvation of our beings.

<u>Raising of Lazarus</u>

At which time O life giver having come
to the tomb of Lazarus, at which time
O life giver having come to the tomb of
Lazarus, with the sound of the one Who brings
good news You were crying out saying, "Lazarus
rise up come out." * Indeed the one who died
arose from the grave, and the same one Yourself
You gave the gift of immortality to Your beloved,
and with Your Godly voice You called
from the grave. And for the sake of Whom the
children of the Hebrews were blessing Your immortal
kingdom. And we in the company of the same
say, "Hosanna, blessed be Your coming, blessing in
the highest, blessed are You Who is to come in
the Name of the Lord."**

*John 11:43
**Matthew 21:9

MIDDAY INTROITS

Palm Sunday

Rejoice, Jerusalem, and adorn your bridal
chamber, Zion, for behold your king Christ
has been seated upon a new donkey, by showing
meekness He comes and enters your bridal chamber.
And we cry out, "Hosanna, blessed is He Who has
come in the Name of the Lord,* Who has
great mercy."

Easter First Day and all Sundays of Eastertide

Christ has risen from the dead,
through death He trampled down death,
and through His resurrection He gifted
unto us life, glories to Him unto the
eternities, Amen.

The Fifty Days After Easter *(Eastertide)*
Monday, Wednesday, Friday

The mystery of our salvation is
awesome and wonderful, Who from
the Father without beginning inexpressibly
took bodily form from the virgin,
through endurance of the cross and
through His voluntary death He gifted unto us
the graces of life.

*Matthew 21:9

MIDDAY INTROITS

The Fifty Days After Easter (Eastertide)
Tuesday, Thursday, Saturday

For Christ God of the eternities rose from the dead, maker and resurrection of the nations of mankind, Whom the armies of angels and all of the lively angels of the heavens unceasingly bless. In whose company by crying out we say, glory to Your awesome resurrection Lord.

Ascension Thursday and Weekdays of Ascension-tide

The multitudes on high were amazed, by seeing You seated in the fiery chariots, having been trembling they said, "Who is this that having gone, comes from Edom"*

---

* Isaiah 63:1a

MIDDAY INTROITS

Ascension Sunday

Which You sit on the inexpressible throne and from
the bodiless angelic beings You are blessed,
incomprehensible Word of God, You appeared upon
the earth true man having fulfilled the mystery
of the law of the house of God, of the cross and
of death You endured, and You exhibited Your
miraculous resurrection with powerful force,
today You ascended with glories into the heavens
and Your body, born of the virgin, You illuminated
wonderfully, who having seen, Isaiah foretold saying,
"Who is this Who has come out from the earth."
Having been astonished the powers of the heavens
were crying out to each other, "princes, lift up your
gates and the king of glories shall enter."* Now, that
in everything You are capable and mighty, and grace
us to meet You in the clouds in Your coming again,
that only You are lover of mankind.

Pentecost

God we confess You the Holy Spirit and
we bow down in worship, Whom You are
the cause of life to we beings and
peace-maker of the world, Who filled
the ignorance of the disciples with
multitudes of knowledge and You were
inexpressibly shown to them through
split fiery tongues, we cry out unto the Lord,
spare us and give us life.

* *Psalm 23:9 KJV 24:9*

Monday after Pentecost

Today through the split fiery tongues You were
rested upon the apostles, by enlightening them,
and now we pray to You God Holy Spirit, Whom
You are cause of life to we beings and
peace-maker of the world, spare us and
give us life.

Tuesday after Pentecost

And for the sake of Whom we confess God the
Holy Spirit united with the Father and with the Son,
and for us we request from the giver above
for spiritual peace, Lord glory to You.

Transfiguration

Today the Lord appears to the disciples
upon Mount Tabor, and the apostles having
been terrified were crying out saying,
"Let us make three tents, one for the Lord, and
one for Moses, and one for Elijah." * And now
we the flock of Your Word sing in the company
with Your true witnesses, send unto us Your
light of graces in Your coming again and give
us life.

---

* Matthew 17:4

MIDDAY INTROITS

Feasts of the Holy Cross*

Before Your honorable all victorious cross, we fall down bowing down in worship and request the forgiveness of our offences, for through it You lifted the condemnation of the nations of mankind. And now for the sake of Your holy Godly sign, grace the heavenly peace to the entire world.

Feast of Holy Etchmiadzin

Our Lord and savior Jesus Christ, Whom through prayers and mediation of Your witness who has undergone many torturous sufferings, and who is our father, Saint Gregory the Illuminator, with great glory and multitudes of bright angelic armies, You descended from the heavens onto the plain of Ararat, in visitation of Your small flock this nation of the Armenians,

---

* *The present church calendar also prescribes the recitation of this Introit beginning from the Sunday of Carnival (Poon Paregentan) through all Sundays of Great Lent. This is a more recently prescribed variable during the season of Great Lent. It was prescribed as such during the tenure of Catholicos Simeon of Yerevan 1763-1780. The historical Introit until this time was the Introit for Ordinary Resurrection Sundays found on page 429.*

and in the demonstration of Your
special love and great mercy, and
with a golden hammer You struck the depths
of the abysses, and expelled the regiments
of the infernal depths of hells, and where
with luminous adornment You miraculously
made the Mother See* Holy Etchmiadzin,
and You made it an inexhaustible storehouse of
Godly graces, while being parent,
instructor and perfecter of all the
churches of the Armenias.** Now, keep her,
pure, firm and bright, and for our churches
keep them in splendor and keep their children servants
of the Lord until the completion of the world,
by Whom Your most holy Name is
continually glorified unto the eternity of
eternities. Amen.

<u>Feasts of the Holy Church</u>

Grace peace unto Your Holy Church,
peace and stability from enemies in war,
and establish in one faith the catholic ***
church, we confess You Lord and God,
grant us life.

---

*   *literally "seat"*

**   *this is plural, because of geopolitical reasons there has always been more than one Armenian state existing simultaneously in their historic lands throughout the millennia.*

*** *catholic means universal in its Greek origin. It has no connection to the Roman Catholic Church in this context. The text above used the term "gatooghige" the Armenicized form of the Greek. Armenian has borrowed this term for unknown reasons as the Armenia language already has its own words for universal, "diezeragan" and general, "unthanoor" which is already used in many other liturgical phrases. Either one of these would be better choices.*

MIDDAY INTROITS

The Forerunner St. John the Baptist

By supposing to obstruct Your preceding and fore-running of the Word of God, whom by the hand of the woman the first created man was cast out from paradise. And now he having ignited Herodias with unrighteousness, and those guests sitting for Herod were pleased by the dances of the girl's feet, that your head was cut off, whom you laid hands upon the head of all, Christ. But you who from the wilderness with a voice of crying, call out to Him Who you have laid hands on, to gift peace and great mercy.

MIDDAY INTROITS

St. Stephen the First Martyr

Holy catholic church rejoice today rejoice and
delight, with the remembrance of Saint Stephen
the first martyr for Christ witnessing for the Father.
Who through prayers was opening the heavens
which Adam closed, and with an angelic look he was
seeing the appearance of the Father in the form of Adam
Who has been sitting in the seat of glories. Which the
multitude of rocks being amassed as flowers,
crowned him with rings of bouquets instead of thorns and
cane. And the martyred blood was mixed
with the saving blood of Christ flowing
from the side. For the sake of whom having surpassed
glories more than all of the saints,
and he was requesting for our sake from
the giver above for the gifts of lives
without ends and the great mercy.

St. Stephen the First Martyr

Saint Stephen having been chosen from
the womb, Saint Stephen having been
chosen from the womb, true witness of
the apostolic preachings who upon the
wicked stone throwers prayed to Christ God
by saying, "do not charge them with this sin."*
Now through his advocation grace us,
Lord, Your great mercy.

---

* Acts 7:60b

MIDDAY INTROITS

<u>Saint Gregory the Illuminator</u>

Rejoice today rejoice, the Holy Church delights,
by celebrating with great festivity the general
wish of this your remembrance, you who have
become superior amongst our fathers, holy patriarch and
illuminator of this house of Torkom, Saint Gregory.
Whom through your intolerable sufferings
you astonished this entire world. Through
your unparalleled hardships you amazed the
fiery angels, and those who in large battalions
having bowed down from the heavens to the earth
hurried to see the exhibition of your martyrdom.
And with incomparable endurance you
subdued the arrogant king with his
own armies under your feet. And with your
God pleasing prayers you enlightened their virgin
minds, and made ministers of the gospel
of Christ. And in the company of the same, with
new spiritual birth you brought the nations
of the Armenians into the light of the knowledge of God.

(continued on page 442)

And especially for the sake of whom you
shined brilliantly amongst all of the saints, and
you received the apostolic seat and honor, and
in the company of the same you were crowned
by Christ God. Now, O our father and enlightener
of our souls, we your church with one mind
and in agreement request of you, that on
this your wonderful feast day, you shall
advocate especially to Christ our God, that the
churches and remnants of Your people shall be
protected in peace, by saving them from the
spiritual and bodily enemies, and that we
always by conducting your remembrances,
may glorify the Father and the Son and
the Holy Spirit unto the eternities. Amen.

Saint Gregory the Illuminator

Gregory holy high priest, who taught
the faiths and expelled the armies of
the demons, you taught mankind to preach
the trinity, you were crowned in the
kingdom, now be advocate to the Lord
for our sake.

MIDDAY INTROITS

Apostles

Apostles and witnesses of Christ God,
with the power of the almighty spirit by
calling everyone universally into adoption of life,
they encouraged us to sing glories in unison
to the Holy Trinity unto the eternities. Amen.

Sons of Thunder, James the Apostle and John the Evangelist

Today alarming sounds of thunder rang
out from the heavens upon the earth, calling
us into adoption of the Zion above,
foundations of faith and boasting of the Church,
those who through their dew drops of blood cleansed
the earth from wicked idolatries, and they
always request from Christ the atonement for
those who celebrate the feast of their name day. Now,
through their petitions, Lord, in having saved Your people,
spare them, Whom only You are lover of mankind.

MIDDAY INTROITS

Days of Prophets

Lord, Who founded Your Church upon the rock of faith, and in it You assigned the apostles and prophets, pastors and doctors of the Church in strengthening of the saints, and through sufferings of witnesses You expelled her enemy, God as lover of mankind keep her in peace.

Days of the Church Fathers

You adorned the patriarchal seat on the earth, you made the apostolic honor from heaven, servant of Christ, O fortunate are you amongst fathers holy patriarch. For the seeds of your teachings, sprouted out forth ears* of piety, in recompense for the fruit of happiness and salvation through grace for we faithful, for the sake of whom, advocate to the Lord, for the sake of our beings.

---

* *The literal meaning is "ears of corn" but this metaphorical meaning translates to ears of piety.*

MIDDAY INTROITS

Days of Christian Kings

As after the God loving king of Israel
Hezekiah, God raised up Josiah, who
cast out all idolatries, and as the pious
Constantine, who obstructed the heresy of
Arius, and raised up the great Theodosius
having become inflamed with Godly envy against
those who blasphemed the Holy Spirit.
Now, O God-like and orthodox holy king,
pray to the Lord while He is saving us from
man-worshiping blasphemy, and that we
shall celebrate your remembrances by
requesting from Christ reconciliation and
the great mercy.

MIDDAY INTROITS

Days of Christian Kings

As after the God loving king of Israel Hezekiah,
God raised up Josiah, who cast out all old idolatries
of the people, and as recently He raised up
the first born of kings, the pious Apkar,*
who from a distant land knew the
heavenly king Christ, and became His proclamation
of Godliness throughout the ends of the
entire earth. And after him the great Tiridates**
who unto the end expelled the demon mad
idol worshipping from the world of the Armenians,
and adorned them with true and orthodox faith.
Now, O God-like and pious holy king, pray
to the Lord, while He is saving us from wicked
tyrants, and we that in celebrating your remembrance,
may we request from Christ peace and great mercy.

Days of Martyrs

In the temple of the saints and for the
remembrance of the holy martyrs, by raising up
our hands we pray, with their advocation and
prayers, make our lives peaceful God as
lover of mankind.

---

* Also spelled "Abgar"
** Known as Tirdat or Durtad in the Armenian language.

MIDDAY INTROITS

Days of Hermetic Monks

Hermits of Christ, you who endured tortures of
the wicked, and you obstructed the madness
of idols, you who have been ranked in the
company of the angels in the heavens, you have
the boldness from Christ, advocate to give life
to our beings, we request from you.

For the Followers and Martyrs of Saint Hripsime

Those who shined forth to us from the west
as the sun, and enlightened all
together the world of the Armenians, they
removed the darkness of the ignorance
of idolatry and enlightened all souls with
faith of the knowledge of God. With their
advocation, Christ God, gift peace
unto this Your world, and to our beings
forgiveness of sins, as Lord lover of humanity.

For the Followers and Martyrs of Saint Gayane

The Holy Church celebrates
your victorious festival delight,
because through holiness you obtained
virginhood, and in body
you demonstrated the festival to the
bodiless angelic beings.

MIDDAY INTROITS

Days of the Holy Virgins

Brides wed to Christ the heavenly
bridegroom, daughters of the Zion above,
request from Christ reconciliation and the
great mercy.

St. Vartan the Commander and his 1,036 Martyrs of the Great War

To the world in battle, to the world in battle
and in the great war, the Godless having been the adversary
in war. Truly the fortunate martyrs obstructed the madness
of the Godless and were found victorious. Whereas
of those who have possessed the Godly power,
physical bodily warfare did not neutralize
them. Now, Christ God, through their advocation
spare us and have mercy.

Days of the Holy Soldiers

Soldier and true witness, brave martyr
for Christ, Saint *(* insert name)* whom you exchanged
your body in exchange for ransom of your
soul, and did not consider the threats of
Godless tyrants. But through the influence of above
observing the burning of their souls,
for the sake of those who set fire to
the temple of the idols and disallowed their
worship. Now, for those who celebrate in the victorious
war, soldiers of Your martyrdom advocate to the
Lord for the sake of our beings.

MIDDAY INTROITS

<u>Day of the Forty Young Soldiers who were martyred in Sebaste* 320A.D.</u>

Through going into the glories of Your
glories, Your catholic** Church Christ
shines extremely bright, for those
who have been crowned by You having rushed
to the heavens, of the martyrs in Sebaste
in shame and in casting stones they were
slandered to their faces. And those
were encouraging each other, but
one who (renounced) would thaw out and
warm up by passing through the warm baths
but would be lost, but another who was
trembling, courageously (took the place of the lost one),
while praying to Christ he had dedicated himself
to the wheels*** of heavenly angels of Godly treasures
which shall wrap around him. ****
Now, receive through their advocation and the adoption of
these our people into the hope of Your beloved,
Lord glory to You.

---

* *Sepastia in Armenian. Ethnically cleansed of Armenians and Greeks by the Ottoman Turks through genocide from 1915-1923.*

** *catholic means universal in its Greek origin. It has no connection to the Roman Catholic Church in this context. The text above used the term "gatooghige" the Armenicized form of the Greek. Armenian has borrowed this term for unknown reasons as the Armenia language already has its own words for universal, "diezeragan" and general, "unthanoor" which is already used in many other liturgical phrases. Either one of these would be better choices.*

*** *"Wheel" is used in Ezekiel Ch 10 and referenced by St. John Chrysostom Grk. (Golden Mouth Eng. Vosgeperan Arm.) to describe a group of heavenly angelic bodies.*

**** *To understand what actually transpired in this historical narrative see:*
  fortymartyrs.org
  Forty Martyrs of Sebaste wikipedia.org
  earlychurchhistory.org/martyrs/forty-martyrs-of-sebaste/

MIDDAY INTROITS

Day of the Three Young Men in the Furnace

You Who are rested upon the cherubim and You are praised with hymns by the armies of fiery angels, You descended into Babylon and saved the three young men from the flame of violence. Those who while shouting were crying out a new song, "bless all works and raise up on high."* King of glories and maker of all, Who humanely had compassion upon the holy boys and saved them from the flaming blaze, those who offended the violence of the king and extinguished the force of the fire, and we in the company of the same cry out, save us from the flame of the eternities. For You only are very compassionate Lord, glory to You unto the eternities. Amen.

Daniel 3:57 KJV 3:35

Days of the Archangels

To whom the intelligible forces, heavenly patriarchates, angels and archangels, thrones and Lordships, principalities and states, Seraphim and Cherubim, bless with an unceasing voice, and we shall bless the same most holy trinity and the one Godly being.

MIDDAY INTROITS

Days of the Archangels

Today this earthly priestly hierarchy of the church
wonderfully rejoices, by the performing of the heavenly
celebrations of the festival of those heavenly priestly hierarchies.
And in the company of the ranks of the bodiless
heavenly beings and of the spiritual beings, and we
physical bodied and earthly beings being in
a unanimous voice glorify the glorified
One amongst you. Now, O holy
Gabriel and Michael, great archangels
of the One raised on high, and all of the
armies of the heavens, those who always
stand before the throne of Godliness,
be an unceasing advocate to the
Lord for our sake, regarding us all in
your company in the kingdom in the heavens,
and singing glories with a unison voice.

MIDDAY INTROITS

All Saints Day

Through the advocation of the Holy God-Bearer,
of Saint John the Forerunner,
of Saint Stephen the First Martyr, and of our
Saint Gregory the Illuminator, and of the holy
apostles and prophets, of patriarchs and of
doctors of the church, of martyrs and kings, of
hermetic monks and virgins, of forefathers and hermits,
and of all Your saints ancient and new, known
and unknown, of whom today is their remembrance,
grant us peace and heavenly mercy Lord lover of
humanity.

Proclamation

Student Chancel

Deacon

And again in peace let us request of the Lord. Receive, save, and have mercy.

Priest

Blessing and glory to the Father and to the Son and to the Holy Spirit. Now and always and unto the eternity of eternities. Amen.

Peace unto all.

Choir

And with Your spirit.

Deacon

Let us bow down in worship of God.

Choir

Before You Lord.

MIDDAY ANTHEM 453

Chant the Midday Anthem (or Response) "Jashoo Pokh." This precedes the Midday Hymn "Jashoo Sharagan" opening verse. The Midday Anthem is chanted according to the proper day as prescribed by the Church Calendar. (In present common practice only the first sentence is chanted by the deacon and then the choir begins singing the Midday Hymn by repeating this first sentence in the hymn.

Midday Anthem chanted for the following Days: The Annunciation, Birth of Christ, Presentation of Christ, Transfiguration, Assumption of Mary, and for all feasts of the Holy Mother of God (God-Bearer).

Senior Chancel
Lk 1:46-55

My soul shall magnify the Lord, and my spirit shall rejoice with God my savior.

He paid visit upon the humility of His maid servant, from now on all nations shall regard me as fortunate.

The Mighty One has made very great things through me, and Holy is His Name.

You made mercy from generation unto generation upon those who fear in Him, he made power with His right arm.

He scattered those who are arrogant in thoughts of their hearts, and pulled down the mighty ones from their thrones.

He uplifted the humble, He filled those who are impoverished, with goodness, and He sent the wealthy away empty.

He defended Israel His servant, by remembering His mercy.

As He spoke unto our fathers, in the company of Abraham and his child, unto eternity.

Midday Anthem chanted for the following Days: Salt and Bread Days (Weekdays of Great Lent), Palm Sunday, Feasts of the Cross, Feasts of the Church, and for all other regular Sundays.

Ps 92:1-5 KJV 93:1-5

The Lord ruled as king, He was clothed in splendor,
He was clothed with strength brought forth from within Him.

The world was established, for it shall not be shaken,
Your throne is prepared from the beginning, You are unto the eternities.

The rivers rose up, Lord, and the rivers lifted up their voices,
and the rivers shall rise up to their currents.

From the sound of the abundant waters the waves of the sea became wonderful.

454 MIDDAY ANTHEM

You are wonderful, Lord, in the heights,
we very much believed in Your testimonies.

Holiness is befitting to Your house, Lord, unto lengthy days.

Glory to the Father and to the Son and to the Holy Spirit.

Now and always and unto the eternity of eternities. Amen.

Midday Anthem chanted from Easter until Pentecost

Ps 147:12-20 KJV 147:12-20

Praise the Lord Jerusalem.

And bless your God, Zion.

He strengthened the bolts on your gates, and
blessed your sons within you.

Who put your borders in peace,
with the fat of the wheat He filled you.

He sends His word to the earth,
His messages run quickly.

He places down snow as wool, and scattered
mist as dust.

He throws out ice as morsels, who is
able to stand before His cold.

He sends out His word and melts them,
the winds shall blow and the waters shall flow.

He tells His word unto Jacob, justice
and righteousness unto Israel.

He has not done this for all nations Lord,
and He has not revealed His judgments to them.

Glory to the Father, and to the Son, and to the Holy Spirit.

Now and always and unto the eternity of eternities.

MIDDAY ANTHEM 455

Midday Anthem chanted for all Feast Days of the Saints

Ps 114:1-9 KJV 116:1-8

I loved that the Lord shall hear the voice of my prayers, for He descended His ear upon me, and through all of my days I called out unto Him.

The pangs of death have me surrounded, and the afflictions of hells* found me.

I found trouble and anguish, and called upon the Name of the Lord.

O Lord, save my being, our merciful God be merciful and Lord keep the children.

I became humble and the Lord gave me life, return my being to Your rest, for the Lord helped me.

He saved my being from death, my eyes from tears, and my feet from stumbling, I shall be pleasing before the Lord in the land of the living.

Glory to the Father, and to the Son, and to the Holy Spirit.

Now and always and unto the eternity of eternities.

Midday Anthem chanted for all days during the one week fasts when a Feast Day or Saint's Day is not celebrated. It is also chanted for all fasting Wednesdays and Fridays throughout the year.

Ps 116:1-2 KJV 117:1-2

All nations bless the Lord, praise Him all peoples.

His mercy shall strengthen upon us, and truth of the Lord shall remain unto eternity.

Glory to the Father, and to the Son, and to the Holy Spirit.

Now and always and unto the eternity of eternities.

* *Hades*

MIDDAY HYMN

Senior Chancel

 The **Midday Hymn (Jashoo Sharagan)** *according to the proper tone of the day as prescribed by the Church Calendar is sung at this point. The following are only examples and the listing is incomplete. To find the correct* **Midday Hymn** *which is to be sung, the Hymnal must be followed for the appropriate day's Midday Hymn. Look in the pages following the corresponding day's* **Hymn of the Fathers (Hartz Sharagan)** *prescribed for the day by using Hymnal's index. Frequently their tones will differ.*

Midday Hymn for Resurrection or Ordinary Sundays

A Tz
―――

Christ the king of glories, Who
for our sake took bodily form
from the holy virgin and by enduring
the cross, in unison let us give praise
with song.
Who took to himself the burial of three days,
having risen from the dead with Lordship,
in unison let us give praise with song.
Powerfully He destroyed the gates of hells,*
He adorned His church with majesty,
in unison let us give praise with song.

* *Hades*

MIDDAY HYMN 457

Midday Hymn for Feast Days of the Holy Archangels

T̄ G

Today the holy Church of Christ having
become gladdened, celebrates with merriment
the feast of the Jerusalem above,
with voice of holy reverence* glorifying Christ.
Today the sons of the earthly Zion,
in unison, make merriment with celebration
of the first born sons of the Zion above,
with voice of holy reverence* glorifying Christ.
Today the ranks of the bodiless heavenly beings
having taken to song, dance with men, spiritual
songs to the immortal bridegroom in the
bridal chamber, with voice of holy reverence*
glorifying Christ.

* *This is a reference to the seraphim singing "Holy, Holy, Holy" in Isaiah 6:3.*

Midday Hymn for Days of the Prophets

Ā Tz

Inexpressible ray of light, incomprehensible
Lordship, beforehand You made wonderful the
vision of the prophets, by descending
into the lower parts with Godly administration.*
Those who founded the temple of faith through
the grace of the Holy Spirit, into which the
Word of God entered with the seven sun rays,
by descending into the lower parts with
Godly administration.*
He appeared to the world with true
humanity, who the inviters, of the One Who
is of the same existence of the Father and Spirit,
proclaimed to us, by illuminating the universes
with Godly administration.*

* *Theologians use the term "redeeming economy"*

MIDDAY HYMN

Midday Hymn for all Wednesdays which are Fasting Days

T G

We send to You glorification heavenly Father,
remember those of ours who are sleeping,
and make them rest in the company of Your saints.
You only begotten Who is of the same existence of
the Father and of the Holy Spirit,
remember those of ours who are sleeping,
and make them rest in the company of Your saints.
You Who are true are sharing in glory of the Father
and of the Holy Spirit,
remember those of ours who are sleeping,
and make them rest in the company of Your saints.

Midday Hymn for Days of the Apostles

A G

You who are lovers of the Maker of
those whom have been made, holy apostles of Christ,
advocate to the Lord for our sake.
Which your proclamations are for the
entire world, holy apostles of Christ,
advocate to the Lord for our sake.
You who are the crowns of all of the
churches, holy apostles of Christ,
advocate to the Lord for our sake.

Midday Hymn for Fridays which are Fasting Days

T G

Who in existence without beginning You
came to the world, took bodily form
from the virgin for the sake of our debts,
make rest those of ours who are sleeping.
Who of the same existence from the Father of light You
shined light unto us and life, only begotten
Son of the Father, make rest those of ours who are sleeping.
You Who are above the minds and thoughts, and having endured
of the cross You save the whole earth,
make rest those of ours who are sleeping.

MIDDAY HYMN 459

Midday Hymn for Monday, Tuesday, and Thursday during the one week fasts when a Saint's Day is not celebrated.

K Tz

Christ God remember those sleeping in Your holy Name.
The prices of Your blood, Lord, remember and
make them rest in the company of Your saints.
And in Your coming again, remember those of
ours who are sleeping and make them rest in the
company of Your saints.

Midday Hymn for Fridays during the one week fasts.

P G

Who from nothing the creator of
existence, co-maker, the Word God of the
Father, grace forgiveness to Your servants
who are sleeping, at which time You come to
judge that which You created with pure hands.
Whom from the Father You were sent
and took bodily form from the holy virgin,
grace forgiveness to Your servants
who are sleeping, at which time You come to
judge that which You created with pure hands.
Who upon the cross You died by
asphyxiation, You dissolved the ruling power of death,
grace forgiveness to Your servants
who are sleeping, at which time You come to
judge that which You created with pure hands.
Whom You are the crowner of Your saints,
and distributor of good without end,
grace forgiveness to Your servants
who are sleeping, at which time You come to
judge that which You created with pure hands.

MIDDAY HYMN

Midday Hymn for Days of Martyrs

K̄ Ḡ

True hermits and witnesses of Christ,
those of you who took to yourselves suffering
and death for the sake of the Lord, we have you as
advocate to Christ for the for the sake of our beings.
For through the flowing of your blood the
holy churches shined brightly, and you lifted
out the shadowy darkness of idolatry, we have you as
advocate to Christ for the for the sake of our beings.
The heavenly armies having descended in
honor of the sacrifice of your death, and by
presenting the spotless crowns from the
Father of light, we have you as
advocate to Christ for the for the sake of our beings.

MIDDAY HYMN

Midday Hymn for the Annunciation

K̄ Ḡ

God-Bearer altar of light, limitless
sun of lives, you who became the
east sun of justice, and you shined
light upon those who sit in darkness,
for the sake of which all of us always
magnify you.
Pure temple and noncombustible blackberry
bush, which having taken the inextinguishable flame
of Godliness you carried it in you, through
whom the carried flame extinguished our
burning natures, for the sake of which all of us always
magnify you.
Living ark of the testaments of this
new covenant, by whom came up to
the earth, the good news of the Word having
been impressed in you and having been
prepared by the Holy Spirit, was given,
for the sake of which all of us always
magnify you.

MIDDAY HYMN

Midday Hymn for the Birth of Christ

K̄ T̄z

We magnify the holy God-Bearer with blessings.
The good news bearing angel announced the savior
having been born of the holy virgin.
He says, "O cheerful one rejoice, for the Lord of Lords
is with you."

Midday Hymn for the Presentation of the Lord to the Temple

T̄ Ḡ

The Word without beginning from the
beginningless Father, and having taken beginning
from the virgin by being clothed in body, by
being enclosed in the womb and with existence
in the company of the Father and having
been born by the prescribed time, God and man.
Having entered in under the laws, the immaterial
One with existence of earthly material, that He
may present those born of the earth to
the Father, the Son of God Who is in the
bosom of the Father, the infant of forty days
is raised up in the bosom of the elderly one,
and was openly made known, God and man.
And for the sake of Whom Simeon rejoiced
with spirit, and he was crying out in the temple,
now this Your servant may be delivered, Lord,
in peace according to Your word, for I saw
the universal savior, God and man.

MIDDAY HYMN

Midday Hymn for Palm Sunday

T̄ G

Word of the Father without beginning,
Who rests upon the cherubim, today
having sit upon a new donkey, blessed is
the King Who has come, the invincible King.
The Son before the eternities, Who sits upon
the four formed beings, this day was glorified
by the elderly and by children, blessed is
the King Who has come, the invincible King.
Come new people, in the company of the
ranks of the multitudes of the bodiless
heavenly beings, let us glorify Him with
song ringing out with a sweet voice, blessed is
the King Who has come, the invincible King

Midday Hymn for Easter

Ā Tz

Christ is risen from the dead, alleluia.
Come people sing unto the Lord, alleluia.
To Him Who has risen from the dead, alleluia.
To Him Who has illuminated the world, alleluia.

MIDDAY HYMN

Midday Hymn for the Ascension of Christ

A Tz

Who with the ascension today with
Godly Lordship in the Fatherly chariot,
with the ministering of the angelic orders,
those who were singing while saying,
"Princes lift up your gates and the King of
glories shall enter." *
The Lordships above were amazed, and with
frightful voices they were crying out to
one another, "Who is this King of glories, **
having come in body and with marvelous power,
"Princes lift up your gates and the King of
glories shall enter." *
The governments above were harmoniously singing
with a wonderful voice, they were singing a
new song by saying, "He Himself is the King of
glories,*** savior of the world and liberator
of the nations of mankind,
"Princes lift up your gates and the King of
glories shall enter." *

---

* *Ps 23:7 KJV 24:7*
** *Ps 23:8a KJV 24:8a*
*** *Ps 23:10a KJV 24:10a*

MIDDAY HYMN 465

Midday Hymn for Pentecost

P Tz

Who having sprung forth before
from the continuously flowing spring,
individually from the Son, supremely the
Holy Spirit, today from the heavens having poured
out intensely unto the ranks of the apostles, filler
of all, let us bless Him* by bowing down in worship.
Who unto the One without beginning and
from the One Who Exists always, of the same
existence with indistinct inseparability of
the Son, co-maker the Holy Spirit, today with
fire, the tongues** were divided unto the preachers,
to bring the nations of mankind into the light,
by dividing of the various graces,
let us bless Him* by bowing down in worship.
Who above the waters with existence give existence
to that which He* had made, without space*** from
the Father and the Son co-ruler the Holy Spirit, today all
nations became born again, the water of life having sprung
forth into Jerusalem, let us bless Him* by bowing down in worship.

---

* He/Him refers to the Holy Spirit. Using the word "it" would be incorrect because the Holy Spirit is the third person of the Trinity.

** Languages

***This statement would support a "Big Bang Theory" of creation with an expanding universe. This being eluded to 1,000 years before the detection of "Big Bang" radio waves. If there were a "Big Bang" it would not be contrary to Armenian Church theology.

MIDDAY HYMN

Midday Hymn for the Transfiguration "Vartavarr"

T G

Be cheerful, crown of virgins mother of
the Lord, today your Son shined forth the
Fatherly glories, make our beings eternal
unto He Himself.
Moses and Elijah wait on Him, Tabor and Hermon
rejoice in His Name, make our beings eternal
unto He Himself.
Isaiah saw You as a light cloud, and
the Father in the cloud professes your Son as His,
make our beings eternal unto He Himself.

MIDDAY HYMN

Midday Hymn for the Assumption and other
feast days of the God-Bearer*

<u>P Tz</u>

Unfading flower, uncondemned offshoot,
having sprouted out again from the root
of Jesse, Isaiah beforehand proclaimed you
to be the vessel of the sevenfold rays of the graces
of the spirit, God-Bearer and virgin, we magnify you.
Delicious taste of fruit, rational branch, from which
the cluster of grapes was gathered for us, to
the inexhaustible gladness of those who are sorrowful
from tasting of the tree of knowledge, pure holy woman,
we all magnify you.
Having dwelled in the body in conduct of
a pure life, today having assembled
from the apostles, with signs from above
you were changed up (from this world) to the
kingdom of your Son and our God, advocate
for we who confess, we magnify you.

* *Literally- "changing from this world to the next"*

MIDDAY HYMN

Midday Hymn for Feasts of the Holy Cross

K G

Let us always sing in the highest, the
victorious and new blessing to the king Christ,
and believing people.
Who came while enlightening the chosen Holy
Church, and crowned her with the cross,
let us sing glories to Him.
And today let us celebrate the dedication
of the holy cross, and let us offer eternally
glory and honor to the Deliverer.

MIDDAY HYMN

Midday Hymn for the Feast of the Ark of the Covenant

A G

Who from the beginning established the
Church with wisdom, wisdom of the Father
in which by the first visual image Moses had signified
with the tabernacle of heaven resting on Mount Sinai,
by enlightening with the glories to God.
Whom from the holy virgin, the mystery of Your
pure Lordship, the ark through impression of
the Godly covenant of the testaments of the
Word of God, of glories to the uncreated One
for place of rest.
In which natures coming back into lives by
You taking the example of turning
back to Jordan and the force of death
and of hells, with the destruction of
Jericho by the ark of the cross having
worked miracles for the New Israel,
the children servants of the Lord shall sing
blessing to You Lord.

Midday Hymn for Feast days of the Holy Church

T Tz

You Who established Your church through
Your Word Christ upon the apostolic rock,
to sing unto Him spiritual songs.
The table of holiness having been
erected inside it, distributes His body and
blood, and from it gives unto us
renewal, for the forgiveness of our sins.
The Holy Spirit having descended with
an appearance of dove like form upon
the body and blood of the Lord,
for the healing of our souls.

470 MIDDAY HYMN

Midday Hymn for Feasts of the Holy Church Fathers

T̄ T̄z

Today the heavenly beings in
our company by celebrating the remembrance
of the holy doctors of the church, those who enlightened
the children of the faith and are placed in the company
of the order of angels.
Today the order of the apostles and prophets
being co-celebrators with the daughters of
the Zion above, in remembrance of the
holy doctors of the church, those who
revealed the mystery of their profound thought.
Today the priests and ministers of the
holy church honor the remembrance of
the holy doctors of the church, through whom
they were adorned with the heavenly graces,
in their company they sing glories unto eternity.

MIDDAY ANTHEM

Sing the "Thrice Holy" also known as "Holy God" (Soorp Asdvadz) according to the proper day or season. The verse is sung three times. See pages 305-306 for the appropriate verse of the day.
(Then return to page 471)

Senior Chancel

Proclamation

<u>Deacon</u> **Student Chancel**
And again in peace let us request of the Lord. Receive, save, and have mercy.

<u>Choir *(continue in alternation)*</u>
Lord have mercy.

For the sake of peace of the entire world and for the stability of the holy church, let us request of the Lord.

Lord have mercy.

For the sake of all holy and orthodox bishops, let us request of the lord.

Lord have mercy.

For the sake of the life of our patriarch Lord *(* insert name)*, and for the salvation of his soul, let us request of the Lord.

Lord have mercy.

For the sake of doctors of the church, priests, deacons, choristers* and the order of all the children who are servants of the church,** let us request of the Lord.

Lord have mercy.

For the sake of pious kings and God loving princes, generals and their armies, let us request of the Lord.

Lord have mercy.

---

* *Actual translation is "scribe or clerk"*
** *Even though "children" is used, this term includes those of all ages who serve the church whether they be adults or children.*

MIDDAY PROCLAMATION

For the sake of the souls who are at rest, who with true and right faith are sleeping in Christ, let us pray to the Lord.

Remember Lord and have mercy.

And again in one voice for the sake of our true and holy faith, let us pray to the Lord.

Lord have mercy.

Let us make ourselves and one another as the Person of the Lord God Almighty.

Let us become as Your Person Lord.

Our Lord God had mercy upon us, according to Your great mercy, let us all say in unison.

Lord have mercy. Lord have mercy. Lord have mercy.

Petition

Priest

For You, existing God are merciful
and the lover of humanity, and to You is
befitting glory, Lordship and honor
now and always and unto the eternity
of eternities. Amen.

MIDDAY PSALM 473

The Midday Psalm (Jashoo Psalm) is chanted as the introduction to the first Midday reading in the Lectionary whether it be a Prophetic reading or a reading from the Epistles. These Psalms are more complete than those which occur in the current Lectionary being used. However, the totally complete sets of Psalms can only be found in the Book of Psalms (Saghmosaran) or completely referenced and prescribed in (Lectionary of the Armenian Apostolic Church by Rev. Dr. George A. Leylegian)

Student Chancel
Midday Psalm for the Fifty Days from Easter through Pentecost

(For this period there are three Psalm responses before the readings beginning with Psalm 1,2, and 3 on Easter then Psalm 4,5, and 6 for the next day and continuing as such until Pentecost where Psalm 148,149, and 150 will be chanted. The Book of Psalms (Saghmosaran) must be used during these days because only one example is shown here.
After each Psalm response, Alleluia must be chanted three times.)

Ps 1:1 KJV 1:1
Fortunate is the man, who did not walk in the counsel of the wicked, who did not stand in the path of sinners, and did not sit in the chair of infectious disease. Alleluia, alleluia, alleluia.

Ps 2:1 KJV 2:1
Why did the heathens become agitated, and people think in vain. Alleluia, alleluia, alleluia.

Ps 3:2 KJV 3:1
Lord, for my oppressors are many, and many are rising against me. Many were saying regarding me that there is no salvation in his God. Alleluia, alleluia, alleluia.

Midday Psalm for the Ascension of Christ
Ps 46:6,2 KJV 47:5,1
God ascended with blessing, and our Lord
with the sound of the trumpet.

Clap your hands, all you heathens,
cry out unto God in a voice of joyfulness.

Reading from the Book of Acts of the Apostles 24:14b-18a
(This is an example only. Follow the Lectionary)

In that manner I serve the God of our fathers, having believed in everything, that which has been written in the laws and in the prophets. I have hope in God and for Whom they indeed await, that there is going to be resurrection of the just and of the sinners. And in Whom I indeed labor, to keep a clear conscious towards God and towards man at all times. I came for many years to make alms to my nation, and I gave for offerings, by those who found me having been purified in the temple.

MIDDAY PSALM

Midday Psalm for Pentecost Psalm 148, 149, and 150 using the "Fifty Days Following Easter" Example (or an alternative, Psalm 142 below)

Ps 142:10b, 1 KJV 143: 10b, 1

Your good spirit shall lead me
into upright land.

Lord, hear my prayers, place Your
ear upon my requests with Your truth.
Alleluia, alleluia, alleluia.

Midday Psalm for the Feast of the Ark of the Covenant

Ps 131:8,1 KJV 132:8,1

Rise Lord to Your rest, You and the ark
of Your holy covenant.
Lord remember David and all his meekness.

Midday Psalm for the Transfiguration of Christ

Ps 14:1-5 KJV 15:1-5

Lord, who shall stay in Your tabernacle, or who
shall dwell upon Your Holy mountain.

He who walks spotlessly works justice,
he speaks the truth in his heart.

Who with his tongue is not of the deceitful,
and does not do evil to his friend.

He does not take up insults upon those near to him,
he despises those who do evil works before him.

He glorifies those who fear of the Lord,
who make oath to their friend and does not lie.

He does not lend his silver out with interest,
and does not take bribes against them,
he who does these things, unto eternity he
shall not be shaken.

MIDDAY PSALM

Midday Psalm for the Assumption* of the God-Bearer

Ps 131:8,1 KJV 132:8,1
Rise Lord to Your rest, You and the ark
of Your holy covenant.
Lord remember David and all his meekness.

Midday Psalm for Feasts of the Holy Cross

Ps 4:7b-8a, 2 KJV 4:6b-7a, 1
A sign of the light of Your faces was placed
before us, and You gave joy to our hearts.

While I cry out You heard me, God,
according to my righteousness, from oppression
You made me calm, have mercy upon
me and hear my prayers.

*Midday Psalm for St. Gregory's Vision (Shoghakat)
and other Feasts of the Church*

Ps 47:9b-10, 2 KJV 48:8b-9, 1
God cast down the foundations of it** unto eternity,
we received Your mercy God in the midst of Your people.

The Lord is great and is greatly blessed, in the city of our
God, in His holy mountain.

Midday Psalm for the Annunciation to the God-Bearer

Ps 67: 12, 2 KJV 68:11, 1
The Lord shall give the Word, to those that
announce of the good news with much power.

God shall arise and all of His enemies
shall become scattered, those who hate Him
shall flee from His faces.

---

* *Literally-changing up from this world to the next*
** *"it" refers to the city which is mentioned earlier in the verse.*

MIDDAY PSALM

Midday Psalm for the Birth of Christ

Ps 2: 7b,1 KJV 2:7b,1

The Lord said to me, "You are my Son
and today I have begotten You."*

Why did the heathens become agitated, and
people think in vain.

Midday Psalm for the Presentation of Christ to the Temple Forty Days After His Birth

Ps 97:3b, 1a KJV 98:3b, 1a

All ends of the earth saw the salvation of our God.

Bless the Lord in a new song, for He has made wonders.

Midday Psalm for Palm Sunday

Ps 97:8b-9a, 1a KJV 98:8b-9a, 1a

The mountains shall rejoice before the Lord, for He comes, for the Lord has come in judging the earth.

Bless the Lord in a new song, for He has made wonders.

*Literally- Have given birth to You.

MIDDAY PSALM

Midday Psalm for Regular Sundays

Ps 64:2-14 KJV 65:1-13

To You is befitting blessing God in Zion,
and prayers shall be given unto You in Jerusalem.

Hear my prayers, for all bodies shall come to You.

The words of the lawless were forced upon us,
and You will atone for our profaneness.

Fortunate is he who You chose and received,
and they may dwell in Your courts.

We will be filled from the goodness of Your house,
Your temple is Holy with wonderful righteousness.

Hear us God our savior, hope of all ends of the earth,
and that of the distant sea.

Who prepares the mountains with His strength,
and is clothed with might.

Who troubles the greatness of the sea,
and softens the sound of its waves.

The heathens shall be troubled, and the
inhabitants of the earth shall become
afraid of Your signs.

MIDDAY PSALM

The outgoings of the morning with the evenings shall rejoice, You were pleased in the earth, You made it drink,* and You made abundant greatness of it.

The river of God became filled with water, You prepared their food, for preparation is in this manner.

You made its furrows drink,* and You made its crops abundant.

While gently showering it, its sprouts shall become joyful, the crown of the year of Your sweetness shall be blessed.

Your fields shall be filled with fatness, beautiful places of the desert shall become fattened.

The hills were clothed with joyfulness, and the rams of the sheep were clothed.**

The valleys shall abundantly produce the wheat, they cry out and bless.

gave it water
*** "with wool" is implied.*

MIDDAY PSALM

Midday Psalm for Feast Days of the Archangels

Ps 103:4,1 KJV 104: 4,1
connection-response

Who made His angels in the spirits,
and His ministers from burning flames.

My being, bless the Lord, Lord my God
You became very great.

Midday Psalm for Feast Days of the Apostles and Prophets

Ps 18:5,2 KJV 19:4,1
connection-response

Their speech went forth into all lands,
and their words unto all ends of the world.

The heavens tell of the works of God, and the firmament tells of that which has been made of His hands.

Midday Psalm for Feasts of the Patriarchs and Doctors of the Church

Ps 131:9, 1-2 KJV 132:9, 1-2
connection-response

Your priests shall be clothed with justice, and Your saints will rejoice with joy.
Lord remember David, and all his meekness.

How he gave oath to the Lord, and gave vows to the God of Jacob.

Midday Psalm for all Feast Days of Holy Martyrs

Ps 115: 15-16a, 10 KJV 116: 15-16a, 10
connection-response

Death of His saints is honorable before the Lord, O Lord,
I am Your servant, servant and son of Your maid-servant.

I believed and of that I spoke I became exceedingly humbled.

MIDDAY EPISTLE

The Epistle Reading from I John 4:7-21

Student Chancel

> *(This is an example only. See the Lectionary or Church Calendar for the correct day's reading.)*

Beloved, let us love one another, for love is from God, and every one that loves, having been born of God and knows God, and he who does not love, does not know God, for God is love. And from this the love of God appeared to us, for God sent His only begotten Son to the world that through Him we shall be living. From this is love, not that we loved God, but that He loved us, and He sent His son for the atonement of our sins. Beloved, if God loved us in that manner, then we also are obligated to love one another. There is none of anyone having ever seen God, if we may love one another,

God has been perfected in us. By that
we know that we have dwelled in Him and
He in us, for He gave us of His spirit. And
we saw and we testify, that the Father sent His
Son the savior of the world. That someone
shall be confessing, that Jesus is the Son of God,
God dwells in him, and he in God, and we
believed, and we knew the love of God, which
He has towards us. God is love, and he
who exists in love, has dwelled in God,
and God dwells in him. In that His love
is perfected in us, that we have boldness
on the day of judgment, and because
as He is, in the same manner we
also are in this world. Fear does not exist
in love, but the love which has been perfected
drives out fear, because fear is under sufferings,
but those who fear, are not perfected in love.
Let us love God, because He
loved us first. If someone may say
that, "I love God," and yet may hate his
brother, he is lying, he who does not
love his brother whom he sees, how
is it possible to love God Whom no one
has seen, and we have this commandment
given from Him, "For he who loves
God, he also loves his brother."

482 MIDDLE MIDDAY PSALM (ANTHEM)

These are Psalms chanted in alternation before the particular Middle Prophetic or Epistle Reading. All begin with "Alleluia, Alleluia."

Not all Middle Midday Psalms listed are in their entirety. However, the totally complete sets of Psalms can only be found in the Book of Psalms (Saghmosaran) or completely referenced and prescribed in (Lectionary 2019 Armenian Apostolic Church by Rev. Dr. George A. Leylegian)

Student Chancel

Middle Midday Psalms which are chanted beginning on the First Wednesday, during the Fifty Day period after Easter. They are chanted after the reading from the book of Acts which is right before the Epistle reading.

Wednesday After Easter
Ps 147:12-20 KJV 147: 12-20

Praise the Lord Jerusalem.

And bless your God, Zion.

(See Pg. 454 for the complete text)

Thursday After Easter
Ps 98: 5,1 KJV 99:5,1

You make our Lord God elevated on high, you bow down in worship to the stool of His feet for it is holy.

The Lord ruled as king, the peoples became angry, You Who sit upon the cherubim, the earth shook.

(Consult the Book of Psalms for the complete text of Ps 98 KJV 99)

Friday After Easter
Ps 97: 3b, 1 KJV 98: 3b, 1

All ends of the earth saw the salvation of our God.

Bless the Lord in a new song, for He has made wonders.

(Consult the Book of Psalms for the complete text of Ps 97 KJV 98)

MIDDLE MIDDAY PSALM (ANTHEM)

Saturday After Easter
Ps 66: 2-8, 2 KJV 67: 1-7, 1

God, have mercy upon us and bless us, make
Your faces appear unto us and have mercy upon us.

To know Your ways upon the earth,
Your salvation unto all nations.

(See Pg. 92-93 for complete text)

New Sunday the Eighth Day of Easter
Ps 64: 2-14, 1 KJV 65:1-13, 1

To You is befitting blessing God in Zion,
and prayers shall be given unto You in Jerusalem.

(See Pg. 477-478 for complete text)

Second Monday Following Easter
Ps 64: 2-14, 1 KJV 65:1-13, 1

To You is befitting blessing God in Zion,
and prayers shall be given unto You in Jerusalem.

(See Pg. 477-478 for complete text)

Second Tuesday Following Easter
Ps 5: 2-13, 13b KJV 5:1-12, 12b

Lord, as of armament with Your pleasure
You crowned us.

Give ear to my words, Lord, and
understand my cry.

(Consult the Book of Psalms for the complete text of Ps 5 KJV 5)

MIDDAY EPISTLE

Reading for the Seventh Sunday following Easter, known as the "Second Palm Sunday" which commemorates Christ's entrance into heaven on the first Sunday after His Ascension. Isaiah 63:1-6

(This is an example only. See the Lectionary or Church Calendar for the correct day's reading.)

But who is this who having hurried
comes from Edom, in his red colored
garments from Bozrah, with a beautiful
robe and powerful force. And I speak of
justice and rights of salvation.
Why are your garments red and your
clothes as he who is treading the full winepress.
I treaded the winepress alone, and of the
heathens no one was with me.
I trampled upon them with passion, and
crushed them with anger, and I brought them down
to the earth, and I soaked all of my garments,*
for the day of restitution has arrived upon
them, and the year of salvation having come
and arrived. I looked, and there was no one
who was helping, I thought, and there was
no one who was coming to my shoulders,**
my arm saved them*** and only my passion
endured, I trampled them with my anger, and
I sacrificed them with my passion, and I brought
them down to the earth.

---

* *"in their blood," is inferred*
** *or back*
*** *refers to shoulders but contextually means "my arm saved me."*

MIDDLE MIDDAY PSALM (ANTHEM)

Middle Midday Psalms chanted before the Epistle readings during the one week fasts throughout the year.

Monday Ps 144:13 KJV 145:13
Your kingdom, kingdom of all eternities,
and Your Lordship from generation to generation.

Melody Change
The Lord is faithful in all His words,
and He is just in all His works.

Tuesday Ps 5: 8b, 12c-13 KJV 5: 7,11c-12
I shall bow down in worship in Your Holy
Temple with Your fear.

Melody Change
The beloved of Your name shall boast in You,
for You shall bless the just, Lord, with Your
pleasure You crowned them as armor.

Wednesday Ps 85: 2b-3 KJV 86 : 2b-3
Give life to your servants, my God,
Whom I hoped in You.

Melody Change
Have mercy upon me, Lord, for I cry out to You daily.

Thursday Ps 98: 5,1 KJV 99:5,1
You make our Lord God elevated on high, you
bow down in worship to the stool of His feet for it is holy.

Melody Change
The Lord ruled as king, the peoples became angry,
You Who sit upon the cherubim, the earth shook.

Friday Ps 97:3b, 1 KJV 98: 3b, 1
All ends of the earth saw the salvation of our God.

Melody Change
Bless the Lord in a new song, for He has made wonders.

486 MIDDLE MIDDAY PSALM (ANTHEM)

Middle Midday Psalms during Great Lent (Salt and Bread Days)

<u>Monday Ps 50: 11, 3 KJV 51: 10, 2</u>
Turn me, Lord, from my sins, atone all of my
unrighteousness from me.

<u>Melody Change</u>
Have mercy upon me, God, according to
Your great mercy, according to Your many
compassions atone my unrighteousness.

<u>Tuesday Ps 127: 1-2, KJV 128: 1-2</u>
Fortunate are all, who fear of the Lord
and walk in His ways.

<u>Melody Change</u>
You shall eat of the labor of your hands,
fortunate are you, may it be good.

<u>Wednesday Ps 37:22, 10 KJV 38: 21, 9</u>
Do not leave me, Lord my God,
and do not be made afar from me,
look while helping me, Lord of my salvation.

<u>Melody Change</u>
Lord, before You are all of my desires,
and my groaning is not hidden from You.

<u>Thursday Ps 70: 9, 2 KJV 71: 9,1</u>
Do not cast me out, Lord, in the time of old age,
do not leave me while in the diminishing
of my strength.

<u>Melody Change</u>
In You, Lord, I hoped unto eternity,
I will not be ashamed, save and give
me life in Your justice.

MIDDLE MIDDAY PSALM (ANTHEM) 487

<u>Friday</u>
<u>Ps 118:169, 149 KJV 119: 169,149</u>
May my requests draw near before You, Lord,
according to Your word make me wise.

<u>Melody Change</u>
Hear my voice, Lord, according to Your mercy,
Lord, and give me life in Your rights.

Middle Midday Psalm for Resurrection Days

<u>A Tz</u>
<u>Ps 65: 4,2 KJV 66: 4, 1-2</u>
All of the earth shall bow down in worship
of You, and they shall say psalms to You.

Melody Change
All of the earth cry out to God, say psalms to
His Name, and give glories of blessing to Him.

<u>A G</u>
<u>Ps 33: 4,2 KJV 34: 3,1</u>
Make great the Lord our God,
and together let us make His Name elevated
on high.

<u>Melody Change</u>
I shall bless the Lord at all times, at all times
His blessing is in my mouth.

488 MIDDLE MIDDAY PSALM (ANTHEM)

P Tz Ps 95:1-2a KJV 96: 1-2a
Bless the Lord in a new song, the entire
earth bless the Lord.

Melody Change
The entire earth bless the Lord, bless
the Lord and bless His Name.

P G Ps 67: 5a, 19c, 20a KJV 68: 4a, 19
Bless our God, bless and say psalms
to the Lord God.

Melody Change
Lord God be blessed, blessed be the Lord daily.

K Tz Ps 146: 5, 1 KJV 147: 5, 1
Great is the Lord and great is His power,
no limit exists to His wisdom.

Melody Change
Bless the Lord, for psalms are good,
to our God, let them be a sweet blessing.

K G Ps 46: 7,2 KJV 47: 6,1
Say psalms to our God, say psalms
to our king, say psalms.

Melody Change
Clap your hands, all you heathens, cry
out unto God in a voice of joyfulness.

T Tz Ps 64: 5b, 2 KJV 65: 4b, 1
Your temple is holy with wonderful justice.

Melody Change
To You is befitting blessing God in Zion,
and prayers shall be given to You in Jerusalem.

MIDDLE MIDDAY PSALM (ANTHEM) 489

<ins>T G Ps 117: 24, 1   KJV 118: 24, 1</ins>

This day is which the Lord has made,
let us rejoice and let us be glad in it.

<ins>Melody Change</ins>

May you all profess to the Lord that
He is good, for His mercy is eternal.

Middle Midday Psalm for Great Lenten (Salt and Bread) Sundays

<ins>Ps 75: 12, 2   KJV 76: 11, 1</ins>

Place and fulfill vows unto the Lord our God.

God is well known is Judea,
and His Name is great in Israel.

*Canonical Psalms for Holy Friday
during the Order of Crucifixion service
(These are chanted in alternation)*

First Psalm

<ins>Ps 34: 11, 1   KJV 35: 11, 1</ins>

Witnesses of evil rose up over me,
and they were interrogating me of things
which I did not know.

Lord judge, those who judge me,
fight against those who fight against me.

Second Psalm

<ins>Ps 37: 18, 2   KJV 38: 17, 1</ins>

In sufferings I am prepared, and my pains
are before me at all times.

Lord, do not reprimand me with Your passion,
and do not discipline me with Your anger.

MIDDLE MIDDAY PSALM (ANTHEM)

Third Psalm

Ps 40: 7a-b, 2 KJV 41: 6a-b, 1

He entered in to see, he was speaking vanity in his heart, and he gathered the lawless to himself.

Fortunate is he who considers the poor and impoverished, in the day of evil the Lord saves him.

Fourth Psalm

Ps 21: 19, 2 KJV 22: 18, 1

They divided my garments amongst themselves, and over my robe they threw dice.

God my God, look to me, why have You left me, why was I far from my salvation, for the sake of the words of my offences.

Fifth Psalm

Ps 30: 6a, 2 KJV 31: 5a, 1

Into Your hands I commit my spirit.

In You, Lord, I hoped, unto eternity I will not be ashamed, save and give me life in Your justice.

MIDDLE MIDDAY PSALM (ANTHEM) 491

Sixth Psalm

Ps 68: 22, 2, KJV 69: 21, 1

They gave me bitters for my food
and in my thirst they made me drink vinegar.

Give me life God, for the waters
have come unto my person, I
have sunk into the depths of
the abysses where rest does not
exist for me.

Seventh Psalm

Ps 87: 5b-6a, 2 KJV 88: 4b-5a, 1

I became as a man without a helper,
and free unto the dead.

Lord God of my salvation, from the
day unto the night I cried out before You.

Eighth Psalm

Ps 101: 6b-7a, 2-3a, KJV 102: 5b-6a, 1-2a

My bone is bound to my body,
I resembled a pelican in the desert.

Lord, hear my prayers, may my cry come
unto You, and do not turn Your faces from me.

MIDDAY EPISTLE *(Example)*

Student Chancel
> The Reading from I Timothy 1:1-11 written by the Apostle Paul
>
> *(This reading is an example only. The Lectionary needs to be used to find the correct reading for the day.)*

Paul, apostle* of Jesus Christ,
according to the command of God our savior,
and of Christ Jesus our hope, to Timothy a beloved
son in faith. Grace, mercy,
and peace from God the Father and
from our Lord Jesus Christ.
As I requested of you to stay in Ephesus,
while I was going to Macedonia, that you shall
give a command to certain people not to teach
strange doctrines, and to not give regard
to fables and endless genealogies,
which especially stir up questions, and not
the administration of God through faith.
For the first of the commandments is love,
from a holy heart and good thoughts, and
of unhypocritical faith, from whom certain
people erred having gone astray into
the vanity of words, they wish to be
teachers of the laws, they themselves do
not understand what they are speaking,
and not for those things which
they have affirmed. We know that the law
is of good, if someone shall bear it through
example, but you will know this, for the law is on
account of the lawless and disobedient, of the
wicked and sinners, of the unholy and impure
of those who despise their father and mother,
of murderers, of the sexually immoral, of
male homosexuals, of seducers of men, of liars,
of perjurers, and if anything else shall
be contrary to right-minded teaching,
which is according to the gospel of glories
of the fortunate God, in which I have been faithful.

* *Literally "having been sent" in Armenian. "Person sent" in Greek.*

MIDDAY ALLELUIA

(These are Psalms which are chanted before Gospel readings only. They all begin with the chanting of Alleluia Alleluia)

Senior Chancel

Midday Alleluias for Fasting Days which are chanted according to the proper tone of the day.

A Tz
Ps 142: 10c KJV 143: 10c

Your good spirit shall lead me into upright land.

or

Ps 142: 11 KJV 143: 11

For the sake of Your Name, Lord, may You give me life, with Your righteousness may You take my being out of difficulty.

A G
Ps 6: 2 KJV 6: 1

Lord, do not reprimand me in Your passion, and do not discipline me in Your anger.

or

Ps 118: 133 KJV 119: 133

Make my footsteps straight for me according to Your word, and may all sins not rule me.

MIDDAY ALLELUIA

P Tz
Ps 54:5 KJV 55:4

My heart was troubled within me, and the fear of death fell upon me.

P G
Ps 6:5 KJV 6:4

Turn, Lord, and save my being, grant me life, Lord according to Your mercy.

K Tz
Ps 24:11 KJV 25:11

For the sake of Your Name, Lord, atone my sins, for they have been a great many.

K G
Ps 6:3 KJV 6:2

Have mercy upon me Lord, for I am sick, heal my being, for my bones are troubled.

T Tz
Ps 24: 6 KJV 25: 6

Remember, Lord, Your compassions, and Your mercies, which are from the eternities.

or

Ps 24: 7-8a KJV 25: 7-8a

Do not remember the sins of my youth, and of my ignorance, but remember me, Lord, according to Your mercy, for the sake of Your sweetness, for You are sweet and upright.

MIDDAY ALLELUIA

<u>T G Ps 137: 8b KJV 138: 8b</u>
Lord, Your eternal mercy,
do not neglect the works of Your hands.

or
<u>Ps 24: 7-8a KJV 25: 7-8a</u>
Do not remember the sins of my youth,
and of my ignorance, but remember me,
Lord, according to Your mercy, for the sake
of Your sweetness, for You are sweet and upright.

or
<u>Ps 141: 6 KJV 142: 5</u>
I cried out to You, Lord, and I said
You are my hope and my portion
in the land of the living.

Alleluias for the One Week Fasts during the year.

If Monday, Tuesday, and Thursday are of the Tone (A Tz) or (T G) only, chant the appropriate Alleluia below. For all other days and Mondays, Tuesdays, and Thursdays of different tones, chant the appropriate Alleluia for these Fasting Days according to the proper tone as shown on page 493-494.

<u>Monday Ps 94: 1 KJV 95: 1</u>
Come let us rejoice in the Lord,
let us cry out to God our savior.

<u>Tuesday Ps 95: 1 KJV 96: 1</u>
Sing to the Lord a new song, all of the earth sing to the Lord,
sing to the Lord and make His Name elevated on high.

<u>Thursday Ps 88: 20b-21 KJV 89:19b-20</u>
I shall make the one who was chosen
from my people elevated on high,
I have found David my servant,
and with my holy oil I have anointed him.

MIDDAY ALLELUIA

Midday Alleluia for Great Lenten Sundays (Salt and Bread Sundays)

Ps 99: 2-5 KJV 100:1-5
All lands cry out unto the Lord, serve unto the Lord with gladness.
Enter before Him with joy, let us know that He is Lord our God.
(Chant the entire Psalm in alternation which is found on page 364.)

*Midday Alleluia for Resurrection Days
according to the proper Tone of the Day*

A Tz Ps 101: 14 KJV 102: 13
You having risen up shall have compassion upon Zion,
the time for compassion upon her, the time has arrived.

or

Ps 46: 8 KJV 47:7
God is the great king over all the earth,
say psalms to Him with wisdom.

A G Ps 149:1 KJV 149:1
Bless the Lord in a new song,
blessing to him in the assemblies of the saints.

P Tz Ps 46:2 KJV 47:1
Clap your hands, all you heathens,
cry out unto God in a voice of joyfulness.

or

Ps 84: 7 KJV 85:6
God, You give us life again, and may
Your people rejoice in You.

P G Ps 7:7-9a KJV 7:6-8a
Rise up, Lord my God, to Your orders,
which You commanded, and the assemblies
of peoples shall be around You, for
the sake of this return to the heights,
Lord, and Lord for judgment of His people.

MIDDAY ALLELUIA

<u>K Tz Ps 149: 2   KJV 149: 2</u>
Israel became glad in his maker,
the sons of Zion shall rejoice in their king.

<u>K G Ps 65: 5   KJV 66:5</u>
Come and see the works of God, for they are
frightful by design, over all the sons of man.

<u>T Tz Ps 84: 2   KJV 85: 1</u>
You were pleased, Lord throughout Your land,
and You have overturned the captivity of Jacob.

<u>T G Ps 67: 2   KJV 68:1</u>
God arose and all of His enemies scattered,
those who hate Him fled from His faces.

Midday Alleluia for Easter
<u>Ps 121: 2   KJV 122:2</u>
Having arrived our feet stood in your gates, Jerusalem.

Midday Alleluia alternative for Easter only but prescribed for the Sundays of the Fifty Days following Easter until Pentecost. Psalm 147:12-20 KJV 147:12-20 chanted in alternation.

Praise the Lord Jerusalem.

And bless your God, Zion.

He strengthened the bolts on your gates, and blessed your sons within you.

Who put your borders in peace, with the fat of the wheat He filled you.

He sends His word to the earth, His messages run quickly.

He places down snow as wool, and scattered mist as dust.

He throws out ice as morsels, who is able to stand before His cold.

He sends out His word and melts them, the winds shall blow and the waters shall flow.

He tells His word unto Jacob, justice and righteousness unto Israel.

He has not done this for all nations Lord, and He has not revealed His judgments to them.

MIDDAY ALLELUIA

Midday Alleluias Mondays through Saturdays between Easter and Ascension

Monday Ps 147: 12-20 KJV 147: 12-20
Praise the Lord Jerusalem.
And bless your God, Zion.
(Continue in its entirety as on page 497.)

Tuesday Ps 20:2 KJV 21:1
Lord in Your strength the king may be glad,
in Your salvation may he rejoice exceedingly.
(Continue the Psalm in its entirety as found in the Book of Psalms "Saghmosaran")

Wednesday Ps 64:2-14 KJV 65: 1-13
To You is befitting blessing God in Zion,
and prayers shall be given unto You in Jerusalem.
(Continue in its entirety as on page 477-478.)

Thursday Ps 14: 1-5 KJV 15: 1-5
Lord, who shall stay in Your tabernacle, or who
shall dwell upon Your Holy mountain.
(Continue in its entirety as on page 474.)

Friday Ps 92: 1-5 KJV 93: 1-5
The Lord ruled as king, He was clothed in splendor,
He was clothed with strength brought forth from within Him.
(Continue in its entirety as on page 453.)

Saturday Ps 80: 2-17 KJV 81: 1-16
Rejoice to God, He is our helper,
cry out to the God of Jacob.

Take a psalm, and give blessing,
say psalms to Him in a voice of sweetness.

Blow the horn on the new moon, on the day
of our festival.

This is the command for Israel, and they
are the rights of the God of Jacob.

MIDDAY ALLELUIA

The testimony of Joseph, which was placed
in him, as he was coming out from the
land of the Egyptians, whose language he heard
yet did not know.

He removed their shoulders of the burdens,
and his hands of serving the basket and shovel.

In oppression you cried out to me, and
I saved you, I heard you from the secret place
of the storm, and I tested you over the waters of
contradiction.

Listen my people and I witness to you,
and Israel that you may listen to me.

Never again shall they be new gods to you,
and you shall not bow down in worship
to the god of a foreigner.

I am your Lord God, who took you
out from the land of the Egyptians,
open your mouth, and I will fill it.

My people did not listen to my voice,
and Israel which did not look in me.

I raised them up and let them to go in the
footsteps of the wills of their hearts,
for they walked according to the wills
of themselves.

For if the people of mine had listened
to me, or if Israel had walked in my ways.

I would have humbled her enemies as nothing,
and I would throw my hands over her oppressors.

Enemies of the Lord lied to Him, and their
times shall be unto the world.

He fed them from the fat of the wheat,
and honey from the stone satisfied their hunger.

Midday Alleluia for Sundays from the First Sunday After Easter "New Sunday" until the Ascension.

Ps 147: 12-20 KJV 147: 12-20

Praise the Lord Jerusalem.

And bless your God, Zion.
(Continue in its entirety as on page 497.)

Midday Alleluia for the Ascension of Christ until Pentecost

Ps 23: 7 KJV 24: 7

Princes, lift up your gates, the gates of eternity
shall be lifted up and the King of Glories
shall enter.

MIDDAY ALLELUIA

Midday Alleluias for the Days of Pentecost

Sunday Ps 32: 5b-6 KJV 33: 5b-6
The earth has been filled with
the mercy of the Lord, and through
the word of the Lord the heavens
became established, and through the
spirit of His mouth, all of their hosts.

Monday Ps 94:1 KJV 95:1
Come let us rejoice in the Lord,
let us cry out to God our savior.

Tuesday Ps 95:1a, 99:3a, KJV 96:1a, 100:2a
Sing unto the Lord a new song,
serve the Lord with gladness.

Wednesday Ps 142:11 KJV 143:11
For the sake of Your Name, Lord, may You give me life,
with Your righteousness may You take my being
out of difficulty.

Thursday Ps 6:3 KJV 6:2
Have mercy upon me Lord, for I am sick,
heal my being, for my bones are troubled.

Friday Ps 131:1 KJV 132:1
Remember Lord, David, and all of his meekness.

Saturday Ps 67:27 KJV 68:26
Bless God in His assemblies, and the Lord
from the fountains of Israel.

Midday Alleluia for the Feast of the Ark of the Covenant

Ps 131:8 KJV 132:8
Rise Lord to Your rest, You and the
ark of Your holy covenant.

MIDDAY ALLELUIA

Midday Alleluias for the Transfiguration of Christ (Vartavarr)

Sunday Matthew 17:5
A brilliant cloud was showing over them, a voice was from the cloud which says, "This is my beloved Son with Whom I was pleased."

Monday Ps 94:4b-6 KJV 95:4b-6
The heights of the mountains are His, the sea is His and He made it, and His hands created the dry land. Come we shall bow in worship to Him, we shall fall and weep before the Lord our maker.

Tuesday Ps 88: 12-13 KJV 89:11-12
Yours are the heavens and Yours is the earth, this world in its entirety You established. You made the north and the south, Mount Tabor and Mount Hermon will rejoice in Your name.

Midday Alleluias for Feasts of the Dedication of the Church of the Holy Sepulcher in Jerusalem, the Holy Cross, and the Holy Church

Saturday Ps 131:13-14 KJV 132:13-14
The Lord loved Zion, and chose to dwell in it, He says, "This is my rest unto the eternity of eternities, in it I shall dwell, for I was pleased with it."

Sunday Ps 85:16b-17a KJV 86:16b-17a
Give strength to Your servant,
give life to the son of Your maid,
and make unto me the sign of goodness.

Monday Ps 59:6 KJV 60:4
You gave a sign to those who fear
You, that they shall live in the faces of the bow.

Tuesday Ps 131:13-14 KJV 132:13-14
The Lord loved Zion, and chose to dwell in it, He says, "This is my rest unto the eternity of eternities, in it I shall dwell, for I was pleased with it."

MIDDAY ALLELUIA

Wednesday Ps 25:8 KJV 26:8
Lord, I loved the elegance of Your
house, and the dwelling place of Your glories.

Thursday Ps 83:2-3 KJV 84:1-2
How beloved are Your dwellings, Lord of hosts,
I desire and long for my being in Your courts.
My Heart and body shall rejoice unto the living God.

Friday Ps 59:6 KJV 60:4
You gave a sign to those who fear
You, that they shall live in the faces of the bow.

Saturday Ps 59:7 KJV 60:5
As they saved Your beloved, give life with Your right hand and hear us.

Midday Alleluias for Feasts of the Church

Ps 86:2 KJV 87:1-2
His foundation is in His holy mountain, the Lord loves the
gates of Zion more than all of the dwellings of Jacob.

or

Ps 86:3 KJV 87:3
Glorification was spoken regarding You, behold the City of God.

or

Ps 14:1-2 KJV 15:1-2
Lord, who shall stay in Your tabernacle, or who shall dwell upon Your
Holy mountain. He who walks spotlessly works justice, he speaks the
truth in his heart.

Midday Alleluia for Feasts of the Cross

Ps 4:7b-8a KJV 4:6b-7a
A sign of the light of Your faces was placed
before us, and You gave joy to our hearts.

MIDDAY ALLELUIA

Midday Alleluias for the nine day Feast of the Assumption* of Mary the God-Bearer.
(The three Alleluias repeat cyclically every third day for the nine days)

<u>Sunday Luke 2:11 Ps 109:3b KJV 110:3b</u>
Today Whom from the Father, the Son before the
eternities was born, Who is anointed Lord, in the City of David.
In the splendor of Your saints, from the womb before the
morning star** I gave birth to You.

<u>Monday Luke 1:28b, 42b</u>
O cheerful one rejoice, the Lord is with you,
blessed are you amongst women, and blessed
is the fruit of your womb.

<u>Tuesday Ps 131:8 KJV 132:8</u>
Rise Lord to Your rest, You and the ark of Your holy covenant.

Midday Alleluia for the Annunciation to Mary the God-Bearer

<u>Luke 1:28b, 42b</u>
O cheerful one rejoice, the Lord is with you,
blessed are you amongst women, and blessed
is the fruit of your womb.

Midday Alleluia for the Birth of Christ

<u>Christmas Eve "The Lighting of the Lamps" (Jrakalooytz)</u>
<u>Luke 1:35b</u>
The Holy Spirit shall come upon you, and
the power of the One raised up on high
shall be a shadow upon you.

---

* *Literally-changing from this world to the next.*
** *Morning star has a double meaning. It is another term for Lucifer (Satan).*

MIDDAY ALLELUIA 505

Midday Alleluias for the Eight Days of the Birth of Christ

Christmas Day Luke 2:11 Ps 109:3b KJV 110:3b
Today Whom from the Father, the Son before the eternities was born, Who is anointed Lord, in the City of David. In the splendor of Your saints, from the womb before the morning star** I gave birth to You.

Second Day Acts 7:55
The holy Stephen having been strengthened through the Holy Spirit, and having been chosen from the womb, true witness, lover and having been sent to the sender, from Christ you received the crown of the angels.

Third Day John 1:29
The Forerunner John having been astonished, from the womb, unto the womb he bowed down in worship, he became servant to the Word of God, and having heard the frightful sound, he was crying out saying, "Behold the Lamb of God, Who takes away the sins of the world."

Fourth Day Luke 1:28b, 42b
O cheerful one rejoice, the Lord is with you, blessed are you amongst women, and blessed is the fruit of your womb.

Fifth Day Luke 1:76
You child, shall be called prophet on high, you will go before the Lord to prepare His pathways.

Sixth Day Ps 39:3 KJV 40:2
He pulled me from the pit of misery, from the clay and from the mud. He firmly propped my feet upon a rock, and straightened my path.

or

Ps 109:4b-5a KJV 110:4b-5a
That You are priest eternally according to the order of Melchizedek, and the Lord is at Your right hand.*

* *This verse may possibly be a remnant from a stational service performed in the Holy Land which is no longer being performed. It is no longer used on this day.*

MIDDAY ALLELUIA

Seventh Day Ps 131:11 KJV 132:11

The Lord swore to David in truth, and did not lie to him, one from the fruit of his womb will be seated upon his throne.

Eighth Day Luke 1:28b, 42b

O cheerful one rejoice, the Lord is with you, blessed are you amongst women, and blessed is the fruit of your womb.

Midday Alleluia for the Presentation of Christ to the Temple After Forty Days.

Ps 10:5a KJV 11:4a

The Lord in His Holy Temple,
the Lord in His throne in the heavens.

Midday Alleluia for Palm Sunday

Ps 117:27 KJV 118:27

Lord our God had appeared to us, make
feasts of rejoicing beforehand up to
the corners of the altar table.

Midday Alleluia for Feasts of the Archangels

Ps 32:5b-6 KJV 33:5b-6

The earth has been filled with
the mercy of the Lord, and through
the word of the Lord the heavens
became established. And through the
spirit of His mouth, all of their hosts.

MIDDAY ALLELUIA

Midday Alleluia for the Feast Day of John the Baptist

Luke 1:76
You child, shall be called prophet on high, you will go before the Lord to prepare His pathways.

Midday Alleluia for the Feast Day of the Beheading of John the Baptist

John 1:29
The Forerunner John having been astonished, from the womb, unto the womb he bowed down in worship, he became servant to the Word of God, and having heard the frightful sound, he was crying out saying, "Behold the Lamb of God, Who takes away the sins of the world."

Midday Alleluia for Feast Days of All Prophets

Ps 67:27 KJV 68:26
Praise God in His assemblies, and the Lord from the fountains of Israel.

Midday Alleluia for Feast Days of All Apostles

Ps 44:17b-18a KJV 45:16b-17a
You shall make them princes throughout the entire earth, and I shall make Your Name remembered through all generations of generations.

or

Ps 18:5 KJV 19:4a
Their speech went forth into all lands, and their words unto all ends of the world.

MIDDAY ALLELUIA

*Midday Alleluia for the Feast Day of
David and the Apostle James the Greater*

Ps 131:1 KJV 132:1
Remember Lord, David, and all his meekness.

Midday Alleluia for Feast Days of the Old Testament Patriarchs

Ps 147:19 KJV 147:19
He tells His word unto Jacob, justice
and righteousness unto Israel.

Midday Alleluia for Feast Days of St. Gregory the Illuminator

Ps 39:2 KJV 40:1
With patience I waited for the Lord, and He looked
to me, and heard my prayers.

*Midday Alleluia for Feast days of the Church Fathers
and for the Doctors of the Church (Vartabeds)*

Ps 131:9 KJV 132:9
Your priests shall be clothed with justice,
and Your saints will rejoice with joy.

Midday Alleluia for Feast Days of the Hermits

Ps 83:5 KJV 84:4
Fortunate are those who have dwelled in the
house of the Lord, unto the eternity of eternities
they shall bless You.

MIDDAY ALLELUIA

Midday Alleluia for Feast Days of the Holy Virgins

Ps 44:10b, 15b KJV 45:9b, 14b
The queen shall stand at your right hand, in garments adorned with gold embroidery and ornamented. She shall be taken to the king, the virgins behind her, and her companions shall be taken to him.

Midday Alleluia for Feast Days of Christian Kings

Ps 20:2 KJV 21:1
Lord in Your strength may the king be glad, in Your salvation he shall rejoice exceedingly.

Midday Alleluia for the Feast Day of the Forty Young Soldiers Martyred in Sebaste 320 A.D. and for the Feast Day of the 20,000 Martyrs who were burned in the Churches of Nicomedia 304 A.D.

Ps 65:12b KJV 66:12b
We passed through fire and water, and You took us out to a place of comfort.

Midday Alleluia for Holy Thursday

Ps 22:5a KJV 23:5a
You have prepared the table before me, before the eyes of my oppressors.

Midday Alleluia for the Gospel Reading at Daybreak

(This is actually chanted in the Holy Friday Evening Entombment Service and during the early morning gravesite visitations of mourners)

Ps 29:6b KJV 30:5b
Throughout the evening weeping shall rest,
in the morning let there be gladness.

MIDDAY ALLELUIA

Midday Alleluias for Feast Days of Martyrs according to Tone of the Day

A Tz Ps 36:28a KJV 37:28a
The Lord loves justice, and does not abandon His saints,
but keeps them unto eternity.

or
Ps 36:39 KJV 37:39
The salvation of the just is from the
Lord, He is their guardian in times of distress.

A G Ps 149:5-6a KJV 149:5-6a
The saints shall become boastful with glory,
and will rejoice in their rest, and they shall
make God elevated on high with their mouths.

or
Ps 96:11 KJV 97:11
He shined light upon the just,
those upright in heart became joyful.

P Tz Ps 149:5-6a KJV 149:5-6a
The saints shall become boastful with glory,
and will rejoice in their rest, and they shall
make God elevated on high with their mouths.

P G Ps 33:18 KJV 34:17
The just cried out to the Lord, and the Lord
heard them, He saved them from all troubles.

K Tz Ps 43:23 KJV 44:22
For Your sake we die every day,
we were accounted as the sheep to slaughter.

K G Ps 5:12a-c KJV 5:11a-c
Let all of those who have hoped in You
be joyful, they shall eternally
rejoice, and You shall dwell in them.

MIDDAY ALLELUIA AND GOSPELS

<u>T Tz Ps 91:13 KJV 92:12</u>
The just shall flourish as the date palm trees,
they shall be many as the cedars of Lebanon.

<u>T G Ps 33:20-21 KJV 34:19-20</u>
The oppressions to the just ones are many,
the Lord saves them from all of them, and He keeps
all of their bones, and not one of them shall be destroyed.

The Midday Gospel Reading is read according to the proper day as shown by the Lectionary.
Then the Nicene Creed is Chanted.
(The following four Gospel Readings are examples only, consult the Lectionary for the correct Gospel of the day.)

<u>Deacon</u>	Alleluia Stand
<u>Priest</u>	Peace unto all.
<u>Choir</u>	And with Your spirit.
<u>Deacon</u>	May you listen with awe.

<u>Reader (priest or deacon)</u> **Senior Chancel**
The Holy Gospel of Jesus Christ According to Matthew 5:1-12

<u>Choir</u>	Glory to You Lord our God.
<u>Deacon</u>	Attention
<u>Choir</u>	God says.

<u>P G</u>
<u>T G</u>
Of our Lord Jesus Christ

And having seen the people, He went up
to the mountain, and as He sat there,
His disciples approached to Him, and
having opened His mouth He was teaching
them, and He says, "Fortunate are the poor in spirit,
for to them is the kingdom of the heavens.

Fortunate are those who mourn,
for they shall be consoled. Fortunate are
the meek, for they shall inherit the earth.
Fortunate are those who have hungered
and become thirsty for justice, for they shall
become filled. Fortunate are the merciful
for they shall find mercy. Fortunate are
those who are with holy heart, for they
shall see God. Fortunate are the peacemakers,
for they shall be called sons of God. Fortunate
are those who are persecuted for the sake of justice,
theirs is the kingdom of the heavens. Fortunate
are you at which time they shall insult and
persecute you, and every evil word which
they say concerning you for my sake is
false. Rejoice and be glad, for your rewards
in the heavens are many, for in this manner
they persecuted the prophets who were
before you."

The Holy Gospel According to Mark 3:13-19

P Tz
T Tz

Our Lord Jesus Christ

He goes up to the mountain, and He calls to Himself
those whom He Himself willed, and they went to Him.

MIDDAY GOSPELS

And He made the twelve, that shall be
around Him, and that He may send them
out to preach, and to have the authority
to heal afflictions and to take out demons.
And He placed upon Simon the name Peter,
and to James the son of Zebedee and to John the
brother of James, He placed upon them of the names
Boanerges, which is Sons of Thunder, and Andrew
and Phillip and Bartholomew and Matthew the
tax collector, and Thomas and James the son
of Alpheus, and Thaddeus and Simon the
Cananite, and Judas Iscariot, who also betrayed Him.

The Holy Gospel According to Luke 14:12-15

A G
K G

Our Lord Jesus Christ

And He says to the host, "At which time you
shall make a meal or dinner, do not call
your friends, nor your brothers, nor your
relatives, nor your neighbors, nor the great men,

for will they also not call you in return,
and to you shall be repayment. But at which
time you shall make a reception, call the poor
and the disabled, and the lame and the blind,
and you shall be fortunate, for they do
not have anything in return for repaying you,
and return to you shall be made in the
resurrection of the just." As one of the guests
heard this, He says to him, "Fortunate is he
who shall eat a meal in the kingdom of God."

The Holy Gospel According to John 10:11-16

A Tz
K Tz

Our Lord Jesus Christ says.

I am the good shepherd, the good shepherd
lays down his being on behalf of the sheep. But
the hired hand who is not the shepherd, of whom the
sheep are not his, as he sees the wolf that comes,
he leaves the sheep and flees,

and the wolf snatches and scatters them,
because he is the hired hand, and there is not
a care for him for the sake of the sheep. I am
the good shepherd, and I know mine, and by my
own I am known. As the Father knows me,
I also know the Father, and I lay down my
being on behalf of the sheep. These and
more other sheep are mine, which are not
from this sheep pen, and they are also necessary
for me to bring to this place, and they shall
hear my voice, and they shall be with one
one flock one shepherd.

<u>Choir</u>
Glory to You our God.

The Nicene Creed

Senior Chancel

We believe in one God in the Father almighty,
in the maker of heaven and earth,
of things visible and invisible.

And in One Lord Jesus Christ the Son of God,
the one having been born from God the Father, only begotten,
that is from the existence of the Father.

God from God, light from light, true God, from true God,
birth and not made.

He himself of the same nature
of the Father, through Whom all things became
in the heavens and upon the earth, visible and
invisible.

Who for the sake of our humanity, and for the
sake of our salvation, having descended from the
heavens He took bodily form, He became human,
He was born perfectly of Mary the holy virgin
through the Holy Spirit.

By whom He took body, soul, and mind, and
everything which that is of man, truly and not
in theory*.

Having suffered, having been crucified, having
been buried, on the third day having
resurrected, having ascended to the heavens
with the same body, He sat at the right
hand of the Father.

He is to come with the same body and glories
of the Father, to judge the living and
the dead, of Whose kingdom no end exists.

We believe also in the Holy Spirit, in the
uncreated and the perfect, Who spoke through the laws,
the prophets, and the gospels.**

Who descended into the Jordan, preached
into the apostles, and dwelled in the saints.

---

*or "ideation"

** *The personal pronoun "Who" must be used when referring to the Holy Spirit because it is the third person of the Trinity. Impersonal pronouns "Which or That" would be theologically incorrect.*

NICENE CREED

We believe also in only one universal
and apostolic* church, in one baptism for
the repentance, atonement, and forgiveness of sins.

In the resurrection of the dead, in the eternal
judgment of souls and bodies, in the kingdom
of the heavens and in the lives eternal.

* "holy" is added here in some editions

The Condemnation**

_____
Deacon
But those who say there once was a time
which there was not the Son, or there once was
a time which there was not the Holy Spirit, or that
they became from nothing or who say that the
Son of God or the Holy Spirit to be of a different existence,
or that they are changeable or alterable, the
universal and apostolic Holy Church condemns those such.

** More commonly known as the "Anathema"

The Glorification*** said by St. Gregory the Illuminator

_____
Priest
But may we glorify Him Who was before the eternities,
by bowing down in worshiping of the Holy Trinity and of the
one Godly Being, of the Father and of the Son and of the Holy Spirit,
now and always and unto the eternity of eternities. Amen.

***More commonly known as "Doxology"

MIDDAY CONCLUSION

Proclamation

Student Chancel

<u>Deacon</u>

And again in peace let us request of the Lord.

<u>Choir</u>

Lord have mercy.

<u>Deacon</u>

And again in faith let us request and ask
from the Lord God and from our savior Jesus
Christ, at these hours of worship service and prayers, that He
may make them worthy of acceptance, may the Lord
hear the voice of our requests, may the requests of
our hearts be accepted, may He forgive our offences, may
He be merciful upon us. May our prayers and
requests at every hour enter before His great
Lordship, and may He grant us to labor in good
deeds in unison, with one faith and with
justice, that He may make His graces of mercy
come upon us, almighty Lord, may You
give life and be merciful.

<u>Choir</u>

Give life Lord.

MIDDAY CONCLUSION

<u>Deacon</u>

To pass this hour and upcoming day in peace, with faith let us ask from the Lord.

Grace unto us Lord.

The angel of peace to be guardian of our beings. Let us ask from the Lord.

Grace unto us Lord.

For atonement and forgiveness of our offences. Let us ask from the Lord.

Grace unto us Lord.

For the great Holy Cross and able strength for assistance of our beings. Let us ask from the Lord.

Grace unto us Lord.

And again in one voice for the sake of our true and holy faith. Let us pray to the Lord.

Lord have mercy.

Let us make ourselves and one another as the person of the Lord God almighty.

Let us become as Your Person Lord.

Lord our God be merciful to us, according to Your great mercy, let us all say in unison.

Lord have mercy. Lord have mercy. Lord have mercy.

Prayer

<u>Priest</u> **Senior Chancel**

Our Lord and savior Jesus Christ, Whom You are great with mercy and abundant with gifts of Your kindness. Whom You through Your will at these hours endured of the sufferings of the cross and of death, for the sake

MIDDAY CONCLUSION

of our sins. And You gifted abundantly the gifts of the Holy Spirit to the fortunate apostles. Give a share to us also, Lord, we request of You, for the Godly gifts, for the forgiveness of sins and for the receiving of the Holy Spirit. So that we may become worthy with thanksgiving to glorify You with the Father and with the Holy Spirit, now and always and unto the eternity of eternities. Amen.

Peace unto all.

Choir
And with Your spirit.

Deacon
Let us bow in worship of God.

Choir
Before You Lord.

Priest
Through Your peace, Christ our savior, Who is above all thoughts and words, fortify us and keep us fearless from all evil. Make us equal along with Your true worshippers, those who with spirit and with truth bow down in worship to You. Because, the most Holy Trinity is befitting glory, Lordship and honor, now always and unto the eternity of eternities. Amen.

Blessed be our Lord Jesus Christ. Amen.

Lord God may He bless all. Amen

> Our Father Who art in heaven, Hallowed be Thy name.
> Thy kingdom come, Thy will be done on earth as it is in heaven.
> Give us this day our daily bread.
> And forgive us our debts, as we forgive our debtors.
> And lead us not into temptation, but deliver us from evil.
>
> For Thine is the Kingdom, and the power,
> and the glory forever and ever. Amen.

MIDDAY CONCLUSION 521

<u>Choir</u>
Only One is holy, only One is Lord, Jesus Christ
in the glories of God the Father. Amen.

<u>Priest</u>
Blessed be the Holy Father, true God.

<u>Choir</u>
Amen.

<u>Priest</u>
Blessed be O Holy Son, true God.

<u>Choir</u>
Amen.

<u>Priest</u>
Blessed be O Holy Spirit, true God.

<u>Choir</u>
Amen.

<u>Priest</u>
Blessing to the Father and to the Son and to the Holy Spirit.
Now and always and unto the eternity of eternities. Amen.

<u>Choir Ps 112:1 KJV 113:1</u>
(Sing this verse three times)

The Name of the Lord shall be blessed,
from this time forth unto eternity.

<u>Priest</u>
You are fulfillment of the laws and the prophets,
Christ God our savior, You Who fulfilled all the
Fatherly laws of the House of God,*
fill us also with Your Holy Spirit.

---

* *The Armenian terms "Dnorenootyoon, Dnorinapar" derived from Greek "Oikonomia" give a loose translation for the term "Redeeming Economy" used by theologians. It may also be loosely translated as "Administrative."*

522 MIDDAY CONCLUSION

Deacon Ps 33:2   KJV 34:1
I shall bless the Lord at all times,
at all times His blessing is in my mouth.

Priest
May You be blessed by the graces of the Holy Spirit.
Go in peace, and may the Lord be with you,
with you all, Amen.

The Blessing of the Table is performed during mealtime in which food and drink are partaken for the nourishment of our physical bodies. The Table is prepared with bread and other dishes and each person stands in his own place at the table. When the Elder of the group or the Priest enters, he recites the Psalm below.

Elder or Priest
Connection-response
Ps 144:15a-b KJV 145:15

The eyes of all hope in You,
and You give food to them on time.

acolytes and choir
Ps 144:1-21 KJV 145:1-21

I raise You up on high my God, and my
king, I also bless Your Name eternally and unto
the eternity of eternities.

I shall bless You daily, and I shall praise
Your Name eternally and unto the eternity of eternities.

Great is the Lord and He is extremely blessed,
and of His greatness there is no measure.

Generations and generations shall praise Your works,
and they shall tell of Your powers.

The magnificence of the holiness of Your
glories shall be spoken of, and Your wonders
shall be told of.

BLESSING OF THE TABLE

They shall say of Your awesome strength,
and they shall tell of Your greatness.

They shall spring forth the many memories
of Your sweetness, and through Your justice
they shall rejoice.

The Lord is compassionate and merciful,
patient and abundantly merciful.

The Lord is sweet to all, and His compassion
over all of which He has made.

All of Your works Lord, shall confess to You,
and Your saints shall bless You.

They shall say of the glories of Your
kingdom, and they shall tell of Your powers.

For the sons of man to know Your
powers, and the glories of the magnificence
of Your kingdom.

Your kingdom, kingdom of all eternities,
and Your Lordship from generation to generation.

BLESSING OF THE TABLE

The Lord is faithful in all of His
words, and He is just in all of His works.

The Lord supports all those who stumble,
and He stands up all those who have sunken.

The eyes of all hope in You,
and You give food to them on time.

You give to them and they are fed,
You open Your hands, and You fill all
with the kindness of Your wills.

The Lord is just in all His ways, and
holy in all of His works.

The Lord is near to all of those
who call upon Him in truth.

The Lord does fulfill the wills of those who
fear in Him, He hears their prayers,
and gives them life.

The Lord keeps all those who love Him,
and the Lord destroys all of the sinners.

My mouth shall speak the blessings of the Lord,
all which is living shall bless His Holy Name
eternally, and unto the eternity of eternities.

Glory to the Father and to the Son and to the Holy Spirit.

Now and always and unto the eternity of eternities. Amen.

BLESSING OF THE TABLE

<u>Priest</u>

The Lord is merciful and compassionate, He gives food to those of His who fear in Him.

<u>Deacon</u>

And again in peace let us request of the Lord.

Let us pray to the almighty God, that He may gift us food of gladness, and may He fill our hearts from the fullness of His creatures which He has made. Our Lord God almighty give life and have mercy.

<u>Priest</u>

Bless, Christ our God, with spiritual blessings the food and drink of Your servants, and grace health to the soul and body. So that enjoying with religious modesty for bodily needs, of Your unpassing good things, and let us be partakers of Your kingdom of the heavens in the company of all Your saints. And with thanksgiving let us glorify You with the Father and the most Holy Spirit, now and always and unto the eternity of eternities, Amen.

BLESSING OF THE TABLE 527

Our Father Who art in heaven, Hallowed be Thy name. Thy kingdom come, Thy will be done on earth as it is in heaven. Give us this day our daily bread. And forgive us our debts, as we forgive our debtors. And lead us not into temptation, but deliver us from evil.

For Thine is the Kingdom, and the power, and the glory forever and ever. Amen.

The one who blesses the table stands, takes the bread and breaks it with the guest of honor, who is seated beside him. Or, he may sit beside those who have prepared the meal, and everyone else may sit beside them. He then recites the prayer "Eat in Peace" (Jashagetzek Khaghaghootyamp)* and then they sit and eat. If this takes place in a monastery or in a desert hermitage one of the brotherhood will sit in the highest place and read from the Bible while everybody eats without making noise. If someone has a question or a problem that needs to be discussed, whoever is able to answer the question may do so and then they should return to eating without talking or making any noise. After they finish eating, they will again stand in their own places and the priest will recite the following.

<u>Priest</u>
Lord Jesus, we were filled in Your goodness.

<u>Acolytes & Choir</u>
Let us give thanks to the Lord our God.

<u>Ps 32:18-22 KJV 33:18-22</u>
The eyes of the Lord are upon those who fear Him,
and who hope in His mercy.

* *Jashagetzek khaghaghootyamp uz-geragoors vor barkevyal e mezi Dyarrne: Orhnyal e Der i barkevs yiur: Amen:*

Eat in peace this meal which has been gifted to us from the Lord. Blessed is the Lord in His gifts. Amen.

BLESSING OF THE TABLE

Save their beings from death, and to
feed them in famine.

Our beings shall wait for the Lord, for He
is our helper and defender.

Our hearts shall be glad in Him, and
we shall hope in His Holy Name.

Lord may Your mercy be upon us,
as we hoped in You.

Glory to the Father and to the Son and to the Holy Spirit.

Now and always and unto the eternity of eternities. Amen.

Priest

Glory to You, Lord, the feeder and the
One Who makes us glad, Christ the One Who
fills, from You we are satisfied.

Deacon

And again in peace let us request of the Lord.

Let us give thanks upon the fullness
of the gifts of the Lord our God. Who
feeds us abundantly day by day with
kindness according to His wills. That of spiritual
goodness and of the kingdom of the heavens,
may He make His servants partakers
according to our wait in hope. Almighty
Lord our God, give life and have mercy.

BLESSING OF THE TABLE

Prayer

<u>Priest</u>

Blessed are You, Lord our God, Who feeds us from childhood, and You give food of all flesh,* fill our hearts with cheer and gladness, in order that we may have all sufficiency having increased in works of good in Christ Jesus our Lord. To Whom is befitting glory, Lordship, and honor, now and always and unto the eternity of eternities. Amen.

Peace unto all.

<u>Acolytes & Choir</u>

And with Your spirit.

<u>Deacon</u>

Let us bow down in worship of God.

<u>Acolytes & Choir</u>

Before You Lord.

<u>Priest</u>

Glory to You, Lord, glory to You, king of glories, You Who gave us food of gladness, and filled our hearts from the fullness of Your most sufficient mercy, and now fill us with Your Holy Spirit, in order that we may be found pleasing before You, and we may not be ashamed, for You come and compensate each one according to their deeds, and to You is befitting glory, Lordship, and honor, now and always and unto the eternity of eternities, Amen.

* *meats*

BLESSING OF THE TABLE

<u>Priest</u>

Blessed be our Lord Jesus Christ. Amen.

Our Father Who art in heaven, Hallowed be Thy name. Thy kingdom come, Thy will be done on earth as it is in heaven. Give us this day our daily bread. And forgive us our debts, as we forgive our debtors. And lead us not into temptation, but deliver us from evil.

For Thine is the Kingdom, and the power, and the glory forever and ever. Amen.

May God bless those who eat, to the servants and to the sponsors may He gift recompense of goodness, and may Christ God bless all, He Who fed and filled us, to Him be glory unto the eternities, Amen.

EVENING HOUR

The order of the common hour of Prayers of the Evening Hour which are performed before the Son of God who descended from the cross and was shrouded in fine linen and placed in the tomb:

Blessed be our Lord Jesus Christ. Amen.

Our Father Who art in heaven, Hallowed be Thy name.
Thy kingdom come, Thy will be done on earth as it is in heaven.
Give us this day our daily bread.
And forgive us our debts, as we forgive our debtors.
And lead us not into temptation, but deliver us from evil.

For Thine is the Kingdom, and the power,
and the glory forever and ever. Amen.

Priest Ps 54:17-18a KJV 55:16-17
I cried out to God, and He heard me in the evening,
in the morning, and at noon.

Student Chancel

Deacon Ps 54:9a KJV55:8 Micah 7:7 & poetic phrases
I waited for my God, and was
expecting the One Who gives life, Who saves
His servants and grants life.

Priest
Glory to the Father and to the Son and to the Holy Spirit.

Deacon
Now and always and unto the eternity of eternities. Amen.

Senior Chancel

* During the fifty days after Easter only, the first Psalm and Gospel Reading as prescribed by the Lectionary are chanted at this point.

534 EVENING HOUR

<u>Deacon</u>
And again in peace let us request of the Lord. Receive, save, and have mercy.

<u>Priest</u>
Blessing and glory to the Father and to the Son and to the Holy Spirit. Now and always and unto the eternity of eternities. Amen.

Peace unto all.

<u>Choir</u>
And with Your spirit.

<u>Deacon</u>
Let us bow down in worship of God.

<u>Choir</u>
Before You Lord.

Psalm 85:1-17 KJV 86:1-17
(Read in alternation)

Senior Chancel

Descend Your ear Lord and hear me,
for I am poor and indigent.

Keep my being holy Lord, and save Your servant,
my God, Whom in You I hope.

Have mercy upon me, Lord, for I cried out to You all of the day, make the being of Your servant glad, for unto You, Lord, I lifted up my being.

For You, Lord, are sweet and upright,
abundantly merciful to all who cry
out to you.

Give ear, Lord, to my prayers and look
upon the voice of my requests.

In the day of my trouble I cried out to You,
and You heard me.

No one is like You of the gods, Lord,
and no one is as of Your works.

EVENING HOUR

All nations which You have made shall
come and bow down in worship before
You, and they shall make Your Name
glorious unto eternity.

You are great, Lord, and make wonders,
and You only are God.

Lead me in Your way, and I shall
walk in Your truth, and my heart
shall be glad, to fear from Your Name.

I shall confess to You, Lord my God,
with all my heart, I shall make Your
Name glorious unto eternity

Your mercy upon me has been great,
Lord, and You saved my being
from the eternals of hells.*

God, the lawless have risen upon me, and
assemblies of mighty ones sought for my
being, and they did not account You as
God before them.

But You, Lord my God, are compassionate and
merciful, patient, abundantly merciful and true, look
upon me and have mercy upon me.

Give strength to Your servant, give
life to the son of Your maidservant,
and make unto me a sign of goodness.

Those who hate me shall see it and shall
be ashamed, for You Lord helped me and
comforted me.

Glory to the Father and to the Son and to the Holy Spirit.

Now and always and unto the eternity of eternities. Amen.

---

* *Hades*

EVENING HOUR

Petition

Priest
Glory to You, God, glory to You, for the sake of all, Lord, glory to You.

Deacon
And again in peace let us request of the Lord. Receive, save, and have mercy.

Priest
Blessing and glory to the Father and to the Son and to the Holy Spirit. Now and always and unto the eternity of eternities. Amen.

Peace unto all.

Choir
And with Your spirit.

Deacon
Let us bow down in worship of God.

Choir
Before You Lord.

Psalms Read in Alternation

Student Chancel

Ps 139:2-14 KJV 140:1-13

Deliver me, Lord, from the evil man, save me from the unjust man.

They thought unlawfulness in their hearts, they prepared for war all of the day.

They sharpened their tongues as the snake, and the venoms of the serpents under their tongues.

Keep me, Lord, from the hands of the sinful, and save me from the evil man.

They thought to obstruct my footsteps, the arrogant hid a snare for me.

They stretched out ropes as a snare for my feet, around my paths they placed for me stumbling blocks.

EVENING HOUR

I said, "Lord You are my God, give ear
Lord to the voice of my prayers."

Lord, Lord strength of my salvation,
covering for my head in the day of battle.

Do not deliver me up, Lord, to the desires of
sinners, those who plotted against my sake,
do not cast me away.

That they may never be raised up, and
their plots may not be fulfilled,
may the end of their accomplishment, the
labor of their lips cover them.

May You cast upon them burning coals
of fire, and destroy them, may they not be
able to live from the torment.

May the smooth talking man not prosper
on the earth, the man who is a sinner,
his evils shall hunt him to destruction.

I know that You make, Lord, justice for
the poor and rights for the needy.

The just shall be thankful from Your Name,
the upright shall dwell before Your faces.

EVENING HOUR

Ps 140:1-10 KJV 141:1-10

Lord, I cried out to You and You heard me,
look upon the voice of my prayers
when I cry out to You.

Let my prayers be upright as incense before You,
Lord, the raising up of my hands as an evening offering.

Lord, place a guard for my mouth,
and a sturdy door for my lips,
that my heart may not go astray with
words of evil.

While making excuses for the causes of sins
through men, who commit unlawfulness,
and let me not be an associate of their
chosen ones.

Let the just discipline me with mercy,
and make reprimand, may the oil of
the sinner not anoint my head,
nor my prayers be of his wills.

Their judges prison is next to the rock,
may they hear my words and become kind.

As the thickness of the soil that has been
spread upon the earth, their bones
shall be scattered next to the hells.*

Hades

EVENING HOUR

Towards You Lord, are my eyes, Lord,
I hoped in You, Lord, do not take
from me my soul.

Keep me from the snare which was hidden
for me, and from the stumbling block of
the committer of unlawfulness.

May the sinners fall into his nets,
I am alone until I shall pass through.

<u>Ps 141:2-8 KJV 142:1-7</u>

With my voice I cried out to the Lord,
with my voice I requested of the Lord.

I shall spread my prayers out before the Lord,
and I shall tell my troubles before Him.

While my soul was diminishing from me,
You, Lord, knew my path, and in the
way in which I walked, a snare was
hidden for me.

I was looking to the right and was seeing,
there was also no one who knew me, from me
my escape was lost and no one was found
as a seeker of my being.

I cried out to You, Lord, and I said,
"You are my hope and portion in the
land of the living."

Look, Lord, upon my prayers,
for I became extremely humbled,
keep me alive from my persecutors,
for they have become stronger than me.

Lord, take my being out of prison,
from Your Name I am satisfied.

And the just wait for You, until You
shall recompense them.

Glory to the Father and to the Son and to the Holy Spirit.

Now and always and unto the eternity of eternities. Amen.

Hymn for Entrance into the Lord's Day

(Sunday Eve which is Saturday Evening.)

Student Chancel

Alleluia, Alleluia.

Glad light holy of glories immortal, of the
heavenly Father of the holy giver of life Jesus Christ.

We having come at the setting of the sun,
we saw the light of this evening.

We bless the Father and the Son and the
Holy Spirit of God. And we all say Amen.

Make us worthy at all times, to
bless with voice of song the Name of
glories the all Holy Trinity.

Which gives life, for the sake of which and this
world glorifies You.

EVENING HOUR 541

Petition for Weekdays

<u>Priest</u>

Blessed Lord, Whom You have dwelled in the heights, and blessed are the glories of Your greatness, You Who established the brilliant lights in the heights, You shined light from the heavens trough all of the universes. You made the light giving sun for the day, the light giving moon and stars for the night, and the light of the lamp, You are praiseworthy light, holy and first light, the darkness flees from You, and Your living light, Lord, shine in our hearts. And let us say in unison, blessed is Your holy Name of glories, and to You we sing blessings and glories to You, to the Father and to the Son, and to the Holy Spirit, now and always and unto the eternity of eternities. Amen.

EVENING HOUR

Proclamation

Student Chancel

<u>Deacon</u>

Having arrived at this hour of the evening we
all with the raising up of our hands
glorify You, Lord our God, You Who graced
us to pass this day in peace and
to arrive at this hour of the evening. Make us
worthy, Lord, with holy heart, with angelic
song to offer thanksgiving to the Lord God
almighty, give life and have mercy.

<u>Choir</u>

Give life Lord.

<u>Deacon</u>

Lord our God be merciful to us,
according to Your great mercy,
let us all say in unison.

<u>Choir</u>

Lord have mercy. Lord have mercy. Lord have mercy.

Petition

<u>Priest</u>

Having arrived at this hour of the evening
we all unceasingly glorify the Father and
the Son and the Holy Spirit, now and
always and unto the eternity of eternities, Amen.

EVENING HOUR

Evening Psalm Anthems (Messetis)

Senior Chancel

Evening Psalm Anthems for The Birth of Christ, The Annunciation to St. Mary, The Assumption of St. Mary, and all other feasts days of the Holy God-Bearer.

First Day
Ps 2:7,1 KJV 2:7,1

The Lord said to me, "You are my Son,
and today I have begotten You.*"

Why were the heathens agitated, and the
people plot in vain.

Second Day
Luke 1:46-48

My soul shall magnify the Lord, and
my spirit shall rejoice with God my savior.

For He looked upon the humility of His maid
servant, behold from now on, all nations
shall regard me as fortunate.

Third Day
Ps 71:6,2a KJV 72:6,1

He will descend as rain upon fleece,
as dew that sprinkles upon the land.

God give Your righteousness to the king,
and Your justices to the son of the king.

---

* Literally- Have given birth to You.

EVENING HOUR

Evening Psalm Anthems for the Resurrection of Christ

A Tz
Ps 23: 8b,1   KJV 24:8b,1

Lord powerful and almighty, Lord powerful in war.

The earth is the Lord's with its fullness,
the world and all of its inhabitants.

A G
Ps 44:7,2a   KJV 45:6,1a

Your throne, God, unto the eternity
of eternities, staff of uprightness, staff of
Your kingdom.

My heart sprung forth the good word, I say of my
works to the king.

P Tz
Ps 96:1,4   KJV 97:1,4

The Lord ruled as king, the earth shall
rejoice, may multitudes of islands be glad.

His lightnings appeared to the world, the
earth saw and trembled.

P G
Ps 99:2-3c   KJV 1,2

Sing to the Lord a new song,
all of the earth, serve unto the
Lord with gladness.

Enter before Him with joy,
let us know that He is our Lord.

EVENING HOUR 545

K Tz Ps 45:9,2 KJV 46:8,1

Come and see the works of God, Who made
signs and skillful art upon the earth.

God our refuge and strength, helper over
troubles which have found us exceedingly.

K G Ps 113:3 set 2, 113:1 set 1 KJV 115:3, 114:1

Our God in the heavens and on the earth,
all that which He willed He made.

When Israel was going out from Egypt,
of the house of Jacob from a foreign people.

T Tz Ps 79:18, 2a KJV 80:17, 1

Let Your hand be upon the man, Your right hand upon the
Son of Man, whom You have strengthened Him in You.

You Who shepherd Israel, look, You
Who leads Joseph as a flock.

T G Ps 49:1 KJV 50:1

God of gods the Lord spoke,
and called the earth.

From the rising of the sun to the
setting of the sun.

Evening Psalm Anthem for Pentecost

Ps 117:26-27 KJV 118: 26-27

Blessed are You Who comes in the Name of the Lord,
blessed are You Who are to come.

Lord our God appeared to us, make feasts of rejoicing
beforehand up to the corners of the altar table.

EVENING HOUR

Evening Psalm Anthem for Feasts of the Holy Church

<u>Ps 133:1 KJV 134:1</u>

All servants of the Lord bless the Lord here.

You Who stand in the house of the Lord,
and in the courts of our God.

Evening Psalm Anthem for Feasts of the Holy Cross

<u>Ps 59:5,6 KJV 60:4,5</u>

You gave a sign to those who fear
You, that they shall live in the faces
of the bow.

As they saved Your beloved,
give life with Your right hand and hear us.

Evening Psalm Anthem for Entrance into the Lord's Day
(Sunday Eve which is Saturday Evening.)

<u>Ps 114:1 KJV 116:1</u>

I loved that the Lord shall hear the
voice of my prayers,

For He descended His ear upon me,
and through all of my days I called out unto Him.

Evening Psalm Anthems for Feasts of the Holy Martyrs

<u>A Tz</u>
<u>Ps 32:22,1 KJV 33:22,1</u>

Let Your mercy, Lord, be upon us,
as we hoped in You.

Righteous ones, rejoice, in the Lord,
for the upright blessing is befitting.

EVENING HOUR

A G
Ps 36:28a, 39 KJV 37:28, 39

The Lord loves justice and does
not abandon His saints.

The salvation of the just is from the
Lord, He is their guardian in times of distress.

P Tz
Ps 67: 36a, 19b-20a KJV 68:35, 19a

God is wonderful over His saints, God of Israel.

Blessed Lord God, blessed is the Lord daily.

P G
Ps 120:2,1 KJV 121:2,1

My help shall come from the Lord, Who made
the heavens and the earth.

I lifted my eyes up to the mountains,
from where help shall come to me.

K Tz
Ps 88:8, 6 KJV 89:7, 5

God is glorified in the council of
His saints, great and feared, over all
those who are around Him.

May the heavens confess of Your wonders, Lord,
and Your truth in the assemblies of the saints.

EVENING HOUR

<u>K G</u>
<u>Ps 17: 2-3 KJV 18:1-2</u>

I shall love You lord my strength.
Provider of my affirmation, my refuge and my salvation.

God my helper and I hope in Him, He is
my refuge, my horn of salvation, and He is
acceptable to me.

<u>T Tz</u>
<u>Ps 144:18-19 KJV 145:18-19</u>

The Lord is near to all of those
who call upon Him in truth.

The Lord does fulfill the wills of those who
fear in Him, He hears their prayers,
and gives them life.

<u>T G</u>
<u>Ps 91:13-14 KJV 92:12-13</u>

The just shall flourish as the date palm trees,
they shall be many as the cedars of Lebanon.

May those that are planted in the house of the Lord,
also may they flourish in the courts of our God.

Evening Psalm Anthems for Days of Repentance

<u>A Tz</u>
<u>Ps 4:4b, 2a KJV 4:3, 1</u>

The Lord shall hear me when I cry out to Him

While I cry out, You heard me God,
according to my righteousness.

EVENING HOUR

A G
Ps 12:5, 1b, 3, 4a KJV 13:4, 1b, 2b, 3a
Do not let the enemy say, "I was
victorious over him," or that my
oppressors will rejoice if I am shaken.

Until when, will You turn Your faces from me,
until when, will the enemy rise above me,
look and listen to me, Lord my God.

P Tz
Ps 36:30, 1 KJV 37:30, 1
The mouth of the just tell of wisdom
and rights shall be spoken of his tongue.

Do not envy the wicked, nor those who
commit lawlessness.

P G
Ps 118:65, 68 KJV 119:65, 68
You have done kindness with Your servant,
Lord, according to Your word.

You are kind, Lord, and advise me with Your kindness.

K Tz
Ps 12:4a, 1 KJV 13:3,1
Look and listen to me, Lord my God.

Until when, Lord, do You forget me until the end,
until when, will You turn Your faces from me.

K G
Ps 118:156, 153 KJV 119: 156, 153
Your compassions are many, Lord,
and according to Your laws give me life.

See my humiliation and save me,
for I did not forget Your laws.

EVENING HOUR

T Tz
Ps 69: 2-3a KJV 70:1-2
God, look at me while helping,
and Lord, hurry while assisting me.

May those who were demanding my being
become humiliated and shamed.

T G
Ps 63:2-3 KJV 64:1-2
Hear, God, my prayers while me praying
to You, from fear of the enemy save my being.

May You hide me from the assemblies
of the evil ones, from the multitude of those
who commit unrighteousness.

Evening Psalm Anthems for Days of Great Lent
(Salt and Bread Days)

Mondays of Lent
Ps 50:11, 3 KJV 51:10, 1
Turn me, Lord, from my sins,
and atone all of my unrighteousness
from me.

Have mercy upon me, God, according to
Your great mercy, according to Your many
compassions atone my unrighteousness.

Tuesdays of Lent
Ps 127:1-2 KJV 128:1-2
Fortunate are all, who fear of the Lord
and walk in His ways.

You shall eat of the labor of your hands,
fortunate are you, may it be good.

EVENING HOUR

Wednesdays of Lent
Ps 37:22, 10 KJV 38: 21, 9

Do not leave me, Lord my God,
and do not be made afar from me,
look while helping me, Lord of my salvation.

Lord, before You are all of my desires,
and my groaning is not hidden from You.

Thursdays of Lent
Ps 70: 9, 2 KJV 71: 9,1

Do not cast me out, Lord, in the time of old age,
do not leave me while in the diminishing
of my strength.

In You, Lord, I hoped unto eternity,
I will not be ashamed, save and give
me life in Your justice.

Fridays of Lent
Ps 118:169, 149 KJV 119:169, 149

May my requests draw near before You, Lord,
according to Your word make me wise.

Hear my voice, Lord, according to Your mercy,
Lord, and give me life in Your rights.

EVENING HOUR

Evening Psalm Anthem for Holy Thursday

Ps 25:6,8 KJV 26:6,8

I will wash my hands with holiness, and
I shall go around Your altar Lord. Lord.

I loved the elegance of Your house, and
the dwelling place of Your glories.

Anthem Response for Holy Thursday

Ps 140:2 KJV 141:2

Let my prayers be upright as incense
before You, Lord.

Receive our evening prayers, Lord, and the
spreading out of our hands.

Evening Psalm Anthem for Holy Friday

Ps 68:22-23 KJV 69:21-22

They gave me bitters for my food
and for my thirst they made me drink vinegar.

Let their tables before them become a snare,
for a recompense and a stumbling block.

Anthem Response for Holy Friday

Ps 140:2 KJV 141:2

Let our prayers be upright as incense
before You, Lord

The raising up of our hands as an
evening offering.

Senior Chancel

* During Great Lent, Old Testament and Epistle Readings are read at this point as prescribed in the Lectionary.

EVENING HOUR

Order of "Let our Prayers be Upright"

Senior Chancel

<u>Ps 140:2 KJV 141:2</u>
Let my prayers be upright.
As incense before You, Lord.
The raising up of my hands.
As an evening offering.

Response specific for those singing on the right chancel of the Church.

<u>Ps 140:2 KJV 141:2</u>
Let my prayers be upright as incense before You, Lord,
the raising up of my hands, as an evening offering.

Lord, I cried out to You and hear me.
Look at the voice of my requests while I
am crying out to You.

Proclamation

Proclamation for the Entrance into Sunday (Sunday Eve which is Saturday Evening) and for all Feast Days of the Lord*

<u>Deacon</u> **Student Chancel**
Let us all say in unison, Lord have mercy.

<u>Choir *(continue in alternation)*</u>
Lord have mercy.

For the sake of peace of the entire world and
for the stability of the holy church, let us
request of the Lord.

Lord have mercy.

---

* The Proclamation "Mother Holy"(Mayr Soorp) may be chanted as the above Proclamation for Feast Days of the Holy Mother of God in some local parish traditions. see pages 299-301

EVENING HOUR

Student Chancel
For the sake of all holy and orthodox
bishops, let us request of the Lord.

Lord have mercy.

For the sake of the life of our patriarch Lord *(* insert name)*,
and for the salvation of his soul, let us request of the Lord.

Lord have mercy.

For the sake of doctors of the church, priests, deacons,
choristers* and the order of all the children who are
servants of the church,** let us request of the Lord.

Lord have mercy.

For the sake of pious kings and God loving princes,
generals and their armies, let us request of the Lord.

Lord have mercy.

For the sake that the Lord almighty shall make
obedient before them all of the wars of the enemies,
let us request of the Lord.

Lord have mercy.

For the sake of our fathers and brothers who are in
captivity and in evil servitude, let us request of
the Lord.

Lord have mercy.

For the sake of travelers and passengers at sea,
that they may arrive at the harbor of goodness,
let us request of the Lord.

Lord have mercy.

---

* *Actual translation is "scribe or clerk"*

** *Even though "children" is used, this term includes those of all ages
who serve the church whether they be adults or children.*

EVENING HOUR

For the sake of those who are sick and all of those who are afflicted, for their speedy recovery, let us request of the Lord.

Lord have mercy.

For the sake of temperate weather, gentle rains and abundance of fruits, let us request of the Lord.

Lord have mercy.

For the sake of pilgrims and those who bring fruit for the holy Church of God, let us request of the Lord.

Lord have mercy.

And for the sake of those who are delivered up into the hands of the unlawful for the sake of the Name of Christ, let us request of the Lord.

Free them Lord and have mercy.

For the sake of the souls of those who are at rest, who sleep in Christ with the true and right faith, let us request of the Lord.

Remember Lord and have mercy.

For the sake of the Lord God saving us from the enemy, visible and invisible, let us request of the Lord.

Lord have mercy.

Petition

<u>Priest</u>
We have as advocates St. Mary the God-Bearer, the glorified and blessed ever Holy Virgin, St. John the Baptist, St. Stephen the first martyr, the Holy Apostles and Prophets, the brave and victorious Holy Martyrs, and the great confessor of Christ our patriarch St. Gregory the Illuminator of the land of the Armenias.

EVENING HOUR

<u>Deacon</u>
And remember all of the saints, and
with them let us request of the Lord.

<u>Choir *(continue in alternation)*</u>
Lord have mercy.

To pass this approaching evening and this coming
night in peace, with faith let us ask from the Lord.

Grace unto us Lord.

The angel of peace to be guardian
of our beings. Let us ask from the Lord.

Grace unto us Lord.

For atonement and forgiveness of our offences.
Let us ask from the Lord.

Grace unto us Lord.

For the great Holy Cross and able
strength for assistance of our beings.
Let us ask from the Lord.

Grace unto us Lord.

And again in one voice for the sake of
our true and holy faith.
Let us pray to the Lord.

Lord have mercy.

Let us make ourselves and one another as
the person of the Lord God almighty.

Let us become as Your Person Lord.

Lord our God be merciful to us,
according to Your great mercy,
let us all say in unison.

Lord have mercy. Lord have mercy. Lord have mercy.

EVENING HOUR 557

Proclamation for Feast Days of the Saints and for Fasting Days

Deacon **Student Chancel**
And again in peace let us request of the Lord.

Let us request of the almighty God, the Father of our Lord Jesus Christ, the king of peace for the sake of peace, and for the one holy catholic* and Apostolic Church, that the Lord our God may give us many years in peace, and may peacemaking kings be sent to us, for the sake of His great holy and awesome Name, the heads of states, the military captains, the commanding generals, the people, may He protect our comings in and our goings out, and may He crush all the wars of the enemy, may the Lord almighty give life and have mercy.

Choir
Give life Lord and have mercy.

Deacon
To pass this approaching evening and this coming night in peace, with faith let us ask from the Lord.

Choir *(continue in alternation)*
Grace unto us Lord.

The angel of peace to be guardian
of our beings. Let us ask from the Lord.

Grace unto us Lord.

For atonement and forgiveness of our offences.
Let us ask from the Lord.

Grace unto us Lord.

For the great Holy Cross and able strength for assistance of our beings.
Let us ask from the Lord.

Grace unto us Lord.

* *catholic means universal in its Greek origin. It has no connection to the Roman Catholic Church in this context. The text above used the term "gatooghige" the Armenicized form of the Greek. Armenian has borrowed this term for unknown reasons as the Armenia language already has its own words for universal, "diezeragan" and general, "unthanoor" which is already used in many other liturgical phrases. Either one of these would be better choices.*

And again in one voice for the sake of our true and holy faith. Let us pray to the Lord.

Lord have mercy.

Let us make ourselves and one another as the person of the Lord God almighty.

Let us become as Your Person Lord.

Lord our God be merciful to us, according to Your great mercy, let us all say in unison.

Lord have mercy. Lord have mercy. Lord have mercy.

Prayer

Senior Chancel
Priest

Hear our voices, Lord our God,
receive our prayers, the lifting up
of our hands and the words of our prayers,
by making holy our evening offering of a
sweet fragrance, to prepare it for Your pleasures.
Increase in us, Lord almighty, faith, hope, love, and
all deeds of virtue, in order that Your
wills of piety, we always may be religious
with piety in the day and in the night,
may we become worthy for the sake of the
salvation of our beings, and to pray to You
for the sake of the spiritual life, Lord, and
to find the graces and mercy, and by
giving thanks let us glorify the Father and the
Son and the Holy Spirit, now and always and
unto the eternity of eternities, Amen.

Peace unto all.

Choir	And with Your spirit.
Deacon	Let us bow down in worship of God.
Choir	Before You Lord.

EVENING HOUR

<u>Priest</u>
Through bowing down in worship of You,
Lord our God, we are satisfied from You for
the sake of passing from within the length of this day
in peace. Give us, Lord, we pray to You, to
pass this evening and this upcoming night without sins
and without stumbling, to stand firm and stay
in faith, in hope, in love, and in the
keeping of Your commandment. By requesting
peace for the entire world, and the stability of
Your holy Church, and for the salvation of
our beings. In order that by receiving our requests
from You, and let us always send the great elegant
glorification in the heights to Your all powerful
Lordship, Christ our God, now and always
and unto the eternity of eternities, Amen.

Sing the "Thrice Holy" also known as "Holy God" (Soorp Asdvadz)
according to the proper day or season. The verse is sung three times.
(Turn to page 305-306 for all variable verses.) (Then return to page 559)

Senior Chancel

For the Holy Friday Midday (Jashoo) Hour, for all Days of the Saints,
Feasts of the Cross, Feasts of the Church, and for Fasting Days.*
(this is an example only)

Holy God, holy and mighty, holy and immortal,
You Who were crucified for our sake,
have mercy upon us.

The Ascription** of Thomas the Apostle

Glorified and blessed ever holy virgin
God-Bearer, Mary mother of Christ,
offer our prayers to your Son and to our God.

---

* *This hymn is attributed to Nicodemus and Joseph of Arimathea having sung this for the first time when removing Christ's body from the cross.*

** *Attributable composition of Thomas the Apostle*

EVENING HOUR

Petition

<u>Priest</u>

To save us from temptation and from all of our dangers.

Proclamation

Senior Chancel

<u>Deacon</u>

And again in peace let us request of the Lord.

For the sake of the voice of our prayers being heard by the Lord God, with the advocation of the holy God-Bearer, and for mercy and compassion of the Lord God to descend upon us. Our Lord God almighty, give life and have mercy.

Petition

<u>Priest</u>

Blessing and glory to the Father and to the Son and to the Holy Spirit. Now and always and unto the eternity of eternities. Amen.

Peace unto all.

<u>Choir</u>

And with Your spirit.

<u>Deacon</u>

Let us bow down in worship of God.

<u>Choir</u>

Before You Lord.

EVENING HOUR 561

Psalm 120:1-8 KJV 121:1-8 (chanted in alternation)
Senior Chancel

I lifted up my eyes to the mountains,
from where help shall come to me.

My help shall come from the Lord,
Who made the heavens and the earth.

Do not bring your foot to trembling
and may your keeper not sleep.

As the keeper of Israel does not
slumber and does not go to sleep.

The Lord shall keep you, and the Lord
shall receive you with His right hand.

The sun shall not harm you in the day,
and nor the moon in the night.

The Lord shall keep you from all evil,
the Lord shall keep your being.

The Lord shall keep your coming in and
your going out, from this time forth unto eternity.

Glory to the Father and to the Son and to the Holy Spirit.

Now and always and unto the eternity of eternities. Amen.

Senior Chancel

 The *"Lifted Up Hymn" (Hampartzi Sharagan) is inserted here. The appropriate "Lifted Up Hymn" (Hampartzi Sharagan) for the day can be found in the Hymnal according to the proper day as shown by the Calendar. The correct "Lifted Up Hymn"(Hampartzi Sharagan) is usually found in the Hymnal following the day's proper "Midday Hymn" (Jashoo Sharagan.)*

On the following pages are examples only of the "Lifted Up Hymn" (Hampartzi Sharagan). The Calendar then the Hymnal must first be consulted to find the correct "Lifted Up Hymn" (Hampartzi Sharagan) of the day.

EVENING HOUR

*"Lifted Up Hymn" (Hampartzi Sharagan) for
Saturday night (Sunday Eve)*

<u>A Tz</u>

You are holy Lord of hosts
You Who has dwelled in the heavens
and You are praised by Your saints.
The heavenly forces the seraphim and the cherubim,
unceasingly bless Your holy Name.

Priests in the company of the same ministers
and people bow down in worship of Your Lordship.

O light Who is before the eternities
You were sent from the Father, and with the
intelligible light You filled those whom have
been made, blessed are You king of the eternities.
You Who from the beginning established the light anew,
and through Your resurrection You expelled the
darkness of ignorance, blessed are You king of the eternities.
And from where we who have been enlightened,
in the company of the bright joyful
angels may we sing in the resurrection
of this evening with joy, blessed are You king of the eternities.

EVENING HOUR

Heavenly citizen John, the great one of
the births of women, with voice in the desert
he preached the ceremonious announcement
of the sunrise of the light of justice.
True prophet and consecrator of the Son of God,
preceding forerunner and teller of the
Godly laws, he opened up the roads for
the King of eternities.
Having become furious the lawless drunkard Herodias,
as a gift she requested the head of the prophet,
to extinguish the morning star shining lamp.

Glory to the Father and to the Son and to the Holy Spirit.
With the advocation of the holy God-Bearer
gift, to those who bow down in worship of the
all Holy Trinity, the resurrection of hope for
life unto the eternities.

Now and always and unto the eternity of eternities. Amen.
Keep the faithful people of the Holy Trinity,
and those who have refuge in
the tabernacle* of Your glories, without agitation
in peace.

---

*or altar

EVENING HOUR

For Feast Days of the Apostles the following verses of the "Lifted Up Hymn" (Hampartzi Sharagan) are sung right after the verse "And from where we" (Oosdi yev mek) on page 562. On these days, the below verses are substituted for "Heavenly citizen" (Yergnakaghakatzin) and its successive verses.

A Tz

We request from You abundantly merciful,
from the hand of Your holy apostles,
Lord spare our beings.
With prior knowledge You chose
these persons who had been made worthy,
the spirit of Your graces having been impressed
in them, through whom repulsed having expelled
the rebel enemy, with their advocation,
Lord spare our beings.
For the sake of whom and we believers
let us carry out the remembrance of the holy apostles,
we pray to You Whom only You are compassionate,
give generously to us Your great mercy,
Lord Whom You give life to all who have been made.

EVENING HOUR

Glory to the Father and to the Son and to the Holy Spirit.
Now mother of God pray for our sake to the One
having been born of you, that by keeping in the
company of the same, through His holy resurrection
we may be renewed, always advocate
to him to give life to us.

Now and always and unto the eternity of eternities. Amen.
And the voice of Judah having been
raised up in requesting from the Lord, for all,
the desirable holy cross, and with faith
cried out "come let us bow down in
worship of this holy Godly sign," by
magnifying the One born of the virgin.

K G

Lover of mankind we bless Your
resurrection, by crying out glory to You Lord.
Whom the seraphim bless and the cherubim
praise, by crying out glory to You Lord.
By the unceasing mouth, by sounding out
without rest, by crying out glory to You Lord.

EVENING HOUR

K G

And having taken our blessings to the
angels we sing and say glories to Your
resurrected Lord.
You Who were crucified for
our sake You were buried and arose, You
delivered from sins.
Holy God, holy and mighty,
holy immortal King.

K G

Today the ranks of martyrs having rejoiced
became cheerful before the Lord Christ the
Son of God.
The voice from the heavens
having witnessed says, "blessed ones come to my
Father, inheritors of the heavenly altars.
Fill the place of the fallen rebellious enemy,
whom have fallen from the place of the heavens."

T G

Lord my prayers shall enter into Your
holy temple, and send unto us Lord
help from Your holy mountain.
Lord may Your right hand protect over those whom
You have created, and send unto us Lord
help from Your holy mountain.
Lord receive our prayers of the evening, through the
advocation of Your birth giver, and send unto us Lord
help from Your holy mountain.

EVENING HOUR

Proclamation

Senior Chancel

<u>Deacon</u>

For the sake of peace for the whole world, and
for the establishment of the Holy Church let us
pray to the Lord. Let us all say in unison.

<u>Priest</u>

Lord have mercy. Lord have mercy. Lord have mercy.

Prayer

Student Chancel

Compassionate Father, good care taker, maker of all
which has been made, receive the requests of Your servants
at this evening hour, Whom You are abundant
towards all, with the gifts of Your kindness.
Have mercy, Lord, to the entire world, and
to Your holy church, to the infirmed, to those
afflicted, to the travelers, to the passengers
at sea, to the confessors, to those repenting,
and to the souls of those who are at rest.
For You, Lord almighty, know our needs and
necessities more than which we request
and understand, and to You in the company
of the Son and most Holy Spirit is befitting
glory, Lordship and honor, now and always and
unto the eternity of eternities. Amen.

EVENING HOUR

 The "Feast Eve Hymn" (Nakhadonag Sharagan) is sung at this point only if it is the Eve of a Feast Day and if it is prescribed by the Church Calendar. On eves of particular feasts, verses of one of the following day's Hymns (Sharagans): "Blessing Hymn" (Orhnootyoon), "Hymn of the Fathers"(Hartz), "Hymn of Magnification" (Medzatzoostze), "Hymn of Mercy"(Voghormya), or "Lord of the Heavens" (Der Hergnitz), are sung as prescribed. The service begins with, "And again in peace let us request of the Lord..." by the deacon who censes the church twice during the hymn. All clergy must be vested in a Cope (Shoorchar) and it is sung in the center chancel area below the bema of the altar.

However

For Days of Great Lent (Salt and Bread Days) recite The Prayer of Manasseh the King "Lord almighty" (Der amenagal) and its proclamation and following prayer which is found on pages 334-339. Then chant the following Psalm of Dismissal beginning with Psalm 90 KJV Psalm 91 "He Who dwells..." (Vor pnagyaln...). But for other Fasting Days and Feast Days of Martyrs, chant only Psalm 90 KJV 91.

For Sunday Eve (Saturday night) recite the Psalms beginning with Psalm 133 KJV Psalm 134 "Bless here..." (Asd orhnetzek...) found on pages 574-575.

Anthem of Dismissal
(Psalm 90 KJV Psalm 91, Psalm 122
KJV Psalm 123, Psalm 53 KJV Psalm54)

Student Chancel

Ps 90:1-16 KJV 91:1-16

He who dwells in aid of the One on high, he shall rest under the shadow of God in the heavens.

He shall say to the Lord, You are my receiver, God is my refuge, and I hope in Him.

He shall save me from the snare of the hunter, and from words of trouble.

EVENING HOUR

Into His backbone you will be received,
in the shadow of His wings you shall have hope.

May His truth be as armor around you.

You shall not fear the fright of the night,
nor the arrow which flies in the day.

Nor from things that walk in the dark,
nor from obstacles of the demon at midday.

Thousands shall fall at Your side, and
tens of thousands at Your right hand, which
no one shall come near You.

But only with Your eyes You shall look,
and You shall see the restitution of the sinners,
because You, Lord, You are my hope.

The One on high made for you a refuge,
no evil shall come near to you, and plague
shall not approach to Your dwelling.

He having commanded to His angels for your sake
while keeping you in all your ways.

They received you in their arms, that you
will never strike your foot upon a stone.

You shall walk over serpents and vipers, and
by the foot you shall trample the lion and
the dragon.

Because he hoped in Me and I shall save him,
I shall be a shield to him, for he knew My Name.

He shall cry out to Me, and to him I shall be heard,
and I shall be in him in trouble.

I shall save and glorify him, I shall fill him with
long days and I shall show him my salvation.

EVENING HOUR

Ps 122:1-4 KJV 123:1-4

To You, Lord, I lifted up my eyes,
You Who has dwelled in the heavens.

As the eyes of the servant to the hand of his master
and as the eyes of the maid servant to the hand
of her mistress.

Likewise our eyes are to You, Lord, our God,
until You shall have mercy upon us.

Have mercy upon us, Lord, have mercy upon us,
for we were filled exceedingly with contempt.

Moreover our beings were filled
with insults, of those who were insulting us,
and with contempt of the arrogant.

EVENING HOUR

Ps 53:3-9 KJV 54:1-7

God, in Your Name grant me life, and in
Your power make me just.

God, hear my prayers, place Your ear upon the
words of my mouth.

Foreigners rose up over me, and the mighty ones
demanded my being, and they did not regard
You as God before them.

Behold God my helper,
and Lord receiver of my soul.

While returning the evil unto my enemies,
destroy them with Your truth.

Of my will I shall offer sacrifices to You,
I shall confess of Your Name, Lord, for it is good.

You saved me from all troubles, and
my eye has seen my enemies.

Glory to the Father and to the Son and to the Holy Spirit.

Now and always and unto the eternity of eternities. Amen.

EVENING HOUR

Petition

<u>Priest</u>

Let us make the uplifted Christ our refuge,
that no evils may reach us, and torments
may not come near our dwellings.

Proclamation

Student Chancel

<u>Deacon</u>

And we by requesting mercy from the Lord
in unison, let us all say in unison.

Prayer

Senior Chancel

<u>Priest</u>

Lord have mercy. Lord have mercy. Lord have mercy.

Hope of life, receiver of prayers, atoner
of sins and fulfiller of requests, Christ our God,
receive our requests in this evening hour,
with the advocation of the holy God-Bearer and
with the prayers of all Your saints.
Hear us, Lord, and have mercy,
pardon, atone, and forgive our sins,
make us worthy with thanksgiving to glorify
You in the company of the Father and in the
company of the Holy Spirit, now and always
and unto the eternity of eternities. Amen.

EVENING HOUR 573

The Recitation of Sargavak Vartabed

The real first name of this 12th century theologian remains unknown. He was both an ordained Deacon "Sargavak" and was conferred with the degree Doctor of the Church "Vartabed." It was common for many Vartabeds not to be ordained as Priests, but it was imperative that they be ordained Deacons so they would be able to read and to preach the Holy Gospel.

Student Chancel

Deacon

Remember, Lord, Your ministers, our parents, our teachers, our brothers, our friends, those that feed us, those that have made vows, travelers, those who give rest, those who are laborers, those who are confessors and those repentant, those who are forced captives, those who are ill, those who are oppressed, those who are princes, those who are doers of evil, those who are doers of kindness, those who are enemies, those who are hateful and those who have joined us through faith.

Senior Chancel

Priest

Remember Lord and have mercy.

Kind and abundantly merciful God, with Your unforgetting knowledge and unlimited love for mankind, remember all of those who have faith in You, and have mercy upon all. Help and save each one from dangers and temptations. Make us worthy with thanksgiving to glorify the Father and the Son and the Holy Spirit, now and always and unto the eternity of eternities. Amen.

Blessed be our Lord Jesus Christ. Amen.

Our Father Who art in heaven, Hallowed be Thy name. Thy kingdom come, Thy will be done on earth as it is in heaven. Give us this day our daily bread. And forgive us our debts, as we forgive our debtors. And lead us not into temptation, but deliver us from evil.

For Thine is the Kingdom, and the power, and the glory forever and ever. Amen.

EVENING HOUR

Anthem for Sunday Eve (which is Saturday Evening)

Student Chancel
Ps 133:1-3 KJV 134:1-3
Bless the Lord here, all servants of the Lord,
who stand in the house of the Lord and in the
courts of our God.

In the night raise your hands to
the sanctuary, and bless the Lord.

May the Lord bless us from Zion,
He Who made the heavens and the earth.

Ps 137:1-8 KJV 138:1-8
I shall confess You, Lord with all of my heart,
before the angels I shall say psalms unto You.

For You heard the words of my mouth,
I shall bow down in worship to Your Holy Temple,
and I shall confess of Your Name for the
sake of Your mercy and truth.

You made Your holy Name great in all,
the day in which I cry out to You,
hear me quickly, and You shall make
strength abundant to my being.

All the kings of the earth shall confess to You,
for they heard the words of Your mouth,
and they shall bless Your ways.

The glories of the Lord are great, the Lord is on high,
He sees the humble, He knows the heights* from afar.

That I shall walk in the midst of troubles, from the
anger of the enemy You shall give me life.

You stretched out Your hand and Your right hand
saved me, and the Lord shall compensate in
exchange for me.

Lord, Your eternal mercy, do not neglect the
works of Your hands.

* *"the arrogant ones" is the inferred meaning.*

EVENING HOUR 575

Ps 53:3-9 KJV 54:1-7

God, in Your Name grant me life, and in
Your power make me just.

God, hear my prayers, place Your ear upon the
words of my mouth.

Foreigners rose up over me, and the mighty ones
demanded my being, and they did not regard
You as God before them.

Behold God my helper,
and Lord receiver of my soul.

While returning the evil unto my enemies,
destroy them with Your truth.

Of my will I shall offer sacrifices to You,
I shall confess of Your Name, Lord, for it is good.

You saved me from all troubles, and
my eye has seen my enemies.

Glory to the Father and to the Son and to the Holy Spirit.

Now and always and unto the eternity of eternities. Amen.

Student Chancel
* During the fifty days after Easter only, the Dismissal Psalm and Gospel Reading as prescribed by the Lectionary are chanted at this point.

Proclamation

Deacon **Student Chancel**
Let us request in unison with faith from
the Lord that He may make the graces
of His mercy be upon us. May the Lord
almighty give life and have mercy.

Choir
Give life Lord.

Lord have mercy, Lord have mercy, Lord have mercy.

576 EVENING HOUR

Prayer*

Senior Chancel
<u>Priest</u>
King of peace, helper and savior of our
beings, Christ our God, having fortified,
keep Your people under the shadow of
Your Holy and revered Cross, in peace,
save us from the visible and invisible enemy.
Make us worthy with thanksgiving to glorify
You with the Father and with the Holy Spirit, now
and always and unto the eternity of eternities. Amen.

Proclamation for Feasts of the Holy Cross

Student Chancel
<u>Deacon</u>
Through the Holy Cross let us request of the Lord,
that through it He may save us from sins, and that
He may grant us life by the grace of His mercy.
Almighty Lord our God, give life and have mercy.

Prayer

Senior Chancel
<u>Priest</u>
Protect us, Christ our God, under the shadow of
Your Holy and revered Cross in peace,
save us from the visible and invisible enemy.
Make us worthy with thanksgiving to glorify
You with the Father and with the Holy Spirit, now
and always and unto the eternity of eternities. Amen.

---

* or Prayer "To Your most powerful" page 316
** Two more variable sets of Proclamations and Prayers may be recited on pages 575-576 according to feast day or season. For Feasts of the Church recite: Proclamation "Through the Holy Church" pg. 578 with Prayer "In this temple" pg. 580. For Feasts regarding the Birth of Christ or the Holy God-Bearer recite: Proclamation "Holy God-Bearer pg. 241 and Prayer Receive Lord pg. 242. The Church Calendar must always be consulted first.

INSTRUCTION FOR WORSHIP

Instruction for Worship, commonly called "The Office of Adoration on Entering the Church" occurs in the church when a Diocesan Prelate, Patriarch, or Catholicos is invited or has returned from a mission. This service is performed only on these occasions.

First the Hymn "Majestic God" (Hrashapar Asdvadz) is sung, then the Hymn "Be Cheerful" (Oorakh Ler) is sung while the pontiff is in procession into the church.

<u>Ps 121:1-9 KJV 122:1-9</u>

I became joyful, those who were saying
to me, let us go to the house of the Lord.

Having arrived, our feet were standing
at your gates, Jerusalem.

Jerusalem having been built as a city,
and with it dwellings all around it.

There nations were going up,
nations of the Lord, in testimony for Israel,
confessing of the Lord, of the Lord.

There they set down thrones of judgment,
they set down thrones in the house of David.

Ask the greeting of Jerusalem, and from
abundance, those of you who love the Lord.

Let there be peace in Your strength,
and abundance in your sturdy towers.

For the sake of my brothers and my friends
I spoke peace, for the sake of you and for
the sake of the house of the Lord our God
we requested goodness from You.

Ps 85:16b-17 KJV 86:16b-17

Give strength to Your servant,
give life to the son of Your maid,
and make unto me the sign of goodness.

Those that hate me shall see and shall
be ashamed, for You, Lord, helped me
and comforted me.

Glory to the Father and to the Son and to the Holy Spirit.

Now and always and unto the eternity of eternities. Amen.

Proclamation for Feast Days of the Church

Student Chancel

Deacon

Through the Holy Church let us request of the Lord,
that through it He may save us from sins, and that
He may grant us life by the grace of His mercy.
Almighty Lord our God, give life and have mercy.

INSTRUCTION FOR WORSHIP

Prayer

Senior Chancel

Priest

Beside the door of this holy church,
and before this holy sign acceptable
to God and having become bright,
having become humble with fear we
bow down in worship, we bless and
glorify Your Holy and wondrous, and victorious
Lordship. We offer to You blessing and
glories, to the Father and to the Son and to the
Holy Spirit, now and always and unto the eternity of
eternities. Amen.

Anthem

Senior Chancel

Ps 99:2-5 KJV 100:1-5
(Chanted in Alternation)

All lands cry out unto the Lord,
serve unto the Lord with gladness.

Enter before Him with joy,
let us know that He is Lord our God.

He made us and we were not ourselves,
we the people and the flock of sheep of His pasture.

Enter through His gates with confession,
and with blessing to His dwellings.

Be confessing to the Lord, and bless His name.

The Lord is sweet, His mercy is eternal,
from generation to generation is His truth.

Glory to the Father, and to the Son, and to the Holy Spirit.
Now and always and unto the eternity of eternities. Amen.

580 INSTRUCTION FOR WORSHIP

Proclamation

Student Chancel

<u>Deacon</u>

Let us bless the almighty God,
the Father of our Lord Jesus Christ,
Who made us worthy to stand in the
place of glorification and to sing
spiritual songs. Almighty Lord our God,
give life and have mercy.

Prayer

Senior Chancel

<u>Priest</u>

In this temple, and before this holy sign
acceptable to God having become bright,
and this holy table, having become humbled
with fear we bow down in worship,
we bless and glorify Your Holy and wondrous
and victorious (*resurrection**). We offer to You
blessing and glories with the Father and with the
Holy Spirit, now and always and unto the
eternity of eternities. Amen.

** The name of the proper season according to the Church Calendar is inserted here.
(e.g. Birth, Revelation, Coming, Lordship etc...)*

INSTRUCTION FOR WORSHIP

Or the following Prayer may be recited.

Senior Chancel

<u>Priest</u>
In this dwelling of holiness and in this
place of glorification, this dwelling of angels
and place of atonement for man, having
become humbled, with fear we bow down
in worship, we bless and glorify Your Holy
and wondrous, and victorious *(resurrection*)*.
And in the company of the heavenly armies we
offer blessing and glories with the Father and
the Holy Spirit, now and always and
unto the eternity of eternities. Amen.

Անցո՛ գրաժակս գայս ինէնէ․ բայց ոչ
որպէս ես կամիմ, այլ որպէս Դու կամիս։

The order of the common hour of prayers of the Peace Hour which is performed preceding bedtime and is performed before the Spirit of God and before the Word of God who was placed in the tomb, then descended into hell and made peace of the souls.

If the Peace Hour is performed immediately following dinner, it begins with the Lord's Prayer followed by the Thanksgiving Psalm for the meal Psalm 33:2-8 KJV 34:1-7. If it is not performed after dinner, skip to Psalm 87:2-3 KJV 88:1-2 on page 584 after the Lord's Prayer.

Blessed be our Lord Jesus Christ. Amen.

Our Father Who art in heaven, Hallowed be Thy name. Thy kingdom come, Thy will be done on earth as it is in heaven. Give us this day our daily bread. And forgive us our debts, as we forgive our debtors. And lead us not into temptation, but deliver us from evil.

For Thine is the Kingdom, and the power, and the glory forever and ever. Amen.

Priest Ps 33:2-8 KJV 34:1-7
I shall bless the Lord at all times,
at all times His blessing is in my mouth.

Deacon **Senior Chancel**

My being shall boast in the Lord,
the meek shall hear and shall be cheerful.

Make great the Lord with me,
and together let us make His Name elevated on high.

I asked from the Lord and He heard me,
He saved me from all my troubles.

Approach the Lord, and take the light,
and may your faces not be ashamed.

This poor man cried out to the Lord,
the Lord heard him, and saved him from
all his troubles.

PEACE HOUR

An army of angels of the Lord surrounds
those who fear Him, and He protects them.

Priest
Glory to the Father and to the Son and to the Holy Spirit.

Deacon
Now and always and unto the eternity of eternities. Amen.
And again in peace let us request of the Lord. Receive, save, and have mercy.

Priest
Blessing and glory to the Father and to the Son and to the Holy Spirit, now and always and unto the eternity of eternities. Amen.

Psalm of Degrees or Song of Ascents (Yerk Asdijanatz).

Song of Worshippers and Pilgrims processioning up the stairs to Solomon's Temple in Jerusalem while being sung in alternation. Psalm 119:1-3 KJV 120:1-3 below is an excerpt only. The entirety of the canon set Psalm 119-130 KJV 120-131 is chanted at this point as found in the Book of Psalms.

(Some versions of the Common Hours of Prayer do not include this Psalm at this point. Some choose not to say Alleluia before chanting it because it is categorized as a Song.)

In my troubles I cried out unto the Lord,
He saved my being from deceitful lips
and an evil tongue.

What shall be given to you or what shall be added,
deceitful tongue.

(Continue with the full canon set as described above.)

* *Some versions of the Common Hours of Prayer begin the Peace Hour at this point, as is done in most churches, inserting the Lord's Prayer here and skipping the preceding Psalms.*

Priest Ps 87:2-3 KJV 88:1-2
Lord God of my salvation, from the day unto the night I cried out before You.

PEACE HOUR

<u>Deacon</u>
May my prayers enter before You, may Your ear descend upon my request.

<u>Priest</u>
Glory to the Father and to the Son and to the Holy Spirit.

<u>Deacon</u>
Now and always and unto the eternity of eternities. Amen.
And again in peace let us request of the Lord. Receive, save, and have mercy.

<u>Priest</u>
Blessing and glory to the Father and to the Son and to the Holy Spirit, now and always and unto the eternity of eternities. Amen.
Peace unto all.

<u>Choir</u>
And with Your spirit.

<u>Deacon</u>
Let us bow down in worship of God.

<u>Choir</u>
Before You Lord.

Psalms read in alternation.

Senior Chancel
<u>Ps 4:2-10 KJV 4:1-10</u>
While I cry out You heard me, God, according to my righteousness, from oppression You made me calm, have mercy upon me and hear my prayers.

Sons of man until when will you be hard hearted, why do you love vanity, and seek falsehood.

Know that the Lord made wonders for His holy one, and the Lord shall hear me while I cry out unto Him.

We become angry and you, do not sin! That which you say in your hearts, repent in your beds.

Offer sacrifices of righteousness,
and hope in the Lord.

Many were saying, "who shall show
us the goodness of the Lord,"
a sign of the light of Your faces was placed
before us, and You gave joy to
our hearts.

More than from the fruit of grain,
wine, and olive oil You filled it *(my heart)*.

With peace, in this and the same we shall
sleep and awaken, for only You alone Lord
with Your hope has made us to dwell.

<u>Ps 6:2-10 KJV 6:1-10</u>

Lord do not reprimand me in Your passion
and do not discipline me in Your anger.

Have mercy upon me Lord, for I am sick,
heal my being, for my bones are troubled.

My being is greatly troubled, and You, Lord, until when?

Turn, Lord, and save my being, grant me life,
Lord according to Your mercy.

PEACE HOUR

For there is no one in death who remembers You, nor in hells* who will confess of You.

I became fatigued in my groanful lamentations, I washed my mattress every night, and with my tears I wet my bed.

My eye became disturbed from anger, I am worn out by all my enemies above.

Stay far away from me, all you who commit unlawfulness.

The Lord heard the sound of my weeping, the Lord heard my prayers, and the Lord received my requests.

May all of my enemies become very ashamed and troubled, may they turn back and become shamed and troubled very quickly.

Hades

PEACE HOUR

<u>Ps 12:1-6 KJV 13:1-6</u>

Until when, Lord, do You forget me unto the end, until when will You turn Your faces from me.

Until when do I place thoughts upon my being, and the daily pains in my heart.

Until when, will the enemy rise above me, look and listen to me, Lord my God.

Give light, Lord, to my eyes that
I will never sleep unto death.

Do not let the enemy say, "I was victorious over him," or that my oppressors will rejoice if I am shaken.

I hoped in Your mercy Lord, my heart rejoiced in Your salvation, I shall bless the Lord my supporter.

<u>Ps 15:2-11 KJV 16:1-11</u>

Keep me, God, for I trusted in You, I said to the Lord, "You are my Lord and things good to me are from You."

Your saints who are in Your land,
You made all my wills in them wonderful.

Their illnesses shall become frequent, then after this they shall hurry.

PEACE HOUR

I shall not meet in their assemblies
of blood, and I shall not remember
their names upon my lips.

Lord You are my portion of inheritance and
my cup, Whom from this returns
my inheritance to me.

The parcels that came to me are
amongst the finest, and my inheritance
has been pleasing to me.

I shall bless the Lord, Who made me wise,
my kidneys also until the night have counseled me.

Beforehand I was seeing the Lord before me
at all times, for He is at my right hand,
that I shall not be shaken.

For the sake of this my heart became glad,
and my tongue rejoiced, and again my
body shall dwell with hope.

Because You shall not leave my being
into the hells,* and You shall not give
Your holy one to see the corruption.

You showed me Your paths of life,
You filled me with the gladness of Your faces,
from the kindness of elegance of Your right
hand until the end.

Hades

PEACE HOUR

Ps 16:1-15 KJV 17:1-15

Hear Lord for justice, and look upon
my requests, place Your ear upon my prayers,
for they are not through deceitful lips.

From Your faces rights came forth to me,
and my eyes shall see the uprightness.

You tested my heart and examined it
in the night, You tested me, and
unrighteousness was not found in me.

May my mouth not speak the works of the
son of man,* for the sake of the words of Your lips
I shall keep Your strict ways.

Make my paths firm in Your ways, that my
steps shall not stumble.

I cried out to You, Lord, for You heard me, God,
descend Your ear to me, and hear of my words.

You made Your mercies wonderful, O save
those who have trusted in You at Your right hand
from those whom are adverse.**

*This is not referring to Christ or angels but refers to humans on earth.

**adversaries or enemies

PEACE HOUR

Keep me as a pupil of the eye,* You shall
cover me in the shadow of Your wings,
from the faces of the wicked
who tormented me.

Enemies have surrounded my being,
in the detention of their own fat,
and their mouth spoke arrogance.

They drove me back, and now having
returned they surrounded with weapons,
they paid attention to casting me down
to the ground.

To me they were considered as a lion
that is ready to hunt, as a cub of
the lion which sits in ambush.

Rise up, Lord, arrive at them and
abolish them, save my being from
the wicked, from the sword, and from
the hand of the enemy.

Lord, destroy them from the earth,
divide and abolish them in their lives.

Your hidden things filled their bellies, they
were satisfied with food and they left the
remainder to their children.

I shall appear with justice to Your faces,
I shall be satisfied to see Your glories.

---

* *Apple of the eye.*

PEACE HOUR

__Ps 42:1-5 KJV 43:1-5__

Judge me God, and do justice to me
at my judgment.

From a nation which is not holy,
save me from deceitful sinful men.

You, God, are my strength, why have You
forgotten me, why do I walk sadly while
being oppressed by my enemy.

Lord, send Your light and Your truth,
that they may lead me, and may lift me
up to Your holy mountain and to Your
dwelling places.

I shall enter before the table of God, to God,
Who makes my childhood cheerful.

I shall be confessing to You with blessings of
the harp,* God my God.

Now, my being, why are you sad? Or why do
you trouble me? Hope to God, confess to Him,
the savior of my faces is God.

---

*Implied, the word "Orhnotyoon" can mean both blessing
and musical instrument. i.e. harp.*

PEACE HOUR

<u>Ps 69:2-6 KJV 70:1-5</u>

God, look at me while helping,
and Lord hurry while assisting me.

May those who were demanding my being
become humiliated and shamed, for those who
were thinking evil towards me, may they
be turned back and be humiliated. *

May those who are shameful be turned back instantly,
who were saying to me woe, woe.

May everyone rejoice and be glad in You,
those who seek You, Lord.

May those who love Your salvation say at all
times, God is great.

I am poor and indigent, God, help me, You are my
helper and savior, and You my Lord, do not delay.

<u>Ps 85:16b-17 KJV 86:16b-17</u>

Give strength to Your servant,
give life to the son of Your maid,
and make unto me the sign of goodness.

Those that hate me shall see and shall
be ashamed, for You, Lord, helped me
and comforted me.

Glory to the Father and to the Son and to the Holy Spirit.

Now and always and unto the eternity of eternities. Amen.

---

* *This is also Ps 34:4 KJV 35:4*

594 PEACE HOUR

Hymn "Grace Unto Us Lord" (Shnorhya Mez Der)
(Based on Isaiah 9:1-6 and 58:10)

Senior Chancel

Choir

Grace unto us Lord, in the night Your heavenly peace,
and protect us from the deceits of the enemy,
through the night of Your all victorious holy cross.

Lord God of my salvation, from the day
and unto the night I cried out before You.

May my prayers enter before You Lord, may
Your ear descend upon my requests.

Lord may a guardian from You come to us,
and may he protect us at all times.

Send unto us Lord the power of the holy cross,
which may protect us at all times.

Make us worthy, Lord, in this evening with peace,
and make us to pass it without temptation.

Make us to be worthy Lord, in this night with peace,
and by keeping us without sins.

PEACE HOUR

The Lord God is with us, may the heathens*
know and be conquered, for God is with us.

And hear this from one end of the earth to
the other, for God is with us.

And may you who have become powerful be
conquered, for God is with us.

And that though again you became powerful,
again may you be delivered into conquest,
for God is with us.

And the intention which you ponder,
the Lord abolishes, for God is with us.

And the word which you speak shall not
remain with you, for God is with us.

And because we will not be frightened with fear
from you, we will not become troubled,
for God is with us.

And let us make the Lord our God glorious, and
let Him be for us to fear, for God is with us.

And behold me and my children, which God gave to me,
for God is with us.

And the people who were sitting in the dark,
saw a great light, for God is with us.

---

* *"heathen" is used in a negative connotation in this case. This and the following six verses refer to an earthly enemy in war.*

PEACE HOUR

And you who having dwelled in darkness
and in the shadows of death, light
shall be shined forth unto you, for God is with us.

And because a child was born, and a son was
given to us, for God is with us.

And of Whom His Lordship is upon His shoulders,
for God is with us.

And Whom His Name is called: Angel of Great Counsel,
for God is with us.

And Wonderful Co-Counselor, for God is with us.

And God Mighty Prince, for God is with us.

And Prince of Peace, Father vested in Eternity,
Lord God is with us.

And glory to the Father and to the Son and to the Holy Spirit.
Now and always and unto the eternity of eternities. Amen.

Petition

<u>Priest</u>

While approaching this evening we raise
our hands in holiness, that which we have sinned
today in thought, in word, or in deed, through
repenting in our beds, by confessing the
secrets in our hearts to God the knower
of secrets, through hope in Your mercy. And in
unison may we cry out, "remember us, Lord," at which
time You come with Your kingdom, and
have mercy on us.

PEACE HOUR

Proclamation

Senior Chancel

<u>Deacon</u>
And again in peace let us request of the Lord.

Let us be thankful from the Lord, Who through His mercy led us into the works of the day, and graced us, in unison to come and arrive to resting in this night. And let us pray at every hour to God the lover of mankind, to be protector of our beings, and He through His mercy shall protect us, and having led us He may make us to arrive to His rest of goodness, Whom the true God Jesus Christ promised to His beloved, may the Lord almighty give life and be merciful.

<u>Choir</u>
Give life Lord and have mercy.

<u>Deacon</u>
For passing the resting of this night in peace. With faith let us ask from the Lord.

<u>Choir</u>
Grace unto us Lord.

The angel of peace to be guardian of our beings. Let us ask from the Lord.

Grace unto us Lord.

For atonement and forgiveness of our offences. Let us ask from the Lord.

Grace unto us Lord.

For the great Holy Cross and able strength for assistance of our beings. Let us ask from the Lord.

Grace unto us Lord.

PEACE HOUR

And again in one voice for the sake of
our true and holy faith.
Let us pray to the Lord.

Lord have mercy.

Let us make ourselves and one another as
the person of the Lord God almighty.

Let us become as Your Person Lord.

Lord our God be merciful to us,
according to Your great mercy,
let us all say in unison.

Lord have mercy. Lord have mercy. Lord have mercy.

Prayer

Student Chancel

<u>Priest</u>

Kind Lord, Whom through Your great compassion
You prepared the eternal rest for those
who have labored with virtue, and You
called to You with a sweet voice those who
are heavy burdened and weary with sins,
by promising to them rest. And grace unto
us, Lord, to pass this night with undisturbed
peace, and those who have labored from the
weight of sins, secure with Your mercy,
and make worthy of the eternal rest
with all of Your saints. And let us glorify
You with thanksgiving with the Father
and most Holy Spirit, now and always and
unto the eternity of eternities. Amen.

Peace unto all.

PEACE HOUR

<u>Choir</u>

And with Your spirit.

<u>Deacon</u>

Let us bow in worship of God.

<u>Choir</u>

Before You Lord.

<u>Priest</u>

Giver of good things, and fountain of peace, Lord our God, make our minds and thoughts at peace from all Satanic disturbances, in this night and at all times. So that we, having been guided through these passing ways of life, may arrive to Your eternal kingdom of the heavens, which You prepared from the beginning of the world for Your saints. And in their company, through giving thanks may we glorify the Father and the Son and the Holy Spirit, now and always and unto the eternity of eternities. Amen.

600   PEACE HOUR

Senior Chancel
           Psalm 26:1-14 KJV 27:1-14

           (Read in Alternation)

Lord my light and my life, from who will I fear?
Lord refuge of my life, from whom will I tremble?

When those of the evil ones were approaching towards me to
eat my body, my oppressors and my enemies
became weak and fell.

If upon me war shall be prepared, my
heart shall not fear, if upon me battle shall
arise, and yet with this, in You Lord, I trusted.

One thing I asked from the Lord, and I pray
the same, for me to dwell in the house of
the Lord all the days of my life.

For me to see the elegance of the Lord,
and to command in His temple.

He hid me in His tabernacle in the day
of evil, under the shelter He made me
(hide) in the secret of His tabernacle.

Upon a rock He raised me up on high,
and now raise my head up over my enemies.

PEACE HOUR

I shall go around and shall offer in His
tabernacle an offering of blessing,*
I shall bless* and say psalms to the Lord.

Hear, Lord, my voice that I cried unto You,
have mercy upon me and hear me,
for my heart said to You and my faces
sought Your faces, Lord, they sought.

Do not turn Your faces from me, and do not
turn away from Your servant in anger.

Lord, be my helper, do not reject me, and
do not abandon me, God my savior.

My father and mother abandoned me,
and the Lord received me.

Make me knowledgeable in the law, Lord, in Your way,
lead me in Your upright paths.

For the sake of my enemies, do not deliver me up
into the hands of my oppressors.

---

* *"blessing in song" is implied.*

PEACE HOUR

Witnesses of sins have risen up over me,
and they lied to me in their lawlessness.

I believed in seeing goodness of the Lord in
the land of the living, and patience for the
Lord gave encouragement, your heart shall
become strong and have patience for the Lord.

Glory to the Father and to the Son and to the Holy Spirit.

Now and always and unto the eternity of eternities. Amen.

Hymn by His Holiness Nerses the Graceful
Catholicos of the Armenians

Senior Chancel

"Look with Love" (Nayatz sirov)

P Tz

Look with love O compassionate Father to
those created works of Your hands, and give the
armies of angels as guardian for the weak, save
our beings from temptations of the night
wandering demons, that in the day and in the night
we will give unceasing glories to You.

They were uncreated without beginning
inexpressible birth the Son and the Word,
Who made the day for work and the night for
rest in sleep, while the eyes of the body sleep
give us to be awake according to the spirit,
that in the day and in the night
we will give unceasing glories to You.

PEACE HOUR

Rabbi of rational souls, fountain of light,
distributor of graces, while closing the doors
of the natures of the body give light to the eyes of our hearts,
from the nights we arrive early to You to give blessing in
the company of the fiery angels, that in the day and in the night
we will give unceasing glories to You.

O Holy of Holies Trinity cleanse us for Your
dwelling, grace us, in the company of the children
with the bridegroom,* to rest in Your company
in the bed; give the request of the friend,
the borrowing of three loaves,
that in the day and in the night
we will give unceasing glories to You.

You created the visible light, You separated the day
and the night, in the night Lord shine forth upon us
intelligible rays, give at all times
the protection of the shadow of Your
right hand, that in the day and in the night
we will give unceasing glories to You.

Your fire of Your love having been cast down upon the
earth shall kindle in our souls, the thoughts
of our hearts shall be cleansed, the light
of Your knowledge shall shine, from the sleep
of death awaken us, kindle our minds
with Your flame, that in the day and in the night
we will give unceasing glories to You.

---

* *Christ*

PEACE HOUR

We look to You O unapproachable light,
having been hidden from the sense of light,
Who for our sake You were placed in the
pit and You slept in the tomb, wakeful
nature sleep with us, repulse the operation
of the evil one, that in the day and in the night
we will give unceasing glories to You.

O of You Who exists of the light without shadow,
with requests we stand before You, Who with closed
doors of the evening You appeared to the eleven,
in the company of Thomas we call out to You,
we profess You Lord and God, and descend unto
us in this night and give Your greeting to our souls.

We having gathered to You Lord we pray, look upon
us to help, we request, O keeper of Israel be a
shadow for our beings, peacemaker lodge with us and
may we sleep undisturbed, that during the mornings
we may arrive early to bless You in the
company of the Father and with the Spirit.

PEACE HOUR

Of the roar of the horn of Gabriel which is
on the last night, make us worthy to listen
and to be on Your right hand of Your sheep,
with the inextinguishable light of the lanterns
as the five wise virgins, that in the company
of the bridegroom we brides with faith may
enter the bridal chamber in glories.

Expel from within us, Lord, with the sign of Your
cross the adversary* and invisible beast* and do not
give unto corruption Your inheritances.

Advocate for our sake, Mary the God-Bearer,
who gave birth to the Lord God Who shepherded
Israel with His almighty and wonderful glories.

Petition

<u>Priest</u>

Lord, do not turn Your faces from me, I pray
to You kind Lord, be my helper. Lord do
not reject me, and do not abandon me,
God my savior.

* Satan

PEACE HOUR

Proclamation

Student Chancel

<u>Deacon</u>

Let us pray to almighty God,
and request from Him, that he may send
the angel of peace, who having come shall
protect us in this fearful night from demonic
disturbances, and to keep entirely our souls and
bodies until the completion of the time of our years.
Almighty Lord our God, may You give life
and have mercy.

Prayer

Senior Chancel

<u>Priest</u>

He Who graces good things, generous in all
immortal Lord, we pray to You, remove
from our beings the gloomy and dark
thoughts. Keep us from the deceits of
slander, and grace unto us with faith
to take refuge in the all Holy Trinity,
in the Father and in the Son, and in
the Holy Spirit, now and always and
unto the eternity of eternities. Amen.

For Great Lenten Days (Salt and Bread Days) recite the following Psalm 118 KJV 119 beginning on page 607 and continue. However, for ordinary days and other regular fasting days, recite only the Lord's Prayer then end the service here.

PEACE HOUR 607

Psalm 118 KJV 119 is chanted on Great Lenten Days
(Salt and Bread Days)

(This Psalm was originally composed in 22 sections. Each section contains 8 verses and each section began with a successive letter of the Hebrew alphabet.)

Student Chancel

Section 1 vs. 1-8

Fortunate are those spotless in the way,
and who walk in the laws of the Lord.

Fortunate are those who examine His testimony,
they will seek Him with all their heart.

Those that commit unlawfulness,
shall not walk in His ways.

You commanded Your commandments to
me while keeping them extremely.

I wish that my ways would have been successful for me,
for me to keep Your justices.

In that time I was not ashamed
while taking heed to Your commandments.

I shall confess You, Lord, in my upright heart,
as I shall learn the righteousness of Your justice.

I kept Your laws, do not leave me unto the end.

Section 2 vs. 9-16

By what may a young man strengthen his ways,
but by keeping Your words.

I sought You with all my heart, do not reject
me from Your commandments.

I hid Your words in my heart, so that I
may not sin against You.

Blessed are You, Lord, teach me Your justices.

With my lips I shall tell all of the righteousness
of Your mouth.

I became cheerful in the ways of Your testimonies,
as in all richness.

In Your commandments I was cared for,
and I took heed in Your ways.

I spoke Your laws, and did not forget Your words.

Section 3 vs. 17-24

Compensate your servant, that I
may live and keep Your words.

PEACE HOUR

Awaken my eyes, and I may look to
the wonders of Your laws.

I am an emigrant on the earth, do not hide
Your commandments from me.

My being longs for, while desiring for me,
Your laws at all times.

You reprimanded the arrogant, those who
strayed from Your commandments have been cursed.

Remove from me the insults and despite,
for I sought Your testimonies.

Though princes sat and spoke ill of me,
but Your servant was pondering upon Your laws.

For Your testimonies were my speech, and Your
justice my counsels.

<u>Section 4 vs. 25-32</u>

My being drew near to the soil,
Lord, give me life according to Your word.

I told my ways to You, and You heard me,
teach me Your justices.

Make me wise in the ways of Your justices,
and I shall examine Your wonders.

My being has remained sleepless while becoming
weary, affirm me in Your words.

Remove from me the ways of sins, and have
mercy on me unto Your laws.

I chose Your ways of truth, and I did not
forget Your laws.

I drew near to Your testimonies, Lord,
do not make me ashamed.

I ran to the ways of Your commandments,
for You made me calm.

Section 5 vs. 33-40

Make me knowledgeable in the law,
Lord, in the ways of Your righteousness,
and I shall seek it at all times.

Make me wise, and I shall examine Your laws, and
I shall keep it with all of my heart.

Lead me in the paths of Your commandments,
for through them I was pleased.

Make my heart descend into Your testimonies,
and not into greed.

PEACE HOUR

Turn my eyes away that I shall not see
vanity, give me life in Your ways.

Affirm Your word to Your servant in Your fear.

Take away from me the insults which I have
also presumed, for Your judgments are kind.

Behold I desired Your commandments,
in Your justice give me life.

Section 6 vs. 41-48

May Your mercy come upon me, Lord,
and Your salvation according to Your word.

I shall give answer those who insult me by words,
for I trusted in Your words.

Do not remove from my mouth the word
of truth completely, for I hoped in Your laws.

I kept Your laws at all time,
eternally and unto the eternity of eternities.

I was walking in tranquility, for I sought
Your commandments.

I was speaking Your testimonies before
kings, and I was not ashamed.

I was pondering in Your commandments
which I loved.

I raised up my hands to Your commandments
which I loved, and I was pondering to Your justice.

<u>Section 7 vs. 49-56</u>

Remember the word of Your servant,
and in which You caused me to hope.

He shall comfort me in my depression,
because Your word gave me life.

The arrogant have violated my rights
extremely, but from Your laws I did
not go astray.

I remembered Your laws unto the eternities,
Lord, and I was comforted.

Sadness has taken hold of me because
of the sinners, and those who abandoned
Your laws.

Your laws are praiseworthy to me,
in the place of my pilgrimage.

I remembered Your Name in the night, Lord,
and I kept Your laws.

This has been a way in life for me,
because I sought Your justices.

<u>Section 8 vs. 57-64</u>

You are my portion, Lord, I have said
to keep Your laws.

PEACE HOUR

I prayed to Your faces with all my heart,
have mercy upon me according to Your word.

I pondered my ways, and turned my feet to
Your testimonies.

I became prepared and did not become agitated,
for I kept Your commandments.

Ropes of sins bound me, but I did not forget Your laws.

In the middle of the night I was arising to
confess to You, for the sake of Your righteousness
and justice.

I was a participant of all who fear You,
of those who have kept Your commandments.

The earth has been filled with the
mercy of the Lord, teach me Your justices.

Section 9 vs. 65-72

You have done kindness with Your servant,
Lord, according to Your word.

Teach me kind advice and knowledge,
for I believed in Your commandments.

Before I had been humbled, I sinned,
for the sake of this I kept Your words extremely.

You are kind, Lord, and with Your kindness
teach me Your justices.

The unrighteousness of the arrogant were
multiplied upon me, but with all my
heart I examined Your commandments.

Their hearts are as slimy as milk,
but I spoke Your laws.

It is good for me, that You humbled me,
more than thousands of gold and of silver.

<u>Section 10 vs. 73-80</u>

Your hands make, and they create me,
make me wise, and I will learn Your
commandments.

Those who fear You shall see me, and they
shall be glad, for I trusted in Your words.

I have known, Lord, that Your judgments
are with justice, in true You humbled me.

Let be Your mercy while comforting me,
according to Your word this Your servant.

PEACE HOUR

Let Your compassions come to me and I
shall live, and Your laws were my speech.

May the arrogant who groundlessly violated
my rights be shamed, but I was cared
for in Your commandments.

Those who fear You advised me, and those
who know Your testimonies.

Let my heart be spotless in Your justice,
that I shall not be ashamed.

<u>Section 11 vs. 81-88</u>

My being was longing to Your salvations,
for I hoped in Your words.

My eyes awaited for Your word, I said,
"when shall He comfort me?"

I became as a wineskin in the clear sky,*
I did not forget Your justices.

How many are the days of Your servant?
When will You make rights for me against
my persecutors.

To me they told unlawful intentions,
but not as Your laws.

All of Your commandments are true,
in vain they persecuted me, help me.

---

* *a leather wineskin exposed to sunny dry weather becomes dried and shriveled;
thus the analogy.*

And they were nearly destroying me from the earth,
but I did not abandon Your commandments.

According to Your mercy give me life,
and I shall keep the testimonies of Your mouth.

<u>Section 12 vs. 89-96</u>

Eternal, Lord, Your word stands in the heavens,
from generation to generation is Your truth.

You established the earth, and it stands.

The day remains to Your command, for all
things are Your servants.

If Your laws were not my speech,
perhaps I again would have already been
destroyed in my depression.

Eternally I did not forget Your justices,
for by them You gave me life.

I am Yours and You gave me life, for
I sought Your justices.

The sinners waited to destroy me,
for I took to mind Your testimonies.

I saw the end of all which had been accomplished,
Your commandments were extremely calming for me.

Section 13 vs. 97-104

As I loved Your laws, daily they were my speech.

You made me more wise than my enemies
in Your commandments, for they were eternal
for me.

I became more knowledgeable than all my teachers,
for Your testimonies were my speech.

I became more wise than my elders,
because I examined Your commandments.

I held back my feet from the ways of evils,
in order that I may keep Your words.

I did not go astray from Your laws,
for You made me knowledgeable in the laws.

Such that Your words are sweet to my palate,
more than honey to my mouth.

Having understood Your commandments, I hated
all ways of evils, because You made me knowledgeable
in the law.

Section 14 vs. 105-112

Your words are a lamp for my feet,
and they give light to my paths.

I took an oath and affirmed it, that
I shall keep all the laws of Your justice.

I have become humbled to the extreme, Lord,
give me life according to Your word.

Be pleased, Lord, according to the wills of my mouth,
and teach me Your righteousness.

My being is in Your hands at all times,
and I did not forget Your laws.

The sinners set a snare for me,
I did not wander away from Your commandments.

I eternally inherited Your testimonies,
for it is joy to my heart.

I descended my heart to perform Your
eternal justices, for the sake of recompense.

Section 15 vs. 113-120

I hate the lawless ones, and I loved Your laws.

You are my helper and savior, and I hoped
in Your words.

Evil ones, be gone away from me! And
I shall examine the commandments of my God.

PEACE HOUR

Help me according to Your word
and give me life, and do not make me
ashamed of my hope.

Help me, and make me live, and I will
ponder on Your righteousness at all times.

You rejected all those who became rebels
to Your justices, because their thoughts
are of unrighteousness.

I had considered all sinners of the
earth offenders, for the sake of this I loved
Your commandments.

Nail my body with Your fear, for I will fear
from Your judgments very much.

Section 16 vs. 121-128

I have done righteousness and justice.
Do not hand me over to the hands of my oppressors.

Receive Your servant in goodness, do not let
the arrogant disgust me.

My eyes awaited for Your salvation, Lord, and for
the word of Your justice.

Make with Your servant, Lord, according to
Your mercy, teach me Your justice.

I am Your servant, make me wise, and
I may know Your testimonies.

It is time to give adoration to the Lord,
they have annulled Your laws.

For the sake of this I loved Your
commandments, more than all the gold
and topaz.

All of Your commandments were favorable
to me, for I hated the ways of evils.

<u>Section 17 vs. 129-136</u>

Your testimonies are wonderful, for the sake of this
my being loved them.

I opened my mouth and took the spirit,
my being desired for Your commandments.

Look upon me and have mercy upon me,
according to righteousness of those that love
Your Name.

Make my ways straight for me according to Your word,
and may all my sins not rule me.

Save me from the defamation of man,
and I shall keep Your commandments.

Show Your faces upon this Your servant,
and teach me Your justices.

Streams of water came down from my eyes,
because they did not keep Your laws.

Section 18 vs. 137-144

You are just, Lord, and Your judgments
are upright.

You commanded justice for Your testimonies,
and they are exceedingly true.

Your zeal wore me out, for my enemies
forgot Your words.

Your word is exceedingly chosen,
and Your servant loved it.

I am a child who has been despised,
and I did not forget Your justices.

Your justice, justice unto the eternities,
and Your laws are true.

Oppression and affliction found me,
and Your commandments were my speech.

Your testimonies are eternal with justice,
make me wise and give me life.

PEACE HOUR

Section 19 vs. 145-152

I cried out to You with all my heart,
hear me, Lord, for I sought Your justice.

I cried out to You and save me,
and I shall keep Your testimonies.

Beforetime I arrived early, I cried out, and I trusted in Your words.

My eyes got up early in the mornings,
while speaking Your words to me.

Hear my voice, Lord, according to Your mercy,
Lord, and give me life in Your rights.

You are near, Lord, and all Your commandments are true.

From the beginning I knew of Your testimonies,
because You established them eternally.

Section 20 vs. 153-160

See my humiliation and save me,
for I have not forgotten Your laws.

PEACE HOUR

Judge my judgment and save me,
according to Your word give me life.

Salvation is far from the sinners,
because they did not keep Your laws.

Your compassions are many, Lord,
according to Your laws give me life.

Many are those who persecute and oppress me,
I have not gone astray from Your testimonies.

I was looking upon the cruel and was languishing,
because they did not keep Your commandments.

See, for I loved Your commandments,
Lord, through Your mercy give me life.

The beginning of Your words is truth,
all laws of Your justice are eternal.

<u>Section 21 vs. 161-168</u>

Princes persecuted me in vain.
And my heart feared from Your words.

I rejoiced in Your word,
as one who finds many spoils.

I hated and despised sins,
and I loved Your laws.

I shall bless You seven times a day, for the
sake of Your righteousness and judgment.

Much peace is for those who love Your laws, and
for them there exists nothing that can make them stumble.

I awaited for Your salvation Lord, and I
loved Your commandments.

My being kept Your testimonies,
and loved them greatly.

I kept Your commandments and testimonies,
for all of my roads are before You.

<u>Section 22 vs. 169-176</u>

May my requests draw near before You, Lord, according
to Your word make me wise.

May my prayers enter before You, Lord, and through
Your word save me.

May Your blessings spring forth from my lips,
at which time You will teach me Your justice.

PEACE HOUR

My tongue shall speak Your words, for all of
Your commandments are with justice.

Let it be Your hand which is giving me
life, for I chose Your commandments.

I became desirous of Your salvation, Lord,
and Your laws were my word.

May my being live, may it bless You,
and Your laws shall help me.

I was wandering as a lost sheep, search for this
Your servant, for I have not forgotten
Your commandments.

Glory to the Father, and to the Son, and to the Holy Spirit.

Now and always and unto the eternity of eternities.

Hymn
"We Request from You" (I ken haytzemk)

Student Chancel
(During Great Lent Only)

K Tz

From You we request, Father of
compassions and God of consolations,
having neared to this dreary hour
of the night, comfort us from
the sorrows of sins, and grace,
cheer through deeds of righteousness,
through the prayers of the holy God-Bearer
and all of the just.

PEACE HOUR

According to the call of Your sweetest Godly command, Son of God, we having come before You in this evening, having labored and having been overburdened, lighten our beings from the weight of our sins and strengthen our beings to willingly take up the sweet yoke of Your commandments, through the prayers of the holy God-Bearer and all of the just.

We request of You with spirit having arrived at this hour of rest, Spirit of God, lover of humanity, at which time You renew the faces of the earth, and again You receive the spirits of mankind, adorn with new feathers* those of ours who are asleep who have been born of You through the holy font, through the prayers of the holy God-Bearer and all of the just.

rejuvenate

PEACE HOUR

The portrait of Your spotless bearer we send
forth before Your unvengeful Lordship, at
which time You come with glories of the
Father, to judge the enemy of Your cross,
forgive our offences with the advocation
of Your mother and virgin, we pray to You,
Lord, protect us with the shadow of Your
holy cross.

Make us also participants, Lord, with
Your holy apostles who became worthy
to see You in Your resurrection, make
us worthy, Lord, to see You in Your
second coming, blessing to the sender
in the highest.

While sitting in Your court, awesome judge,
with the prayers of the holy God-Bearer,
remember those of ours who are asleep,
at which time You come with inexpressible glories,
for the glories are Yours unto eternity, Amen.

628   PEACE HOUR

Modulated Chants
(Sung after the Hymn)

Student Chancel

These Chants are traditionally sung beginning on the Wednesday of the fourth week of Great Lent. One verse is usually sung beginning with the first verse, singing the second verse the fifth week, and the third verse the sixth week all on their appropriate weekday. The melodies are complex and sung slowly.

Wednesday

T̄ Ḡ

Holy Mary, golden vessel and ark of
the testaments, who from above you
gifted the Bread of Life to those of
hungering natures, always advocate to
Him for the sake of the atonement of our sins.

Ranks of the bodiless angels are fortunate in you,
most blessed virgin Mary, Whom the Word of the
same existence, in the company of the Father,
without seed, was carried in you, always advocate to
Him for the sake of the atonement of our sins.

For the sake of Whom, we believers
also bow down and worship You Christ,
and with tears we request from You,
with the advocation of the God-Bearer,
shine Your Godly light upon our beings,
awesome king we bless You in the
resurrection of this evening.

PEACE HOUR

Thursday

T G

Apostles of God, those having been chosen
from the beginning before this world, those of
you who were worthy to see that which was unseen by
the fiery angels, advocate to the Lord for the sake
of children who are servants of the church.*

Friends of Christ, majors of the Godly councils,
those who took men up from the flowing
sea of sins into lives immortal,
advocate to the Lord for the sake of children
who are servants of the church.*

Supreme more than ever, you arrived to
inexpressible fortune, those who
in the coming of the Lord shall sit on
the twelve thrones of Christ,
advocate to the Lord for the sake of children
who are servants of the church.*

---

* *Even though "children" is used, this term includes those of all ages who serve the church whether they be adults or children.*

PEACE HOUR

Friday

T G

Having enclosed it they were guarding
the ways to the tree of lives
of the uncreated fertile paradise,
cherubic troops with fiery seraphim, today having
glistened You showed to the earth the
God adorned wood of lives and of
Your salvation, the children who are
servants of the Holy Church bless You.*

Regarding the burning blackthorn tree branches,
burnt offering of the ram instead of Isaac,
but upon You the spotless lamb was sacrificed,
for reconciliation with the Father while
taking up our sins, the children who are
servants of the Holy Church bless You.*

Boasts of Paul, having professed You Godly
place of the Word and sacrificial altar,
for through You we were saved from the
biting and bodiless beast, upon You flowing
drops of incorruptible blood from
Your side erased the sins, the children who
are servants of the Holy Church bless You.*

---

* *Even though "children" is used, this term includes those of all ages who serve the church whether they be adults or children.*

PEACE HOUR

Monday

T G

Chosen heavenly flock, which the Good Shepherd
has left in the heavens, and He
has come in seek of us whom have gone astray,
by which having filled the number
of one hundred, You made cheerfulness
in the heavens for Your heavenly beings,
we request of You, be an advocate to the Lord,
for the sake of the atonement of our sins.

Seers of the unseen, ponder the depths of God,
those who having descended with the only begotten
to minister in administration, those announcers of
the good news of the birth to the shepherds,
and preaching of the messages of
life to the oil-bearing women,
we request of You, be an advocate to the Lord,
for the sake of the atonement of our sins.

Guardians of the world,
armies of the Lord
surrounding those with fear,
mediators of death and resurrection,
the great ones Michael and Gabriel,
who stand always before the most Holy Trinity,
we request of You, be an advocate to the Lord,
for the sake of the atonement of our sins.

PEACE HOUR

Tuesday

<u>T Tz</u>

Heavenly bridegroom, intelligible shadowless light,
You Who descended from the heavens
into love of Your bride the church, of which
Your friend and best man spoke to You,
with petitions of the same, have mercy.

Of the four formed beings inaccessible
and unseen by the seraphim,
holy of holies and Lord of all,
You descended into the Jordan,
by requesting cleansing of water from
Your servant while washing away the sins of Adam,
with petitions of the same, have mercy.

Whom You Lamb of God, the lifter of sins,
were witnessed of by the Forerunner,*
supreme amongst the just You were made known great
from the birth of woman and lantern of the laws,
and who preached Your salvatory
coming to the hells,**
with petitions of the same, have mercy.

* *John the Baptist*
** *Hades*

PEACE HOUR

Petition

<u>Priest</u>

For the souls of those who are at rest, Christ God, make them rest and have mercy, and for we sinners grace upon us the forgiveness of offences.

Proclamation

Student Chancel

<u>Deacon</u>

And again in peace let us request of the Lord, for the sake of the souls who are resting we request, Christ our savior, that He rank them amongst the just, and give life to us with the grace of His mercy. Our almighty Lord God, give life and have mercy.

<u>Priest</u>

Lord have mercy, Lord have mercy, Lord have mercy.

Prayer

Senior Chancel

Priest

Christ Son of God, humane and compassionate, have compassion with Your love as creator upon the souls of Your servants who are resting. Remember them on the day of the great coming of Your kingdom. Make them worthy of mercy, atonement, and forgiveness of sins. Make them shine brightly placing them in the order of saints in the rank at Your right side. For You are Lord and creator of all, judge of the living and of the dead. And to You is befitting glory, Lordship and honor, now and always and through the eternity of eternities, amen.

Blessed be our Lord Jesus Christ. Amen.

Our Father Who art in heaven, Hallowed be Thy name.
Thy kingdom come, Thy will be done on earth as it is in heaven.
Give us this day our daily bread. And forgive us our debts,
as we forgive our debtors.
And lead us not into temptation, but deliver us from evil.

For Thine is the Kingdom, and the power,
and the glory forever and ever. Amen.

REST HOUR

The order of the common hour of Prayers of the Rest Hour which are performed before God the Father, who by the shield of the right hand of the Only Begotten Son of God, protects us from the darkness of this night.

Blessed be our Lord Jesus Christ. Amen.

Our Father Who art in heaven, Hallowed be Thy name.
Thy kingdom come, Thy will be done on earth as it is in heaven.
Give us this day our daily bread.
And forgive us our debts, as we forgive our debtors.
And lead us not into temptation, but deliver us from evil.

For Thine is the Kingdom, and the power,
and the glory forever and ever. Amen.

Priest Ps 42:3-5 KJV 43:3-5
Lord, send Your light and Your truth, that they may lead me, and may lift me up to Your holy mountain and to Your dwelling places.

Student Chancel
Deacon
I shall enter before the table of God, to God,
Who makes my childhood cheerful.

I shall be confessing to You with blessings of
the harp,* God my God.

Now, my being, why are you sad? Or why do
you trouble me? Hope to God, confess to Him,
the savior of my faces is God.

Priest
Glory to the Father and to the Son and to the Holy Spirit.

Deacon
Now and always and unto the eternity of eternities. Amen.
And again in peace let us request of the Lord. Receive, save, and have mercy.

Priest
Blessing and glory to the Father and to the Son and to the Holy Spirit,
now and always and unto the eternity of eternities. Amen.

* Implied, the word "Orhnotyoon" can mean both blessing and musical instrument. i.e. harp.

REST HOUR

Student Chancel

Psalms

(read in alternation)

Ps 118:41-48 KJV 119:41-48
Section 6

May Your mercy come upon me, Lord,
and Your salvation according to Your word.

I shall give answer those who insult me by words,
for I trusted in Your words.

Do not remove from my mouth the word
of truth completely, for I hoped in Your laws.

I kept Your laws at all time,
eternally and unto the eternity of eternities.

I was walking in tranquility, for I sought
Your commandments.

I was speaking Your testimonies before
kings, and I was not ashamed.

I was pondering in Your commandments
which I loved.

I raised up my hands to Your commandments
which I loved, and I was pondering to Your justice.

REST HOUR

Ps: 118:49-56 KJV 119:49-56 Section 7

Remember the word of Your servant,
and in which You caused me to hope.

He shall comfort me in my depression,
because Your word gave me life.

The arrogant have violated my rights
extremely, but from Your laws I did
not go astray.

I remembered Your laws unto the eternities,
Lord, and I was comforted.

Sadness has taken hold of me because
of the sinners, and those who abandoned
Your laws.

Your laws are praiseworthy to me,
in the place of my pilgrimage.

I remembered Your Name in the night, Lord,
and I kept Your laws.

This has been a way in life for me,
because I sought Your justices.

Ps 118:113-120 KJV 119:113-120 Section 15

I hate the lawless ones, and I loved Your laws.

You are my helper and savior, and I hoped
in Your words.

Evil ones, be gone away from me! And
I shall examine the commandments of my God.

Help me according to Your word
and give me life, and do not make me
ashamed of my hope.

Help me, and make me live, and I will
ponder on Your righteousness at all times.

You rejected all those who became rebels
to Your justices, because their thoughts
are of unrighteousness.

I had considered all sinners of the
earth offenders, for the sake of this I loved
Your commandments.

Nail my body with Your fear, for I will fear
from Your judgments very much.

Ps 118:169-176 KJV 119:169-176
Section 22

May my requests draw near before You, Lord, according
to Your word make me wise.

May my prayers enter before You, Lord, and through
Your word save me.

May Your blessings spring forth from my lips,
at which time You will teach me Your justice.

My tongue shall speak Your words, for all of
Your commandments are with justice.

REST HOUR

Let it be Your hand which is giving me
life, for I chose Your commandments.

I became desirous of Your salvation, Lord,
and Your laws were my word.

May my being live, may it bless You,
and Your laws shall help me.

I was wandering as a lost sheep, search for this
Your servant, for I have not forgotten
Your commandments.

Ps 35:12-13 KJV 36:11-12

Do not let the foot of arrogances come upon us,
nor let the hand of sinners cause us to tremble.

Over there all those whom commit unrighteousness
have fallen, may they be cast down and be made not
able to recover.

Habakkuk 3:18 – 19

I hoped in the Lord, I shall rejoice and
be glad in God my savior.

Lord Lord gave me strength and stood
my feet up in firmness, He stood
me upon the neck of the enemy,
and quickly quickly made me rest.

REST HOUR

Ps 90:1-16 KJV 91:1-16

He who dwells in aid of the One on
high, he shall rest under the
shadow of God in the heavens.

He shall say to the Lord, You are my
receiver, God is my refuge, and I hope in Him.

He shall save me from the snare of the
hunter, and from words of trouble.

Into His backbone you will be received,
in the shadow of His wings you shall have hope.

May His truth be as armor around you.

You shall not fear the fright of the night,
nor the arrow which flies in the day.

Nor from things that walk in the dark,
nor from obstacles of the demon at midday.

Thousands shall fall at Your side, and
tens of thousands at Your right hand, which
no one shall come near You.

But only with Your eyes You shall look,
and You shall see the restitution of the sinners,
because You, Lord, You are my hope.

The One on high made for you a refuge,
no evil shall come near to you, and plague
shall not approach to Your dwelling.

REST HOUR

He having commanded to His angels for your sake
while keeping you in all your ways.

They received you in their arms, that you
will never strike your foot upon a stone.

You shall walk over serpents and vipers, and
by the foot you shall trample the lion and
the dragon.

Because he hoped in Me and I shall save him,
I shall be a shield to him, for he knew My Name.

He shall cry out to Me, and to him I shall be heard,
and I shall be in him in trouble.

I shall save and glorify him, I shall fill him with
long days and I shall show him my salvation.

<u>Ps 122:1-4 KJV 123:1-4</u>

To You, Lord, I lifted up my eyes,
You Who has dwelled in the heavens.

As the eyes of the servant to the hand of his master
and as the eyes of the maid servant to the hand
of her mistress.

Likewise our eyes are to You, Lord, our God,
until You shall have mercy upon us.

Have mercy upon us, Lord, have mercy upon us,
for we were filled exceedingly with contempt.

Moreover our beings were filled
with insults, of those who were insulting us,
and with contempt of the arrogant.

REST HOUR

<u>Ps 53:3-9 KJV 54:1-7</u>

God, in Your Name grant me life, and in
Your power make me just.

God, hear my prayers, place Your ear upon the
words of my mouth.

Foreigners rose up over me, and the mighty ones
demanded my being, and they did not regard
You as God before them.

Behold God my helper,
and Lord receiver of my soul.

While returning the evil unto my enemies,
destroy them with Your truth.

Of my will I shall offer sacrifices to You,
I shall confess of Your Name, Lord, for it is good.

You saved me from all troubles, and
my eye has seen my enemies.

REST HOUR

A Canticle, Song from the Prophet Daniel 3:52-56
Blessing of the Three Young Men in the Furnace 29-34
Blessed are You, Lord God of our fathers,
being praised and most elevated on high
unto eternity.

And blessed be Your Holy Name of glories,
being praised and most elevated on high
unto eternity.

Blessed be You in the temple of Your
glories of holiness, being praised and
most elevated on high unto eternity.

Blessed be You upon the throne of
Your kingdom, being praised and
most elevated on high unto eternity.

Blessed be You which You sit upon
the cherubim and look into the abysses,
being praised and most elevated on high
unto eternity.

Blessed be You upon the establishment
of the heavens, being praised and
most elevated on high unto eternity.

Ps 150:1-6 KJV 150:1-6
Bless God in His sanctuary, bless Him
in the expanse of the skies,* in His power.

Bless Him in His power, bless Him in His
multitudes of greatness.

Bless Him in the sound of song, bless Him
with harps and instruments.**

firmament

**tambourines and timbrels*

Bless Him with rejoicing, praise Him
with cheerfulness.

Bless Him with sweet words, praise Him in
sound to hear.

Bless Him in a voice of thanksgiving,
every soul bless the Lord.

The Prayer of the Elderly Simeon
Lk 2:29-32

Now, release this Your servant in peace
Lord, according to Your Word, for my
eyes have seen Your salvation, which
You have prepared before all peoples.

Light has been revealed to the heathens,*
and glory to Your people of Israel.

Ps 137:7b-8 KJV 138:7b-8

You stretched out Your hand and Your right hand
saved me, and the Lord shall compensate in
exchange for me.

Lord, Your eternal mercy, do not neglect the
works of Your hands.

Ps 141:8 KJV 142:7

Lord, take my being out of prison,
from Your Name I am satisfied.

And the just wait for You, until You
shall recompense them.

---

* *Heathen is not an offensive term in this case. It means all peoples who are not believers in the God of Israel. The term "Gentiles" could be used but heathen is more precise.*

REST HOUR

<u>Song of Mary the God-Bearer</u>
<u>Lk 1:46-55</u>

My soul shall magnify the Lord, and
my spirit shall rejoice with God my savior.

He paid visit upon the humility of His
maid servant, from now on all nations
shall regard me as fortunate.

The Mighty One has made very great
things through me, and Holy is His Name.

You made mercy from generation unto
generation upon those who fear in Him,
He made power with His right arm.

He scattered those who are arrogant in
thoughts of their hearts, and pulled down
the mighty ones from their thrones.

He uplifted the humble, He filled those who
are impoverished, with goodness, and He
sent the wealthy away empty.

He defended Israel His servant,
by remembering His mercy.

As He spoke unto our fathers, in the
company of Abraham and his child,
unto eternity.

REST HOUR

<u>Ps 85:16b-17 KJV 86:16b-17</u>
Give strength to Your servant,
give life to the son of Your maid,
and make unto me the sign of goodness.

Those that hate me shall see and shall
be ashamed, for You, Lord, helped me
and comforted me.

Glory to the Father and to the Son and to the Holy Spirit.

Now and always and unto the eternity of eternities. Amen.

Petition

<u>Priest</u>
My soul is in Your hands at all times, and I have trusted
in Your holy cross, heavenly king, I have the multitude of
Your saints as advocates to You. Whom You are patient
towards all, do not ignore the ones who have taken refuge
in You, but keep them in peace through Your holy and
revered cross.

Proclamation

Student Chancel
<u>Deacon</u>
Let us pray to almighty God,
and request from Him, that he may send
the angel of peace, who having come shall
protect us in this fearful night from demonic
disturbances, and to keep entirely our souls and
bodies until the completion of the time of our years.
Almighty Lord our God, may You give life
and have mercy.

<u>Choir</u>
Give life Lord and have mercy.

REST HOUR 649

<u>Deacon</u>
To pass the resting of this night in peace,
with faith let us ask from the Lord.

<u>Choir *(continue in alternation)*</u>
Grace unto us Lord.

The angel of peace to be guardian
of our beings. Let us ask from the Lord.

Grace unto us Lord.

For atonement and forgiveness of our offences.
Let us ask from the Lord.

Grace unto us Lord.

For the great Holy Cross and able strength for assistance of our beings.
Let us ask from the Lord.

Grace unto us Lord.

And again in one voice for the sake of our true and holy faith. Let us pray to the Lord.

Lord have mercy.

Let us make ourselves and one another as the person of the Lord God almighty.

Let us become as Your Person Lord.

Lord our God be merciful to us, according to Your great mercy, let us all say in unison.

Lord have mercy. Lord have mercy. Lord have mercy.

Prayer

Senior Chancel
<u>Priest</u>
Lord our God, keep us with peace in this night and at all time. Keep our minds and thoughts, having been affixed in Your holy fear, in order that at every hour we may be protected from the snares of the enemy.
And may we lift up blessing and glories to the Father and to the Son and to the Holy Spirit, now and always and unto the eternity of eternities. Amen.

REST HOUR

Priest

Peace unto all.

Choir

And with Your spirit.

Deacon

Let us bow down in worship of God.

Choir

Before You Lord.

Priest

Unto the angel of peace, make our beings unto yourself, Lord of hosts, Who having come may keep us undisturbed in the day and in the night, in our wakefulness and in our rest, for You are the creator of light and maker of the night. And now we pray to You, Lord our God, to grace unto us to pass the rest of this night in peace, and to arrive to the service of the morning to the bowing down in worship and to the glorification of the all Holy Trinity, now and always and unto the eternity of eternities. Amen.

REST HOUR 651

Senior Chancel

Ps 4:9-10, 2-10 KJV 4:8-10, 1-10

With peace, in this and the same we shall
sleep and awaken, for only You alone Lord
with Your hope has made us to dwell.

While I cry out You heard me, God,
according to my righteousness, from oppression
You made me calm, have mercy upon
me and hear my prayers.

Sons of man until when will you be hard hearted,
why do you love vanity, and seek falsehood.

Know that the Lord made wonders for His holy one,
and the Lord shall hear me while I cry out unto Him.

We become angry and you, do not sin!
That which you say in your hearts,
repent in your beds.

Offer sacrifices of righteousness,
and hope in the Lord.

Many were saying, "who shall show
us the goodness of the Lord,"
a sign of the light of Your faces was placed
before us, and You gave joy to
our hearts.

More than from the fruit of grain,
wine, and olive oil You filled it *(my heart)*.

With peace, in this and the same we shall
sleep and awaken, for only You alone Lord
with Your hope has made us to dwell.

REST HOUR

The Gospel of Rest (Hanksdyan)

Deacon	Alleluia Stand
Priest	Peace unto all.
Choir	And with Your spirit.
Deacon	May you listen with awe.

Reader *(priest or deacon)* Senior Chancel
The Holy Gospel of Jesus Christ According to John 12:24-26*

Choir	Glory to You Lord our God.
Deacon	Attention
Choir	God says.

Our Lord Jesus Christ says

Amen Amen** I say to You, unless a grain of wheat
has fallen to the earth and shall die, it alone exists,
then if after it shall die, it makes a multitude of fruits.
He who loves his being, releases it, he who hates
his being in this world, he shall keep it into
life eternal. If someone shall adore me, he shall
come after me, and where I am, there also shall
be my minister, if someone shall adore me,
my Father shall honor him.

---

* *In some traditions, the Gospel is read according to the tone of the day found in the Chancel Gospel (Adeni Avedaran).*

** *"Amen" is actually Hebrew. The exact translation is "Let it be, Let it be" As a side note, the original translators of the Armenian Bible, St. Mesrob et al. decided to use the Hebrew "Amen" rather than the authentic Armenian "Yeghitzi" throughout scripture and to conclude prayers with, in the Armenian language.*

REST HOUR 653

Proclamation

Student Chancel

<u>Deacon</u>

Glory to You our God.

Through the Holy Cross let us request of the Lord,
that through it He may save us from sins, and that
He may grant us life by the grace of His mercy.
Almighty Lord our God, give life and have mercy.

Prayer

Senior Chancel

<u>Priest</u>

Protect us, Christ our God, under the shadow of
Your Holy and revered Cross in peace,
save us from the visible and invisible enemy.
Make us worthy with thanksgiving to glorify
You with the Father and with the Holy Spirit, now
and always and unto the eternity of eternities. Amen.

REST HOUR

Blessed be our Lord Jesus Christ. Amen.

Our Father Who art in heaven, Hallowed be Thy name.
Thy kingdom come, Thy will be done on earth as it is in heaven.
Give us this day our daily bread.
And forgive us our debts, as we forgive our debtors.
And lead us not into temptation, but deliver us from evil.

For Thine is the Kingdom, and the power,
and the glory forever and ever. Amen.

Petition

<u>Priest</u>

We fall before you, holy God-Bearer, and we request of you
O spotless virgin, advocate for the sake of our beings,
and pray to your Only Begotten Son to save us from
temptation and from all of our dangers.

REST HOUR 655

Here follows the reading of one of the 365 Prayers of Lamentation composed by Saint Gregory of Narek in the 10th century. Several of these prayers have been included as examples.
(These are sung in this service)

The following prayers of St. Gregory of Narek were graciously provided by Dr. Abraham Terian from his book "From the Depths of the Heart (Annotated Translation of the Prayers of St. Gregory of Narek)" Published by Liturgical Press, Collegeville, Minnesota 2022.

The Powerful Petition against the Terrors of the Night written by St. Gregory of Narek Discourse No. 12

Student Chancel

12.3
Accept kindly, mighty Lord God, the prayers of my embittered soul.
Draw near with compassion to my unsightly person.
Dispel, Giver of all gifts, my appalling sadness.
Remove from me, merciful One, my unbearable burdens.
Cast into the outer realm, resourceful One, my mortal habits.

Hold me back, ever-victorious One, from the deceiver's desires.
Disperse, exalted One, the fraudster's fog.
Block, Giver of life, the destroyer's ways.
Undo, Seer of secrets, the oppressor's evil gains.
Defeat, inscrutable One, the assailant's attacks.

Inscribe the skylight of my abode with your lordly name.
Support the ceiling of my chapel with your hand.
Mark the threshold of my room with your blood.
Exhibit your sign on the door-lintel of your petitioner.
Strengthen with your hand the frame on which I rest.
Keep the cover of my bed free from defilement.

Preserve my tormented soul by your will.
Steady the breath of life you bestowed upon my body.
Surround me with a band of your heavenly host.
Assign them to guard against the legion of demons.

REST HOUR

12.4

Grant me that blissful rest of death-like sleep in the depth of this night, through the prayers of intercession by the Holy Mother of God and of all the elect. Veil thoroughly the window of my mental faculties, securing them from nightmares, floating anxieties, concerns of daily life, sleepless dreaming, and aimless wanderings. Remembering the hope placed in you, keep them safe from harm.

And when I wake from my sound sleep, fully alert, grant that I stand spiritually refreshed before you. Then will I raise heavenward cries of supplication scented with faith in you, O most blessed King of ineffable glory; so will I join the choirs of glorifiers assembled in heaven. For you are glorified by all creatures, for ever and ever. Amen.

REST HOUR 657

The Powerful Prayer written by St. Gregory of Narek
Discourse No. 41

Senior Chancel

41.1

Son of the living God, blessed in all things, inscrutably begotten of your astounding Father: Nothing is impossible for you. Upon the dawning of the shadowless rays of your glorious mercy, sins fade, demons are chased away, transgressions are erased, shackles are loosened, chains are broken, the dead are brought to life, ailments are cured, wounds are healed, corruption ceases, sadness withdraws, sighs retreat, darkness flees, fog disperses, haze recedes, gloom scatters, obscurity clears, darkness dissipates, the night passes, anxiety is banished, evil is wiped out, despair is chased away. Besides, your omnipotent hand rules, Reconciler of all.

41.2

You who came not to destroy the souls of people but to give life, forgive with your abundant mercy my countless transgressions; for you alone are ineffable in heaven and inscrutable on earth, in the substance of existence unto the very ends of the universe, the beginning of everything and the fullness in everything, blessed in the highest heaven.
Glory to you with the Father and the Holy Spirit, forever. Amen.

REST HOUR

*Petition for Protection Against the Demons
written by St. Gregory of Narek
Discourse No. 94 (No. 93 in some editions)*

Senior Chancel

94.1

Eternal God, benevolent and almighty, Creator of light and Author of night, Life in death and Light in darkness, Hope for the expectant and Forbearance for doubters. In your resourceful wisdom you turn the darkness of death into dawn, O Sunrise in its fullness and unsetting Sun. The night's darkness cannot cover the glory of your Lordship, before which all creation kneels in worship —those in heaven and on earth and in the netherworld.

You who hear the sighs of those who are bound and attend to the prayers of the humble and accept their supplications, my God and my King, my Life and my Refuge, my Hope and my Trust, Jesus Christ, God of all, the Holy One who dwells in the souls of the saints, consolation for the afflicted and pardon for sinners, you who know all things before they happen, send the protective strength of your right hand and save me from the terror of the night and from the evil demon, so that by the very remembrance of your astounding and holy name—always kissed with the lips of my soul and the desires of my breath—I might live protected along with those who call on you with all their hearts.

94.2 And with the seal of your sign, which you renewed by staining it with your divine blood, thereby baptizing us into the grace of adoption and into the glory of your image, in which you fashioned and created us, with these divine gifts may Satan be confounded and his machinations foiled; may his snares be removed and forces defeated; may his sharp-edged weapons fall short; may his haze be lifted, his darkness dispelled, his fog cleared away. May your arm shield me and your right hand seal me, for you are compassionate and merciful, and your servants are called by your name.

To you with the Father and your Holy Spirit, glory and power for ever and ever. Amen.

REST HOUR

A Petition to the Mother of the Lord the Holy God-Bearer written by St. Gregory of Narek Discourse No. 80.

Senior Chancel

80.1

And now, after so much despair and distressing heartbreak, with my endlessly agonized soul grieving because of the dreadful enormity of divine wrath, I pray to you, Holy Mother of God, an angel from humankind, a cherub in bodily appearance, heavenly queen, pure as air, clean as light, clear as the image of Venus at its height, superior to the untrodden dwelling place of the Holiest of All, the promised, blessed place, that breath-taking Eden, the tree of immortal life guarded by the flaming sword, strengthened and protected by the exalted Father, prepared and purified by the resting of the Holy Spirit, adorned by the Son who made his tabernacle in you, the only Son of the Father and your firstborn, your Son by birth and Lord by creation, given your impeccable purity, O perfect goodness—your absolute holiness, O caring intercessor.

Accept the petitions in these supplications by me, who confess faith in you, and with the words of my earlier encomium to your greatness, present them as an offering intermingled with your own pleas. Weave the bitter weeping of my sinful self with your own beatific and incense-perfumed requests, O plant of life with the blessed Fruit. Thus being always helped and having become a recipient of your beneficence, and trusting in and being enlightened by your immaculate birthing, I shall live for Christ, your Son and Lord.

80.2

Confessed Mother of the living, assist me on your wings of prayer, so that my departure from this earthly valley may be painless, leading to life in the prepared dwellings, that my death might be light, though I am weighed down by iniquity.

Healer of Eve's labor pains, make the day of my anguish a festive day; intercede, plead, beseech, for I believe your ineffable purity and that your word is accepted.

Blessed among women, help me with your tears, for I am imperiled.

Mother of God, ask on bended knee for my reconciliation.

Altar of the Most High, care for me, for I am miserable.

Heavenly temple, lend me a hand, for I have fallen.

Handmaid and Mother of God, glorify your Son, by performing upon me the divine miracle of pardon and mercy.

REST HOUR

80.3
May your honor be magnified through me, and may my salvation be manifested through you.

Should you take notice of me, O Mother of the Lord,
Would you pity me, O holy one?
Would you rescue me, for I am lost, O immaculate one?
Would you care for me, for I am brought low, O happy one?
Would you commend me, for I have been shamed, O gracious one?
Would you intercede for me, for I am hopeless, O ever Holy Virgin?
Would you welcome me, a reject, O exalted of God?
Would you show me compassion, O lifter of the curse?
Would you steady me, a drifter, O serenity?
Would you calm me down, for I am worried, O peacemaker?
Would you direct me, for I have strayed, O praised?
Would you appear before the assembly for me,
 O vanquisher of death?
Would you mellow my bitterness, O kindness?
Would you tear down the separating barriers, O conciliation?
Would you lift away my uncleanness, O eradicator of corruption?
Would you save me, for I am condemned to death, O living light?
Would you end the sound of my wailing, O rejoicing?
Would you support me, for I am wrecked, O salve of life?
Would you look upon me, for I am ruined, O spirit-filled?
Would you visit me with compassion, O gift of his will?

80.3 (continued)

You alone are blessed on the pure lips and tongues of the happy ones. Please, let a droplet of milk from your virginity drop on me, to foster me to life, O Mother of our exalted Lord Jesus, Creator of heaven and the whole earth, whom you bore wholly in the flesh, in his full divinity, who is glorified with the Father and the Holy Spirit, uniting his essence and our nature inexplicably. He is all and in all, one of the Trinity. To him be glory for ever and ever. Amen.

Ս. ԳՐԻԳՈՐ ՆԱՐԵԿԱՑԻ

REST HOUR

The prayer "With Faith I Confess" for each individual believer in Christ, written by His Holiness Nerses the Graceful, Catholicos of the Armenians 12th century.
(The prayer contains 24 verses, one for each hour of the day and night.)

Senior Chancel

1. With faith I confess, and bow down in worship
   of You, Father and Son and Holy Spirit,
   uncreated and immortal nature,
   maker of angels and of man and
   all which exists,
   have mercy upon those whom You have
   made and upon me a multitudinous sinner.

2. With faith I confess, and bow down in worship
   of You, inseparable light, unified Holy Trinity and one
   Godly being, maker of light
   and disperser of darkness, disperse from
   my soul the darkness of sins and ignorance,
   and enlighten my mind at this hour to
   pray in pleasure to You,
   and to receive my requests from You,
   have mercy upon those whom You have
   made and upon me a multitudinous sinner.

3. Heavenly Father true God,
You Who sent Your beloved Son
in search of the wandering sheep, I have sinned
unto the heavens and before You, receive me
as the Prodigal Son, and clothe me with the
first robe, of which I had become naked in sins,
have mercy upon those whom You have
made and upon me a multitudinous sinner.

4. Son of God true God,
Whom You had descended from the Fatherly bosom,
and took body from the virgin Mary
for the sake of our salvation,
You were crucified, You were buried and raised from
the dead, and You ascended with glories to the Father,
I have sinned unto the heavens and before You,
remember me as the thief at which time
You come with Your kingdom,
have mercy upon those whom You have
made and upon me a multitudinous sinner.

5. Spirit of God true God,
   Who descended into the Jordan (River) and the upper room,
   and You enlightened me through baptism
   of the holy font, I have sinned unto the heavens and
   before You, cleanse me anew
   with Your Godly fire, as You did with the
   fiery tongues of the holy apostles,
   have mercy upon those whom You have
   made and upon me a multitudinous sinner.

6. Uncreated nature, I have sinned against You
   with my mind, with my soul and body,
   do not remember my previous sins for the sake
   of Your Holy Name,
   have mercy upon those whom You have
   made and upon me a multitudinous sinner.

7. Seer of all, I have sinned against You
   by thought, word, and deed, erase
   the writing of my offences, and write my
   name in the book of lives,
   have mercy upon those whom You have
   made and upon me a multitudinous sinner.

8. Examiner of secrets, I have sinned against You
   willingly and unwillingly, knowingly and
   unknowingly, grace forgiveness
   upon this sinner, for from birth of the
   holy font until this day I have sinned
   before Your Godliness
   with my senses and all of the
   members of my body,
   have mercy upon those whom You have
   made and upon me a multitudinous sinner.

REST HOUR

9. All-caring Lord, place Your holy fear
as a guard for my eyes to no longer
look in lust, and for my ears
not to have the appetite to listen to words of evil,
and for my mouth not to speak lies,
and for my heart not to think evil,
and for my hands not to commit unrighteousness,
and for my feet not to walk in
the ways of lawlessness, but
straighten their motion to always be
according to all of Your commandments,
have mercy upon those whom You have
made and upon me a multitudinous sinner.

10. Christ living fire, the fire of Your
love which You cast down upon the earth,
inflame my being, that the stain of my
soul shall burn, and shall purify the conscience
of my thoughts, and shall cleanse the sins of my body,
and light of Your knowledge shall be lit in my heart,
have mercy upon those whom You have
made and upon me a multitudinous sinner.

11. Jesus wisdom of the Father, give to me
wisdom to think and to speak and to perform
works of goodness before You at all times,
save me from evil thoughts, from evil words,
and from evil deeds,
have mercy upon those whom You have
made and upon me a multitudinous sinner.

12. Willing of good things, willing Lord, do
    not let me to walk in the wills of my being,
    but lead me always to be according to
    wills of loving good,
    have mercy upon those whom You have
    made and upon me a multitudinous sinner.

13. Heavenly king, give to me Your kingdom
    which You have promised to Your beloved,
    and strengthen my heart to hate sins,
    and to love You only, and to do Your wills,
    have mercy upon those whom You have
    made and upon me a multitudinous sinner.

14. Caretaker of all which has been made,
    through the sign of Your holy cross protect my
    soul and body: from the deceptions of sins,
    from the temptations of demons, and from unrighteous men,
    and from all dangers to the body and soul,
    have mercy upon those whom You have
    made and upon me a multitudinous sinner.

15. Christ protector of all, may Your right
    hand be a shadow over me in the day
    and in the night, while sitting at home,
    while traveling on the road, while sleeping
    and while arising, that I may never be shaken,
    have mercy upon those whom You have
    made and upon me a multitudinous sinner.
    have mercy upon those whom You have
    made and upon me a multitudinous sinner.

REST HOUR

16. My God, You Who opens Your hands
 and You fill all of those whom You have made
 with Your mercy, I commit my being to You,
 care for and prepare the needs of my soul
 and body from this time forth unto eternity,
 have mercy upon those whom You have
 made and upon me a multitudinous sinner.

17. Returner of the wanderers, turn me from
 my evil habits to good habits, and affix upon
 my soul the frightful day of death, the fear of hell,*
 and the love of the kingdom,
 that I may repent of my sins, and I shall
 commit deeds of justice,
 have mercy upon those whom You have
 made and upon me a multitudinous sinner.

18. Fountain of immortality, flow forth from
 my heart tears of repentance as the harlot,
 that I may wash away the sins of my being
 before my going up to this world,
 have mercy upon those whom You have
 made and upon me a multitudinous sinner.

19. Grantor of mercy, grant
 with upright faith, with works of good,
 and with the communion of Your holy
 body and blood for me to come to You,
 have mercy upon those whom You have
 made and upon me a multitudinous sinner.

---

* *Gehenna*

20. Kind Lord, may You commit the angel of good
for me to give up my spirit with sweetness,
and without disturbance to pass through the
wickedness of the evil spirits,
which are in the inner heavens,
have mercy upon those whom You have
made and upon me a multitudinous sinner.

21. Christ true light, make my soul
worthy with gladness, to see the
light of Your glories on the day of *(my)* calling,
and to rest with hope of good
in the abodes of the just until
the great day of Your coming,
have mercy upon those whom You have
made and upon me a multitudinous sinner.

22. Just judge, at which time You come
with glories of the Father to judge the
living and the dead, do not deliver up
into judgment with Your servant,
but save me from the eternal fire, and
make me to hear the fortunate call
of the just in Your kingdom of the heavens,
have mercy upon those whom You have
made and upon me a multitudinous sinner.

23. Most merciful Lord, have mercy upon all
those who believe in You, upon those who are mine
and upon those who are strangers, upon those
whom I know and upon those that I do not know,
upon those who are living and upon those who are dead,
and grace forgiveness to my enemies and to those who hate me,
their offences which were committed against me,
and turn their feet from the evils which
they have for me, that they may become worthy of Your mercy,
have mercy upon those whom You have
made and upon me a multitudinous sinner.

REST HOUR

This last verse is sung.

24. Glorified Lord, receive the prayers
    of Your servant, and fulfill in good
    my requests, with the advocation of:
    the holy God-Bearer, and of John the Baptist,
    and of Saint Gregory our Illuminator, and of
    the holy apostles, of the prophets,
    of the doctors of the church, of the martyrs,
    of the patriarchs, of the hermits, of the virgins,
    and of all of Your heavenly and earthly saints.
    Also to You glory and bowing down in worship
    of the inseparable O Holy Trinity, unto the
    eternity of eternities. Amen.

* *"Lord Have Mercy" (Der Voghormya) by local tradition in some parishes, may be sung while kneeling at this point, however, this is not in the rubrics.*

Petition

<u>Priest</u>

For the sake of the advocation of the holy God-Bearer,
receive our requests and give us life.

REST HOUR

Proclamation

<u>Deacon</u> **Student Chancel**
Holy God-Bearer and all of the saints
make advocation to the Father in the
heavens, that having willed it He may
have mercy, and having compassion
He shall give life to those whom He has
made. Our Lord God almighty give
life and have mercy.

Prayer

<u>Priest</u> **Senior Chancel**
Receive, Lord, our requests with the advocation
of the holy God-Bearer, pure bearer of Your
Only Begotten Son, and with the requests of
all of Your saints, and with the grace of this
day*

* *The following substitution may be made in its place which is a mention of the Saint or Saints whose names are remembered on this particular day according to the Calendar.*

(Saints' name) of whom today are remembered:

Hear us, Lord, and have mercy, pardon,
atone, and forgive our sins. Make us worthy
with thanksgiving to glorify You with the
Son and with the Holy Spirit, now and
always and unto the eternity of eternities. Amen.

Blessed be our Lord Jesus Christ. Amen.

Our Father Who art in heaven, Hallowed be Thy name. Thy kingdom come, Thy will be done on earth as it is in heaven. Give us this day our daily bread. And forgive us our debts, as we forgive our debtors. And lead us not into temptation, but deliver us from evil.

For Thine is the Kingdom, and the power,
and the glory forever and ever. Amen.

REST HOUR

Petition

<u>Priest</u>
Receive these prayers and requests of the
Rest Hour, God lover of humanity,
in the pleasures of Your kind wills,
grace forgiveness of our sins and multitude of offences,
and to You glories unto the eternities. Amen.

(The continuation is chanted along with the "Amen" response in a very beautiful and heavy melody)

<u>Priest</u>
Glory to You, Lord our God,
You Who gifted this day to pass
with goodness and peace.

<u>Choir</u>
Blessed be God.

(continue in alternation)

God lover of humanity,
in this upcoming night which is to come upon us,
save us from sins, free us from evils,
and lead us unto good works.

Amen.

Make worthy, all of the believers in
Your Holy Name, of the blessings
and glorifications of the morning,
and keep them in peace.

Amen.

Lord our God, give Your peace to the
entire world, lift up the wrath and punishment
from those who have been made.

Amen.

Have mercy upon our fathers and brothers,
to those living and to those at rest.

Amen.

Have mercy upon the builders of the church,
sponsors, donors, servants,
and to those who are at rest
under the shadow of the holy church.

Amen.

Lord God, help the Christian kings
and pious princes,
their armies and their children,
by keeping them in peace.

Amen.

Lord our God, keep our *(church)* leaders and
our brotherhoods whole and undisturbed
in the wills of Your mercy.

Amen.

By the sign of Your holy and revered cross,
expel the visible and invisible enemy
from our borders and from within our dwellings.

Amen. *(Depending on the version sung,
this "Amen" may be sung by the priest.)*

Save us from the fire of eternities,
and glories to You unto the eternities. Amen.

(recited normally)

<u>Priest</u>

Be blessed by the graces of the
Holy Spirit, go, rest in peace,
and may the Lord be with you,
with you all. Amen.

The End

NOTATIONS

LORD'S PRAYER

The following is a translation for purposes of comparison only. As stated earlier in the book, the Traditional King James Version translation of the Lord's prayer is the closest to the Classical Armenian and because it is universally familiar, for the entire text of the book the author uses the Traditional King James Version. As with the Traditional King James Version, the Classical Armenian uses Matthew 6:9-13.

Our Father Whom You are in the heavens,
let Your Name be holy.
May Your kingdom come,
may Your wills be
as in the heavens and on the earth.
Give us this day our daily bread.
And forgive us our debts,
and as we forgive our debtors.
And do not lead us into temptation,
but save us from evil.*
For Yours is kingdom and power and
glories unto the eternities. Amen.

---

* *Depending on the version of the Classical Armenian, both "evil" and "Evil One" are used.*

REFERENCES 679

Adeni Zhamakirk with Saghmosaran and Donatzooytz: St. James' Press, Jerusalem. fourth edition 1915.

Zhamakirk (Hand held Edition): St. Vartan Press, New York, N.Y. 1986.

Zhamakirk (Hand held Edition): St. James' Press, Jerusalem. eighth edition 1985.

Kirk Saghmostaz Tavti. Book of the Psalms of David: St. James' Press, Jerusalem. 1870.

Avak Shapat: Photogravure Zaven and Fils Printing, Beirut, Lebanon. 1988.

Jashotz Kirk: St. James' Press, Jerusalem. 1967.

Avedaran Jashoo with Donatzooytz (Second Volume): St. James' Press, Jerusalem 1970.

Sharagan Book: Holy Etchmiadzin Printing Press, Vagharshabad, Armenia. second edition 1888. (Reprinted in 1999 in Holy Etchmiadzin. third edition)

Sharagan Book: Hovhanoo Miuhendisian Printing Press, Constantinople 1853. (Reprinted in 1986 by St. Vartan Press, New York, N.Y.)

Divine Liturgy of the Armenian Apostolic Orthodox Church: by Bishop Tiran Nersoyan, The Delphic Press, New York, N.Y. 1950.

The Book of Hours or The Order of the Common Prayers of the Armenian Apostolic Orthodox Church. Matins, Prime, Vespers and Occasional Offices: by Archbishop Tiran Nersoyan, Ouzoonian House Publishing, Evanston, IL. 1964.

Rest Service of the Armenian Church: by Archbishop Torkom Manoogian, St. Vartan Press, New York, N.Y. 1981.

A Dictionary of the Armenian Church: by Malachia Ormanian translated by Bedros Norehad, St. Vartan Press, New York, N.Y. 1984.

Class Syllabus and Notes to the "Study of Ritual (Dzisakidootyoon) of the Armenian Church" fall and spring semesters of academic year 2002-2003. Yerevan State University Department of Theology. Professor Khoren Balian.

Hamaparpar Armenian Biblical Concordance Old and New Testaments: St. James' Press, Jerusalem 1895.

Rituale Armenorum: by Fredrick Cornwallis Conybeare, Oxford at the Clarendon Press 1905.

REFERENCES

Lectionary 2019 Armenian Apostolic Church: by Rev. Dr. George A. Leylegian, 2019.

From the Depths of the Heart (Annotated Translation of the Prayers of St. Gregory of Narek), by Dr. Abraham Terian, Liturgical Press, Collegeville, Minnesota 2022.

New Dictionary Armenian-English: by Rev. M. Bedrossian, Librairie du Liban 1875. Reprinted 1985.

An Introduction to Classical Armenian: by Robert W. Thompson, Caravan Books, Delmar, N.Y. 1989.

Websites

https://www.arak29.am

https://www.arak29.org

English-Armenian dictionary (nayiri.com)

Hayeren Gavarragan Parraran (Etymological Dictionary): by Hrachia Acharian, Lazaryan Jemaran Arevelyan Lezvatz, Tiflis, Georgia 1913.
http://www.nayiri.com/imagedDictionaryBrowser.jsp?dictionaryId=7

The University of Texas at Austin Linguistics Research Center
https://lrc.la.utexas.edu/eieol/armol

https://biblehub.com

Hebrew Interlinear Bible (OT)
https://www.scripture4all.org/OnlineInterlinear/Hebrew_Index.htm

If any errors or mistyped words are discovered by the reader, please make a photocopy of the page with the error and give an explanation of what the correction should be, so that for future editions, the errors will be corrected. Kindly mail corrections to:

Holy Trinity Armenian Apostolic Church
c/o Deacon Gregory R. Eritzian
2226 Ventura St.
Fresno, CA 93721

www.ingramcontent.com/pod-product-compliance
Lightning Source LLC
LaVergne TN
LVHW022233080526
838199LV00106B/292